How Do Judges Decide?

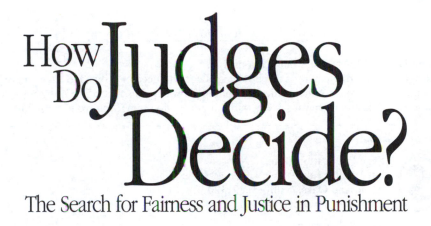

How Do Judges Decide?

The Search for Fairness and Justice in Punishment

Cassia C. Spohn

University of Nebraska at Omaha

Sage Publications
International Educational and Professional Publisher
Thousand Oaks ▪ London ▪ New Delhi

For Jerry, Joshua, and Jessica

For information:

Sage Publications, Inc.
2455 Teller Road
Thousand Oaks, California 91320
E-mail: order@sagepub.com

Sage Publications Ltd.
6 Bonhill Street
London EC2A 4PU
United Kingdom

Sage Publications India Pvt. Ltd.
M-32 Market
Greater Kailash I
New Delhi 110 048 India

Printed in China

Library of Congress Cataloging-in-Publication Data

Spohn, Cassia.
 How do judges decide? : the search for fairness and justice in punishment / by Cassia C. Spohn.
   p. cm. — (Key questions for criminal justice)
Includes bibliographical references and index.
 ISBN 0-7619-8760-6 (alk. paper)
 1. Sentences (Criminal procedure)—United States. 2. Punishment—United States. 3. Judicial process—United States. I. Title. II. Series.
 KF9685 .S68 2002
 345.73'077—dc21

                                          2001005430

01 02 03 04 05 10 9 8 7 6 5 4 3 2 1

Acquiring Editors:	Stephen D. Rutter and Jerry Westby
Editorial Assistants:	Kirsten Stoller and Vonessa Vondera
Production Editor:	Claudia A. Hoffman
Typesetter/Designer:	Larry K. Bramble
Indexer:	Molly Hall
Cover Designer:	Michelle Lee

KHerr.

Contents

Acknowledgments

This book reflects 20 years of contemplating, teaching, and researching judicial decision making and sentencing. It reflects my quest to understand the complex process by which decisions regarding punishment are made and to assess the fairness of the outcomes that result. The project has been informed by the work of a diverse group of scholars: criminologists, political scientists, sociologists, philosophers, and lawyers. They, of course, bear no responsibility for any omissions, errors, or misinterpretations.

I would like to thank Bob Meier, the Chair of the Department of Criminal Justice at the University of Nebraska at Omaha, for his support and encouragement. I also am grateful to the University's Committee on Research, which has supported my research throughout my tenure at UNO, and to the National Science Foundation, which funded the multisite sentencing study that provided the data for much of my recent research. I also wish to thank the judges, prosecutors, and defense attorneys in Chicago, Miami, and Kansas City who talked with me candidly and at length about the sentencing process and whose comments are interspersed throughout this book.

I owe special thanks to my spouse, Jerry Cederblom, with whom I have spent many hours discussing (and, yes, debating) philosophies of punishment; he introduced me to the work in his field, patiently explained complicated concepts and theories, and provided invaluable suggestions for writing (and rewriting) Chapter 1. He also shouldered more than his fair share of family responsibilities during the year in which I was immersed in this book.

I also would like to thank Steve Rutter, the former publisher of Pine Forge Press, who conceived the idea for this book and brought me on board. I am also grateful to Carla Freeman, whose careful editing clarified my meaning, corrected my mistakes, and improved my writing. Thanks also to Jerry Westby, a senior acquisitions editor at Sage, who shepherded the book to completion.

Preface

In the minds of many Americans, the word *sentencing* evokes an image of a solemn and slightly mysterious process in which a wise, fair, and impartial judge determines the appropriate sentence for each offender who has been convicted of a crime. In this view, the judge deliberately fashions a sentence that reflects the facts and circumstances of the case, the background and blameworthiness of the offender, and the judge's own philosophy of punishment. Judges use their discretion to choose from a continuum of sanctions that range from life imprisonment—or possibly death—at one end to probation at the other, with a diversity of intermediate sanctions in between. According to this view, the sentences meted out by judges are appropriate, unbiased, and just.

The reality of the sentencing process is somewhat different. The sentences imposed on offenders convicted of crimes in state and federal courts are the result of a collaborative exercise involving legislators and criminal justice officials other than the judge. The judge plays a significant and highly visible role in the process, but other officials play important supporting roles. In some jurisdictions, the judge retains discretion to tailor sentences to fit individuals and their crimes, whereas in other jurisdictions, the judge's options are constrained by sentencing guidelines that prohibit consideration of the offender's background characteristics or by mandatory minimum sentencing statutes that dictate the sentence to be imposed. The sentences that result from this process may not reflect a coherent philosophy of punishment or a reasoned assessment of crime seriousness and offender culpability. Similarly situated offenders convicted of comparable crimes may be sentenced differently, offenders convicted of different crimes may get the same sentence, and the sentence imposed may depend upon the offender's race, ethnicity, gender, or social class.

The sentencing reforms enacted during the past 30 years were designed to ameliorate these problems. They were designed to bring order to a system of sentencing characterized as "irrational," "lawless," and desperately in need of improvement. Reformers challenged the principles underlying the indeterminate sentence and called for changes designed to curb discretion, reduce disparity and discrimination, and achieve proportionality and parsimony in sentencing. A number of states adopted determinate sentencing policies that offered judges a limited range of sentencing options and included enhancements for use of a weapon, presence of a prior criminal record, or infliction of serious injury. Other states and the federal government adopted sentence guidelines that incorporated crime seriousness and prior criminal record into a sentencing "grid" that judges were to use in determining the appropriate sentence. Other reforms enacted at both the federal and state level included mandatory minimum penalties for certain types of offenses, three-strikes-and-you're-out laws that mandated long prison terms for repeat offenders, and truth-in-sentencing statutes that required offenders to serve a larger portion of the sentence before being released.

Although the reforms enacted during the past three decades did transform the sentencing process in the United States, the degree to which they "improved" the process is debatable. Advocates of sentencing reform contend that the changes enacted during the past three decades have resulted in more punitive, more effective, and fairer sentence outcomes. Critics of the sentencing reform movement, on the other hand, assert that although sentences today are definitely harsher than they were in the past, attempts to structure the sentencing process and constrain judicial discretion did not produce the predicted reduction in crime or eliminate unwarranted disparities in sentencing.

This book provides a comprehensive overview of the sentencing process in the United States. We begin with a discussion of the goals or purposes of sentencing. Chapter 1 explores the meaning of "punishment" and describes and analyzes the different justifications for punishment: retribution, deterrence, incapacitation, rehabilitation, and restoration. This chapter also explains how each theoretical perspective would answer the question "Why do we punish those who violate the law?" We then discuss the allocation or distribution of punishment; that is, according to each theory, who should be punished and how much should they be punished? Using hypothetical cases, we show that the different theoretical perspectives would not necessarily produce the same sentence outcomes.

Chapter 2 focuses on the options available to the judge at sentencing and the sentencing process. We discuss the death penalty, incarceration, and the alternatives to incarceration: probation, boot camps, house arrest and electronic monitoring, community service, and monetary penalties. We explain that a jail or prison sentence is an option in most cases and that imprisonment is required by mandatory minimum sentencing statutes for certain types of offenders and certain types of crimes. We discuss the differences between indeterminate and determinate sentences and provide a brief introduction to presumptive sentencing guidelines. We also explain that the sentences imposed on offenders actually result from a "collaborative exercise" that involves decision makers other than the judge. We show how sentences are shaped by decisions made by state legislators, prosecutors, jurors, corrections officials, and appellate court judges.

In Chapter 3, our focus shifts to the judge. We contend that decisions made by legislators and other criminal justice officials limit the judge's options and constrain his or her discretion but that the ultimate responsibility for determining the sentence rests with the judge. We discuss the findings of studies that attempt to explain "how judges decide": in other words, how judges arrive at the appropriate punishment for criminal offenders. We acknowledge that the "key determinants" of sentences are the seriousness of the offense and the offender's prior criminal record, but we contend that the characteristics of the offender, the victim, and the case also play a role. We also discuss the results of research examining the relationship between judges' background characteristics and their sentencing decisions. We ask whether women judges, black judges, and Hispanic judges dispense a "different kind of justice."

Chapters 4 and 5 examine disparity and discrimination in sentencing. We begin by noting that there are important differences between disparity and discrimination and by illustrating that both disparity and discrimination can take different forms. In Chapter 4, we present evidence of gender disparity in sentencing and discuss the results of research designed to determine whether these disparities reflect discrimination in favor of women. We explain that the question of whether female offenders should be treated the same as male offenders has generated considerable controversy, and we discuss the explanations proffered for the more lenient treatment of female offenders. In Chapter 5, we discuss the results of research on racial and ethnic disparities in sentencing. We demonstrate that racial minorities are substantially more likely than whites to be locked up in state and federal prisons, and we examine the various explanations for this disproportionality. We also discuss the effect of race on the imposition of the death penalty. We conclude that gender and race/ethnicity continue to influence the sentences that judges impose.

In Chapters 6 and 7, our focus shifts to the sentencing reform movement and its impact. In Chapter 6, we explore the motivations of those who lobbied for sentencing reform, and we describe the changes in sentencing policies and practices that have occurred since the mid-1970s. We focus on determinate sentencing and sentencing guidelines, mandatory minimum sentencing statutes, three-strikes-and-you're-out laws, and truth-in-sentencing laws. We explain what each reform was designed to do and discuss the degree to which the reforms have resulted in compliance or circumvention.

In Chapter 7, we examine the impact of the sentencing reform movement. We attempt to determine whether the sentencing reforms enacted during the past 30 years have resulted in more punitive, more effective, and fairer sentence outcomes. We begin by exploring the degree to which the changes in sentencing policy have resulted in more punitive sentences. We ask whether offenders today are being sentenced to prison at higher rates and for longer periods of time than they were in the past. We then focus on whether the sentencing reforms, which were based on the argument that more punitive penalties would deter and incapacitate would-be offenders, causing crime rates to fall, have led to the predicted reduction in crime. Finally, we ask whether sentences today are fairer or more equitable than they were in the past: Is there less disparity and gender or racial bias today than there was 30 years ago?

— *Cassia Spohn*

Chapter One

The Goals
of Sentencing

Punishment is an institution in almost every society.
Only very small and very isolated communities are at a loss
about what to do with transgressors, and even they recognize
the punishment of children by parents . . . It is an institution
which is exemplified in transactions involving individuals,
transactions that are controlled by rules, laying down what
form it is to take, who may order it, and for what.

Nigel Walker[1]

Deciding how much to punish is an agonizing process,
in which conflicting aspirations compete.

Andrew von Hirsch[2]

W hat should be done with an individual who has been found guilty of a crime? Should he or she be punished? If so, what is the purpose of the punishment? And if punishment is justified, what should it be? Should that person be required to pay a fine or provide restitution to the victim? What amount should be paid? Should he or she be placed on probation? For how long and under what conditions? Should the sentence be incarceration in jail or prison? Or should the individual receive the "ulti-mate punishment" and be put to death?

Questions such as these have been pondered and debated by philoso-phers and legal scholars since the beginning of time. The answers to the question "Why punish?" have varied, with some scholars contending that a crime has been committed and the offender deserves to be punished for it[3] and others arguing that offenders should be punished "to promote good (and/or prevent evil) in the future."[4] Answers to questions regarding the type and amount of punishment that should be imposed—which ultimately depends on the answer to the question "Why punish?"—are similarly var-ied. The death penalty, for example, was once viewed as an appropriate pen-alty for a variety of crimes other than murder; today, its use for even the most heinous of crimes has been called into question. Controversy also sur-rounds the use of incarceration. Some scholars contend that only those who commit the most serious crimes or who pose the greatest danger to society should be imprisoned and then only for relatively short periods of time. Others claim that lengthy incarceration is an appropriate penalty for all but the least serious offenders. Finally, there is considerable disagreement about what to do with offenders for whom incarceration is not appropriate.

Questions regarding the purpose and distribution of punishment are not simply academic questions. In fact, the answers to these questions provide the foundation on which sentencing policies and practices rest. Legislators, who determine the penalties associated with particular crimes or categories of crimes, cannot make these determinations in the absence of beliefs about the justification of punishment. A legislator's views of the goals of punish-ment, in other words, affect his or her decisions as to whether burglary should be punished more or less harshly than robbery or whether manufac-turing drugs should be penalized more or less severely than possession of drugs. Judges and corrections officials, who must decide what to do with particular offenders, are similarly constrained by their views about the pur-poses of punishment. A judge's assessment of the appropriate penalty for a serial rapist or the parole board's decision whether to release a serial rapist will be influenced by personal beliefs about what the punishment is de-signed to achieve. To understand the sentencing process and to evaluate sentence outcomes, then, we must first consider the diverse and often con-flicting goals of sentencing.

In this chapter, we address the question of crime and punishment, which David Garland recently characterized as "one of the most pressing prob-lems of our age."[5] We begin by describing and analyzing five different justi-fications for punishment: retribution, deterrence, incapacitation, rehabilitation, and restitution/restoration. We explain how each theory would answer the question "Why punish?" We then discuss the allocation or distribution of punishment—that is, according to each theory, who should be punished and how much?

Why Punish?

In "The Brothel Boy,"[6] Norval Morris tells the story of District Officer Eric Blair, a young and inexperienced Burmese magistrate who must decide the fate of a young man charged with the rape and murder of a 12-year-old girl. The "brothel boy," perhaps mimicking the behavior of the adults in the brothel where he worked, offered the girl money to have sex with him. She refused, they struggled, and she fell, hitting her head on a sharp rock. Several days later, she died. District Officer Blair wonders whether this unfortunate young man—who is described as "illiterate," "stupid," and "quite retarded"—should be punished at all and, if so, what his punishment should be. While acknowledging that the youth should be blamed for what he did, the magistrate questions whether he is guilty of the crimes with which he is charged. "The boy meant no harm, no evil," he states. "The more I thought about him and his crime, the less wicked it seemed, though the injury to the girl and her family was obviously extreme; but it was a tragedy, not a sin."[7]

As he attempts to understand the accused and his crime, Officer Blair discusses the case with Dr. Veraswami, a Burmese physician. Unlike Blair, Veraswami has no doubts about "what should be done with him." "He will be hanged, of course," Veraswami tells Blair. Officer Blair argues that the brothel boy "meant no harm insofar as he understood what was happening" and therefore is "less worthy of being hanged than most murderers."[8] Dr. Veraswami disagrees:

> He was conscious of what he was doing. And being conscious, backward and confused though he iss, mistreated and bewildered though he wass, he must be held responsible. You must convict him, punish him, hang him . . . you must treat him ass a responsible adult and punish him.[9]

When Officer Blair asks the doctor if there was no room under the law for mercy, for clemency, the doctor replies, "Justice, Mr. Blair, iss your job. Justice, not mercy."[10] Eventually, of course, the brothel boy is hanged.

According to Dr. Veraswami, justice requires that the brothel boy be punished. But why is this so? Why is punishment, rather than forgiveness or revenge, the appropriate response to his offense? What purpose does punishment serve in this case?

As noted above, questions such as these have long intrigued philosophers and legal scholars. In the sections that follow, we define punishment and discuss the justifications for it.

The Concept of Punishment

Before we can answer the question "Why punish?" we must explain what is meant by *punishment*. According to H. L. A. Hart, an English philosopher, there are five necessary elements of punishment:

- It must involve pain or other consequences normally considered unpleasant.

- It must be enacted for an offense against legal rules.

- It must be imposed on an actual or supposed offender for his offense.

- It must be intentionally administered by human beings other than the offender.

- It must be imposed and administered by an authority constituted by a legal system against which the offense is committed.[11]

Stated more simply, punishment involves infliction by the state of consequences that are considered to be unpleasant on a person who has been convicted of a crime. According to this definition, the judge who sentences a man convicted of murder to 30 years in prison is imposing a punishment on him. The prison sentence is an "unpleasant consequence"; the penalty is imposed on a man found guilty of murder, which is an "offense against the legal rules"; and the penalty is intentionally imposed by a judge who has the legal authority to order and implement it.

It may be easier to illustrate the concept of punishment by explaining what punishment is *not* rather than what it *is*. According to Hart's definition, individual and group acts of vengeance do not constitute punishment. Neither the man who avenges his sister's rape by physically assaulting her alleged attacker nor the mob that snatches the condemned man from the local jail and lynches him is imposing punishment. Although both cases involve "pain or other consequences normally considered unpleasant," neither incorporates all the necessary elements of punishment. In the case of the man who avenges his sister's rape, the person attacked may not actually have committed the crime, and the brother does not have the legal authority to administer the consequences. And even if we assume that the condemned man has been found guilty of a crime, the lynching mob does not have the authority to seize him and put him to death.

In the two scenarios described above, the unpleasant consequences do not constitute punishment because they are not administered by someone with the authority to do so. But not all government-administered consequences, no matter how painful or unpleasant, constitute punishment. Consider, for example, the forced relocation of more than 100,000 Japanese Americans living in California during World War II. Although the order was issued by the president of the United States, and the consequences—internment in relocation camps and in some cases, loss of property—were certainly unpleasant, the Japanese Americans were not guilty of an "offense against the legal rules." They were rounded up and forced to relocate because of a belief that they constituted a threat to national security, but they had committed no crime. Another example would be a government-ordered quarantine of persons with an infectious disease. In this case, the government legitimately confines these individuals to their homes—not because of any crime they have committed but because doing so will control the spread of the disease. In both of these situations, there was no crime and therefore, there can be no punishment.

Some scholars add a sixth essential feature to Hart's five-part definition of punishment. They contend that the person ordering or administering the unpleasant consequences must have a "justification" for doing so.[12] As Walker notes, "A justification is called for because what is involved is the imposition of something unpleasant regardless of the wishes of the person on whom it is imposed."[13] It is to this issue, the justification of punishment, that we now turn.

The Justification of Punishment

Consider the following hypothetical situation. A federal district court judge sentences Jason Miller, a first-time offender convicted of selling 5 grams of crack cocaine to an undercover narcotics officer, to 15 years in prison. When asked why she imposed this sentence, the judge replies, "Fifteen years is the mandatory sentence under the federal sentencing guidelines—it is the sentence prescribed by the law." Is this a sufficient justification for the punishment imposed? It is certainly true that the judge has the legal authority to impose the prescribed penalty. This does not explain, however, why this punishment—indeed any punishment at all—is justified in this case. The judge's response tells us nothing about the purpose for which the punishment is imposed.

Justify *

Why do we punish those who violate the law? Although the answers to this question vary widely, they can be classified into two distinct categories: *retributive* (desert-based) justifications and *utilitarian* (result-based) justifications. According to retributive theory, offenders are punished because they have done something wrong—something blameworthy—and therefore deserve to be punished.[14] Retributive justifications of punishment, in other words, "rest on the idea that it is right for the wicked to be punished; because man is responsible for his actions, he ought to receive his just deserts."[15] In contrast, utilitarian justifications of punishment emphasize the prevention of crimes in the future. Punishment is seen as a means of (a) deterring offenders from reoffending or discouraging others from following their examples (deterrence) or (b) preventing offenders from committing additional crimes by locking them up (incapacitation) or reforming them (rehabilitation). Whereas retributivists equate punishment with desert, utilitarians justify punishment by the results it is designed to achieve.

BOX 1.1

WHY DO WE PUNISH THOSE WHO VIOLATE THE LAW?

Retribution

We punish those who violate the law because they have done something wrong. Justice demands that the guilty be punished.

> *Every guilty deed*
>
> *Holds in itself the seed*
>
> *Of retribution and underlying pain.*
>
> — Henry Wadsworth Longfellow (1875:viii)

Deterrence

The purpose of punishment is to prevent those who are punished from committing additional crimes in the future (specific deterrence) or to deter others from committing similar crimes (general deterrence).

> *Not that he is punished because he did wrong, for that which is done can never be undone, but in order that in future times, he, and those who see him corrected, may utterly hate injustice, or at any rate, abate much of their evil-doing.*
>
> —Plato, *Laws II* 934, as cited in Gottfredson and Gottfredson (1988:143)

Incapacitation

The purpose of punishment is to isolate high-risk offenders in order to limit their opportunities for committing crimes in the future.

The longer a murderer, rapist, child-molester, or armed robber is detained the fewer the people he will victimize in the future.

—Nigel Walker (1991:38)

Rehabilitation

The purpose of punishment is to reform the offender and thus to reduce his propensity to commit crimes in the future.

In revenges or punishments men ought not to look at the greatness of evil past but at the greatness of the good to follow, whereby we are forbidden to inflict punishment with any other design than for the correction of the offender and the admonition of others.

—Thomas Hobbes (1651:xxviii)

Restoration

The purpose of punishment is to repair the harm to the victim and the community, to heal the victim and the community, and to restore harmony between victims and offenders.

The original goal of restorative justice was to restore harmony between victims and offenders. For victims, this meant restitution for tangible losses and emotional losses. For offenders, it meant taking responsibility, confronting shame, and regaining dignity.

—Leena Kurki (2000:236)

These justifications of punishment are summarized in Box 1.1 and discussed in detail in the sections that follow. We begin with a discussion of retribution, which we refer to as *desert*. We then discuss the various utilitarian, or *result*, rationales: deterrence, incapacitation, and rehabilitation. We conclude with a discussion of *restorative justice*, a utilitarian justification for punishment that emphasizes repairing harm and rebuilding relations among victims, offenders, and communities.

Retribution: A Theory of Desert

The retributivist's answer to the question "Why punish?" is straightforward. We punish the man who violates the law because he has done something wrong; justice demands that he be punished. Stated another way, "We are justified in punishing because and only because offenders deserve it."[16] Although some might suggest that this sounds like vengeance, Hospers emphasizes that retribution should not be confused with vengeance. "It is not punishment for punishment's sake, nor the infliction of pain for pain's sake, that is the justification for punishing. . . . It is rather punishment for the sake of justice."[17] In the case of Jason Miller, the offender convicted of selling crack cocaine, if the judge sentencing him were a retributivist, she would justify punishing him by pointing out that he was guilty of a crime and therefore deserved to be punished.

The basis for this principle—that is, the answer to the question "Why does the guilty man deserve to be punished?"—is more complex. One school of thought holds simply that there is "intrinsic good in the guilty suffering."[18] Just as those who believe in an afterlife think it is morally justified for those who lead good lives to be rewarded whereas those who lead wicked lives must suffer, advocates of this position believe that punishment of those who violate the law is inherently right.[19] Man, in other words, "is a responsible moral agent to whom rewards are due when he makes right moral choices and to whom punishment is due when he makes wrong ones."[20] Indeed, as illustrated by Kant's famous example of the last murderer (see Box 1.2), those who hold this view suggest that society has not just the right, but the *duty*, to punish the morally culpable offender.

Another school of thought maintains that all members of a civilized society agree, either explicitly or implicitly, to follow the rules that govern the society.[21] They agree that people will not attack or kill one another, steal one another's property, or behave in other ways that cause harm. This agreement benefits all members of the society. Therefore, someone who vi-

---

BOX 1.2

EXECUTING "THE LAST MURDERER"

The categorical imperative to punish is illustrated by Kant's example of "the last murderer."

Even if a civil society resolved to dissolve itself with the consent of all its members—as might be supposed in the case of a people inhabiting an island resolving to separate and scatter themselves throughout the whole world—the last murderer lying in prison ought to be executed before the resolution was carried out. This ought to be done in order that everyone may realize the desert of his deeds, and the bloodguiltiness may not remain upon the people; for otherwise they might all be regarded as participators in the murder as a public violation of justice.

—Kant (1887:198)

What is Kant's point? Why would it be necessary to execute "the last murderer lying in prison"? What purpose would it serve?

olates the rules, by killing or stealing, for example, gains an unfair advantage over law-abiding members of society. Punishment, by penalizing the offender, rectifies this unfair advantage; it restores the equilibrium. As Walker notes, "Penalties put matters right, either by removing what the offender has gained or by imposing a disadvantage."[22]

In summary, the retributive justification of punishment focuses on what the offender "deserves" as a result of his criminal behavior. It is a backward-looking approach that focuses exclusively on the offender's past wrongdoing as the reason for punishment.

Utilitarian Justifications for Punishment

In contrast to desert theory, which, as noted above, is a backward-looking approach, the utilitarian justifications for punishment are forward looking: deterrence, incapacitation, and rehabilitation. Rather than looking back to the crime that has been committed, these justifications focus on the future criminal behavior of both the person being punished and other members of society. Thus, punishment does not occur because a crime has been committed and the offender deserves to be punished for it; rather, "The punishment is *in order to* promote good (and/or prevent evil) in the future."[23] According to the utilitarian theorist, if punishment cannot achieve this, "It is immoral; merely the adding of one evil (punishing) to another (the crime)."[24] Strictly speaking, then, if no "good consequences" would result from punishing an individual, no punishment would be justified.

Although all utilitarian justifications of punishment are based on the general principle that the purpose of punishment is to prevent or reduce crime, each theory would answer the question "Why punish?" somewhat differently. We explore these differences in the sections that follow.

Deterrence. Imagine that our hypothetical judge imposing a sentence on Jason Miller for selling crack cocaine believed that the purpose of punishment was deterrence. How would the rationale for punishing him differ from that of the judge who based his or her sentence on retribution? Rather than focusing on Jason's guilt and blameworthiness, this judge would stress the deterrent effects of punishment, emphasizing that the sentence would prevent him and other would-be drug dealers from selling drugs in the future.

As developed by 18th-century utilitarian philosophers such as Jeremy Bentham[25] and Cesare Beccaria,[26] deterrence theory suggests that crime results from a rational calculation of the costs and benefits of criminal activity.

Individuals commit crimes, in other words, when the benefits outweigh the costs. Because an important "cost" of crime is apprehension and punishment, deterrence theorists suggest that potential offenders will refrain from committing crimes if they believe that the odds of getting caught and being severely punished are high and are not outweighed by any anticipated gain from the crime. According to this perspective, "The threat and imposition of punishment is called for in order to secure compliance—not full compliance, but more compliance than there might be were there no legal penalties at all."[27] Some punishment, in other words, deters better than none.

Deterrence can be either specific or general. Specific deterrence occurs when individuals who have been legally punished cease offending because they fear future punishment. General deterrence occurs when potential offenders "learn of the consequences of criminal involvement [for actual offenders] and decide not to risk subjecting themselves to such punishment."[28] If, for example, Jennifer Peterson is sentenced to 30 days in jail for drunk driving and, as a result of being punished, never again gets behind the wheel of a car after she has been drinking, we would say that specific deterrence has occurred. If those who learn of her sentence similarly resolve to refrain from drinking and driving, we would conclude that general deterrence has occurred.

Some scholars also differentiate between absolute and restrictive deterrence. In the case of absolute deterrence, a potential offender is completely deterred by the fear of punishment; this person commits no crimes at all. Restrictive deterrence, on the other hand, occurs when potential offenders attempt to minimize the risk or severity of punishment by committing less serious offenses or by reducing the number of offenses they commit. Absolute deterrence occurs when a potential drug dealer is "scared straight" after a cousin is sentenced to 15 years in federal prison for selling crack cocaine to an undercover narcotics officer. Restrictive deterrence occurs when a drug dealer sizes up potential customers and, reasoning that some of them will turn out to be undercover narcotics officers, refuses to sell drugs to those who "do not effect the right appearance, are not emaciated or poor, do not have the right skin color, or do not know the proper argot."[29] In the first case, fear of punishment leads the potential drug dealer to refrain from crime altogether. In the second case, fear of punishment leads the drug dealer to make fewer sales (i.e., commit fewer crimes).

Although the use of deterrence as a justification for punishment has been criticized on a number of grounds, the most compelling argument against it is that it does not necessarily require the person being punished to be guilty. Because general deterrence rests on would-be offenders' perceptions of the certainty and severity of punishment, it can be achieved even if the person being punished is innocent.[30] Consider, for example, a judge who knows that a person charged with a series of armed robberies is innocent but believes that sending him to prison for a long time will deter others. If the judge is a utilitarian who believes that the consequences of punishment are paramount, he or she might rationalize punishing the innocent person by pointing to the "good effects" the punishment is designed to achieve: that it will deter those contemplating armed robbery and thus will protect potential victims of this violent crime. In this case, in other words, the judge might reason that the negative consequences to the innocent person are outweighed by the positive consequences to society. But is this justice? As Hospers points out, "The question of what is *just* punishment and the question what punishment will have *good effects* are two distinct questions; and the answer to the first need not be the same as an answer to the second."[31]

Incapacitation. A second forward-looking utilitarian justification of punishment is incapacitation, which is sometimes referred to as *isolation, neutralization,* or *predictive restraint.* Incapacitation involves locking up or otherwise physically disabling dangerous or high-risk offenders to prevent them from committing crimes in the future. In other words, offenders judged to be bad risks should be physically restrained. Under this theory, the judge sentencing Jason Miller, the crack dealer, would reason either (a) that those who sell crack cocaine are a danger to society and are likely to continue selling drugs if not physically prevented from doing so or (b) that Jason Miller, by virtue of his criminal history and background, is a dangerous and high-risk offender. In either case, the judge would justify the prison sentence on the grounds that imprisonment would eliminate (or at least severely restrict) Jason's ability to continue selling crack cocaine.

As illustrated by this hypothetical case, the justification for punishment can rest on two related but conceptually distinct views of incapacitation. The first is *collective* incapacitation, which refers to the incapacitation of all offenders found guilty of a particular type of crime, regardless of their prior records or other personal characteristics. Offenders convicted of certain types of crimes (for example, armed robberies, aggravated rapes, or drug sales involving large amounts of crack cocaine) are deemed dangerous and are locked up to protect society from them. In this case, "It would not matter whether an offender had an alcohol problem, had family ties in the community, or was a high school graduate."[32] Being convicted of a crime categorized as dangerous would be sufficient to qualify the offender for a prison sentence.

Selective incapacitation focuses on the offender as well as the crime. Whereas collective incapacitation means incarcerating those whose crimes are deemed dangerous, selective incapacitation involves incarcerating primarily "those who, when free, commit the most crimes."[33] It involves predicting that an individual offender, or offenders with certain characteristics, will commit additional crimes if they are not locked up. In this case, the offender's prior record and background characteristics might be relevant. Suppose research reveals that burglars with a history of drug abuse have significantly higher recidivism rates than burglars who have not abused drugs. Under a policy of selective incapacitation, drug-addicted burglars would be sent to prison; burglars with no history of drug abuse might receive some alternative to incarceration.

Most of the criticism directed at incapacitation as a justification for punishment reflects critics' concerns about our ability to predict who will become a repeat offender. To the extent that these predictions are accurate, the punishment can be justified on utilitarian grounds. As Packer notes, "Utilitarian ethics can approve the use of punishment for incapacitative purposes, on the view that the pain inflicted on persons who are punished is less than the pain that would be inflicted on their putative victims and on society at large if those same persons were left free to commit further offenses."[34] In this case, in other words, the punishment is justified because the good results achieved outweigh the harm done to the offender.

The problem is that not much evidence exists in support of the assumption that our predictions of dangerousness and risk are accurate. Although researchers can identify the *characteristics* associated with a higher-than-average rate of recidivism, they cannot predict whether any particular offender with these characteristics will offend again. In fact, the statistical techniques available to us produce "a disturbingly high incidence of 'false positives.'"[35] That is, many of the offenders predicted to become recidivists will not offend again. Overprediction is particularly problematic for crimes of violence, which are relatively rare and are thus more difficult to predict. In identifying a significant number of offenders who will probably commit violent crimes in the future, the forecaster inevitably includes many who will not actually do so. As Tonry notes, the conventional wisdom is that "for every three persons predicted to commit serious violent offenses, only one will do so, and the other two will be 'false positives.'"[36]

This suggests that the rationale for selective incapacitation is weak. Proponents of preventive confinement contend that the benefits achieved by incapacitating truly dangerous individuals outweigh the costs of confining individuals mistakenly judged to be dangerous,[37] but critics assert that this assumption is "highly questionable." They argue that the benefits of selective incapacitation would not outweigh the costs "once the magnitude of the 'cost' of confining large numbers of false positives is fully taken into account."[38] Retributive theorists further contend that even if the supporters of selective incapacitation could prove that the benefits were greater than the costs, the system still would be "unacceptable in absolute terms because it violates the obligation of society to do *individual* justice."[39] The use of selective incapacitation as a justification for punishment, then, is criticized on both utilitarian and retributive grounds. As Tonry indicates, "Almost every analyst of predictive sentencing is uncomfortable with some of its features."[40]

Rehabilitation. The third utilitarian justification for punishment is rehabilitation. Sometimes referred to simply as *treatment*, rehabilitation is "any measure taken to change an offender's character, habits, or behavior patterns so as to diminish his criminal propensities."[41] Like deterrence and incapacitation, the goal of rehabilitation is crime prevention. Rehabilitation does not achieve this goal by making the offender fearful of additional punishment (deterrence), or by isolating him so that his opportunities for crime are limited (incapacitation), but does so by reforming him. The techniques used to reform or rehabilitate offenders include individual or group counseling, education, job training, substance abuse treatment, and behavior modification programs.

The advocate of rehabilitation, then, justifies punishment on the grounds that it will "'cure' an offender of his or her criminal tendencies."[42] Suppose, for example, that a presentence investigation revealed that Jason Miller, the crack dealer, was selling drugs primarily to obtain money to support his own habit. If she were an advocate of rehabilitation, the judge imposing the sentence might place him on probation and order him to undergo drug treatment as a condition of probation.[43] The judge would justify the punishment on the grounds that it was designed to solve Jason's substance abuse problem and thus reduce the odds that he would commit crimes in the future.

Like selective incapacitation, rehabilitation requires identification and prediction. Selective incapacitation involves identifying the offender characteristics associated with recidivism and then using these characteristics to predict which offenders will be most likely to reoffend. Rehabilitation requires the identification of the forces that caused the offender's criminality and then predicting the type of treatment most likely to prevent that individual from committing future crimes. Critics of the rehabilitative ideal charge that because our ability to identify causal forces and design effective treatments is limited, punishment cannot be justified on the basis of rehabilitation.[44] Although they acknowledge that some treatments work with some types of offenders, these critics contend that no generic treatments routinely produce major reductions in recidivism. There are no treatments, in other words,

> That can inform the judge, when confronted with the run-of-the-mill robbery, burglary, or drug offense, what the appropriate sanction should be, and provide even a modicum of assurance that the sanction will contribute to the offender's desistance from crime.[45]

According to these critics, our inability to match treatments to offenders means that rehabilitation cannot serve as the primary justification for punishment. Herbert Packer goes even further; he claims that "so long as our ignorance in these matters persists, punishment in the name of rehabilitation is gratuitous cruelty."[46]

Supporters of rehabilitation disagree.[47] In contrast to Packer, they argue that treatment is a humane or benevolent response to crime and that rehabilitation "is the only justification of criminal sanctioning that obligates the state to care for an offender's needs or welfare."[48] Although they admit that the ultimate goal of rehabilitation is crime prevention, advocates of the treatment ideology contend that this can best be accomplished "if society is willing to punish its captives humanely and to compensate offenders for the social disadvantages that have constrained them to undertake a life of crime."[49] According to this point of view, rehabilitation, rather than deterrence or incapacitation, is the preferred method of crime prevention because it responds to the needs of the offender: It "punishes but endeavors as well to rehabilitate society's wayward members."[50]

Restoration. The final utilitarian justification for punishment is restoration or *restorative justice*. Unlike the other three utilitarian perspectives, which emphasize punishment for crime prevention and focus almost exclusively on the offender, restorative justice views punishment as a means to repair the harm and injury caused by the crime, focusing on the victim and the community as well as the offender.[51] The goal of restorative justice "is to restore the victim and the community and to rebuild ruptured relationships in a process that allows all three parties to participate."[52]

Restorative justice achieves its goals through a variety of practices. These practices include victim-offender mediation, family group conferencing, sentencing circles, and citizen supervision of probation. What typically occurs is a face-to-face meeting involving the victim, the offender, the victim's and offender's families, and other members of the community.[53] Participants in the process discuss the effects of the crime on the victim, the offender, and the community and attempt to reach a collective agreement regarding the most appropriate sanction. Although this *process* differs significantly from the traditional criminal justice process, the *outcomes* are often similar to those imposed by judges and other criminal justice officials: apologies, restitution, fines, community service, alcohol or drug abuse treatment, anger management programs, intensive supervision probation, or short jail terms. Advocates of restorative justice contend that the use of these traditional methods does not conflict with "the belief that communities must be more heavily involved and given much greater responsibility in the quest for justice."[54]

It is somewhat difficult to use the case of Jason Miller, the crack dealer, to illustrate how an advocate of restorative justice would answer the question "Why punish?" This is because, at least as practiced in this country, restorative justice is confined to crimes by juveniles or to minor crimes by adults. Suppose, for the sake of illustration, that Jason Miller were convicted in a progressive jurisdiction that was experimenting with restorative justice practices for all nonviolent crimes. Assume that Jason had been operating a crack house and that residents of the neighborhood refused to leave their homes at night for fear of being attacked or robbed by someone high on crack or looking for money to buy crack. In a system guided by the principles of restorative justice, Jason might meet with representatives of the community in a "sentencing circle." The neighborhood residents would have an opportunity to explain how Jason's crime had affected their lives, and the participants would collectively agree on the appropriate punishment—that is, the punishment that would repair the harm done by Jason's crime and heal the community.

The Justification of Punishment: A Summary

Punishment, which involves the intentional infliction of harm or suffering, must be morally justified. It does not suffice to say that punishment is justified because it is prescribed by law. This is a *legal* justification for punishment, not a *moral* justification. Capital punishment, which is legally justified by the existence of statutes authorizing the state to impose the death penalty, may or may not be morally justified, depending on one's view of the purpose of punishment.

A moral justification for punishment rests on ethical principles, not on legal rules. Punishment is justified because of the offender's guilt and blameworthiness (retribution) or in order to achieve good results (utilitarianism). Retributivists look backward to the crime and the criminal. They argue that punishment is justified because it is deserved. Punishment is deserved either because it is inherently right that the guilty suffer for their wrongdoing or because those who violate the rules gain an unfair advantage over those who abide by the rules. Utilitarians, on the other hand, look forward to future consequences or results. They argue that punishment is justified because it leads to good results: It prevents future crime, reforms the offender, or helps the victim and the community heal. The harm done to the offender in the name of punishment, in other words, is outweighed by the good consequences that result from punishment.

Retributive and utilitarian theories of punishment provide significantly different answers to the question "Why punish?" As we see next, their answers to the question "How much to punish?" also vary rather dramatically.

How Much to Punish?

Having defined punishment and discussed the various justifications for punishment, we now turn to a related question: How much punishment is justified? Each theoretical perspective discussed thus far would answer this question differently. In fact, if we asked a panel of judges, each representing a different philosophy of punishment, to determine the appropriate punishment for a particular offender, the resulting sentences would probably vary widely. As von Hirsch has noted, "Deciding how much to punish is an agonizing process in which conflicting aspirations compete."[55]

In the sections that follow, we explain how each theoretical perspective would determine the amount of punishment. We begin with a brief overview of the principles that guide each theory's approach to this issue. (These principles are summarized in Box 1.3). We then use three hypothetical cases to illustrate how judges might use these principles in determining the appropriate sentence. We first present an "easy" case, in which the theories would all produce relatively similar, but not identical, sentences. We then present two more difficult cases, in which the theories might produce wildly divergent outcomes.

The Retributive Approach

The retributivist, who justifies punishment on the grounds of desert, uses the principle of proportionality to determine the amount of punishment.[56] Simply stated, this principle holds that the amount of punishment imposed on the offender should be equal to the amount of harm done by the offender. If the harm is great, the punishment should be severe; if the harm is minor, the punishment should be lenient. Disproportionate penalties—severe sentences for minor crimes or lenient sentences for serious crimes—are undeserved; as such, they are unjustified.[57]

Another way of expressing the retributive principle is, "The punishment should fit the crime."[58] This does not mean, however, that the punishment must "resemble" the crime or that the punisher should inflict on the offender what he or she has inflicted on the victim. Although this "mirror image" theory is often used to justify capital punishment—if someone takes another's life, then his or her life should be taken—it is not necessarily consistent with desert theory.[59] Even if the punishment resembles the crime, in other words, it is not necessarily what the offender *deserves*. Consider the case of a woman who runs a red light and crashes into a car, breaking both of the driver's legs. Although the retributivists would agree that she deserves to be punished for her negligent behavior, they would not agree that she deserves to have her legs broken in a similar fashion. That punishment, according to the retributivist, would be disproportionately severe.

BOX 1.3

HOW MUCH SHOULD WE PUNISH THOSE WHO VIOLATE THE LAW?

Retribution

The amount of punishment imposed on the offender should equal the amount of harm done by the offender. The punishment should be proportionate to the seriousness of the crime and the culpability of the offender.

Deterrence

The punishment should be sufficient to outweigh the benefits of the crime. The amount of punishment should be enough (and no more) to dissuade the offender from reoffending and to discourage potential criminals.

Incapacitation

The amount of punishment should be proportionate to the risk posed by the offender. Dangerous, high-risk offenders should be punished more severely than nonviolent, low-risk offenders.

Rehabilitation

The nature and duration of the punishment should be based on the offender's need for treatment and potential for reform. The punishment should continue until the offender has been rehabilitated.

To say, as retributive theory does, that the amount of punishment should be proportionate to the harm done implies a rank-ordering of crimes and punishments. It implies that the most serious offense should be matched to the most severe punishment and that the least serious offense should be matched to the most lenient punishment. But how are we to determine which offense is most (or least) serious and which punishment is most (or least) severe? Retributive theory suggests that crimes be rank-ordered on the basis of the harm done or risked by the offense and the culpability of the offender. Although this seems fairly straightforward, measuring harm and determining culpability are complicated. For example, most people would agree that armed robbery is a more serious crime than burglary. Both involve theft of property, but armed robbery poses a much greater risk of serious injury than burglary. But how would we rank-order the theft of a car from a shopping center parking lot and a nighttime burglary in which only an inexpensive stereo system is taken? The thief who steals a car has taken a more valuable piece of property, but the nighttime burglar has violated the occupants' privacy and threatened their sense of security. Consider the case in which an offender plants a bomb in a crowded subway station, but the bomb is defused before it causes any damage. Is his crime, which risks a great deal of harm, more or less serious than an assault that seriously injures one person but poses no risk to anyone else?

There are similar problems in determining an offender's culpability, which is defined as the degree to which the offender may be blamed or held responsible for the consequences (or risked consequences) of the act.[60] Most people would agree that someone who commits an intentional act is more blameworthy than someone who is reckless or negligent. The woman who commits a cold-blooded, premeditated murder is more culpable, and therefore her crime is more serious, than the woman who impulsively grabs a kitchen knife and stabs her husband during a domestic disturbance. Other issues, however, are more contentious. For example, should intoxication or mental capacity be taken into consideration in determining culpability? Should the offender's motivation for the crime or the degree to which the victim precipitated the crime matter? Should the offender's blameworthiness depend on whether he or she was a key player or an accomplice? Clearly, determining culpability, like measuring crime seriousness, is complicated.

Even if retributivists could agree on the relative seriousness of offenses, which is by no means assured, they still might not agree on what the specific punishment for each offense should be. Premeditated murder is commonly considered the most serious offense. As such, the retributive theorist would insist that it be punished with the most severe penalty. But what should that penalty be? Death? Life in prison with no possibility of parole? A prison sentence of a fixed number of years? If the most serious offense is punished by a sentence of death, what is the appropriate sentence for a crime in the middle of the seriousness scale? And for the least serious crime? To say, as the retributivist does, that the punishment should be neither disproportionately severe nor disproportionately lenient does not tell us how we should answer these questions.

Retributive theorists also disagree on another issue: the role that prior criminal record should play in determining the appropriate punishment. The pure retributivist would argue that punishment should be based on the harm done by the offense for which the offender is being punished and not on the cumulative harm of past offenses.[61] According to this view, a first offender does not deserve a more lenient punishment or a repeat offender a more severe punishment than would otherwise be imposed for the current offense. Other retributive theorists disagree with this analysis. Von Hirsch, for example, argues that taking prior criminal record into account is justified on retributive grounds because of the fact that "repetition alters the degree of culpability that may be ascribed to the offender."[62] A man who continues to drink and drive after being punished for drunk driving, in other words, "may be regarded as more culpable, since he persisted despite being censured through prior punishment."[63] Because the culpability of the offender affects the seriousness of the offense, the repeat offender has committed a more serious offense and thus deserves a more severe punishment.

To the retributive theorist, then, a just punishment is a deserved punishment, proportionate to the harm caused by the offense. Although disagreements regarding the measurement of crime seriousness, the relationship between crimes and penalties, and the role played by prior criminal record complicate the process, they do not alter this basic principle.

The Utilitarian Approach

The utilitarian, who justifies punishment on the basis of the positive results it produces, would give a variety of answers to the question "How much should we punish?" Utilitarians would generally agree that the amount of punishment should be the amount that would be needed to prevent the offender and other potential criminals from committing crimes in the future. However, each of the three traditional utilitarian approaches, deterrence, incapacitation, and rehabilitation, would use somewhat different criteria to determine how much punishment would be needed to prevent future crime.

If deterrence is viewed as the justification for punishment, then the amount of punishment should be sufficiently "costly" to outweigh the potential benefits of the crime.[64] Deterrence theorists contend that the costs of punishment reflect its *certainty*, *severity*, and *celerity*. Potential offenders "will refrain from committing crimes if they perceive that they are certain to be punished, with a severe penalty, and soon after the offense has been committed."[65] This suggests that punishment should be harsh enough to dissuade offenders from reoffending and to discourage would-be criminals from following their example. But how much is that? Would a lot or a little punishment be required to prevent the rapist from repeating his crime and to deter potential rapists? And the petty thief? What if it could be shown that a relatively lenient punishment is all that is needed to deter the rapist but a fairly severe punishment is needed to prevent petty theft? Would a penalty structure based on deterrence, which might not be calibrated to the seriousness of the offense, be "just?"[66]

The advocate of incapacitation would use a somewhat different calculus in determining the appropriate punishment. Because the goal of incapacitation is to prevent future crime by isolating dangerous or high-risk offenders, the amount of punishment would be proportionate to the risk posed by the offender. An offender whose predicted risk of reoffending is high would be punished more severely than one whose predicted risk is low. Again, this would not necessarily result in a punishment scheme that reflects the seriousness of the offense. Murderers, for example, seldom repeat their crimes, whereas those who use drugs have high recidivism rates. Does this mean that the murderer should receive a mild punishment and the drug offender, a severe one? Related to this notion, if incapacitation requires that we lock offenders up until the end of their "crime-prone" years, how do we predict when that will be? If a crime stems from an addiction or compulsion that an individual cannot control, will he or she need to be locked up forever?[67] Even if we assume that predictions about future criminality are reasonably accurate (a highly questionable assumption), is it justified to punish people more severely for what they are *predicted* to do?

If rehabilitation is the justification for punishment, the nature and duration of the punishment will depend on what is needed to reform the offender. The offender's punishment, in other words, will be an individualized treatment program designed to alter the forces that caused his or her criminality; the offender will be punished (treated) until "cured." Because we can't accurately predict how long it will take to reform the offender, the duration of the punishment is not known in advance. Thus, as in punishment for deterrence and selective incapacitation, there is not necessarily a correlation between the seriousness of the crime and the amount of punishment. Consider, for example, the case of offenders who commit serious crimes but do not need any type of rehabilitation. Because they don't need to be reformed, should they simply be released? What should be done with minor offenders who have serious psychological problems or are longtime heroin addicts? Should they be held indefinitely because they can't be reformed? Would either of these outcomes be fair?

In summary, the three traditional utilitarian perspectives have similar, but not identical, views regarding the amount of punishment that is appropriate. The utilitarian regards the purpose of punishment as crime prevention; thus, the appropriate amount of punishment would be the amount necessary to prevent crime by the offender and by other members of society. This implies that the punishment should be individualized. It should be tailored to the seriousness of the offense, as well as to each offender's likelihood of recidivism, dangerousness, or need for treatment. This implies, in turn, that similarly culpable offenders who commit the same crime may receive different sentences, depending on the amount of punishment needed to deter, incapacitate, or rehabilitate.

As noted at the beginning of this chapter, answers to questions regarding the purpose and allocation of punishment affect sentencing policies and practices. The way judges answer these questions influences the sentences they impose. Although it may be true that judges in the United States "tend to be eclectic, reasoning sometimes as utilitarians but sometimes, when they are outraged by a crime, as retributivists,"[68] their philosophies of punishment do matter. This is illustrated by the hypothetical cases presented next.

Theories of Punishment and Judges' Sentencing Decisions

A Case of Armed Robbery

As Maria Gonzales approached her car, Alexander Cruz put a loaded handgun to her back and demanded her purse. She complied, and Cruz fled with her purse, which contained cash and credit cards. He was apprehended, tried, and convicted of armed robbery. Cruz is 24 years old, unmarried, and unemployed. He has one prior conviction for possession of cocaine, for which he was sentenced to 2 years in prison. He now stands before the sentencing judge.

How would each of the four approaches to punishment affect the judge's decision regarding the amount of punishment Cruz should receive? Suppose first that the judge takes the deserts approach, believing that Cruz should be punished simply because he is guilty of a wrongful, illegal act and that the harm he receives in punishment should be roughly equal to the harm he intentionally inflicted. The judge's attention is focused on what has already happened: Cruz's offense and its harmfulness. The retributive judge is not concerned about other potential robbers and how they might be deterred by the punishment of Cruz, about preventing Cruz from committing more robberies, or about how to reform Cruz.

In thinking about this crime and the potential punishment, the judge focuses on the fact that Cruz's act put Maria Gonzales in a terrifying situation. She probably feared for her life, and she lost a substantial sum of money. Moreover, the fact that Cruz used a loaded gun put Gonzales at risk of suffering even greater harm: serious injury or loss of life. Cruz knew, or could reasonably be expected to have known, that using a weapon in the robbery might have led to Maria Gonzales (or a bystander) being seriously and permanently injured or even killed. Furthermore, Cruz's action harmed other citizens in the community. They are now more fearful and feel that their freedom to move about freely in the neighborhood has been limited.

The judge concludes that all of these "harms" must be reflected in Cruz's sentence. But how do these considerations translate into a specific sentence? It is difficult for the deserts approach to give a precise answer to this question. Theoretically, one could imagine living through all the harm that Cruz's act would typically cause and then imagine living through prison sentences of different lengths. One could ask, would I rather go to prison for 5 years or suffer all the harm that could be expected to result from this offense? If a person would rather suffer the harm of the offense than suffer the sentence, the sentence must be too severe and would not be called for by the deserts theory. To the extent that a person would be indifferent about experiencing the punishment versus suffering all the harm brought about by the offense, the deserts-oriented judge would be satisfied that the sentence was appropriate.

In a more practical approach, the judge (or a legislature or sentencing commission) could lay out a scale of offenses from least serious to most serious and then lay out a scale of punishments. The two scales could be anchored at points where the harm in the offense is most clearly comparable to the harm in punishment. At the extreme end, the punishment of death or life imprisonment would probably be assigned to the offense of first-degree murder. Short of this, the deserts theorist would hope that punishments and offenses could be brought roughly in line so that the harm in each would remain comparable. At the least, the deserts theorist would try to avoid assigning a greater punishment to a less serious crime. If such a scale were devised on the principle of "harm for harm," the judge could consult this scale in determining a sentence for Alexander Cruz.

What if the judge is a utilitarian rather than a retributivist? Instead of focusing on desert, he or she will focus on results. The utilitarian aims for three kinds of results, which have already been described: deterrence, incapacitation, and reform. Of course, a sentencing judge could aim for a combination of these results, but here we consider each of them in turn as they apply to the case of Alexander Cruz.

First, the judge could impose a punishment on Cruz to deter other potential offenders and to deter Cruz himself from committing additional robberies after he is released. In this case, the sentence would have to be sufficiently severe (sufficiently costly) to outweigh the benefits that offenders get from such crimes. The judge might reason that the incentive to commit armed robbery is high: The risks are relatively minor—the offender puts a gun to the victim's head and walks away with money and valuables, usually without a struggle—and the likelihood of profit is high. Because of this, the judge might decide that a relatively severe sentence is needed to deter Cruz and other would-be robbers. He could reason that the harm to Cruz in the name of punishment would be outweighed by the prevention of harm to potential victims.

Second, the judge could aim to incapacitate Cruz for a period of time: to confine him so that he will not be able to commit similar offenses. In this situation, the judge might reason either (a) that armed robbers in general pose a serious risk of reoffending or (b) that Cruz himself, who is in the middle of his crime-prone years, previously served time in prison for possession of drugs, and now stands convicted of a violent crime, is a dangerous, high-risk offender. In either case, the judge would justify locking Cruz up on the grounds that doing so would prevent him from committing crimes in the future. If the presentence investigation revealed that Cruz was addicted to cocaine and had committed the armed robbery to get money to satisfy his habit, the judge might sentence Cruz to the maximum term allowed by law. Cruz's drug addiction, in other words, makes it more likely that he will reoffend, which, according to the theory of incapacitation, justifies a harsher sentence.

Third, the judge could impose a sentence on Cruz in order to reform him: to change his character, his personality, or his behavior and thereby reduce the likelihood that he will reoffend. In this case, the judge would not focus on the seriousness of the crime or the risk posed by Cruz; he or she would focus on the factors that impelled Cruz to commit the crime. The nature and duration of the sentence would depend on whether Cruz robbed Maria Gonzales "just for the thrill of it," to get money to support his drug habit, or for some other reason. It would depend on what the judge (or corrections officials) believed the appropriate treatment was and where that treatment could best be administered. If Cruz were motivated by his drug addiction, a judge aiming for rehabilitation would want to make sure he received substance abuse treatment as part of his sentence. In this case, Cruz might be placed on probation and ordered to complete a residential drug treatment program as a condition of probation. If, on the other hand, it were revealed that Cruz robbed Maria Gonzales at gunpoint because he liked the feeling of power it gave him, a different type of punishment/treatment would be called for. The judge might sentence Cruz to prison for an indeterminate term with the expectation that Cruz would not be released until he reformed.

In the case of Alexander Cruz, then, four judges, each using a different philosophical approach, would arrive at relatively similar punishments. Although the rationale for the punishment would differ, each judge, with the possible exception of the judge whose goal was to rehabilitate, would impose a prison sentence on a repeat offender who has been convicted of a serious crime. As we see below, however, this "easy case" may not be typical.

A Case of Murder

Kathleen Harrison has been found guilty of second-degree murder. She came home from work one evening and found her husband Frank, who was unemployed and was supposed to be taking care of the children and preparing the evening meal, sitting in his easy chair, surrounded by empty beer cans. The children had been unsupervised all afternoon, and Frank had no plans for dinner. Kathleen confronted Frank, an argument ensued, and things quickly got out of hand. At one point, Kathleen grabbed a knife and ordered Frank out of the house. He refused, they struggled, and she stabbed him in the neck. He was taken to a local hospital where he died that night. Kathleen is 32 years old and is the mother of three young children. At the time of the murder, she was working full-time as an elementary school teacher. She has no prior convictions.

In this case, as in the case of Alexander Cruz, the judge using the deserts approach would focus on the harm done by the crime: A man's life has been taken, his children have been traumatized by his death, and his friends and relatives are grief stricken. Because Kathleen Harrison has committed a serious crime, she deserves a severe punishment, one commensurate to the harm caused. The retributive judge might take into consideration the fact that the crime was committed in the heat of passion and that Kathleen Harrison had never before been in trouble with the law; but he or she would not worry about the amount of punishment needed to deter her or others from committing murder in the future or about whether she needed to be isolated or reformed.

In contrast to the Cruz case, in which each of the utilitarian approaches yielded similar sentences to the sentence based on desert, in the Harrison case, the utilitarian judges would come to very different conclusions about the appropriate punishment. The judge whose goal is deterrence would believe it extremely unlikely that Harrison would commit murders in the future. Most murderers do not repeat their crimes, and there would be no reason to suspect that Harrison, who killed in the heat of passion and had no history of violence, would be any different. Moreover, judges know that would-be murderers generally are not deterred by the threat of punishment. If the purpose of punishment is deterrence, then, there is no reason (no justification) for punishing Kathleen Harrison.

A judge aiming for incapacitation would reach a similar conclusion. Kathleen Harrison is not a dangerous, high-risk offender; she does not need to be locked up to protect potential victims of her crimes. The judge who believes that the purpose of punishment is rehabilitation would agree, but for different reasons. Kathleen Harrison has been steadily employed for years, is not addicted to drugs or alcohol, and does not appear to have a personality disorder that would lead her to commit crimes in the future. At most, the judge pursuing the goal of rehabilitation might place Harrison on probation and order her to complete an anger management program.

As we can see, our four judges would not agree on the appropriate punishment for Kathleen Harrison. The retributive judge would impose a harsh sentence because of the harm done by the crime. The utilitarian judges, on the other hand, would not; they would reason that the harm inflicted on Harrison by imprisonment would outweigh any good results that punishing her would produce.

A Case of Drug Possession

Willie Bennett, a 23-year-old waiter at a trendy restaurant, was stopped by the police as he was driving home late one night. The officer said that one of his front headlights was burned out. After ascertaining that

Bennett's license and registration were valid, he asked Bennett whether he could search the car. Bennett consented to the search, which turned up a plastic bag containing half a gram of cocaine. Willie Bennett was arrested. He later pled guilty to possession of cocaine. Bennett, who is not married, has a previous conviction for petty larceny. During the presentence investigation, he admitted that he uses cocaine regularly.

What would our four judges decide to do in this case? The judge who bases the sentence on desert might not punish Bennett at all. This judge, whose goal is to fashion a sentence commensurate with the harm done by the crime, would reason that the use of cocaine, at least in this case, caused no harm. Bennett's behavior, though illegal, did not injure or threaten to injure anyone else. It did not disturb the peace and security of the community or make other citizens fearful. Even if the retributivist judge believed that Willie Bennett, who has been found guilty of a crime, deserves some punishment because of his guilt, he would impose only minimal punishment for this minor offense.

The utilitarian judges would not agree. Rather than focusing on the harmfulness of Willie Bennett's conduct, these judges would be concerned about the consequences of punishing (or not punishing) him. (See Box 1.4 for a different type of utilitarian reasoning.) They would be concerned about preventing crime, including the use of illegal drugs. The judge who sees deterrence as the primary purpose of punishment would argue that if Bennett were not punished, he would continue to use drugs. Moreover, he would reason that the punishment must be severe enough to overcome the temptation to use drugs. This judge would also contend that punishing Bennett severely would send a message to other would-be cocaine users, who then would curtail or reduce their use of illegal drugs.

The judge who views incapacitation as the goal of punishment would also impose a severe sentence. This judge would reason that drug offenders pose a particularly high risk of reoffending; their addiction makes it difficult for them to refrain from using drugs. He might also conclude, on the basis of research showing a strong relationship between drug use and crime, that Bennett is likely to engage in other types of crime if he continues to use drugs. Because Willie Bennett poses a high risk of future criminality, imprisonment, according to the judge who seeks to incapacitate, is the appropriate punishment.

The outcome would be different if Willie Bennett were sentenced by a judge who believed that punishment should rehabilitate. This judge would pursue the goal of crime prevention by insisting that Bennett get treatment for his substance abuse problem. He would send Bennett to prison only if he believed that participation in a prison-based drug treatment program would have the best odds of curing him of his drug addiction. More realistically, the judge would place Bennett on probation, with the requirement that he successfully complete a community-based drug treatment program. The judge would monitor Bennett's progress and would continue his probation until he had been reformed. If Bennett failed to complete the program or was arrested for a new drug offense, the judge could consider other options (a short period of shock incarceration, for example) but the overriding goal would still be Bennett's rehabilitation. Bennett would not be released from the court's supervision until and unless he reformed.

As in the previous case, the four judges sentencing Willie Bennett would reach different conclusions about the appropriate punishment. Depending on the judge's philosophy of punishment, Bennett might receive a long prison sentence, probation plus drug treatment, or no punishment at all.

BOX 1.4

AN UNUSUAL UTILITARIAN JUSTIFICATION

In December of 2000, a judge in Tampa, Florida stated that she had decided not to send a drug offender to prison because she feared that he would become a target for sexual assault. Hillsborough County Judge Florence Foster placed Paul Hamill, who had violated his probation for a previous cocaine conviction, on probation for 2 more years and ordered him to undergo drug treatment.

At the sentencing hearing, Judge Foster stated, "He's a small, thin, white man with curly dark hair, and I suspect he would certainly become a sexual target in the Florida state prison system." She also noted that she had been told that prison officials could not protect someone like Hamill. "I'm not going to send a man like this to Florida state prison," she said. "That is cruel and unusual punishment in my book."

In this case, the judge seems to have concluded that the pain and suffering that would be inflicted on Hamill by incarcerating him outweighed any good consequences that might result. Is this a morally justified reason? Why or why not?

SOURCE: "Judge Says Prison Not Safe for Convict," *Omaha World Herald,* December 29, 2000, p. A-4.

Considered together, these three cases illustrate the complexities inherent in deciding how much to punish. Although the four theories would lead to relatively similar results in some types of cases, they would produce dramatically different results in other cases. As we stated at the beginning of the chapter, our answers to the questions "Why punish?" and "How much to punish?" have important policy implications.

Conclusion

In 1976, the Committee for the Study of Incarceration, which included lawyers, philosophers, social scientists, and criminal justice officials, began its report by asking the question "What should be done with the criminal offender after conviction?"[69] The committee also asked whether "this society ought *ever* to resort to incarceration, and if so, when, under what conditions, and for how long a period of time."[70]

A quarter of a century later, these questions are still being posed and debated. As we have seen in this chapter, the answers depend on one's philosophy of punishment. They depend on whether one regards the purpose of punishment from a retributive or a utilitarian perspective. Retributive, or desert, theorists, who contend that punishment of the guilty is justified because it is deserved, would base their answers to both questions on the degree of harm caused by the offender. Utilitarian, or results, theorists view punishment as a means of accomplishing something else (i.e., crime prevention) and thus believe that punishment is justified only to the extent that it produces good results. They would weigh the costs and benefits of punishment and choose the sanction that maximized benefits and minimized costs.

It should be clear that these philosophical differences have practical effects. A sentencing scheme based on a philosophy of retribution would differ in important ways from one based on utilitarian rationales. Similarly, judges' sentencing decisions will vary, sometimes dramatically, depending on the philosophy of punishment guiding those decisions. As we see in the chapters that follow, we cannot understand the sentencing process and its outcomes unless we understand and appreciate these differences.

Discussion Questions: Chapter 1

1. Explain why individual and group acts of vengeance do not constitute "punishment."

2. How do retributive and utilitarian theorists answer the question "Why punish?"

3. What is the difference between a *legal* justification for punishment and a *moral* justification for punishment?

4. Could the principles underlying restorative justice be applied to offenders who commit serious violent crimes? Why or why not?

5. Consider the following scenario: Jack Brown was celebrating his 21st birthday with two of his close friends. After downing several drinks at a local bar, they hopped in Jack's car, intending to drive to a nearby restaurant for dinner. Jack, who was legally drunk, ran a stop sign and smashed into an oncoming car. He suffered a broken leg. His two friends were killed instantly. Jack Brown was convicted of motor vehicle homicide. How would the four theories of punishment answer the question "Why should Jack Brown be punished?" How would each of them answer the question "What is the appropriate punishment for Jack Brown?"

6. If you were a criminal court judge and could choose only one of the purposes of punishment to guide your sentencing decisions, which one would you choose? Why?

Notes

1. Walker, *Why Punish?* p. 1.
2. von Hirsch, *Doing Justice: The Choice of Punishments*, p. 59.
3. See, for example, Moore, "The Moral Worth of Retribution"; Moore, "Persons and Punishment"; and von Hirsch, *Doing Justice*.
4. Hospers, "Punishment, Protection, and Retaliation," p. 25.
5. Garland, "Punishment and Society Today," p. 5.
6. Morris, *The Brothel Boy and Other Parables of the Law*.
7. Ibid., p. 16.
8. Ibid.
9. Ibid., p. 19.
10. Ibid., p. 21.
11. Hart, *Punishment and Responsibility*, p. 1.
12. See, for example, Packer, *The Limits of the Criminal Sanction*, and Walker, *Why Punish?*
13. Walker, *Why Punish?* p. 2.

14. Hospers, "Punishment, Protection, and Retaliation"; Moore, "Persons and Punishment"; von Hirsch, *Doing Justice*.
15. Packer, *The Limits of the Criminal Sanction*, p. 37.
16. Moore, "The Moral Worth of Retribution," p. 188.
17. Hospers, "Punishment, Protection, and Retaliation," p. 22.
18. Braithwaite and Pettit, *Not Just Deserts: A Republican Theory of Criminal Justice*, p. 157.
19. See, for example, Kant, *The Philosophy of Law*, and Moore, "The Moral Worth of Retribution."
20. Packer, *The Limits of the Criminal Sanction*, p. 9.
21. See, for example, Finnis, *Natural Law and Natural Rights*; Moore, "Persons and Punishment"; Murphy, *Retribution, Justice and Therapy*; and Sadurski, *Giving Desert Its Due*.
22. Walker, *Why Punish?* p. 25.
23. Hospers, "Punishment, Protection, and Retaliation," p. 25.
24. Ibid.
25. Bentham, *Introduction to the Principles of Morals and Legislation*.
26. Beccaria, *On Crimes and Punishments*.
27. von Hirsch, *Doing Justice*, p. 44.
28. Durham, *Crisis and Reform*, p. 134.
29. Jacobs, "Crack Dealers and Restrictive Deterrence: Identifying Narcs," p. 427.
30. Hospers, "Punishment, Protection, and Retaliation," p. 28.
31. Ibid.
32. Durham, *Crisis and Reform*, p. 25.
33. Wilson, "Selective Incapacitation," p. 152.
34. Packer, *The Limits of the Criminal Sanction*, p. 49.
35. von Hirsch and Ashworth, *Principled Sentencing*, p. 103.
36. Tonry, "Selective Incapacitation: The Debate Over Its Ethics," p. 171.
37. Floud and Young, *Dangerousness and Criminal Justice*, p. 49.
38. von Hirsch, "Prediction and False Positives," p. 121.
39. Ibid., p. 122.
40. Tonry, "Selective Incapacitation," p. 176.
41. von Hirsch, *Doing Justice*, p. 11.
42. von Hirsch and Ashworth, *Principled Sentencing*, p. 1.
43. If, however, this hypothetical defendant were convicted of an offense with a mandatory minimum prison sentence, the judge would be prohibited from imposing probation and drug treatment.

44. Skepticism about the effectiveness of rehabilitation programs and criticism of the use of rehabilitation as a justification for punishment grew in the wake of the publication in 1974 of the "Martinson Report," which concluded that "rehabilitative efforts that have been reported so far have no appreciable effect on recidivism." This report was widely—and some would say mistakenly—interpreted to mean that "nothing works." This attitude began to change in the late 1980s in response to research showing that treatment, particularly substance abuse treatment, was effective. For research critical of treatment programs, see Martinson (1974). For reviews of research on the efficacy of drug treatment, see Anglin and Hser (1990), Lipsey (1992), and Lipton (1995).

45. von Hirsch and Maher, "Should Penal Rehabilitationism Be Revived?" p. 43.

46. Packer, *The Limits of the Criminal Sanction*, p. 56.

47. See, for example, Cullen and Gilbert, *Reaffirming Rehabilitation*; East, "Is Reformation Possible in Prison Today?"; and Palmer, "The Effectiveness of Intervention: Recent Trends and Current Issues."

48. Cullen and Gilbert, "Reaffirming Rehabilitation," p. 32.

49. Ibid.

50. Ibid., p. 38.

51. See, for example, Braithwaite, "Restorative Justice: Assessing Optimistic and Pessimistic Accounts"; Bazemore, "Restorative Justice and Earned Redemptions: Communities, Victims, and Offender Reintegration"; Carey, "Restorative Justice in Community Corrections"; Hahn, *Emerging Criminal Justice: Three Pillars for a Proactive System*; and Kurki, "Restorative and Community Justice."

52. Kurki, "Restorative and Community Justice," p. 236.

53. A thorough discussion of these techniques can be found in Kurki, "Restorative and Community Justice," pp. 268-284.

54. Hahn, *Emerging Criminal Justice*, p. 157.

55. von Hirsch, *Doing Justice*, p. 59.

56. von Hirsch and Ashworth, *Principled Sentencing*, p. 182. In *Doing Justice*, von Hirsch referred to this as the "principle of commensurate deserts."

57. von Hirsch, *Doing Justice*, p. 66.

58. Hospers, "Punishment, Protection, and Retaliation," p. 23.

59. Walker, "Why Punish?" p. 69.
60. von Hirsch, *Doing Justice*, p. 82.
61. Walker, *Sentencing: Theory, Law, and Practice.*
62. von Hirsch, *Doing Justice*, p. 85.
63. Ibid.
64. Bentham, "Punishment and Deterrence."
65. Paternoster, *Capital Punishment in America*, p. 219.
66. This issue is further complicated by the fact that most scholarly research concludes that the nature or severity of penalties has little, if any, effect on the crime rate. The voluminous body of research on the deterrent effect of the death penalty reveals, for example, that "capital punishment is no better at deterring would-be murderers than a prolonged period of incarceration" (Paternoster 1991:241). Also, see Cochran, Mitchell, Chamblin, and Seth (1994). Research examining the effect of increased use of imprisonment similarly fails to support the deterrence argument (Blumstein, Cohen, and Nagin 1978; Gibbs 1975; Reiss and Roth 1993).
67. Packer, *The Limits of the Criminal Sanction.*
68. Walker, *Why Punish?* p. 8.
69. von Hirsch, *Doing Justice*, p. 1.
70. Ibid., p. xxiii.

Chapter Two

Sentencing Options and the Sentencing Process

The most difficult task facing a criminal court judge is sentencing a defendant. . . . Judges are aware of the horrible conditions awaiting defendants sentenced to penal institutions, just as they are cognizant of the general ineffectiveness of the probation sentence. Compassionate judges are aware of the inability of either form of sentence to adequately prevent the defendant from returning to society even more embittered and committed to a continued life of crime.

Paul Wice[1]

In February of 2001, Colorado District Court Judge David Lass sentenced Nathan Hall, a former lift attendant at the Vail ski resort, to 90 days in county jail for the ski slope collision that killed Alan Cobb in 1997. Hall, who was 18 years old at the time of the incident, was skiing out of control and at a high rate of speed when he collided with Cobb on an intermediate ski run. He was convicted of criminally negligent homicide.

Judge Lass also sentenced Hall to 3 years of intensive supervision probation following the 90-day jail sentence. In addition, he ordered Hall to perform community service and make financial restitution to Cobb's family for funeral and travel expenses and for psychological counseling. In announcing the sentence, Judge Lass said that although Hall didn't deserve a prison sentence, he did need to be punished for his role in Cobb's death. "He is still a young man, and he has done some immature and irresponsible things," Lass said. "Probably some of the things that have been said by others in this courtroom may be more important than my decision or anything I can say."[2]

As Nathan Hall's case illustrates, an individual who has been convicted of a crime faces a number of different sentence alternatives, depending on the seriousness of the crime and the willingness of the judge to experiment with alternative sentences. The judge has more discretion and thus more opportunities to tailor the sentence to fit the individual offender if the crime is a misdemeanor or a less serious felony. In this type of case, the judge might impose a fine, order the offender to perform community service, place the offender on probation, or impose some other alternative to incarceration. The judge's options are more limited if the crime is serious or if the offender has a lengthy prior criminal record. In this situation, a jail or prison sentence is likely; the only question is how long the offender will serve.

In this chapter, we discuss the options available to the judge at sentencing. We begin with the death penalty, which is the ultimate sanction that society can impose on the guilty. We then discuss incarceration and the various alternatives to incarceration. We conclude the chapter by explaining that the sentences imposed on (and served by) offenders actually result from a "collaborative exercise" that involves legislators and criminal justice officials other than the judge.

The Judge's Options at Sentencing

The Death Penalty

In the United States, 38 states and the federal government have statutes that authorize the death penalty.[3] Imposed for a variety of offenses in the past, including armed robbery and rape,[4] the death penalty today is imposed almost exclusively for first-degree murder. It is, however, a penalty that is rarely applied. In 1999, nearly 15,000 persons were arrested for murder and nonnegligent manslaughter,[5] but only 272 persons were sentenced to death.[6]

A sentence of death does not necessarily mean that the offender will be executed. The offender's conviction or sentence might be overturned by a higher court, the sentence might be commuted to life in prison by the governor, or the offender might die in prison. Of the 6,365 prisoners under the sentence of death from 1977 to 1999, 598 (9.4 percent) were executed and 2,240 (35.2 percent) received some other type of disposition; the remaining 3,527 inmates were still incarcerated. The average amount of time these offenders had been on death row was 7 years and 7 months.[7]

Current death penalty statutes have a number of common features.[8] Most are *guided-discretion statutes* that allow the death penalty to be imposed only if at least one statutorily defined aggravating circumstance is present. Although the aggravating circumstances vary among jurisdictions, the list typically includes such crimes as murder for hire, murder of more than one person, murder of a police officer, murder involving torture, or murder during the commission of another crime, such as armed robbery or sexual assault.

Most jurisdictions also require a bifurcated trial in capital cases. The first stage involves the determination of the defendant's guilt or innocence. If the defendant is convicted of a capital crime—that is, a crime for which the death penalty is an option—a separate sentencing proceeding is held. At this stage, evidence regarding the aggravating and mitigating circumstances of the case is presented. The jury and/or the judge weigh the evidence and decide whether the defendant should be sentenced to death or should receive a lesser sentence of life without parole, life, or a specified term of years. Finally, most death penalty statutes also provide for automatic review of the conviction and death sentence by the state's highest court. If either the conviction or the sentence is overturned, the case can be sent back to the trial court for retrial or resentencing.[9]

The role played by the judge in the capital sentencing process varies from state to state. In some jurisdictions, such as Texas and Louisiana, the jury decides whether the defendant should be sentenced to death or not. In these jurisdictions, the jury's decision cannot be overturned by the trial court judge. In other jurisdictions, such as Alabama and Florida, the jury recommends the sentence, but the judge can overrule the jury. Under Florida law, for example, the jury in a capital case makes an advisory sentence recommendation to the court, but the judge is required to independently weigh the aggravating and mitigating circumstances and determine whether the offender should be sentenced to life imprisonment or death.[10] In some states, such as Nebraska, the death penalty decision is made either by the trial judge or by a panel of judges.

Although, as noted above, the death penalty is used infrequently, its importance as a sentencing alternative cannot be ignored. As we explain in detail in Chapter 5, questions have been raised about the fairness of the death penalty process. Critics charge that the death penalty is imposed in an arbitrary and capricious manner and that there is compelling evidence of racial discrimination in the capital sentencing process.

Incarceration

Unlike the death penalty, which can be imposed only for first-degree murder and a handful of other offenses, a jail or prison sentence is an option in most criminal cases. This includes misdemeanors as well as felonies. The Texas Penal Code, for example, categorizes misdemeanors as Class A, Class B, or Class C; Class A misdemeanors are the most serious, Class C the least serious. Although offenders convicted of Class C misdemeanors cannot be sentenced to jail, those convicted of Class B offenses can be confined in jail for up to 180 days, and those found guilty of Class A offenses can be sentenced to jail for as long as a year.[11] In most jurisdictions, sentences of less than a year are served in a local jail, and those of a year or more are served in a state prison. All offenders who are tried in U.S. District Courts and receive a prison sentence are incarcerated in a federal prison; there are no federal jails.

For some offenses, a prison sentence is not simply an option, it is required. All jurisdictions in the United States now have laws that prescribe mandatory minimum terms of incarceration for selected crimes. For example, 41 states have mandatory sentences for repeat or habitual offenders and for crimes involving possession of a deadly weapon. Most states also require minimum prison sentences for certain types of drug offenses: trafficking, selling drugs to minors, or selling drugs within 1,000 feet of a school.[12] At the federal level, more than 100 crimes are subject to laws requiring 2- to 20-year minimum sentences. Mandatory minimum provisions can be circumvented by prosecutors who refuse to charge offenses that trigger a minimum sentence[13] or by judges who either refuse to convict or ignore the statute and impose less than the mandatory minimum sentence,[14] but these "tough-on-crime" laws limit the options available to the judge at sentencing. They generally require the judge to sentence the offender to prison for a specified period of time.

Judges' options are also limited by the type of sentencing system used in their jurisdiction (see Box 2.1). Some state laws require judges to impose indeterminate sentences.[15] In these states, the legislature specifies a minimum and a maximum sentence for a particular offense or category of offenses. In sentencing an offender, the judge either imposes a minimum and a maximum sentence from within this range or, alternatively, determines only the maximum sentence that the offender can serve. Assume, for example, that the sentence range for armed robbery is 5 to 20 years. In the first scenario, the judge would determine both the minimum and the maximum sentence. He or she might sentence the offender to 5 to 10 years, 10 to 15 years, 5 to 20 years, or any other range of years within the statutory minimums and maximums. In the second scenario, the judge would determine only the maximum penalty; the minimum penalty would be automatically applied. In other words, regardless of whether the maximum penalty was 10 years, 15 years, or 20 years, the minimum would always be 5 years. In either case, the actual amount of time the offender will serve is determined by the parole board on the basis of its judgment as to whether the offender has been rehabilitated or has simply served enough time. An armed robber sentenced to an indeterminate sentence of 5 to 10 years, then, will serve at least 5 years but no more than 10 years, depending on the parole board's assessment of his case.

In other states, judges impose determinate sentences, which are fixed-term sentences that may be reduced if the offender behaves while incarcerated (i.e., through "good-time credits").[16] The offender's date of release is based on the sentence imposed minus any good-time credits. The parole board may supervise offenders who have been released from prison, but it does not determine when offenders will be released. In states that have adopted this type of system, the legislature provides a presumptive range of confinement for various categories of offenses. Although some offenses are nonprobationable, for most crimes, the judge has the discretion to determine whether the offender will be incarcerated and if so, for how long. If, for example, the presumptive range of confinement for robbery is 4 to 15 years and the statute does not specify that offenders convicted of robbery must be sentenced to prison, the judge could impose either a probation sentence or a prison sentence of anywhere from 4 to 15 years. If the sentence was 10 years in prison, the offender would serve that time minus credit for good behavior.

In still other states and at the federal level, judges' incarceration options are limited by presumptive sentencing guidelines.[17] (Sentencing guidelines are discussed in detail in Chapter 6.) In jurisdictions that use this model, a sentencing commission develops guidelines based on the seriousness of the offense and the offender's prior criminal record, which judges are required to use in determining the appropriate sentence. Judges are allowed to de-

---

BOX 2.1

SENTENCING SYSTEMS IN
STATE AND FEDERAL JURISDICTIONS

Indeterminate Sentence

The legislature specifies a minimum and maximum sentence for each offense or class of offenses. The judge imposes either a minimum and a maximum term of years or the maximum term only. The parole board decides when the offender will be released from prison.

Determinate Sentence

The legislature provides a presumptive range of confinement for each offense or class of offenses. The judge imposes a fixed term of years within this range. The offender serves this sentence minus time off for good behavior.

Mandatory Sentence

The legislature requires a mandatory minimum prison sentence for habitual offenders and/or for offenders convicted of certain crimes. Examples include use of a weapon during the commission of a crime, drug trafficking, and selling drugs to minors.

Sentencing Guidelines

A legislatively authorized sentencing commission establishes presumptive sentencing guidelines. The guidelines are typically based on the seriousness of the offense and the offender's prior record. Judges are required to follow the guidelines or explain in writing why they did not.

---

part from the guidelines and impose a more severe or less severe sentence than the guidelines require, but they must provide a written justification for doing so. The judge's decision to depart either upward or downward can be appealed to a state or federal appellate court.

Felony Sentences in 1996

Recent data on the types of sentences imposed on felony offenders reveal that most of them are incarcerated; less than one third receive "straight probation" (i.e., probation only, not jail or prison followed by probation).[18] As shown in Exhibit 2.1, 38 percent of all offenders convicted of felonies in state courts in 1996 were sentenced to prison, 31 percent were sentenced to jail, and 31 percent were placed on probation. The proportion of federal offenders sentenced to prison in 1996 was even higher. Of all federal offenders,

Exhibit 2.1 Sentences Imposed on Felony Offenders in State and Federal Courts, 1996

Type of Sentence	Offenders Convicted in State Courts			Offenders Convicted in Federal Courts		
	Prison	Jail	Probation	Prison ≥ 1 year	Prison < 1 year	Probation
All offenses (percentage)	38%	31%	31%	64%	16%	20%
Violent offenses[a]	57	22	21	85	7	8
Property offenses[b]	34	28	38	29	29	42
Drug offenses[c]	35	37	28	84	7	8
Average sentence length (months)						
All offenses	62	6	41	78	7	39
Violent offenses	105	7	48	107	8	42
Property offenses	49	6	40	35	7	39
Drug offenses	51	6	42	89	9	42
Average Estimated time served in prison: months/percentage						
All offenses	28/45%			67/85%		
Violent offenses	53/51%			91/85%		
Property offenses	21/42%			30/85%		
Drug offenses	21/41%			76/85%		

SOURCE: Adapted from *Felony Sentences in the United States, 1996* (Table 3, Table 7, and Table 11), by U.S Department of Justice, Bureau of Justice Statistics, 1999. Washington, DC: Author.

a. Includes murder, sexual assault, robbery, aggravated assault and other violent crimes.
b. Includes burglary, larceny, motor vehicle theft, forgery, fraud, and embezzlement.
c. Includes drug trafficking and drug possession.

80 percent were sentenced to prison, 64 percent received a sentence of a year or more, and 16 percent received a sentence of less than a year. As one would expect, the likelihood of a prison sentence was highest for offenders convicted of violent crimes. This was especially true of federal offenders: 85 percent of all federal offenders convicted of violent crimes were sentenced to prison for more than a year. Federal offenders convicted of drug offenses also faced high odds of imprisonment. In fact, the incarceration rates for drug offenders and violent offenders convicted in U.S. District Courts were nearly identical.

Exhibit 2.1 also displays the average lengths of prison, jail, and probation sentences. The typical state felony offender received a prison sentence of just over 5 years, whereas the typical federal offender received a sentence of 6.5 years. Again as one would expect, offenders convicted of violent offenses received substantially longer average prison sentences than those convicted of property crimes or drug offenses. The sentences imposed on state property offenders averaged longer than those imposed on federal property offenders. In contrast, the average sentence imposed on federal drug offenders (89 months) was substantially longer than the average sentence imposed on state drug offenders (51 months).

It is important to note that the amount of prison time the offender receives at sentencing is not the amount of time that he or she will actually serve in prison. There are two reasons for this. As noted earlier, many states have indeterminate sentencing systems in which the parole board decides when the offender is fit to be released. In these states, the amount of time served equals the amount imposed at sentencing only in the relatively rare cases in which the defendant is never paroled. In addition, in most states, prison inmates can earn early release for good behavior and automatic good-time credits are awarded in a number of states. Both of these factors reduce the amount of time the offender will serve in prison.

As shown in Exhibit 2.1, state prisoners serve only 45 percent of the sentence imposed. The estimated time to be served is slightly higher for violent offenses and somewhat lower for property and drug offenses. In contrast, the expected time to be served for federal inmates is a uniform 85 percent. By law, all federal inmates—with the exception of those sentenced to life imprisonment, who must serve the sentence in full—must serve a minimum of 85 percent of the sentence imposed. This means that offenders sentenced in federal court receive sentences averaging 16 months longer than the ones imposed by state courts but they will serve 3 years and 3 months longer than state prison inmates. The differences for drug offenses are even larger: Federal drug offenders will serve 4.5 years longer than state drug offenders.

Incarceration, then, is a widely prescribed and frequently imposed sentencing option. In the United States, in fact, it is now the "option of choice" for offenders convicted of felonies in both state and federal courts.

Probation

The primary alternative to incarceration is probation. A straight probation sentence does not entail confinement in jail or prison.[19] Rather, the judge imposes a set of conditions agreed to by the offender, who is then released into the community. The court retains control over the offender while he or she is on probation; if the conditions of probation are violated, the judge can modify the conditions or revoke probation and sentence the offender to jail or prison.

Probation was developed primarily as a means of diverting juvenile offenders and adults convicted of misdemeanors and nonviolent felonies from jail or prison. However, as shown in Exhibit 2.1, just under a third of all state felony defendants and 20 percent of all federal felony defendants were sentenced to probation in 1996. Although straight probation sentences were imposed more frequently when the offender was convicted of a nonviolent crime, a significant minority (21 percent) of offenders convicted of violent felonies in state courts were placed on probation. This included 28 percent of all offenders convicted of aggravated assault, 21 percent of those convicted of sexual assault, 13 percent of those convicted of robbery, and 5 percent of those convicted of murder and manslaughter.[20] As these figures indicate, probation is not reserved exclusively for nonviolent offenders.

Although the proliferation of statutes requiring mandatory minimum prison sentences has reduced the number of offenses for which probation is an option, judges retain wide discretion in deciding between prison and probation for offenses that are not subject to mandatory minimums. Most state statutes allow judges to impose probation unless they believe that (a) the offender is likely to commit additional crimes if released, (b) the offender is in need of treatment that can be provided more effectively in jail or prison, or (c) probation would be inappropriate given the seriousness of the offender's crime. Many statutes also specify the conditions that "shall be accorded weight in favor of withholding sentence of imprisonment."[21] The Nebraska statute, for example, includes such aspects as the offender's motivation or intent, the role played by the offender in the crime, provocation on the part of the victim, the offender's criminal history, and the burden that imprisonment would place on the offender's dependents. Other state statutes similarly specify that probation is the preferred sentence unless the crime is serious and the offender is likely to commit additional crimes if not locked up.

The Conditions of Probation

All offenders placed on probation are expected to meet regularly with their probation officer and to obey all laws. But these are minimum requirements: Most probationers face additional restrictions. A recent national survey of adults on probation found that 36 percent of all probationers had three or four additional conditions attached to the sentence; 46 percent had five or more conditions.[22] As shown in Exhibit 2.2, which lists the conditions imposed on probationers (felony and misdemeanor) in 1995, most offenders were also required to pay court costs, supervision fees, or fines. About a third were required to pay restitution to the victim. About 40 percent of the probationers were required to enroll in some form of substance abuse treatment. Consistent with this, about a third were required to submit to drug testing, and 8.4 percent were required to refrain from using alcohol or drugs. Forty percent of the offenders were also required to maintain employment or enroll in educational or vocational training programs. Relatively few offenders, on the other hand, were subject to requirements designed to monitor or restrict their movement (e.g., curfews, house arrest, electronic monitoring) or orders to stay away from bars or other places of business.

Offenders who violate the conditions of their probation may be called before the court to explain the circumstances of the violation. At the probation violation hearing, the judge can continue or extend the offender's probation, with or without additional conditions. If the violations are serious enough or if the offender repeatedly violates the conditions of probation, the judge may schedule a hearing to determine whether the offender's probation should be revoked and a different sentence alternative imposed, generally incarceration in jail or prison. In 1995, 18 percent of the adult probationers surveyed by the Bureau of Justice Statistics had at least one disciplinary hearing during the course of their probation. Most were brought back to court for "technical violations": for example, failure to meet regularly with the probation officer, failure to pay fines or restitution, or failure to attend or complete a drug treatment program. More than a third, however, violated probation by being arrested for new offenses.[23] Although most of these hearings resulted in a continuation of the offender's probation, just under a third led to revocation of probation and incarceration of the offenders.[24]

Revocation of probation is more likely if the offender is arrested for a new offense, particularly a new felony offense, than if the offender is cited for a technical violation. If, for example, an offender on probation for a felony drug offense tests positive for illegal drugs, the judge might continue his or her probation with a stipulation that the individual submit to more frequent random drug tests and complete a drug treatment program. If, on the other hand, the offender is arrested for possession of cocaine, the judge would probably revoke his or her probation and sentence that individual to prison. Offenders who repeatedly commit technical violations also risk eventual revocation of probation and incarceration.

Exhibit 2.2 Conditions of Sentences of Adult Probationers, 1995

Condition of Sentence	Percentage
Fees, fines, court costs	84.2
Supervision fees	61.0
Fines	55.8
Court costs	54.5
Substance abuse treatment	41.0
Alcohol	29.2
Drug	23.0
Employment and training	40.3
Maintain employment	34.7
Education/training	15.0
Alcohol/drug restrictions	38.2
Alcohol	32.5
Drug	8.1
Restitution to victim	30.3
Community service	25.7
Restrictions	21.1
No contact with victim	10.4
Driving restrictions	5.3
Other treatment	17.9
Sex offenders program	2.5
Psychiatric/psychological counseling	7.1
Other counseling	9.2
Confinement/monitoring	10.1
Boot camp	0.5
House arrest/electronic monitoring	3.7
Curfew	0.9
Restriction on movement	4.2

SOURCE: Adapted from *Characteristics of Adults on Probation, 1995* (Table 8), by U.S. Department of Justice, Bureau of Justice Statistics, 1997. Washington, DC: Author.

Intensive Supervision Probation

We noted above that probation was developed as an alternative to incarceration for juvenile offenders and for first-time adult offenders convicted of misdemeanors. Skyrocketing increases in prison and jail populations coupled with concerns about the costs of incarcerating nonviolent offenders led to increasingly large numbers of felony offenders being placed on probation. Some policymakers and researchers questioned the wisdom of this, citing high recidivism rates for felony probationers. One of the most influential of these studies was an analysis of recidivism among adult felony offenders placed on probation in Los Angeles and Alameda Counties (California).[25] The authors of this study reported that recidivism rates among these probationers were high: 65 percent were arrested and 51 percent were charged and convicted during the 40-month follow-up period. Moreover, 18 percent of the probationers were convicted of serious violent crimes. These results led the researchers to conclude that "felony probation has been a high-risk gamble."[26]

Findings such as this led to a search for "alternative sanctions that punish but do not involve incarceration."[27] One of these alternative, or intermediate, sanctions is intensive supervision probation (ISP), which, as the name suggests, involves closer scrutiny of offenders and more restrictions on their behavior. Candidates for ISP include offenders, typically those convicted of felonies, deemed too serious or dangerous for routine probation but not so serious or dangerous that they must be incarcerated. An unemployed car thief whose crimes are becoming more frequent or escalating in seriousness might be eligible for intensive supervision probation. A serial rapist, on the other hand, would be viewed as too dangerous to qualify for the program, and a college student convicted of possession of a small amount of marijuana would be perceived as a better candidate for routine probation than intensive supervision probation.

Offenders placed on intensive supervision probation are required to meet frequently with their probation officers. Some programs require as many as five face-to-face contacts per week, whereas others require less frequent face-to-face meetings but include routine curfew checks or daily phone calls.[28] In addition, these probationers are routinely ordered to perform community service, maintain employment and/or attend school or job training programs, complete substance abuse treatment programs, submit to random drug tests, and abide by curfews and other restrictions. Offenders in ISP programs may also be subject to house arrest and electronic monitoring.

Intensive supervision probation, then, is a penalty with "more punitive bite than simple probation"[29] that is designed to reform and rehabilitate offenders in the community while minimizing the risk that such offenders pose to the community.

Although the concept of ISP has almost universal support among policymakers and practitioners, questions regarding its effectiveness and its application have surfaced. One issue is whether ISP is more effective than routine probation in preventing or reducing reoffending. Most evaluations conclude that it is not.[30] In fact, a multisite experimental evaluation in which offenders were randomly assigned to ISP or to other sentence alternatives found that offenders sentenced to ISP not only had recidivism rates comparable to other offenders but also had *higher* rates of technical violations and probation revocation.[31] The authors of this study attributed this higher rate of "failure" in part to the nature or structure of the ISP program. In other words, because they were subject to more restrictive conditions as well as heightened surveillance, ISP participants faced a greater risk of failure than did offenders on routine probation.[32] Others suggest that the results of this evaluation indicate that ISP is succeeding, not failing. They suggest that if ISP is seen as a means of incapacitating offenders in the community, then high rates of technical violations and probation revocation signal that probation officers "are watching their clients closely enough to make the commission of new crimes quite difficult."[33]

A second issue is *net widening*, which, in this case, refers to the use of ISP for probation-bound rather than prison-bound offenders. An important goal of ISP is to divert nonserious, nonviolent offenders from the prison system. Thus, offenders selected for participation in ISP should be those who otherwise would have gone to prison. But critics charge that ISP is not used in this way. They charge that judges and probation officials use ISP for offenders who otherwise would have received regular probation. Hence, the term net widening.

According to Morris and Tonry, the "mechanism that serves to widen the net is obvious."[34] Judges who in the past have given the benefit of the doubt to some offenders, sentencing them to probation rather than prison despite reservations about doing so, view more restrictive alternatives such as ISP as more appropriate sentences for these offenders. As Morris and Tonry note, if judges have given "a probationary sentence to the offender for whom imprisonment seemed too severe and probation too lenient, the newly available intermediate punishment will be just what's wanted."[35]

Net widening can be avoided, or at least minimized, by the use of *back-end* rather than *front-end* programs. A front-end program is one in which the sentencing judge makes the decision to sentence the offender to prison, to regular probation, or to ISP probation. This allows the judge to widen the net by using ISP in place of regular probation rather than as a substitute for imprisonment. In contrast, a back-end program selects ISP participants from those already sentenced to prison. In New Jersey, for example, an offender who is sentenced to prison and meets the eligibility criteria for the program can apply for resentencing to ISP. Applicants are carefully screened using risk-assessment tools, and those who qualify are released from prison and placed on ISP for 18 months.[36] This approach seems less susceptible to, but not immune from, net widening. Judges who previously might have placed, albeit reluctantly, medium-risk offenders on regular probation might decide to sentence them to prison instead, anticipating that they will be released into the ISP program.[37] Both front-end and back-end programs, then, may present "almost irresistible temptations to judges and corrections officials to use them for offenders other than those for whom the program was created."[38]

As we will see below, questions about effectiveness and net widening have been raised about many other intermediate sanctions developed to reduce prison overcrowding and supervise offenders in the community.

Other Intermediate Sanctions

It should be clear from the information presented thus far that incarceration (in jail or in prison) and probation (routine or intensive supervision) are the principal sentences imposed on criminal offenders in the United States. Despite their widespread use, however, they are not the only sentencing options. Indeed, a variety of *intermediate sanctions* are available: boot camps, house arrest and electronic monitoring, day reporting centers, community service, restitution, and fines. Like intensive supervision probation, these alternative punishments are intended to fill the void between routine probation and protracted imprisonment. They are designed to free up prison beds and "to provide a continuum of sanctions that satisfies the just deserts concern for proportionality in punishment."[39]

A number of scholars have urged judges to reduce their reliance on prison and probation and to incorporate intermediate sanctions into their philosophy of sentencing.[40] Although they recognize that the alternatives developed thus far will not *replace* prison or probation as the primary punishments imposed on criminal offenders, these scholars have called on judges to sentence fewer nonviolent offenders to prison, to shorten the prison sentences they do impose, and to develop a "comprehensive punishment system" incorporating a wide range of intermediate punishments.[41] As Morris and Tonry contend,

> At present, too many criminals are in prison and too few are the subjects of enforced controls in the community. We are both too lenient and too severe; too lenient with many on probation who should be subject to tighter controls in the community, and too severe with many in prison and jail who would present no serious threat to community safety if they were under control in the community.[42]

Morris and Tonry argue that a just sentencing system is one that includes a wide range of punishments and not just a choice between prison and probation. They further suggest that widespread use of these intermediate sanctions will make it possible "to move appreciable numbers who otherwise would be sentenced to prison into community-based punishments, having a roughly equivalent punitive bite but serving both the community and the criminal better than the prison term."[43]

Austin and Irwin[44] are less sanguine about the prospects for significant reductions in imprisonment through the use of intermediate sanctions. They argue that "well-intentioned alternatives have had marginal impact on reducing prison populations."[45] They attribute this both to the net-widening phenomenon discussed earlier and to the fact that policymakers and the public "are increasingly disenchanted with probation and other forms of community sanctions."[46] Austin and Irwin also contend that even widespread use of intermediate punishments, which primarily target offenders who would otherwise serve only short prison terms, would not significantly reduce the United States prison population, which is increasingly composed of offenders serving long prison sentences. According to these authors, "The single most direct solution that would have an immediate, dramatic impact on prison crowding and would not affect public safety is to shorten prison terms."[47]

In the following sections, we briefly describe four intermediate sanctions: boot camps, house arrest and electronic monitoring, community service, and monetary penalties.

Boot Camps

Correctional boot camp, or shock incarceration, programs target young, nonviolent felony offenders who do not have extensive prior criminal records.[48] Modeled on the military boot camp, the correctional boot camp emphasizes strict discipline, military drill and ceremony, and hard labor and physical training. Most also provide substance abuse counseling and educational and vocational training. Offenders selected for these programs, which typically last 3 to 6 months, are separated from the general prison population. They live in barracks-style housing, address the guards by military titles, and are required to stand at attention and obey all orders. Although the structure and focus of the programs vary widely, their primary goal is to divert young offenders from "a life outside the law using the same tactics successfully employed by the military to turn civilians into soldiers."[49]

Prison boot camps began in Georgia and Oklahoma in 1983. Today, these programs are found in 29 states. Most serve young adult males, but programs that target women and juvenile offenders are becoming increasingly popular.[50] Most programs limit eligibility to offenders who are under 30, but some have a higher upper-age limit. Georgia, which has one of the largest programs, admits offenders aged 17 to 35. Massachusetts takes offenders up to 40 years old. About a third of the programs restrict eligibility to first offenders; the others admit first-time felony offenders or those without prior prison sentences.

Despite their popularity, prison boot camps are controversial. The primary point of contention is the military model on which the programs are based. Critics charge that the harsh discipline characteristic of prison boot camps is not an effective way to change offenders. They also contend that too much time is devoted to military training and hard physical labor and too little to therapeutic treatment, education, and vocational training. Supporters counter that the military atmosphere encourages reform and rehabilitation. They argue that "the stress created in boot camp may shake up the inmates and make them ready to change and take advantage of the treatment and aftercare programs offered."[51]

The controversy surrounding boot camps prompted the National Institute of Justice to fund a number of single- and multisite evaluations of their effectiveness. One of the earliest studies found that boot camp participants in Louisiana did not have lower recidivism rates than either offenders who served time in traditional prisons or offenders who were placed on probation.[52] The results of an evaluation of programs in eight states were similarly disappointing.[53] This study found that although boot camp participants had more positive attitudes than regular prison inmates while they were incarcerated, they did not adjust more positively than traditional inmates to community supervision. Moreover, the recidivism rates of the boot camp participants were generally similar to those of comparable offenders who served their time in state prisons or local jails. In the three jurisdictions in which boot camp participants did have significantly lower recidivism rates, the programs emphasized education and counseling rather than military training. They also required 6 months of intensive supervision of offenders who were released into the community. These results led the author of this study to conclude that "the core elements of boot camp programs—military-style discipline, hard labor, and physical training—by themselves did not reduce offender recidivism."[54]

House Arrest and Electronic Monitoring

In September of 2000, baseball All-Star Darryl Strawberry pleaded guilty to driving under the influence of medication and leaving the scene of an accident. Strawberry, who was serving an 18-month probation sentence for drug and solicitation charges, was on his way to a meeting with his probation officer when he blacked out and rear-ended a car stopped at a red light. He apparently had taken a prescription sleeping medication prior to getting behind the wheel of his car. Florida Circuit Court Judge Florence Foster sentenced him to 2 years' house arrest. He was ordered to remain in his home except for specifically permitted outings.

House arrest, with or without electronic monitoring, is an alternative sanction used primarily for nonviolent offenders such as Darryl Strawberry. Offenders placed on house arrest, which is also referred to as *home confinement*, are ordered to remain at home for designated periods of time. They are allowed to leave only at specified times and for specific purposes: to obtain food or medical services, to meet with a probation officer, and sometimes, to go to school or work. Both back-end and front-end programs exist. In some jurisdictions, such as Oklahoma, offenders are released early from jail or prison sentences if they agree to participate in a home confinement program. In other jurisdictions, such as Florida, house arrest is a front-end program in which offenders who otherwise would be sentenced to jail or prison are instead confined to their homes. Both types of programs "aim simultaneously to offer a community sentence that is seen as burdensome and intrusive . . . and to reduce pressure on overcrowded prisons and jails."[55]

Offenders placed on house arrest are often subject to electronic monitoring, which is a means of ensuring that they are at home when they are supposed to be. The most popular system today is one in which the offender is fitted with a wrist or ankle bracelet that he or she wears 24 hours a day. The bracelet serves as a transmitter. It emits a constant radio signal to a home monitoring unit, which is attached to the offender's home phone. The monitoring unit informs the monitoring center when offenders enter and leave home; it also sends a message if they tamper with or attempt to remove the bracelet. The monitoring officer is informed when the offender deviates from the preapproved schedule: if, for example, he or she returns from school at 9 p.m. but was expected at 4 p.m. Ideally, the officer will respond immediately to a violation notice. The offender can be terminated from the program for tampering with the device, for repeated unauthorized absences from home, and for a variety of other violations.

The use of electronic monitoring began in 1983 in New Mexico and Florida. Although there were only 95 offenders on electronic monitoring in 1986, by the early 1990s, there were more than 400 programs involving 12,000 offenders. During the next decade, the number of offenders placed on electronic monitoring continued to grow. By 1998, approximately 95,000 offenders, including pretrial detainees, juveniles, and adult probationers and parolees, were being monitored electronically.[56] Among adults on probation in 1997, more than 15,000 were being monitored.[57]

Like other intermediate sanctions, house arrest with electronic monitoring is designed to be a cost-effective alternative to jail or prison that does not jeopardize public safety. The results of studies designed to evaluate its effectiveness in meeting these objectives are inconsistent. There have been no multisite studies in which offenders are randomly assigned to house arrest, regular probation, or incarceration, and the studies that have been done have been criticized for "shoddy or weak research designs."[58] Some studies report recidivism rates of less than 10 percent for offenders on electronic monitoring, whereas others report rates of 40 percent or higher.[59] As the authors of a comprehensive review of the research concluded, "we know very little about either home confinement or electronic monitoring."[60]

Community Service Orders

An underused but potentially important intermediate sanction is the community service order. Rather than being sentenced to jail or placed on routine probation, offenders are ordered to perform a certain number of hours of unpaid work at schools, hospitals, parks, and other public and private nonprofit agencies. Thus, an accountant convicted of fraud might be sentenced to provide advice to poor taxpayers, a baseball player convicted of a drug offense might be required to lecture to junior high school students on the dangers of using drugs, and traffic offenders might be required to pick up trash along highways or in public parks. As Morris and Tonry observe, the list of community service projects "is limited only by the imagination of the sentencing judge and the availability of some supervision to ensure that the offender fulfills the terms of the sentence."[61]

Use of community service orders in the United States dates from 1966, when judges in Alameda County, California, began to sentence low-income women found guilty of traffic offenses to unpaid labor in the community. The concept spread rapidly in the United States and elsewhere; but today, community service orders are used much more frequently in the United Kingdom and Europe than in the United States and for a greater variety of offenses. In fact, laws passed in England, Wales, Scotland, and the Netherlands specifically authorize the use of community service orders as an alternative to short-term incarceration.

The most comprehensive community service program in the United States is New York City's Community Service Sentencing Project (CSSP), established in 1979.[62] CSSP is one of the few community service programs in the United States to be designed as an alternative to jail or prison. It places repeat misdemeanor offenders on work crews in their home neighborhoods and supervises them as they complete 10 to 15 days of unpaid labor. Each year, about 1,000 adult offenders are ordered to remove graffiti, clean sidewalks, paint buildings, or perform other types of community service work in low-income neighborhoods. An early evaluation of the program revealed that it was effective. Offenders were diverted from prison, rearrest rates of CSSP participants were similar to those of a matched group of offenders who served short jail sentences, and the program was cost-effective.[63] A more recent evaluation found that 73 percent of the participants successfully completed the program and that very few were arrested for new offenses while they were participating in the program.[64]

With the exception of the program in New York City, which targets misdemeanants only, community service is not widely used as an alternative punishment in the United States. Here, the primary use of community service is as a condition of probation or as a punishment for minor traffic offenses. Some judges are reluctant to use this alternative as a stand-alone sanction for misdemeanors and less serious felonies. This may reflect a belief that requiring an offender to perform community service is not adequate punishment for most crimes. Judges may believe, in other words, that removing graffiti or cleaning up parks for 200 hours is not as onerous as even a short stint in jail. Those who advocate wider use of intermediate sanctions disagree. They contend that community service should not be regarded as merely a "slap on the wrist." Rather, it is a constructive and burdensome penalty "that is inexpensive to administer, that produces public value, and that can to a degree be scaled to the seriousness of crimes."[65] Advocates of restorative justice agree. They suggest that community service can be used "to restore victims to wholeness, to hold offenders accountable," and to repair "the damage to the community fabric resulting from crime."[66]

Monetary Penalties

Monetary penalties, such as fines, fees, and restitution to the victim, are frequently imposed on offenders convicted of misdemeanors and felonies in American courts. Every year, millions of offenders convicted of traffic offenses and less serious misdemeanors are ordered to pay fines that are to some degree calibrated to the seriousness of the crime. Offenders placed on probation are required to pay fees for probation supervision, substance abuse treatment, urinalysis, and use of electronic monitoring equipment. And offenders who steal or damage the property of others or cause physical or emotional injuries are ordered to pay restitution to the victims, often as a condition of probation.

Although these types of monetary penalties are common, their use as stand-alone sentences is not. Fines, for example, are seldom used as alternatives to incarceration for offenders convicted of less serious felonies; they are often used only in conjunction with probation for more serious misdemeanors. Although the fine is "unambiguously punitive,"[67] studies reveal that judges do not regard it as "a meaningful alternative to incarceration or probation."[68] The use of fines also poses dilemmas for the courts. If the amount of a fine is commensurate with the seriousness of an offense, with no consideration given to the ability of the offender to pay the fine, then fines will be relatively more burdensome to the poor than to the rich. Low-income offenders will have a more difficult time coming up with money to pay the fines—indeed, they may resort to more crime to raise the money needed—and those who are unable to pay the fines may be jailed for nonpayment. Wealthier offenders, then, get double benefits: The fines they pay are less punitive punishments, and they evade jail because they have money to pay the fines.

To avoid these potential problems, a number of jurisdictions use what is referred to as a *day fine*. Imported from Europe and Latin America, the day fine is calibrated both to the seriousness of the offense and to the offender's ability to pay. Rather than requiring all offenders convicted of shoplifting to pay $1,000, for example, judges determine how many *punishment units* each offender deserves. Typically, each punishment unit is equal to 1 day's pay or some fraction of a day's pay. Two offenders convicted of shoplifting might each be ordered to pay five punishment units, equal to 5 days' pay. If one offender made $50 per day and the other earned $500 per day, the fines paid by the two offenders would differ. The first would pay $250, the second $2,500.

The day fine has obvious advantages over the traditional fine. Because it can be tailored more precisely to an offender's ability to pay, the day fine is more equitable. It is also more likely to be paid in full, which means that offenders are less likely to be called back to court or sentenced to jail for non-payment. But there are disadvantages as well. Courts that use the day fine must define a unit of punishment in terms other than jail time or standard dollars to be paid, establish the range of units to be imposed on offenders convicted of various offenses, and devise a means of translating these units into dollars. Implementing a system of day fines, in other words, involves "changing—or, at least accommodating—existing habits, customs, and laws."[69]

Whereas fines, whether traditional or day fines, and fees go into state and federal government coffers, restitution is money paid by the offender to the victim or to a victim compensation fund.[70] In requiring restitution, courts attempt to calculate the costs of the crime to the victim and order the offender to repay those costs. Thus, victims might be compensated for financial losses, for medical expenses, or for the costs of traveling to and from the courthouse for criminal proceedings. Because not all offenders, particularly those who are incarcerated, are equally able to pay restitution, most jurisdictions require all offenders to pay a fee to victim compensation funds. Victims can apply to these funds and obtain money to recover their losses. These funds, however, are "notoriously inadequate."[71] They do not cover all crime victims and they seldom pay the full costs of the victimization.

The Future of Intermediate Sanctions

More than a decade ago, Attorney General Richard Thornburgh called for the development of a "portfolio of intermediate punishments." As he pointed out,

> We . . . know that there are many for whom incarceration is not appropriate. But is simple probation sufficient? Particularly when probation officers are carrying caseloads far beyond what is manageable? We need to fill the gap between simple probation and prison. We need intermediate steps, intermediate punishments.[72]

Others have made similar claims and predicted that the repertoire of punishments advocated by the attorney general would be developed and implemented (see Box 2.2). In 1990, for example, Morris and Tonry made the following prediction:

> Concerns for justice and fairness in sentencing will lead, in time, probably within 25 years, to the creation in most American states of comprehensive systems of structured sentencing discretion that en-

compass a continuum of punishments from probation to imprisonment, with many intermediate punishments ranged between.[73]

As we have seen, Morris and Tonry may have been overly optimistic
about the future of intermediate sanctions. As we enter the 21st century,
prison, jail, and probation sentences remain the dominant forms of punishment imposed on criminal offenders, especially those convicted of felonies. In fact, state and federal prison statistics suggest that the trend has
been the *opposite* of what Thornburgh called for and Morris and Tonry
predicted. As shown in Exhibit 2.3, the rate of incarceration, which was
relatively stable from 1925 through 1975, skyrocketed from 1980 to
1998. Despite stable or falling crime rates, the number of offenders incarcerated in state and federal prisons ballooned from 329,821 in 1980 to
1,284,894 in 1999, an increase of nearly 400 percent. At the turn of the
century, 6.3 million people, 3.1 percent of all adult residents, were on
probation, in jail or prison, or on parole in the United States.[74] Rather
than replacing incarceration and probation with "a portfolio of interme-

---

BOX 2.2

INNOVATION (OR BIAS) IN THE COURTROOM?

In 2000, Dayne Brink appeared before Douglas County (Nebraska)
Judge Lyn White for violating his probation in a domestic violence case.
While on probation, Brink allegedly violated the protection order obtained
by his former wife. He was arrested for driving while intoxicated and carrying a concealed weapon and failed to attend a mandatory batterers' intervention program.

Judge White sentenced him to the maximum possible sentence: 180 days
in jail and a $1,000 fine. She also ordered Brink to read Shakespeare's tragic
play, *Othello*, in which a jealous husband kills his wife. When questions were
raised about the propriety of the sentence, Judge White stated that requiring
Brink to read *Othello* was appropriate because it was "rationally related to the
defendant's crime."

Brink appealed his sentence, arguing that it was excessive and that Judge
White was biased against him. District Court Judge Joseph Troia vacated the
sentence and sent the case back to County Court for resentencing by a different judge. In the decision, Troia wrote, "Although the sentence fell within
the statutory parameters, the court finds that the trial court's actions and
comments could cause a reasonable person to question the impartiality of
the judge."

SOURCE: "Judge Takes Self Off Cases," *Omaha World Herald*, 2001, February 13, pp. A1-2.

diate punishments," the United States "has been engaged in an unprecedented imprisonment binge"[75] during the past two decades.

The question, of course, is why this is so. Austin and Irwin suggest that it
can be attributed in large part to the public's fear of drugs and crime, which
led to a movement for more punitive sentences for felony offenders in general and for drug offenders in particular.[76] Tonry argues that it also reflects a
view on the part of judges and policymakers that "only imprisonment
counts" as punishment. He suggests that this emphasis on absolute severity
"frustrates efforts to devise intermediate sanctions for the psychological
(not to mention political) reason that few other sanctions seem commensu-
rable with a multiyear prison sentence."[77] If, in other words, the philosophy
of just deserts demands that felony offenders be punished harshly and only
incarceration is regarded as harsh punishment, then nonincarceration sentences will be viewed as inappropriately lenient. Unless these attitudes
change, it seems unlikely that intermediate sanctions will play anything
more than a supporting role in sentencing policies and practices in the
United States.

Exhibit 2.3. Incarceration Rates, 1925-1998

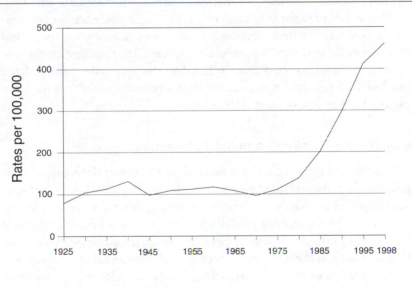

SOURCE: Adapted from Figure 1.1, James Austin and John Irwin. 2001. *It's About Time: America's
Imprisonment Binge*, 3rd ed. Belmont, CA: Wadsworth.

Sentencing as a Collaborative Exercise

Seated on a raised bench, clothed in black robes, and wielding a gavel that he uses to maintain order in the courtroom, the judge pronounces sentence on the defendant, who has been found guilty of robbery and sexual assault. "After considering all of the facts and circumstances in the case," he states, "I have decided to impose the maximum sentence: 15 years in prison. I believe that this is the appropriate sentence given the heinousness of the crime and the fact that the defendant has a prior conviction for aggravated assault."

Scenes such as this are played out everyday in courtrooms throughout the United States. Media accounts of these sentencing proceedings report, "*The judge* sentenced the defendant to prison," "*The judge* gave the defendant 3 years probation and ordered him to pay a $2,000 fine," or "*The judge* sentenced the defendant to death." Although accurate, these accounts are misleading. The judge clearly plays an important role in the sentencing process—in many cases, the lead role—but others play supporting roles. The sentences defendants eventually receive are produced by a collaborative exercise involving legislators, prosecutors, jurors, probation officials, trial court judges, corrections officials, and possibly appellate court judges.

In the following sections, we discuss "the many participants and decisions that together constitute 'sentencing.'"[78] These decisions are summarized in Box 2.3. We first describe how decisions made by Congress and state legislatures structure the sentencing process. We then discuss the role played by criminal justice officials other than the judge. We assume that a crime has been reported, a suspect has been arrested, and the case has been forwarded to the prosecuting attorney.

Legislative Restrictions on Judicial Discretion

Congress and state legislatures make the basic policy decisions regarding sentencing. As explained above, these bodies decide whether the sentences imposed by judges will be indeterminate, determinate, mandatory, or structured by sentencing guidelines. They decide whether and under what conditions the death penalty can be imposed, the circumstances under which probation is the preferred sentence, and to some extent, the types of intermediate sanctions that are available. They also decide, for each offense or class of offenses, what the penalty range will be.

These decisions obviously constrain the discretion of judges. If, as is the case in 12 states, the state legislature has decided not to enact a statute au-

---

BOX 2.3

SENTENCING AS A COLLABORATIVE EXERCISE

Legislature

    –Makes the basic policy decisions regarding sentencing

    –Decides whether and how to use capital punishment

    –Determines the types of sentences that are to be imposed

    –Specifies penalties for offenses or classes of offenses

Prosecuting Attorney

    –Decides whether to file charges and what charges to file

    –Engages in plea bargaining on the charges and/or sentence

    –Recommends a sentence to the judge

Jury

    –Decides whether to convict or acquit

    –Decides whether to convict of original or lesser included charge

    –Recommends or (rarely) determines the sentence

Probation Officer

    –Conducts the presentence investigation

    –Recommends a sentence to the judge

    –Supervises offenders on probation

Judge

    –Has final responsibility for determining the sentence

Corrections Officials

    –Determine where prison sentence will be served

    –Reduce sentence by awarding good-time credits

    –Determine date of release on parole

Appellate Court Judges

    –Decide whether to overturn conviction and/or sentence

---

thorizing capital punishment, a judge in that state cannot sentence an offender to death. Even if he or she believes that capital punishment is an appropriate penalty and is convinced that the offender deserves to die, the judge must abide by the legislature's decision. If the legislature has decided that sentences are to be indeterminate, the judge cannot disregard the law and impose a fixed term of years. Conversely, in states with determinate sentencing, the judge cannot impose a minimum and maximum sentence and order corrections officials to determine when the offender is fit to be released. And in states with mandatory minimum sentences or sentencing guidelines, there is an expectation that judges will comply or explain their reasons for noncompliance.

The laws passed by legislative bodies generally place tighter restrictions on judges' discretion in more serious cases and fewer restrictions in less serious cases. This is particularly true with respect to the decision to sentence the offender to prison or not. Offenses regarded as particularly serious or offenders deemed especially dangerous may be nonprobationable. The Illinois Criminal Code, for example, states that a variety of options (probation, imprisonment, an order directing the offender to repair the damage caused by the crime, a fine, and/or an order directing the offender to make restitution to the victim) are appropriate for "all felonies or misdemeanors." The statute also lists 15 offenses for which "[a] period of probation, a term of periodic imprisonment, or conditional discharge shall not be imposed." These nonprobationable offenses include the following: first-degree murder, any Class X felony (the most serious classification), possession of more than 5 grams of cocaine, residential burglary, aggravated battery of a senior citizen, a forcible felony related to the activities of an organized gang, carjacking, and a second or subsequent conviction for a hate crime.[79]

Judges can circumvent, or at least attempt to circumvent, some of these legislative restrictions in several ways. For example, if a defendant charged with a nonprobationable offense is being tried by a judge, he or she can find the defendant guilty of a lesser included offense that will not trigger the mandatory sentence. Similarly, judges can impose sentences that fall outside the penalty range or guidelines enacted by the legislature and then state, either from the bench or in writing, why they decided to depart. If the defendant is convicted of a collateral charge, such as use of a weapon, which carries a mandatory sentence enhancement, the judge can reduce the sentence for the main charge so the overall sentence is no longer than it would have been if the defendant had been convicted only of the main charge. Generally, however, as U.S. District Court Judge Irving R. Kaufman wrote in 1960, "The judge must take this legislative guide and apply it to the particular circumstances of the case before him. He must work within the legislative formula, even if he does not agree with it."[80]

The Role Played by the Prosecutor

All decision makers in the American criminal justice system have a significant amount of unchecked discretionary power, but the prosecutor stands apart from the rest. The prosecutor decides who will be charged, what charge will be filed, who will be offered a plea bargain, and the type of bargain that will be offered. The prosecutor may also recommend the offender's sentence. As Supreme Court Justice Jackson noted in 1940, "the prosecutor has more control over life, liberty, and reputation than any other person in America."[81]

None of the discretionary decisions made by the prosecutor is more critical than the initial decision to prosecute or not, which has been characterized as "the gateway to justice."[82] Prosecutors have wide discretion at this stage in the process. There are no legislative or judicial guidelines on charging, and a decision not to file charges is ordinarily immune from review. As the Supreme Court noted in *Bordenkircher v. Hayes*,

> So long as the prosecutor has probable cause to believe that the accused committed an offense defined by statute, the decision whether or not to prosecute, and what charge to file or bring before a grand jury generally rests entirely in his discretion.[83]

The discretion exercised by the prosecutor at charging has obvious implications for sentencing. If the prosecutor decides not to file charges, either because he or she believes that the defendant is innocent or that the defendant is guilty but a conviction is unlikely, the case is closed; the defendant will not be convicted or sentenced. If the prosecutor does file charges, the number and seriousness of the charges filed may affect the severity of the sentence imposed by the judge if the defendant is convicted. The death penalty is the most striking example of this. If the prosecutor decides not to request the death penalty, the death penalty will not be an option at sentencing. Conversely, if the prosecutor does seek the death penalty, the defendant may in fact be sentenced to death. The sentences imposed in noncapital cases can similarly depend on the charges filed. Suppose, for example, that the police in Chicago arrest a woman with 6 grams of cocaine in her purse, which, as we have seen, is a nonprobationable offense in Illinois. The prosecutor could charge her with possession of some lesser amount, thereby avoiding the mandatory prison sentence. Sentence severity may also be affected by the prosecutor's decision to charge the defendant as a habitual offender, to add weapons charges that enhance the sentence for the main offense, or to charge the defendant with multiple counts of the same offense.

Plea Bargaining and Its Effect on Sentence Outcomes

Another way the prosecutor affects sentencing is through plea bargaining.[84] The predominance of jury trials in television dramas such as *Law and*

Order and *The Practice* notwithstanding, most convictions result from guilty pleas. In 1996, for instance, 91 percent of all felony convictions in state courts were the result of guilty pleas.[85] The rate was even higher—94 percent—for defendants convicted of felonies in federal courts.[86] Although the actual number of guilty pleas that result from plea bargains is unknown, most experts would argue that some type of negotiation between the prosecutor and the defendant (or the defense attorney) occurs prior to the entry of the guilty plea.

There are several different forms of plea bargaining, and they can be used alone or in combination with one another. Consider the following scenario: A 19-year-old man holds a gun to the head of a convenience store clerk, demands money, and escapes on foot with a bag containing more than $1,000. He is spotted and arrested by the police 30 minutes later. The prosecutor reviewing the case files one count of aggravated robbery, punishable by 3 to 10 years in prison, and one count of use of a weapon during the commission of a felony, which adds an additional 2 years to the sentence. The plea negotiations in this case might center on the charges filed. If the defendant agrees to plead guilty, the prosecutor might reduce the aggravated robbery charge to a less serious charge of robbery or dismiss the weapons charge. Both types of charge reductions would reduce the potential sentence the defendant faces.

The plea negotiations might also revolve around the sentence. In exchange for a guilty plea, the prosecutor might agree to a sentence of 3 years on the aggravated robbery and 2 years on the weapons charge, with the sentences to be served concurrently rather than consecutively. Alternatively, the prosecutor might agree "to stand mute at sentencing" or agree to a "sentence lid." In the first instance, he or she would not recommend any particular sentence or challenge the defense attorney's presentation of mitigating evidence and recommendation for leniency. In other words, the prosecutor would say nothing about the sentence the defendant should receive. In the second instance, the prosecutor would recommend that the judge impose a sentence that would not exceed the sentence lid. In this case, for example, he or she might state that the sentence should be no greater than 3 years in prison.

Both charge reductions and sentence agreements limit the judge's options at sentencing. Judges have little recourse if the prosecutor decides to reduce the number or the severity of the charges in exchange for a guilty plea. Because the charging decision "generally rests entirely in his [the prosecutor's] discretion,"[87] the judge ordinarily cannot refuse to accept the plea to a reduced charge and force the defendant to go to trial. In *United*

States v. Ammidown, for example, the U.S. Court of Appeals ruled that a judge "had exceeded his discretion"[88] by rejecting a plea agreement because he believed that the "public interest" required the defendant to be tried on a greater charge. Although the justices stated that the trial court should not "serve merely as a rubber stamp for the prosecutor's decision,"[89] they ruled that judges cannot reject agreements reached between the prosecution and defense unless they determine that the prosecutors have abused their discretion. Moreover, the court said,

> The question is not what the judge would do if he were the prosecuting attorney, but whether he can say that the action of the prosecuting attorney is such a departure from sound prosecutorial principle as to mark it an abuse of prosecutorial discretion.[90]

Sentence agreements also reduce the judge's discretion, even though the prosecutor does not have any official authority to impose sentence. If, for example, the prosecution and the defense negotiate an agreement whereby the defendant agrees to plead guilty and the state agrees that a probation sentence is the appropriate disposition, the judge must either (a) accept the plea agreement and place the defendant on probation or (b) reject the agreement and allow the defendant to withdraw his guilty plea.[91] As the Supreme Court stated in the case of *Santobello v. New York*, "When a plea rests in any significant degree on a promise or agreement of the prosecutor, so that it can be said to be part of the inducement or consideration, such promise must be fulfilled."[92] Moreover, judges face organizational pressure to approve plea agreements. Like other members of the courtroom workgroup, they view the guilty plea as an efficient and effective method of case disposition. As a result, they are unlikely to reject sentence agreements that make a high rate of guilty pleas possible.

In summary, charging and plea-bargaining decisions made by prosecuting attorneys have significant effects on sentence outcomes. The charges filed by the prosecutor determine the limits of the defendant's legal liability, and concessions made during plea negotiations may reduce the sentence.

The Jury's Role in Sentencing

As we have seen, most criminal convictions result from guilty pleas. Very few defendants exercise their right to a trial, and many of those who do are tried by judges, not juries. In 1993, for example, 90 percent of all offenders convicted of felonies in Cook County (Chicago), Illinois, pled guilty; 9 percent were tried by a judge, and less than 1 percent were tried by a jury.[93] Jury trials comprised a somewhat larger proportion of all dispositions in U.S. District Courts in 1998: 94 percent of these federal defendants pled guilty, 5 percent had a jury trial, and 1 percent had a bench trial.[94]

Although the rarity of jury trials limits the jury's overall influence on sentencing, decisions made by the jury do affect sentence outcomes in cases that are tried before juries. The jury decides whether to convict the defendant or not. The jury may also decide whether to convict the defendant for the offense charged or for a lesser included offense. In a murder case, for example, the jury might have the option of finding the defendant guilty of first-degree murder, second-degree murder, or manslaughter. Like the prosecutor's charging decisions, these conviction decisions affect the sentences that will be imposed. Defendants charged with first-degree murder but convicted of manslaughter will be sentenced more leniently than if they were convicted of the more serious charge.

Most jury trials result in convictions. For example, in 1996, in the 75 largest counties in the United States, 84 percent of all defendants tried by juries were convicted.[95] A jury's decision to acquit the defendant usually means that the state has failed to prove its case beyond a reasonable doubt. Sometimes, however, the jury votes to acquit despite overwhelming evidence that the defendant is guilty. In this case, the jury ignores, or nullifies, the law.

Jury nullification, which has its roots in English common law, occurs when a juror believes that the evidence presented at trial establishes the defendant's guilt, but nonetheless votes to acquit. The juror's decision may be motivated either by a belief that the law under which the defendant is being prosecuted is unfair or by an objection to the application of the law in a particular case. In the first instance, a juror might refuse to convict a defendant charged in U.S. District Court with possession of more than 5 grams of crack cocaine because he or she believes that the long prison sentence mandated by the law is unfair. In the second instance, a juror might vote to acquit a defendant charged with petty theft and also charged as a habitual criminal and facing a mandatory life sentence—not because the juror believes the law itself is unfair but because he or she believes that this particular defendant does not deserve life in prison.[96] Similarly, an African American juror might heed Paul Butler's call for "racially based jury nullification" (see Box 2.4) and refuse to convict African Americans charged with drug offenses and less serious property crimes.[97]

Jurors clearly have the power to nullify the law and vote their conscience.[98] If the jury votes to acquit, the double jeopardy clause of the Fifth

Amendment prohibits reversal of the jury's decision. The jury's decision to acquit, even in the face of overwhelming evidence of guilt, is final and cannot be reversed by the trial judge or an appellate court. In most jurisdictions, however, jurors do not have to be told that they have the right to nullify the law.[99]

The jury's effect on sentence outcomes is not limited to its power to acquit the defendant of all charges or convict the defendant of lesser included charges. In a number of jurisdictions, the jury either determines the sentence or makes a sentence recommendation to the judge. As explained earlier, juries play a prominent role in sentencing in capital cases: In 6 states,

---

BOX 2.4

RACIALLY BASED JURY NULLIFICATION

In a provocative essay published in the *Yale Law Journal* shortly after O. J. Simpson's acquittal on murder charges, Paul Butler, an African American professor at George Washington University Law School, called for "racially based jury nullification." Arguing that there are far too many young black men in prison, Butler urged African American jurors to refuse to convict black defendants charged with nonviolent crimes, regardless of the strength of the evidence arrayed against them. According to Butler, the "black community is better off when some nonviolent lawbreakers remain in the community rather than go to prison" (p. 677).

Butler asserted that black jurors have a moral responsibility "to emancipate some guilty black outlaws" (p. 679). He argued that the criminal justice system is racially biased and suggested that white racism, which "creates and sustains the criminal breeding ground which produces the black criminal," is the underlying cause of much of the crime committed by blacks. Because, in other words, the operation of the criminal law does not reflect or advance the interests of black people, black jurors can—and should—"opt out of American criminal law" (p. 714). They should do this by generally refusing to convict blacks charged with nonviolent victimless crimes such as possession of drugs and, depending upon the circumstances, sometimes refusing to convict blacks charged with property offenses and more serious drug trafficking offenses. According to Butler, "The race of a black defendant is sometimes a legally and morally appropriate factor for jurors to consider in reaching a verdict of not guilty" (p. 679).

SOURCE: "Racially Based Jury Nullification: Black Power in the Criminal Justice System," by Paul Butler, 1995. *Yale Law Journal, 105.*

the jury makes a sentencing recommendation to the judge; in 6 states, the jury decides the sentence but the judge can alter it; and in 18 states, the jury makes the final sentencing decision. The jury's role is more circumscribed in noncapital cases. Texas is the only state in which the jury determines the final sentence, and there are only 3 additional states (Arkansas, Missouri, and Virginia) in which the jury determines the original sentence but the sentence can be altered by the trial judge.[100] This reluctance to entrust the sentencing function to the jury in noncapital criminal cases may reflect legislators' fears that doing so would lead to inconsistent or wildly disparate sentences for similar offenders. Unlike the capital sentencing process, which is tightly constrained by death penalty statutes, the noncapital sentencing process is more discretionary.

The Probation Department and the Presentence Investigation

Prior to sentencing an offender, the judge may order a presentence investigation. In most jurisdictions, the probation department conducts the investigation into the circumstances of the offense and the background of the offender and reports its findings and sentencing recommendation to the judge. Probation officers may interview the offenders, the offenders' families, other persons familiar with the offenders, and the victims. They will also gather information on offenders' prior criminal records, education, employment history, and family circumstances.[101]

The purpose of the presentence investigation is to provide the judge with more detailed information about the crime and the offender. Because most offenders plead guilty, the judge may have relatively little information about the case. In fact, he or she may know nothing more than the minimal facts necessary to support acceptance of the guilty plea. The presentence investigation report typically describes the nature of the offense, the role played by the offender in the offense, the offender's past and current circumstances, and the effect of the crime on the victim and the community. The report may also include the officer's assessment of the offender's remorse (or lack thereof) and risk of future criminal offending. In some jurisdictions, the assessment of the offender's likelihood of recidivism is based on the officer's subjective impressions; in others, it is based on a risk-screening instrument. On the basis of the information gathered, the officer indicates whether the offender is a good candidate for probation or for some other alternative to incarceration.

Studies reveal that judges do follow the sentencing recommendations in presentence reports.[102] One study, for example, found 95 percent agreement between the probation officer's recommendation and the judge's sentence when the officer recommended probation; the rate of agreement was 88 percent when the officer recommended against probation.[103] Researchers disagree, however, about the meaning of these findings. Some argue that probation officers play a key role in the sentencing process and conclude that judges "lean heavily" on their professional advice.[104] Others contend that the probation officer's recommendation typically matches the recommendation of the prosecutor. They assert that the probation officer is "largely superfluous"[105] and plays little more than a "ceremonial" role in the sentencing process.[106]

Rosecrance, who examined the presentence investigation process in California, is even more critical. Based on interviews with probation officers in two California counties, he concluded that "probation presentence reports do not influence judicial sentencing significantly but serve to maintain the myth that criminal courts dispense individualized justice."[107] He found that probation officers based their recommendations primarily on the seriousness of the offense and the offender's prior record. Early in the process, they used these two factors to "type" the defendant—that is, to place the defendant into a dispositional category: diversion, probation, prison, or some other outcome. After determining the appropriate disposition in the case, the probation officer then gathered other information that could "legitimate" this decision. As Rosecrance noted, "Probation officers do not regard defendant typings as tentative hypotheses to be disproved through inquiry but rather as firm conclusions to be justified in the body of the report."[108]

Rosecrance contends that the primary purpose of the presentence report is to give the appearance of individualized justice. As he states, "Although judges do not have the time or the inclination to consider individual variables thoroughly, the performance of a presentence investigation perpetuates the myth of individualized sentences."[109] This suggests that the effect of the presentence report on sentencing is illusory rather than real.

Corrections Officials and Sentencing

The casual observer of the American criminal justice system probably assumes that the sentencing process ends when the judge pronounces sentence from the bench and that the sentence imposed is the sentence that will be served. As we have seen, these assumptions are not necessarily correct. The sentence that the offender serves may be "refined" by corrections officials, who play a number of important roles in the sentencing process.

We already have discussed the role played by probation officers, who conduct the presentence investigation and supervise offenders placed on probation. Corrections officials also make a number of decisions regarding offenders sentenced to prison. In many states, they decide where the offender will serve his or her sentence: in a maximum-, medium- or minimum-security institution or in a correctional facility in the community. In making this decision, they use the information contained in the presentence investigation report, as well as diagnostic and risk-assessment tools that they administer after the offender arrives in the prison system.

In addition, corrections officials can award or withhold good-time credits, which reduce the amount of time the offender will serve. Good-time credits are one way for corrections officials to control inmates. Those who abide by the rules will be awarded the maximum time off, whereas those who violate the rules may have some or all of their credits taken away. Offenders in a few states do not earn good-time credits. In other states, only those convicted of less serious offenses are eligible for time off for good behavior. The rate at which offenders earn good time also varies. In a number of states, good time accrues at a rate of 1 day off for every day served. In other states, offenders can earn a specified number of days off for each month served. Offenders in Maine and Nevada, for example, can earn up to 10 days per month, and those in Massachusetts earn from 2.5 to 12.5 days per month.[110]

In a majority of the states, the parole board also plays an important role in the sentencing process. In states with indeterminate sentencing, the judge sets the maximum (and sometimes the minimum) sentence the offender can serve, but the parole board determines the actual date of release. In states with determinate sentencing or sentencing guidelines, the parole board may or may not have the authority to release offenders prior to the expiration of their sentences. Congress, for instance, abolished discretionary parole release with the passage of the Sentencing Reform Act of 1984.[111] Federal offenders serve the entire sentence minus a maximum of 15 percent off for good behavior. California's determinate sentencing statute also abolished parole release. Pennsylvania and Utah, on the other hand, adopted sentencing guidelines but retained discretionary release on parole.[112]

Although some offenders serve the maximum term, most are released on parole after serving a portion of the sentence. Offenders serving time in states with "truth-in-sentencing" laws, which attempt to reduce the discrepancy between the sentence imposed and the time served, will serve a larger proportion of their sentence than those incarcerated in states without such laws. As explained earlier, the average state inmate serves 45 percent of his or her sentence, whereas the typical federal inmate serves 85 percent. During the 1990s, the number of adults on parole grew by 32.7 percent. There were 531,407 parolees in 1990 and 704,964 in 1998.[113]

The decision to release the offender prior to the expiration of the sentence is made by the parole board. Today, most parole boards are not directly linked to or controlled by the staff of the correctional institution. They are either independent bodies whose members are appointed for fixed terms or consolidated boards that include corrections officials, representatives of social service agencies, and private citizens. The members of the parole board make individualized release decisions, taking into consideration such factors as the seriousness of the offense, the offender's past criminal history, the offender's behavior while incarcerated, and, in the case of a violent crime, the wishes of the victim or the victim's survivors. In many jurisdictions, the board uses written parole guidelines that structure the release decision.[114]

Like probationers, parolees are released into the community and are required to abide by a set of conditions designed to ensure that they do not return to a life of crime. They may be required, for example, to meet regularly with their parole officers, maintain employment, enroll in educational or vocational training, continue substance abuse treatment, and abide by curfews and other restrictions on their behavior. Offenders who are rearrested or who otherwise violate the conditions of their release may be returned to prison to serve the balance of the sentence.

The Role of Appellate Courts

Appellate courts can alter the outcomes of criminal cases by overturning offenders' convictions or sentences. Although offenders do not have a constitutional right to appeal their convictions, every jurisdiction has created a statutory right to appeal to one higher court. The purpose of this is to ensure that proper procedures were followed by police, the prosecutor, the judge, and the jury. A state court defendant who believes that his conviction was obtained improperly can appeal his conviction to the intermediate appellate court or, in states that do not have a two-tiered appellate court system, to the state supreme court. Similarly, a defendant who has been tried and convicted in U.S. District Court can appeal his conviction to the U.S. Court of Appeals. If the appellate court sustains the appeal and rules that procedures were violated, the court will overturn the conviction and send the case back to the trial court. The case then may be retried or dismissed. If the appellate court rules against the offender, he or she can appeal to the next highest court, but that court does not have to hear the appeal.

The ability of appellate courts to alter sentences imposed by trial court judges is more limited. The U.S. Supreme Court has ruled as follows:

> [That] review by an appellate court of the final judgement in a criminal case . . . is not a necessary element of due process of law, and that the right of appeal may be accorded by the state to the accused upon such conditions as the state deems proper.[115]

Although all states with death penalty statutes provide for automatic appellate review of death sentences, only half of the states permit appellate review of noncapital sentences that fall within statutory limits.[116] The standards for review vary. In some states, appellate courts are authorized to modify sentences deemed "excessive," but in other states only sentences determined to be "manifestly excessive," "clearly erroneous," or "an abuse of discretion" can be altered.[117] A defendant sentenced under the federal sentencing guidelines can appeal a sentence that is more severe than the guidelines permit. Federal law also allows the government to appeal a sentence that is more lenient than provided for in the guidelines. If an offender appeals his or her sentence and the appeal is sustained, the sentence must be corrected. An appellate court decision to vacate the sentence does not mean, however, that the offender will escape punishment. As the Supreme Court stated in 1974, "The Constitution does not require that sentencing should be a game in which a wrong move by the judge means immunity for the prisoner."[118] Thus, the case will be sent back to the trial court for resentencing.

The Sentencing *Process*

The sentence imposed on an offender who has been found guilty of a crime is the result of a collaborative exercise that involves legislators and criminal justice officials other than the judge. It results from a sentencing *process*, not from a single sentencing *decision*. Legislators determine the sentencing policies that judges are to apply. Prosecutors and jurors decide whether the offender will face punishment. Prosecutors and occasionally jurors also determine the charges on which the punishment will be based. Prosecutors, jurors, and probation officers may provide sentencing recommendations to the judge, and corrections officials supervise and monitor offenders and determine the amount of time that those who are incarcerated actually serve. Appellate court judges can overturn convictions and vacate sentences.

Although the decisions made by legislators and other criminal justice officials obviously limit the judge's options and constrain his or her discretion, the ultimate responsibility for determining the sentence does in fact rest with the judge. Sentencing guidelines and mandatory minimum sentencing provisions restrict but do not eliminate judicial discretion. Charge reductions by the prosecutor and convictions by the jury on lesser included charges may reduce the offender's potential sentence, and sentence recommendations may influence the judge's decision, but they do not dictate what the sentence will be. The judge determines who goes to prison and who does not and how long the sentence will be. As Judge Irving R. Kaufman wrote, more than 40 years ago:

> If the hundreds of American judges who sit on criminal cases were polled as to what was the most trying facet of their jobs, the vast majority would almost certainly answer, "sentencing." In no other judicial function is the judge more alone; no other act of his carries greater potentialities for good or evil than the determination of how society will treat its transgressors.[119]

Some judges, particularly those at the federal level, might argue that the sentencing reforms enacted during the past 25 years have reduced their position from a leading role to a supporting role in the sentencing process, but most of them would agree that sentencing is, as Judge Kaufman put it, "the judge's problem." We address this issue in Chapter 3.

Discussion Questions: Chapter 2

1. What are the "common features" of current death penalty statutes? How does the capital sentencing process differ from state to state? How does it differ from the noncapital sentencing process?

2. Why is the amount of prison time an offender receives at sentencing not necessarily the amount of time he or she actually will serve in prison?

3. What happens to offenders who violate the conditions of their probation?

4. Critics of some alternatives to incarceration, such as intensive supervision probation, electronic monitoring, and boot camps, contend

that these programs result in "net widening." What is "net widening"? What is the best method of preventing it?

5. Assume that you are a criminal court judge who must determine the appropriate punishment for a first-time offender convicted of possession of cocaine. Your choice is limited to one of the alternatives to incarceration and regular probation discussed in this chapter. Which of these alternatives would be the most appropriate punishment for this offender? Justify your choice using one of the purposes of punishment discussed in Chapter 1.

6. What role does the prosecutor play in the sentencing process? Is there any way to regulate or constrain the prosecutor's discretion?

7. Do you believe that jurors should be told that they have the right to nullify the law? Do you agree or disagree with Butler's contention that black jurors should refuse to convict black defendants charged with drug offenses and nonserious property crimes? Why?

8. What would be the positive and negative consequences of allowing all criminal defendants to appeal their sentences?

Notes

1. Wice, *Judges and Lawyers: The Human Side of Justice*, p. 273.
2. "Skier Receives 90-Day Term In Fatal Crash; Hall Remorseful, Plans Appeal," Steve Lipsher, Denver Post, February 1, 2001, p. A-01.
3. The following states do not have capital punishment statutes: Alaska, Hawaii, Iowa, Maine, Massachusetts, Michigan, Minnesota, North Dakota, Rhode Island, Vermont, West Virginia, and Wisconsin.
4. In 1977, the Supreme Court ruled that the death penalty was a disproportionately severe penalty for the rape of an adult woman [*Coker v. Georgia*, 433 U.S. 584 (1977)].
5. Federal Bureau of Investigation, *Uniform Crime Reports, Crime in the United States*, 1999, Table 29.
6. U.S. Department of Justice, Bureau of Justice Statistics (BJS), *Capital Punishment 1999*, p. 1.
7. Ibid., pp. 11-12.
8. In 1972, the U.S. Supreme Court struck down federal and state laws that permitted wide discretion in the imposition of the

death penalty. In the case of *Furman v. Georgia* [408 U.S. 153 (1972)], the Court characterized death penalty decisions under these laws as "arbitrary and capricious" and ruled that they constituted cruel and unusual punishment in violation of the Eighth Amendment. In the wake of this decision, most states enacted new death penalty statutes. These statutes were of two types: those that required the death penalty for all offenders convicted of specified crimes and those that allowed the death penalty to be imposed depending on the presence of certain aggravating circumstances. In 1976, the Court struck down the mandatory death sentence statutes [*Woodson v. North Carolina*, 428 U.S. 280 (1976); *Roberts v. Louisiana*, 428 U.S. 325 (1976)], but upheld the guided discretion statutes [*Gregg v. Georgia*, 428 U.S. 153 (1972); Jurek v. Texas, 428 U.S. 262 (1976); *Proffitt v. Florida*, 428 U.S. 242 (1976)].

9. U.S. Department of Justice, BJS, *Capital Punishment 1999*, pp. 2-4.

10. Florida Statutes, 2000, Title XLVII, chap. 921.141.

11. Texas Statutes, Revised 2000, Title 3, § 12.03 to 12.23.

12. U.S. Department of Justice, BJS, *National Assessment of Structured Sentencing*, pp. 21-23. See also, Tonry, *Sentencing Matters*, chap. 5.

13. See, for example, Shichor and Sechrest, *Three Strikes and You're Out: Vengeance as Public Policy*; and U.S. Sentencing Commission, *Mandatory Minimum Penalties in the Federal Criminal Justice System*.

14. Heumann and Loftin, "Mandatory Sentencing and the Abolition of Plea Bargaining: The Michigan Felony Firearms Statute."

15. The Bureau of Justice Assistance conducted a national survey of sentencing practices in the United States in 1993 and 1994. They classified 29 states and the District of Columbia as having "primarily" indeterminate sentencing. (A few states use indeterminate sentences for some classes of offenses and determinate sentences for others). See U.S. Department of Justice, Bureau of Justice Assistance, *National Assessment of Structured Sentencing*, pp. 19-21.

16. Ibid. The Bureau of Justice Assistance survey revealed that five states—Arizona, California, Illinois, Indiana, and Maine—used determinate sentencing.

17. Ibid. The Bureau of Justice Assistance categorized 16 states as having sentencing guidelines. Of these, 10 had presumptive guidelines and 6 had advisory or voluntary guidelines.

18. U.S. Department of Justice, BJS, *Felony Sentences in the United States*, 1996.

19. This is in contrast to a "mixed" or "split" sentence, which involves a term of incarceration followed by period of probation.

20. U.S. Department of Justice, BJS, *Felony Sentences in the United States*, 1996, Table 4.

21. Nebraska Statutes, 29-2260.

22. U.S. Department of Justice, BJS, *Characteristics of Adults on Probation*, 1995, p. 7.

23. Ibid., Table 12.

24. Ibid., Table 13.

25. Petersilia, Turner, Kahan, and Peterson, Granting Felons Probation: Public Risks and Alternatives.

26. Ibid., p. 45.

27. Petersilia, *Expanding Options for Criminal Sentencing*, p. 4.

28. Morris and Tonry, *Between Prison and Probation: Intermediate Punishments in a Rational Sentencing System*; Petersilia, *Expanding Options for Criminal Sentencing*.

29. von Hirsch and Ashworth, *Principled Sentencing*, p. 325.

30. See Petersilia and Turner, "Intensive Probation and Parole" and U.S. General Accounting Office, *Intermediate Sanctions: Their Impacts on Prison Crowding, Costs, and Recidivism Are Still Unclear*.

31. Petersilia and Turner, "Intensive Probation and Parole."

32. For a discussion of the "piling up" of intermediate sanctions and its effect on failure rates, see Blomberg and Lucken, "Intermediate Punishment and the Piling Up of Sanctions."

33. Petersilia, *Expanding Options for Criminal Sentencing*, pp. 30-31.

34. Morris and Tonry, *Between Prison and Probation*, p. 225.

35. Ibid.

36. Clear and Hardyman, "The New Intensive Supervision Movement."

37. Ibid., pp. 182-183.

38. Tonry, *Sentencing Matters*, p. 101.

39. Ibid.

40. See, for example, Austin and Irwin, *It's About Time: America's Imprisonment Binge*; Beckett and Sasson, *The Politics of Injustice*;

Mauer, *Race to Incarcerate*; Morris and Tonry, *Between Prison and Probation*; Tonry, Sentencing Matters.

41. Morris and Tonry, *Between Prison and Probation*, chap. 2.
42. Ibid., p. 3.
43. Ibid., p. 32.
44. Austin and Irwin, *It's About Time*.
45. Ibid., p. 245.
46. Ibid., p. 245.
47. Ibid., p. 246.
48. For a detailed description of correctional boot camps, see *Correctional Boot Camps: A Tough Intermediate Sanction*, edited by MacKenzie and Hebert.
49. Ibid., p. vii.
50. U.S. Department of Justice, BJS, *State Court Organization 1998*, Table 47.
51. MacKenzie and Hebert, *Correctional Boot Camps*, p. xi.
52. MacKenzie and Parent, "Shock Incarceration and Prison Crowding in Louisiana."
53. MacKenzie and Brame, "Shock Incarceration and Positive Adjustment During Community Supervision"; MacKenzie, Brame, McDowall, and Souryal, "Boot Camp Prison and Recidivism in Eight States."
54. MacKenzie, Brame, McDowall, and Souryal, "Boot Camp Prison and Recidivism," p. 351.
55. Morris and Tonry, *Between Prison and Probation*, p. 213.
56. National Law Enforcement Corrections Technology Center, *Keeping Track of Electronic Monitoring*, p. 1.
57. U.S. Department of Justice, BJS, Bureau of Justice Statistics, *Correctional Populations in the United States*, 1997.
58. Renzema, "Home Confinement Programs: Development, Implementation, and Impact," p. 49.
59. Lilly, Ball, Curry and McMullen, "Electronic Monitoring of the Drunk Driver: A Seven-Year Study of the Home Confinement Alternative."
60. Baumer and Mendelsohn, "Electronically Monitored Home Confinement: Does It Work?" p. 66.
61. Morris and Tonry, *Between Prison and Probation*, p. 152.
62. A detailed discussion of the program can be found in McDonald, *Punishment Without Walls: Community Service Sentences in New York City*.

63. Ibid.
64. Caputo, "Community Service for Repeat Misdemeanor Offenders in New York City."
65. Tonry, *Sentencing Matters*, p. 121.
66. Hahn, *Emerging Criminal Justice: Three Pillars for a Proactive Justice System*, p. 147.
67. McDonald, Greene, and Worzella, "Day Fines in American Courts: The Staten Island and Milwaukee Experiments," p. 1.
68. Cole, Mahoney, Thornton, and Hanson, as cited in Morris and Tonry, *Between Prison and Probation*, p. 127. Regarding Fines as a Criminal Sanction.
69. McDonald, Greene, and Worzella, *Day Fines in American Courts*, p. 5.
70. For a detailed discussion of the philosophical justification of restitution as a goal of punishment, see Abel and Marsh, *Punishment and Restitution*.
71. Clear, *Harm in American Penology: Offenders, Victims, and Their Communities*, p. 129.
72. Thornburgh, *Opening Remarks*.
73. Morris and Tonry, *Between Prison and Probation*, p. 19.
74. U.S. Department of Justice, BJS, *Prisoners in 1999*.
75. Austin and Irwin, *It's About Time*, p. 1.
76. Ibid., pp. 4-7.
77. Tonry, *Sentencing Matters*, p. 128.
78. Blumstein, Cohen, Martin, and Tonry, *Research on Sentencing: The Search for Reform*, Vol. I, p. 41.
79. Illinois Compiled Statutes Annotated, 730 ILSC § 5-5-3 (1996).
80. Kaufman, "*Sentencing: The Judge's Problem*," at http://www.theatlanticmonthly/unbound/flashbks/death/kaufman.htm
81. Davis, *Discretionary Justice: A Preliminary Inquiry*, p. 190.
82. Kerstetter, "Gateway to Justice: Police and Prosecutorial Response to Sexual Assaults Against Women," p. 182.
83. *Bordenkircher v. Hayes*, 434 U.S. 357, 364 (1978).
84. For a detailed discussion of the guilty plea process, see Nardulli, Eisenstein, and Flemming, *The Tenor of Justice: Criminal Courts and the Guilty Plea Process*.
85. U.S. Department of Justice, BJS, *State Court Sentences of Convicted Felons, 1996*, Table 4.2.

86. U.S. Department of Justice, BJS, *Federal Criminal Case Processing, 1998,* Table 4.

87. *Bordenkircher v. Hayes*, 434 U.S. 357, 364 (1978).

88. *United States v. Ammidown*, 162 U.S. App. D.C. 28, 497 F.2d 615 (1973).

89. Ibid.

90. Ibid. However, it should be noted that other appellate courts have adopted a less restrictive standard. In *United States v. Bean* [564 F.2d 700 (5th Cir. 1977)], the Court of Appeals for the 5th Circuit ruled that "A decision that a plea bargain will result in the defendant's receiving too light a sentence under the circumstances of the case is a sound reason for the judge's refusing to accept the agreement."

91. Rule 11 of the Federal Rules of Criminal Procedure, which applies to cases adjudicated in federal court, states the following: "If the court accepts the plea agreement, the court shall inform the defendant that it will embody in the judgment and sentence the disposition provided for in the plea agreement. . . . If the court rejects the plea agreement, the court shall, on the record, inform the parties of this fact, advise the defendant personally in open court . . . that the court is not bound by the plea agreement, afford the defendant the opportunity to then withdraw his plea, and advise the defendant that is he persists in this guilty plea. . . . The disposition of the case may be less favorable to the defendant than that contemplated by the plea agreement."

92. *Santobello v. New York*, 404 U.S. 257 (1971).

93. Spohn and DeLone, "When Does Race Matter? An Analysis of the Conditions Under Which Race Affects Sentence Severity."

94. U.S. Department of Justice, BJS, *Compendium of Federal Justice Statistics, 1998,* Table 4.2.

95. U.S. Department of Justice, BJS, *Felony Defendants in Large Urban Counties*, 1996, p. 26.

96. Dodge and Harris, "Calling a Strike a Ball: Jury Nullification and 'Three Strikes' Cases."

97. Butler, "Racially Based Jury Nullification: Black Power in the Criminal Justice System."

98. Scheflin and Van Dyke, "Merciful Juries: The Resilience of Jury Nullification."

99. See, for example, *United States v. Dougherty*, 473 F.2d 1113 (D.C. Cir., 1972).
100. U.S. Department of Justice, BJS, *State Court Organization 1998*, Table 46.
101. Clear, Clear, and Burrell, *Offender Assessment and Evaluation*.
102. Carter and Wilkins, "Some Factors in Sentencing Policy"; Hagan, "The Social and Legal Construction of Criminal Justice: A Study of the Presentence Process"; Hagan, Hewitt, and Alwin, "Ceremonial Justice: Crime and Punishment in a Loosely Coupled System"; Kingsnorth and Rizzo, "Decision-Making in the Criminal Courts: Continuities and Discontinuities"; Rosecrance, "Maintaining the Myth of Individualized Justice: Probation Presentence Reports"; Walsh, "The Role of the Probation Officer in the Sentencing Process."
103. Carter and Wilkins, "Some Factors in Sentencing Policy."
104. Walsh, "The Role of the Probation Officer in the Sentencing Process," p. 363.
105. Kingsnorth and Rizzo, "Decision-Making in the Criminal Courts: Continuities and Discontinuities."
106. Hagan, Hewitt, and Alwin, "Ceremonial Justice: Crime and Punishment in a Loosely Coupled System."
107. Rosecrance, "Maintaining the Myth of Individualized Justice," p. 369.
108. Ibid., p. 380.
109. Ibid., p. 381.
110. U.S. Department of Justice, BJS, *State Court Organization* 1998, Table 50.
111. 18 U.S.C. §§ 3551-3626 and 28 U.S.C. §§ 991-998.
112. U.S. Department of Justice, BJS, *State Court Organization* 1998, Table 50.
113. U.S. Department of Justice, BJS, *Probation and Parole in the United States*, 1998, p. 1.
114. For a discussion of the development and implementation of parole guidelines, see Bottomley, "Parole in Transition: A Comparative Study of Origins, Developments, and Prospects for the 1990s," and Gottfredson, Wilkins, and Hoffman, *Guidelines for Parole and Sentencing*.
115. *Murphy v. Com. of Massachusetts*, 177 U.S. 155 (1900).
116. U.S. Department of Justice, BJS, *State Court Organization*, Table 45.

117. Miller, Dawson, Dix, and Parnas, *Prosecution and Adjudication*, p. 1153.

118. *Bozza v. United States*, 330 U.S. 160 (1947).

119. Kaufman, "Sentencing: The Judge's Problem," at http://www.theatlanticmonthly/unbound/flashbks/death/kaufman.htm

Chapter Three

How Do Judges Decide?

Seated at the center of the American criminal process is the trial judge. Robed on a raised bench, attentive but detached, severe but compassionate, involved but disinterested, the judge is the central figure of authority—and mystery—in the mysterious and authoritarian morality play we call criminal justice.

Richard Uviller[1]

In 1993, William Spence[2] pled guilty to two felonies in the Circuit Court of Jackson County, Missouri: assault in the first degree and armed criminal action. Spence, who had heard from a friend that Bill Smith had been harassing his girlfriend at the restaurant where she worked, shot Smith five times in the leg with a .38-caliber revolver. Smith was seriously injured. According to Missouri law, assault in the first degree is a Class A felony; the range of punishment is 10 to 30 years or life in prison. Armed criminal action is also a Class A felony; it is punishable by a mandatory prison term of 3 years to life.

William Spence was 18 years old and lived with his grandmother. His parents were divorced. He was not married, had no children, and had completed only 2 years of high school. He had been employed off and on at the fast food restaurant where his girlfriend worked. In his early teens, he was hospitalized in a psychiatric unit for about a month because of behavior problems at school. He had been arrested at the age of 17 for petty larceny but had no previous felony convictions.

Judge Ann Harding presided at the guilty plea proceeding. Judge Harding questioned Spence to ensure that he understood the nature of the charges against him and the range of penalties for each charge. She also asked him a series of questions designed to ensure that (a) he was pleading guilty voluntarily and (b) he understood that in doing so, he was giving up his right to a trial by jury. After stating that the court was accepting the defendant's guilty plea, Judge Harding sentenced William Spence to 10 years in prison for assault in the first degree and to 3 years in prison for armed criminal action. The sentences were to be served concurrently.

How did Judge Harding arrive at this decision? What factors did she consider as she attempted to decide whether William Spence should be sentenced to prison and if so, the length of time that he should be incarcerated? What factors do judges generally consider as they struggle to determine an appropriate punishment? Do sentences depend on the nature of the crime or the characteristics of the offender and victim? If so, which are most important? Do sentences vary depending on the background characteristics or attitudes of the judge? If so, which characteristics or attitudes come into play?

In this chapter, we address these questions. Our goal is to explain how judges decide—that is, to explain how judges arrive at the appropriate sentence for a particular offender.

Modeling the Sentencing Process

Researchers have conducted dozens of studies designed to enhance our understanding of judges' sentencing decisions and to identify the factors that predict sentence outcomes. These studies generally use one of two different approaches. Some researchers present judges with a set of hypothetical cases and ask each judge to indicate the sentence he or she would impose[3] and perhaps explain why. The advantage of this approach is that each judge is making decisions about identical cases. The researcher can determine whether sentences are consistent from one judge to another and can isolate the characteristics of cases (and judges) that affect sentence severity. The main disadvantage of this approach is that the researcher can include only a limited amount of information about each hypothetical case and cannot ask each judge to respond to hundreds, or even dozens, of cases. The hypothetical cases, therefore, may not reflect the reality of the sentencing process. Related to this, the decision-making context is artificial. Judges are making sentencing decisions about hypothetical, not real, defendants.

A second and more common approach is to collect data on actual cases decided by judges in a particular jurisdiction.[4] Researchers collect information about the crime, the offender, and the case from court files or electronic databases. They analyze the data using statistical techniques that allow them to isolate the effect of one factor (the offender's prior criminal record, for example) while controlling for other factors that influence sentence severity. These factors include crime seriousness, the offender's background characteristics, whether the offender pled guilty or went to trial, whether the offender was free on bond or detained in jail prior to trial, whether the offender had a private attorney or a public defender, and so on. Researchers typically analyze the decision to incarcerate or not separately from the length of sentence imposed on those who are incarcerated. They assert that sentencing is in fact a two-stage process: Judges first decide whether the offender should be incarcerated and then decide how long the sentence should be. They also argue that different case attributes may affect each decision.[5]

In the sections that follow, we discuss the results of empirical research on judges' sentencing decisions. We focus on the role played by characteristics of the offense, the offender, the victim, and the case. We also discuss the results of research examining the relationship between judges' background characteristics and their sentencing decisions. At various points, we use data on sentences imposed on offenders convicted of felonies in Cook County (Chicago, Illinois) Circuit Court in 1993 to illustrate the research findings. These data were collected for a multisite study of sentencing decisions funded by the National Science Foundation.[6]

Sentencing and Case Attributes

Consider the following scenario. Two offenders appear before Judge Susan Jones for sentencing in Cook County. Offender A is a first offender convicted of a Class 3 felony, which is punishable by probation or a prison sentence of 2 to 5 years. Offender B has two previous felony convictions and has been convicted of a more serious Class 1 felony, which is punishable by probation or a prison sentence of 4 to 15 years. Judge Jones places Offender A on probation for 3 years. She sentences offender B to 6 years in prison. Does this seem fair? Most people would say that it does. They would agree that those who commit more serious crimes or have more extensive criminal histories should be punished more harshly.

Now, consider a different pair of cases: two offenders who have been convicted of Class 2 felonies, neither of whom has a prior felony conviction. The presentence investigations ordered by Judge Jones reveal that one offender has been steadily employed for about 2 years and that the other offender has been unemployed for more than a year. The cases are comparable in other respects. Judge Jones decides to give the employed offender the benefit of the doubt. She places him on probation for 3 years and orders him to maintain his job as a condition of probation. She sentences the unemployed offender to prison for 2 years. Is this fair? Should the sentence the offender receives depend on his employability or employment history? Are there legitimate reasons for treating the unemployed, who may pose a higher risk of reoffending, differently than those who are employed?

Consider a third scenario. Judge Jones is sentencing two 18-year-old offenders who have been convicted of a Class 4 drug offense; both of them have one prior arrest for possession of drugs. Offender A, a white female, is placed on probation for 3 years and is ordered to spend the first 18 months in a residential drug treatment program. Offender B, a black male, is sentenced to prison for 18 months. Is this fair? Should the sentence the offender receives depend on gender or race? Are there legitimate reasons for treating males differently than females? For treating white offenders differently than black offenders?

As these scenarios illustrate, judges' sentencing decisions may reflect legally irrelevant as well as legally relevant factors. *Legally relevant* factors are case characteristics and offender attributes that judges are legally authorized to take into consideration. These factors include the statutory seriousness of the charge(s), the number of charges, use of a weapon, the age of the victim, the extent of injury to the victim, and the offender's prior criminal record and current legal status. *Legally irrelevant* factors are case characteristics and offender attributes that judges are either legally prohibited from taking into consideration or that bear no rational relationship to the purposes of sentencing. Race/ethnicity, gender, and social class are obviously legally irrelevant. Both the Equal Protection Clause of the Fourteenth Amendment and state and federal civil rights laws prohibit racial, gender, and class discrimination. Thus, judges are not supposed to consider the offender's (or the victim's) race/ethnicity, gender, or social class.

The categorization of other offender characteristics is more problematic. Is employment status legally relevant? What about age or education? Marital status and responsibility for dependent children? Some jurisdictions allow judges to consider these offender characteristics; other jurisdictions explicitly prohibit judges from considering them. The Illinois Criminal Code, for example, states that judges, in deciding whether to sentence the offender to prison or not, should consider a number of mitigating factors. Included are the following:[7] The character and attitudes of the defendant indicate that he or she is unlikely to commit another crime, the defendant is particularly likely to comply with the terms of a period of probation, or the imprisonment of the defendant would entail excessive hardship to his or her dependents.

Although the statute does not specifically mention the offender's age, education, employment history, or marital status, the way it is worded suggests that these background characteristics might be regarded as legally relevant "factors in mitigation." In contrast, the Minnesota Sentencing Guidelines explicitly prohibit consideration of the offender's employment status. And federal sentencing guidelines state that the offender's age, education, mental and emotional conditions, history of alcohol or drug abuse, employment history, family ties and responsibilities, and community ties are "not ordinarily relevant in determining whether a sentence should be outside the applicable guideline range."[8] Offender characteristics other than race/ethnicity, gender, and social class, then, may be legally relevant or irrelevant, depending on the laws in the jurisdiction.

In sections that follow, we discuss the results of research on the determinants of sentencing. To avoid the confusion inherent in attempting to differentiate between legally relevant and legally irrelevant determinants, we focus first on the role played by the seriousness of the offense and the offender's prior criminal record. We then examine the effect of offender characteristics, victim characteristics, and case-processing characteristics. In this chapter, we focus on characteristics other than gender and race/ethnicity. Gender discrimination in sentencing is discussed in detail in Chapter 4, and discrimination based on race or ethnicity is the subject of Chapter 5.

Offense Seriousness and Prior Record

Studies of judges' sentencing decisions reveal that these decisions are based, first and foremost, on the seriousness of the offense and the offender's prior criminal record.[9] Offenders who commit more serious crimes are sentenced more harshly than those who commit less serious crimes. Offenders with more extensive criminal histories receive more severe sentences than those with shorter criminal histories. As the National Academy of Sciences Panel on Sentencing Research concluded in 1983, offense seriousness and prior criminal record are the "key determinants of sentences."[10]

These conclusions are not surprising. As we have seen, legislators devise penal codes or sentencing guidelines based explicitly on these two factors. Offenders who commit more serious crimes or who repeat their crimes are *legally eligible* for more punishment than first offenders or those who commit less serious crimes. Moreover, as we explained in Chapter 1, judges who see retribution as the primary purpose of punishment believe that sentences *should* be proportionate to the seriousness of the crime and the culpability of the offender. Even utilitarian judges would not contend that these two factors are irrelevant to the sentence that should be imposed. Judges, in other words, are legally and morally justified in taking crime seriousness and prior record into account in making sentencing decisions.

The data presented in Exhibit 3.1, which displays sentence outcomes for offenders convicted of felonies in Chicago in 1993, show that both the likelihood of incarceration and the length of the prison sentence depend on the seriousness of the offense. Offenders convicted of Class X felonies are substantially more likely to be sentenced to prison than those convicted of less serious felonies; they also face significantly longer prison terms. A similar pattern of results is found for the various types of felonies. Most offenders convicted of first-degree murder, forcible rape, and armed robbery are sentenced to prison. In contrast, only about half of those convicted of aggravated assault, larceny, or possession of narcotics are incarcerated. The mean prison sentences imposed on offenders convicted of different types of crimes also vary substantially. They range from an average of just over 24 years (291 months) for murder to just under 2 years (23 months) for possession of narcotics.

In contrast to crime seriousness, which affects both measures of sentence severity, the offender's prior criminal record primarily affects the decision to incarcerate or not. Offenders with no prior felony convictions are sentenced to prison at a much lower rate (27.1 percent) than those with even one prior felony conviction (79.8 percent). The incarceration rate increases to 89.9 percent for offenders with two convictions and to 92.8 percent for those with three or more convictions. The odds of incarceration for the current offense also increase if the offender previously served time in prison. In fact, 89.7 percent of offenders with one prior prison sentence were incarcerated, compared with only 45.7 percent of those who had not previously been imprisoned. And *every offender* who had been to prison four or more times in the past received a prison sentence for the current offense. These results suggest that although judges in Chicago give first offenders

Exhibit 3.1 The Effect of Offense Seriousness and Prior Record on Sentence Outcomes: Offenders Convicted of Felonies in Cook County (Chicago), Illinois, 1993

	Sentenced to Prison (Percentage)	Mean Prison Sentence (Months)
Statutory classification of most serious conviction charge		
Class X	91.8	132
Class 1	67.7	59
Class 2	61.4	49
Class 3	60.0	35
Class 4	43.8	22
Type of conviction charge[a]		
First-degree murder	97.7	291
Forcible rape	96.6	142
Armed robbery	94.4	103
Unarmed robbery	72.5	61
Aggravated assault	56.1	67
Burglary	71.2	58
Larceny	51.1	30
Possess narcotics with intent	63.7	49
Possess narcotics	43.8	23
Number of prior felony convictions		
0	27.1	79
1	79.8	48
2	89.9	51
3 or more	92.8	57
Number of prior prison sentences		
0	45.7	58
1	89.7	51
2	95.2	56
3	94.2	64
4 or more	100.0	55

SOURCE: *A Multi-Site Study of the Effect of Race on Sentencing*, by C. Spohn and M. DeLone. Unpublished data. Funded by the National Science Foundation in 1996.
a. Not all offense types are included.

the benefit of the doubt in deciding between prison and probation, they are likely to impose a prison sentence on repeat offenders, particularly those who have already been in prison. (See Box 3.1 for judges' statements about the factors they take into consideration in deciding between prison and probation.)

The data presented in Exhibit 3.1 demonstrate, in a fairly unsophisticated way, that offense seriousness and prior record influence sentence se-

BOX 3.1

HOW DO JUDGES DECIDE
WHETHER PRISON IS APPROPRIATE?

Judges in Chicago, Miami, and Kansas City were asked, "What factors do you take into account in deciding whether to sentence a felony offender to prison or not?"

A lot of our discretion in sentencing has been removed by legislation mandating a prison sentence. So, the most important consideration is whether the law requires a prison sentence. If not, I look at the seriousness of the offense, the offender's prior criminal record, and the offender's potential for rehabilitation (I consider his demeanor and attitude and whether family members are supportive). I also consider whether something other than prison would benefit the victim—restitution may be more important than incarceration from the victim's point of view. The most important factor is the statute (is prison required or not); if not, decision rests most heavily on prior record.

—A judge in Chicago

In this jurisdiction, about 90 percent of the sentences handed down are the result of a plea bargain. We're somewhat unusual in that we give the attorneys handling the case the power to cut a deal—a binding deal. For the other 10 percent, I hope that a presentence investigation (PSI) is available to me. I read the PSI, listen to the arguments of the attorneys in chambers and in the courtroom, and make a decision. I put crimes into two categories—crimes of violence and crimes that don't involve violence. I also look at the nature of the crime—what occurred, the facts, the harm to innocent parties. I also consider the offender's prior criminal record.

—A judge in Kansas City

I consider the crime itself and whether this person has the potential to be rehabilitated. I look at the types of crimes the offender has been involved in the past (violent crimes, burglaries of occupied dwellings, versus relatively nonserious crimes), the offender's situation at home, whether there is the potential for more violent crimes. Whether the offender is employed or not is very important—a person who has a job looks at life very differently. I also consider whether the offender has a drug or alcohol problem that requires treatment (but not someone who smokes crack). The most important factor is whether the offender will commit more violence in the community (if released).

—A judge in Miami

SOURCE: Personal interviews with the author during 1995.

verity. They indicate that there is a relationship between offense serious-ness and both measures of sentence severity and between prior record and the decision to incarcerate or not. What these data don't tell us, however, is whether the effect of crime seriousness would remain if we controlled for prior record (and vice versa) or whether crime seriousness or prior record is a better predictor of sentence severity. To answer these questions, we need to use statistical techniques that allow us to determine the effect of one vari-able (e.g., crime seriousness) while controlling for other variables (e.g., prior criminal record).

The results of these analyses are presented in Exhibit 3.2. Part A of Ex-hibit 3.2 displays the results of statistical analyses that control simulta-neously for crime seriousness (the statutory classification of the offense) and prior criminal record (the offender's number of prior felony convic-tions). The effect of being convicted for a Class X (Class 1, Class 2, or Class 3) felony is compared with the effect of being convicted for a Class 4 felony, which is the reference category. Consistent with the results presented in Exhibit 3.1, both variables have a statistically significant effect on the deci-sion to incarcerate or not. Crime seriousness also affects the length of the prison sentence, but prior record does not. The probability of incarceration for offenders convicted of Class X felonies, for example, is 49.5 percent greater than the probability for offenders convicted of Class 4 felonies. The prison sentences imposed on offenders convicted of Class X felonies is also more than 8 years (100.8 months) longer than those imposed on offenders convicted of Class 4 felonies. Similar patterns are found for the other three offense classifications. The probability of incarceration for offenders with one prior felony conviction is 33.9 percent greater than the probability for offenders with no prior felonies, but this measure of prior record does not affect the length of the prison sentence.

These results suggest that judges take these two measures of crime seri-ousness and prior record into account when deciding on the appropriate sentence. But there are obviously other indicators of crime seriousness that might affect sentence severity: the type of crime for which the offender was convicted, whether the offender used a gun, the degree of injury to the vic-tim, the amount of property stolen, whether the offender victimized a stranger or a nonstranger, and so on. Similarly, judges might consider other indicators of the offender's past criminal history: whether the offender had ever been convicted of a violent crime, whether the offender was on proba-tion or parole at the time of arrest for the current crime, or whether the of-fender's crimes were increasing in frequency or seriousness.

Part B of Exhibit 3.2 summarizes the results of analyses that include several of these additional indicators of the seriousness of the crime and the offender's prior criminal record. Once again, the statutory classification of the conviction charge has an effect on both the likelihood of incarceration and the length of the sentence. Several of the other measures of crime seriousness also affect sentence severity. Offenders convicted of violent crimes are sentenced more harshly than those convicted of property crimes, and offenders convicted of more than one charge receive more severe sentences than those convicted of only one charge. Use of a gun during the crime increases the odds of incarceration but does not affect sentence length. And each of the three measures of prior record affects the likelihood that the defendant will be sentenced to prison, but none of them influences the length of the prison sentence. These results provide compelling evidence that crime seriousness and prior criminal record are important determinants of sentence severity. Consistent with the results of other studies of sentencing decisions, they indicate that judges impose harsher sentences on offenders who commit more serious crimes and who have more serious prior criminal records.

Offender Characteristics

Prior criminal record is not the only offender characteristic that affects judges' sentencing decisions. Studies have shown that the sentences offenders receive may depend on their demographic characteristics (gender, age, and race/ethnicity), their socioeconomic status (education and income), and their social stability (employment history, marital status, responsibility for dependent children, and history of drug or alcohol abuse). There is evidence, for example, that men are sentenced more harshly than women,[11] that young adults are sentenced more harshly than either teenagers or older adults,[12] and that blacks and Hispanics are sentenced more harshly than whites.[13] In fact, two recent studies concluded that the harshest sentences are imposed on young black and Hispanic males.[14] (See Chapter 4 for a discussion of gender discrimination in sentencing and Chapter 5 for a discussion of racial discrimination.)

There also is evidence that the offender's education, income, and employment status affect sentence severity: Harsher sentences are imposed on the less educated, the poor,[15] and the unemployed. Albonetti's[16] study of drug offenders sentenced in U.S. District Courts from 1991 to 1992, for example, showed that offenders with at least a high school education received shorter prison sentences than those without a high school education. Further analysis revealed that white offenders received a greater "sentence dis-

Exhibit 3.2 Crime Seriousness, Prior Criminal Record, and Sentence Severity: Results of a Multivariate Analysis of Sentences Imposed on Offenders Convicted of Felonies in Chicago, 1993

	Differences in the Probability of Incarceration (Percentage)[a]	Differences in the Length of Sentence (Months)[b]
A. Analysis with two variables		
Statutory classification of conviction charge		
Class X	+49.5	+100.8
Class 1	+27.7	+37.4
Class 2	+15.9	+27.3
Class 3	+13.8	+13.7
Class 4 (reference category)		
Number of prior felony convictions	+33.9	*Not significant
B. Analysis with several variables		
1. Measures of crime seriousness		
Statutory classification of conviction charge		
Class X	+40.8	+81.5
Class 1	+25.1	+29.6
Class 2	+12.8	+17.7
Class 3	*Not significant	*Not significant
Class 4 (reference category)		
Type of conviction charge		
Violent crime	+20.6	+18.6
Drug offense	*Not significant	-14.4
Property crime (reference category)		
Number of conviction charges	+6.6	+10.9
Defendant used a gun during crime	+14.2	*Not significant
2. Measures of prior criminal record		
Number of prior felony convictions	+31.4	*Not significant
Prior violent felony conviction	+17.3	*Not significant
Defendant on probation or parole	+13.0	*Not significant

SOURCE: From *A Multi-Site Study of the Effect of Race on Sentencing*, by C. Spohn and M. DeLone. Unpublished data. Funded by the National Science Foundation in 1996.

  a. Logistic regression was used to analyze the likelihood of incarceration. The odds ratios were converted to probability differences using the following formula: (*odds/odds* + 1) - .50

  b. Ordinary least squares regression was used to analyze sentence length. The values in this column were used to determine the differences in the lengths of sentences.

*Not significant at .05.

count" than either black or Hispanic offenders for having a high school education.

Researchers have reached similar conclusions about the effect of unemployment on sentencing. The authors of a study of sentencing decisions in Chicago and Kansas City found that (a) unemployed offenders were significantly more likely than employed offenders to be sentenced to prison in Kansas City and (b) in Chicago, unemployed offenders faced longer sentences than employed offenders.[17] An analysis of sentencing decisions in two Florida counties found a similar pattern of results: Unemployed defendants were significantly more likely than employed defendants to be sentenced to prison; they were also more likely to be detained in jail prior to trial.[18] A number of scholars suggest that results such as these reflect the fact that judges perceive the unemployed as more dangerous and threatening than the employed.[19] For example, arguing that "many people believe that unemployment causes crime," Box and Hale suggest that judges view the unemployed as a threat and that this "belief alone is sufficient to propel them towards stiffening their sentencing practices."[20]

Relatively few studies test for the effects of offender characteristics such as marital status, responsibility for dependent children, or a history of drug or alcohol abuse. (This is due in large part to the fact that the court files or electronic databases that researchers use for data collection do not consistently record this information.) Kathleen Daly's research on gender bias in sentencing suggests that judges do take offenders' family circumstances into consideration in making pretrial release and sentencing decisions.[21] She found that defendants who were living with a spouse, living with parents or other relatives, or caring for young children were treated more leniently than "non-familied" defendants. According to Daly, this more lenient treatment of familied defendants reflects judges' beliefs that these offenders have more informal social controls in their lives, as well as judges' concerns about maintaining families and protecting innocent children, which she labels the "social costs of punishment."[22]

In summary, judges do appear to take offenders' background characteristics into consideration when determining the appropriate sentence. Race/ethnicity, gender, and social class clearly are illegitimate considerations. Judges are legally precluded from using these "suspect classifications" in sentencing. Indicators of the "social stability" of offenders or measures of the degree to which they have "informal social control" in their lives, on the other hand, may be legally and/or practically relevant. Judges who believe that punishment serves purposes other than retribution and therefore attempt to individualize sentences may believe that the offender's social and economic circumstances are not irrelevant. For example, a judge in Chicago, who stated that the most important determinants of the sentence are crime seriousness and prior record, acknowledged that sometimes social and economic circumstances *are* relevant:

> For example, if the offender is employed and is supporting a family, the defense attorney may have a pretty good argument that if you send this person away, you're going to be putting four people on welfare. It may be true that the defendant is getting a break, but society is getting a break as well. You have to consider what's best for society.[23]

A judge in Kansas City suggested that the influence of the offender's social and economic circumstances would depend on the nature of the crime. That is, these characteristics would come into play only if the crime were nonserious. Consistent with this, a second Kansas City judge noted that the offender's current circumstances would be a factor only in "borderline cases." As he noted,

> If it's a case where I'm considering probation, these things will help me predict the likelihood of success—whether the offender has a family support network, a solid history of employment, or serious drug or alcohol problems. These types of things may "tip the scales" for or against probation.[24]

Michael Tonry, who contends that the notion of "like-situated offenders" is an "illusion,"[25] suggests that judges' *ought* to consider offenders' social and economic disadvantages at sentencing. He argues that allowing judges to use "social adversity" as a mitigating consideration is not incompatible with a "just sentencing system." In fact, he has called for the repeal of all sentencing policies "that forbid mitigation of sentences on grounds of the offenders' personal characteristics or special circumstances."[26] He argues that these policies "damage disadvantaged and minority offenders, especially those who have to some degree overcome dismal life chances."[27] However, as we explain in Chapter 4, allowing judges to use their discretion "to intelligently and compassionately tailor each sentence to the individual situation"[28] may have unintended consequences; it may lead to *unwarranted* disparities in sentencing.

Characteristics of the Victim

In attempting to determine the appropriate sentence, do judges consider the characteristics of the victim or the behavior of the victim at the time of the crime? Are offenders who victimize whites treated differently than those who victimize blacks? Are offenders who victimize strangers sentenced differently than those who victimize relatives, friends, or intimate partners? Do judges mitigate the sentence if the victim "provoked" or "precipitated" the crime? Or when the victim's lifestyle is unconventional? (See Box 3.2)

Evidence regarding the effect of victim characteristics on sentence severity comes primarily from research regarding the imposition of the death penalty and from research examining sexual assault case outcomes. As we explain in more detail in Chapter 5, there is a substantial body of research demonstrating that blacks who murder whites are much more likely to be sentenced to death than blacks who murder blacks or than whites who murder blacks or whites.[29] The most widely cited of these studies found that defendants convicted of killing whites in Georgia were more than 4 times as

---

BOX 3.2

**THE VICTIM'S LIFESTYLE AND
BIAS IN SENTENCING DECISIONS**

On November 28, 1988, Richard Bednarski was sentenced to 30 years in prison for the murder of two gay men. Bednarski testified in court that he and his friends went to a park in Dallas, Texas, to "pester homosexuals." He ended up killing the two men in an execution-style slaying. Bednarski put a gun in one man's mouth and pulled the trigger; he shot the other man point-blank several times.

Jack Hampton, the judge who imposed the sentence, had a reputation as a "hanging judge." He usually gave at least a life sentence for murder. When asked by a reporter for the *Dallas Times Herald* why he hadn't imposed a more severe sentence on Bednarski, Judge Hampton said that the murdered gay men got pretty much what they deserved, since they were "queers" who "wouldn't have been killed if they hadn't been cruising the streets picking up teenage boys."

Publication of Judge Hampton's remarks sparked protests and led to calls for Hampton to be disciplined. The judge then issued a statement in which he said he wanted "to apologize" for "his poor choice of words." He also stated that in his court "everyone is entitled to and will receive equal protection."

SOURCE: "Dallas Judge Apologizes for 'Poor Choice of Words.'" *Montrose Voice*, 1988, December 23, p. 5.

likely to receive death sentences as defendants convicted of killing blacks.[30] Baldus and his colleagues also found that blacks who killed whites had the greatest likelihood of receiving the death penalty. A number of studies also found that black men convicted of sexually assaulting white women are sentenced more harshly than other race of offender/race of victim pairs.[31] One study, for example, found that 86 percent of the black offenders convicted of sexually assaulting whites were sentenced to prison, compared with only 66 percent of the blacks convicted of sexually assaulting blacks and 54 percent of the whites convicted of assaulting whites.[32] This study also found that blacks who murdered whites received substantially longer sentences than did offenders in the other two categories.

Why are blacks who murder or sexually assault whites singled out for harsher treatment? One explanation is that judges apply the law to maintain the power of the dominant group in society and to control the behavior of those who threaten that power.[33] This explanation, in other words, suggests that crimes involving black offenders and white victims are punished most harshly because they pose the greatest threat to the "system of racially stratified state authority."[34] A second explanation emphasizes the race of the victim rather than the racial composition of the offender/victim dyad.[35] This explanation suggests that crimes involving black victims are not taken seriously and/or that crimes involving white victims are taken very seriously. It suggests that the lives of black victims are devalued relative to the lives of white victims. Thus, crimes against whites will be punished more severely than crimes against blacks, regardless of the race of the offender.

Other evidence of the role played by victim characteristics is found in research examining the legal processing of sexual assault cases. This research provides evidence that supports the claims of feminist theorists who assert that outcomes of rape cases reflect (a) decision makers' beliefs about acceptable and unacceptable behavior by women or (b) their stereotypes of sexual assault. Although sentences in sexual assault cases, like those in other types of cases, are strongly influenced by legally relevant factors, such as the seriousness of the crime and the offender's prior criminal record, victim characteristics also come into play. For example, a number of studies reveal that sexual assault case-processing decisions, including decisions regarding sentence severity, are affected by the victim's age, occupation, and education;[36] by "risk-taking" behavior, such as hitchhiking, drinking, or using drugs; [37] and by the reputation of the victim.[38] Sexual assault case outcomes also are affected by the relationship between the victim and the offender: Men convicted of sexually assaulting women who are strangers to them are sentenced more harshly than men convicted of sexually assaulting women who are relatives or friends.[39]

In summary, victim characteristics do affect the sentences that judges impose. Offenders who murder or sexually assault whites—particularly blacks who murder or sexually assault whites—are sentenced more harshly than offenders who murder or sexually assault blacks. The sentences imposed on offenders convicted of sexual assault are less severe if the victim's character, reputation, or behavior suggest that she is not a "genuine victim."

Case-Processing Attributes

Three case-processing attributes have been linked to sentence severity: the type of disposition (plea versus trial), the defendant's pretrial status (released or in custody prior to trial), and the type of attorney representing the defendant (private attorney versus public defender). Critics of the sentencing process charge that (a) defendants who plead guilty are treated more leniently than those who are tried by a judge or jury, (b) defendants who are released pending trial are sentenced more leniently than those detained in jail prior to trial, and (c) defendants represented by private attorneys receive more lenient sentences than those represented by public defenders. Some critics suggest that these findings reflect discrimination against the poor. That is, indigent defendants who are unable to make bail or hire attorneys to defend them are sentenced more harshly than nonindigent defendants. Thus, "Social statuses influence final dispositions through their relationships with earlier decisions, especially those pertaining to counsel and pretrial release."[40]

Is There a Trial Penalty? We noted in Chapter 2 that more than 90 percent of all state and federal defendants plead guilty. We also noted that the prosecutor influences the sentencing process through plea bargaining. But what about those cases in which the prosecutor and the defense are unable to negotiate an acceptable bargain and the defendant refuses to plead guilty? If the defendant is convicted at trial, will the sentence imposed by the judge be harsher than it would have been if he had accepted the state's offer? Will the defendant who insists on a trial be required to pay a "trial penalty" or a "jury tax?"

Critics of plea bargaining argue that this is exactly what happens. In fact, one of the most widely accepted assumptions about the criminal court system is that defendants who go to trial will be sentenced more harshly than similar defendants who plead guilty. Studies have shown that criminal justice officials[41] and defendants[42] believe that it pays to plead guilty. Like

---

BOX 3.3

A "JURY TAX?"

Judge Kovitsky is on the bench in the Bronx County Courthouse. He calls the defendant to the stand. The prosecutor has offered a sentence of 2 to 6 years in prison in return for a guilty plea, but the defendant has refused the offer. The Judge is explaining "the deal" to the defendant:

You've got a job, you've got a home, you're young, you're a nice-looking, bright young man. You've got a lot going for you. You've got more than most people. But you've got one big problem to overcome. YOU BEEN INVOLVED IN THESE F [- - - - -]G ROBBERIES! Now, the district attorney has made you an offer of two to six years. If you take that offer and you behave yourself, this will all be behind you, in no time, and you'll still be a young man with your whole life ahead of you. If you go to trial and you're convicted, you could get eight to twenty-five. Now think about that. The district attorney has made you an offer.

Excerpted from *The Bonfire of the Vanities* by Tom Wolfe. Copyright © 1988 by Tom Wolfe. Reprinted by permission of Farrar, Straus & Giroux, LLC.

Judge Kovitsky in *The Bonfire of the Vanities* (see Box 3.3), they believe that defendants who refuse the prosecutor's offer will be penalized. As a Chicago judge told a defense attorney contemplating a jury trial for a client, "You take some of my time; I'll take some of his."[43]

Studies of sentencing outcomes confirm this. These studies provide evidence supporting the existence of trial penalties in both federal and state courts. For example, two recent studies of sentences imposed on drug offenders in U.S. District Courts found that pleading guilty reduced both the likelihood of a prison sentence and the length of sentence imposed on offenders who were incarcerated.[44] A study of sentences imposed in Chicago, Kansas City, and Miami reached similar conclusions.[45] In Kansas City and Miami, defendants convicted at trial were substantially more likely than those who pled guilty to be sentenced to prison. In all three jurisdictions, those who went to trial faced significantly longer sentences than those who pled guilty. The "trial penalty" was 10 months in Chicago, 35 months in Kansas City, and 45 months in Miami.[46] Research in Pennsylvania also uncovered a substantial trial penalty.[47] Defendants tried by a jury were 25 percent more likely than those who pled guilty to be sentenced to prison. They also received prison sentences that averaged 19 months longer than sentences imposed on defendants who pled guilty.

When confronted with evidence such as this, many judges will suggest that the data reveal not that those who insist on a trial are penalized, but that those who plead guilty are rewarded. The comments of a judge in Chicago, who responded that it was "absolutely" appropriate to sentence defendants who plead guilty more leniently, are typical:

> Confession cleanses the soul and gives the offender a clean slate. Moreover, if he pleads guilty he saves the time and expense of a trial and saves the victim from having to testify. It's not a jury tax, however; it's a benefit awarded for recognizing and accepting responsibility for your conduct.[48]

Another Chicago judge, who stated that "Someone who takes a jury trial should *not* be penalized for exercising a constitutional right," said that he had heard a saying about the so-called trial penalty:

> If the offender pleads guilty, he's going to get a very good deal on the sentence. If he takes a bench trial, he's going to get a deal. If he takes a jury trial, he's going to get what he deserves.[49]

Whether viewed as a penalty imposed on those who insist on a trial or a reward to those who do not, the effect is the same: Defendants tried and convicted at trial are sentenced more harshly than those who plead guilty.

Does Pretrial Status Affect Sentence Severity? Despite the fact that criminal defendants are presumed innocent until proven guilty, a significant number of them are held in jail prior to trial, either because they were unable to make bail or because a judge ordered them to be detained pending adjudication of the charges. In 1996, for example, 37 percent of all felony defendants in the 75 largest counties in the United States[50] and 44.4 percent of all federal defendants[51] were in custody prior to trial. More than 80 percent of the state court defendants were detained because they could not make bail. In contrast, about three quarters of the federal defendants were detained by order of the court, either because they were considered flight risks or because they were considered dangerous to the community or to prospective witnesses or jurors.[52] In both state and federal courts, defendants charged with serious violent crimes had the highest pretrial detention rates. Federal defendants charged with drug trafficking and weapons offenses also had high detention rates.

Concerns about pretrial detention focus on the fact that (a) defendants who are presumed to be innocent are held in jail prior to trial and (b) those who are detained face higher odds of conviction and receive harsher sentences than those who are released prior to trial. These concerns focus, in other words, on the possibility that pretrial detention has "spillover" effects on other case-processing decisions.

A recent analysis of pretrial release of felony defendants by the Bureau of Justice Statistics (BJS) attests to the validity of these concerns.[53] Using data from 1992, BJS compared the conviction and incarceration rates for released and detained defendants in the 75 largest counties in the United States. They found that 79 percent of those detained prior to trial were convicted, compared with only 61 percent of those released. Pretrial status also affected the likelihood of incarceration: 50 percent of the detained defendants were sentenced to prison, compared with only 19 percent of those released prior to trial. There were similar disparities for each of the four types of offenses analyzed. Among offenders charged with violent crimes, for example, the conviction rates were 72 percent for those who were detained and 47 percent for those who were released; 55 percent of the detainees were sentenced to prison, compared with 20 percent of those who were released.

These data suggest that pretrial release does have important spillover effects on case outcomes. However, higher conviction and imprisonment rates for defendants who were detained pending trial could occur because defendants held in jail prior to trial tend to be charged with more serious crimes, have more serious prior criminal histories, and have past histories of nonappearance at court proceedings. The BJS study discussed above, for example, found that defendants charged with murder had the lowest release rate and that defendants with more serious prior records or histories of nonappearance were more likely to be detained prior to trial.[54] Given these findings, it is possible that the relationship between pretrial status and case outcomes would disappear once controls for case seriousness and prior criminal record were taken into consideration.

A number of studies demonstrate that the effect of pretrial status does *not* depend on the seriousness of the crime or the offender's prior record. A study of sentencing decisions in two Florida counties, for example, found that defendants held in jail prior to trial were significantly more likely to be incarcerated following conviction, even after controlling for other predictors of sentence severity.[55] Moreover, pretrial detention increased the odds of incarceration for offenders convicted of drug offenses, property crimes, and violent crimes. A study of sentencing decisions in Chicago, Miami, and

Kansas City reached a similar conclusion.[56] In each city, offenders who were released prior to trial faced substantially lower odds of imprisonment than those who were detained. In Chicago, the probability of incarceration for offenders who were released was 41.7 percent less than the probability for offenders kept in custody. The difference in the probability of imprisonment was 32.0 percent in Kansas City and 10.2 percent in Miami. And a study of sentencing decisions in "Metro City" found that pretrial release affected both the likelihood of incarceration and overall sentence severity.[57]

What explains these results? Why would defendants who are free pending trial be treated differently than those kept in custody? One possibility is that defendants held in jail in the months prior to trial are less able to assist in their own defense: Because they are incarcerated, they may have less contact with their attorneys and thus fewer opportunities to discuss the conditions of plea bargains or to provide the names of character witnesses or other evidence that might be helpful at the sentencing hearing. Their incarceration also makes it difficult, if not impossible, for them to do the sorts of things that might incline the judge to mitigate the sentence: maintain employment, maintain relationships with spouses or children, start educational or vocational training programs, or get help for substance abuse problems. Furthermore, defendants who are incarcerated may be pressured to plead guilty and "get on with their lives." As a result, they may be willing to settle for less favorable outcomes than they would have had they not been incarcerated. Finally, judges and jurors may assume that defendants held in jail prior to trial are more dangerous and pose greater risks than those who are free. They might reason, in other words, that the defendants wouldn't have been locked up if they weren't dangerous.

Whatever the reason, it seems clear that defendants who remain in custody suffer both the pains of incarceration prior to trial and the consequences of pretrial detention at sentencing.

Are Defendants Represented by Public Defenders Penalized at Sentencing? The Sixth Amendment to the U.S. Constitution states, "In all criminal prosecutions, the accused shall enjoy the right to have the assistance of counsel for his defense." Historically, this meant simply that someone who had an attorney could bring the attorney along to represent him. Of course, this was no help to the majority of criminal defendants, who were too poor to hire their own attorneys and were consequently convicted and sentenced without legal representation. The U.S. Supreme Court, recognizing that defendants could not obtain fair trials without the assistance of counsel, began to interpret the Sixth Amendment as requiring the appointment of counsel for indigent defendants. The process began in 1932, when the Court ruled in *Powell v. Alabama*[58] that states must provide attorneys for indigent defendants charged with capital crimes. The Court's decision in a 1938 case, *Johnson v. Zerbst*,[59] required the appointment of counsel for all indigent defendants in federal criminal cases, but the requirement was not extended to the states until *Gideon v. Wainwright*,[60] in 1963. In subsequent decisions, the Court ruled that "no person may be imprisoned, for any offense, whether classified as petty, misdemeanor, or felony, unless he was represented by counsel"[61] and that the right to counsel is not limited to trial, but applies to all "critical stages" in the criminal justice process.[62] As a result of these rulings, most defendants must be provided with counsel from arrest and interrogation through sentencing and the appellate process.

As a result of Supreme Court decisions expanding the right to counsel and the development of federal and state policies implementing these decisions, poor defendants are no longer routinely denied legal representation at trial or at any of the other critical stages in the process. Questions have been raised, however, about the quality of legal representation provided to indigent defendants by public defenders. As Sterling notes,

> The general suspicion is that equal justice is not available to rich and poor alike. Rather, it is believed that indigents receive a lower quality of legal service, which results in their being more likely to suffer harsher penal sanctions than similarly situated defendants who can afford to buy good legal talent.[63]

One of the most oft-quoted statements about public defenders is the answer given by an unidentified prisoner in a Connecticut jail when asked whether he had had a lawyer when he went to court. "No," he replied, "I had a public defender."[64] Some social scientists have echoed this view, charging that public defenders, as part of the courtroom workgroup, are more concerned with securing guilty pleas as efficiently and as expeditiously as possible than they are with aggressively defending their clients.[65] As Weitzer notes,

> In many jurisdictions, public defenders and state-appointed attorneys are grossly underpaid, poorly trained, or simply lack the resources and time to prepare for a case—a pattern documented in cases ranging from the most minor to the most consequential capital crimes.[66]

Other social scientists disagree. Citing studies showing that criminal defendants represented by public defenders do not fare worse than those represented by private attorneys,[67] these researchers suggest that critics "have tended to underestimate the quality of defense provided by the public defender."[68] Wice, in fact, concludes that the public defender is able to establish a working relationship with prosecutors and judges "in which the exchange of favors, so necessary to greasing the squeaky wheel of justice, can directly benefit the indigent defendant."[69] As part of the courtroom workgroup, in other words, public defenders are in better positions than private attorneys to negotiate favorable plea bargains and to mitigate punishment.

A recent report by the BJS suggests that case outcomes for state and federal defendants represented by public attorneys do not differ dramatically from those represented by private counsel.[70] There were only slight differences in the conviction rates of defendants represented by public and private attorneys but somewhat larger differences in the incarceration rates. At the federal level, 87.6 percent of defendants represented by public attorneys were sentenced to prison, compared with 76.5 percent of defendants with private attorneys. The authors of the report attributed this to the fact that public counsel represented a higher percentage of violent, drug, and public-order offenders, whereas private attorneys represented a higher percentage of white-collar defendants. Felony defendants in state courts also faced lower odds of incarceration if they were represented by private attorneys (53.9 percent) rather than public defenders (71.3 percent). In both state and federal courts, on the other hand, defendants represented by public defenders got somewhat shorter sentences than those represented by private attorneys. At the federal level, the mean sentences were 58 months (public defenders) and 62 months (private attorneys); at the state level, they were 31.2 months (public defenders) and 38.3 months (private attorneys).

These results suggest that defendants represented by public defenders do not necessarily fare worse than those represented by private attorneys. The results of Spohn and DeLone's[71] study of sentence outcomes in Chicago, Miami, and Kansas City are similar. The type of attorney representing the offender had no effect on the likelihood of incarceration in any of the three jurisdictions, even after the authors controlled for crime seriousness, prior criminal record, and other predictors of sentence severity. Moreover, there were no differences between the sentences imposed on offenders represented by public defenders and private attorneys in two of the three cities. In fact, the type of attorney had a significant effect only in Miami, and there, offenders with private counsel received sentences that averaged 15 months *longer* than those imposed on offenders represented by public defenders.

These results reveal that type of counsel is not a strong predictor of judges' sentencing decisions. They indicate that "indigent defenders get the job done and done well"[72] and that judges do not look more favorably on defendants who hire their own attorneys.

The findings discussed thus far suggest that although the seriousness of the crime and the culpability of the offender are the *primary* determinants of sentence severity, offenders' background characteristics and case-processing factors also play a role. They suggest that legally relevant case characteristics are not the only determinants of judges' sentencing decisions. In the next section, we examine the relationship between the characteristics of the judge and sentence outcomes.

Sentencing and Characteristics of the Judge

> *Most of the judges in America are white and male. The law is too pale and too male.*
>
> Judge Bruce M. Wright[73]

Do judges from different backgrounds impose different sentences? Do former prosecutors impose more punitive sentences than former defense attorneys? Do judges' sentences become more or less severe the longer they serve? Does judges' religion or political party identification affect their sentencing decisions? Do black judges or female judges dispense a different kind of justice than white judges or male judges?

Researchers have only recently begun to ask these types of questions. This is not surprising, given the homogeneity of the individuals who don judicial robes in courts throughout the United States. The typical federal or state judge is white, male, and middle-aged. Only about 6 percent of all state court judges, for example, are members of racial minorities, and fewer than 15 percent are women.[74] Most state court judges were born and went to law school in the state in which they serve. They typically came to the bench either from private practices of law or from lower-court judgeships, such as a magistrate's position. As Carp and Stidham note, "They tend to be home-grown fellows who are moderately conservative and staunchly committed to the status quo. . . . local boys who made good."[75] Stumpf's conclusion is even more pointed:

If you are young, female, a member of a racial minority, are of the wrong political party, or presumably have few contacts within the organized legal community in your state, the chances of making it to the trial bench are slight.[76]

As shown in Exhibit 3.3, U.S. District Court judges also "come from a very narrow stratum of American society."[77] More than three quarters of the district court judges appointed by Presidents Carter, Bush, and Reagan were men, as were two thirds of those appointed by President Clinton. Similarly, about three quarters of the judges appointed by these four presidents were white. In fact, a majority of the judges appointed by Presidents Carter, Reagan, and Bush were white males. In contrast, just over half of President Clinton's appointees were either women or members of racial minorities.[78] The typical district court judge was about 48 years old at the time of his appointment and came to the bench from either a prior judicial position or a position as a public prosecutor. Not surprisingly, the political party affiliation of judges matches that of the president who appointed them. In fact, about 90 percent of the judges appointed by each president came from that president's political party.

Diversity on the Bench: Would It Make a Difference?

How does the fact that state and federal court judges are "much more alike than they are different"[79] affect the sentencing process? Does the judicial recruitment process produce "a corps of jurists who agree on how the judicial game is played"?[80] Would sentencing patterns and sentencing outcomes be different if more women and members of racial minorities were elected or appointed to the bench? Or if there were more diversity in terms of age, religion, and prior experience?

The answers to such questions are varied. Most of the debate centers on whether increasing the number of black and female judges would produce a different type of justice. One side argues that it would not. They contend that the judicial selection process produces a relatively homogenous bench and that even black and white judges and male and female judges share similar background characteristics. The judicial recruitment process, according to this view, screens out candidates with unconventional views, with the result that women and members of racial minorities selected for judgeships "tend to be 'safe' candidates who are generally supportive of the system."[81] They are judges, in other words, who know how the judicial game is played.

Those who take the "no-difference position" argue that the homogeneity of the bench is reinforced by the judicial socialization process, which

Exhibit 3.3 The Background Characteristics of Presidents' District Court Appointees, 1977-2000

	Clinton (N = 270)	Bush (N = 148)	Reagan (N = 290)	Carter (N = 202)
Gender				
Male	69.6%	80.4%	91.7%	85.6%
Female	30.4	19.6	8.3	14.4
Race/ethnicity				
White	73.7	89.2	92.4	78.7
African American	17.8	6.8	2.1	13.9
Hispanic	7.0	4.0	4.8	6.9
Asian	1.1	–	0.7	0.5
Native American	0.4	–	–	–
White male	49.3	73.0	84.8	68.3
Average age at appointment	48.7	48.1	48.7	49.6
Prior experience				
Judicial	49.7	46.6	46.2	54.0
Prosecutorial	37.9	39.2	44.1	38.1
Neither	31.4	31.8	28.6	30.7
Political party Identification				
Democrat	90.5	5.4	4.8	90.6
Republican	2.4	88.5	91.7	4.5
Other/none	7.1	6.1	3.4	5.0

SOURCE: Information on the gender and race/ethnicity of President Clinton's appointees is provided for all appointments through the end of his second term. Data on experience and political party identification include only judges appointed through 1997. Data on President Clinton's second-term appointments were obtained from the Alliance for Justice, Judicial Selection Project Database, available on the World Wide Web at http://www.afj.org/jsp. Data on appointments made by Presidents Carter, Reagan, Bush, and on President Clinton's first-term were adapted from *Judicial Process in America*, 4th ed. (Table 8.1), by R. Carp and R. Stidham, 1998. Washington, DC: Congressional Quarterly.

produces a subculture of justice that encourages judges to adhere to prevailing norms, practices, and precedents.[82] They say that it also is reinforced by the courtroom workgroup: the judges, prosecutors, and defense attorneys who work together day after day to process cases as efficiently as possible. To expedite sentencing, for example, members of the courtroom workgroup may informally agree on the parameters of acceptable plea negotiations and on the range of penalties appropriate for each type of crime. According to the no-difference position, individual judges might deviate from these norms, but there is no reason to expect women or members of racial minorities to deviate more often than men or whites. Finally, there is the notion that conformity may be encouraged by the nature of the sentencing process; that is, the legal constraints on sentencing decisions may leave little room "for judicial idiosyncrasies to affect outcome."[83]

Some commentators assert that even unconventional or maverick judges are eventually forced to conform. Bruce Wright, an African American who now sits on the New York Supreme Court, stated in 1973: "No matter how 'liberal' black judges may believe themselves to be, the law remains essentially a conservative doctrine, and those who practice it conform."[84] Twenty years later, Judge Wright made an even more pointed comment about some black judges:

> [They] are so white in their imitation of life and in their reactions to Black defendants that they are known as "Afro-Saxons." As soon as these Black judges put on the Black robes, they become emotionally white. But it's not surprising. We have Eurocentric educations. We learn white values.[85]

Those who champion diversity in the courtroom argue that black judges and female judges can make a difference. They suggest that black and female judges bring to the bench beliefs, attitudes, and experiences that differ from those of whites and/or men. Goldman, for example, maintains that members of racial minorities and women will bring to the court "a certain sensitivity—indeed, certain qualities of heart and mind —that may be particularly helpful in dealing with [issues of racial and sexual discrimination]."[86] In remarks following her inauguration as an Associate Justice of the U. S. Supreme Court, Ruth Bader Ginsburg also spoke of the importance of diversity on the bench:

> Justice Sandra Day O'Connor recently quoted Minnesota Supreme Court Justice Jeanne Coyne, who was asked: "Do women judges decide cases differently by virtue of being women?" Justice Coyne re-

plied that in her experience, "a wise old man and a wise old woman reach the same conclusion." I agree, but I also have no doubt that women, like persons of different racial groups and ethnic origins, contribute what a fine jurist, the late Fifth Circuit Judge Alvin Rubin, described as "a distinctive medley of view influenced by differences in biology, cultural impact, and life experience."[87]

Like Justice Ginsburg, advocates of the "difference position" contend that female judges and black judges contribute something unique to the judicial process. In support of the argument that women judges "speak in a different voice," some point to the work of Carol Gilligan,[88] who claimed that women's moral reasoning differs from that of men: Whereas men emphasize legal rules and reasoning based on an ethic of justice, women, who are more concerned about preserving relationships and more sensitive to the needs of others, reason using an ethic of care. Others, who counter that "the language of law is explicitly the language of justice rather than care,"[89] claim that the differences women bring to the bench stem more from their experiences as women than from differences in moral reasoning. They maintain, for example, that women are substantially more likely than men to be victimized by rape, sexual harassment, domestic violence, and other forms of predatory violence and that their experiences as crime victims and/or their fear of crime shapes their attitudes toward and their responses to crime and criminals. Noting that "Human beings are products of their experiences," Martha Fineman suggests that "if women collectively have different actual *and* potential experiences from men, they are likely to have different perspectives—different sets of values, beliefs, and concerns as a group."[90]

How might these gender differences influence judges' sentencing decisions? If, in fact, women are more compassionate—more caring—than men, they might sentence offenders more leniently than men do. A female judge, in other words, might be more willing than a male judge to sentence a nonviolent offender who is struggling to provide for his family to probation rather than prison. Alternatively, the fact that women are more likely to be victims of sexualized violence and are more fearful of crime in general might incline them to impose harsher sentences than men, particularly for violent crimes, crimes against women, and crimes involving dangerous repeat offenders. Still another possibility is that the life experiences of female judges, and particularly black or Hispanic female judges, will make them more sensitive to the existence of racism or sexism. As a result, they might make more equitable sentencing decisions than white male judges.

Similar arguments are advanced by those who contend that increasing the number of members of racial minorities in state and federal courts will alter the character of justice and the outcomes of the criminal justice system. In other words, because the life histories and experiences of members of minorities differ dramatically from those of whites, the beliefs and attitudes they bring to the bench also will differ. Justice A. Leon Higginbotham Jr., an African American who retired from the U.S. Court of Appeals for the Third Circuit in 1993, wrote that "the advantage of pluralism is that it brings a multitude of different experiences to the judicial process."[91] More to the point, he stated that "someone who has been a victim of racial injustice has greater sensitivity of the court's making sure that racism is not perpetrated, even inadvertently."[92] Judge George Crockett's assessment of the role of the black judge was even more pointed:

I think a black judge . . . has got to be a reformist—he cannot be a member of the club. The whole purpose of selecting him is that the people are dissatisfied with the status quo and they want him to shake it up, and his role is to shake it up.[93]

Assuming that black judges agree with Judge Crockett's assertion that their role is to "shake it up," how would this affect their behavior on the bench? One possibility is that black judges might attempt to stop, or at least slow, the flow of young black men into state and federal prisons. If black judges view the disproportionately high number of young black males incarcerated in state and federal prisons as a symptom of racial discrimination, they may be more willing than white judges to experiment with alternatives to incarceration for offenders convicted of nonviolent drug and property crimes. Welch and her colleagues make an analogous argument. Noting that blacks tend to view themselves as liberal rather than conservative, they speculate that black judges might be "more sympathetic to criminal defendants than whites judges are, since liberal views are associated with support for the underdog and the poor, which defendants disproportionately are."[94] Others similarly suggest that increasing the number of black judges would reduce racism in the criminal justice system and produce more equitable treatment of black and white defendants.[95]

In the next section, we review the findings of research examining the effect of characteristics of the judge on sentence severity.

Research on Judicial Characteristics

Although researchers interested in the effect of judicial characteristics on sentence outcomes have focused on the race/ethnicity and gender of the judge, a number of studies examine the influence of the judge's age, time on the bench, religion, political party affiliation, and experience prior to becoming a judge. The results of these studies generally reveal that these background characteristics either do not affect sentence outcomes at all[96] or have only weak effects.[97] They also reveal that these characteristics do not always have the expected effects. Three studies,[98] for example, found that judges with prior prosecutorial experience imposed harsher sentences, whereas one[99] found that former prosecutors imposed more lenient sentences. Similarly, two studies[100] found that judges who had been on the bench longer imposed more severe sentences, but two others[101] found that longer tenure on the bench led to more lenient sentences. Several studies[102] concluded that older judges sentenced defendants more harshly than did younger judges and that judges who were members of fundamentalist churches meted out more severe punishment than those who were not.[103] The fact that most of these effects were relatively weak—coupled with the fact that some of them were the opposite of what was predicted—suggests that these background characteristics do not consistently affect the sentences that judges impose.

But what about the judge's gender and race/ethnicity? As we explained above, there are a number of reasons why we might expect a "different kind of justice" from female, black, or Hispanic judges. At the same time, there are good reasons to predict that minority judges will conform to the sentencing standards set by majority judges. As we will see, the research that has been conducted to date does not tell us, at least not conclusively, which of these expectations is more tenable.

Racial Minorities on the Bench. Turning first to research on the judge's race/ethnicity, we find that these studies have reached contradictory conclusions. Two early studies found few differences in the sentencing behavior of black and white judges. Engle,[104] for example, analyzed Philadelphia judges' sentencing decisions. He found that although the judge's race had a statistically significant effect, nine other variables were stronger predictors of sentence outcomes. He concluded that the race of the judge exerted "a very minor influence" overall.[105] Uhlman's[106] study of convicting and sentencing decisions in "Metro City"(as the author refers to Philadelphia) reached a similar conclusion. Black judges imposed somewhat harsher sentences than white judges, but the differences were relatively small. And both black and white judges imposed harsher sentences on black defendants than on white defendants. Moreover, there was more "behavioral diversity" among the black judges than between black and white judges. Some of the black judges imposed substantially harsher sentences than the average sentence imposed by all judges, and other black judges imposed significantly more lenient sentences. These findings led Uhlman to conclude that "Black and white judges differ little in determining both guilt and the punishment a defendant 'deserves' for committing a crime in Metro City."[107]

A later study of sentencing decisions in "Metro City" reached a different conclusion. Welch, Combs, and Gruhl[108] found that black judges were more likely than white judges to send white defendants to prison. Further analysis led them to conclude that this difference reflected black judges' tendency to incarcerate black and white defendants at about the same rate and white judges' tendency to incarcerate black defendants more often than white defendants. They also found, however, that black judges favored defendants of their own race when determining the length of the prison sentence but whites judges did not. These results led them to conclude that "black judges provide more than symbolic representation."[109] According to these authors,

> To the extent that they equalize the criminal justice system's treatment of black and white defendants, as they seem to for the crucial decision to incarcerate or not, [black judges] thwart discrimination against black defendants. In fact, the quality of justice received by both black and white defendants may be improved.[110]

A study of sentencing decisions by black and white judges on the Cook County Circuit Court reached a similar conclusion.[111] Spears found that black judges sentenced white, black, and Hispanic offenders to prison at about the same rate, whereas white judges sentenced both black and Hispanic offenders to prison at a significantly higher rate than white offenders. In fact, compared with white offenders sentenced by white judges, black offenders sentenced by white judges had a 13 percent greater probability of imprisonment; for Hispanic offenders sentenced by white judges, the difference was 15 percent. Like the "Metro City" study, then, this study found that white judges sentenced members of racial minorities more harshly than they sentenced whites and concluded that having black judges on the bench "does provide more equitable justice."[112]

Spohn's[113] analysis of the sentences imposed on offenders convicted of violent felonies in Detroit Recorder's Court produced strikingly different results and led to very different conclusions. Like Engle and Uhlman, Spohn uncovered few meaningful differences between black and white judges. She found that black judges were somewhat more likely than white judges to sentence offenders to prison but that judicial race had no effect on the length of sentence. Like Engle, she concluded that "the effect of judicial race, even where significant, was clearly overshadowed by the effect of the other independent variables."[114] Spohn also tested for interaction between the race of the judge, the race of the offender, and the race of the victim. That is, she attempted to determine first, whether black and white judges treated black and white offenders differently and second, whether black and white judges imposed different sentences on black offenders who victimized other blacks, black offenders who victimized whites, white offenders who victimized other whites, and white offenders who victimized blacks.

The results of this analysis, which takes crime seriousness, prior record, and other relevant predictors of sentencing into account, are presented in Exhibit 3.4. The adjusted percentages clearly highlight the similarities in the sentences imposed by black and by white judges. Black judges sentenced 72.9 percent of black offenders to prison, whereas white judges incarcerated 74.2 percent, a difference of less than 2 percentage points. The adjusted figures for white offenders were 65.3 percent (black judges) and 66.5 percent (white judges), again a difference of less than 2 percentage points. More important, these data reveal that both black and white judges sentenced black defendants more harshly than white defendants. For both black and white judges, the adjusted incarceration rates for black offenders were 7 percentage points higher than for white offenders. Moreover, black judges sentenced offenders to prison at about the same rate as white judges, regardless of the racial makeup of the offender/victim pair. These findings led Spohn to conclude that there was "remarkable similarity"[115] in the sentencing decisions of black and white judges. They also led her to question the assumption that discrimination against black defendants reflects prejudicial or racist attitudes on the part of white criminal justice officials. As she noted, the findings of her study suggest that the explanation is more complex:

> Contrary to expectations, both black and white judges in Detroit imposed harsher sentences on black offenders. Harsher sentencing of black offenders, in other words, cannot be attributed solely to discrimination by white judges.[116]

Spohn suggested that her findings contradicted the widely held assumption that blacks do not discriminate against other blacks, as well as conventional wisdom about the role of black judges. She concluded "that we should be considerably less sanguine in predicting that discrimination against black defendants will decline as the proportion of black judges increases."[117]

To explain her unexpected findings that both black and white judges sentenced black defendants more harshly than white defendants, Spohn suggested that black and white judges might perceive black offenders as more threatening and more dangerous than white offenders. Alternatively, she speculated that at least some of the discriminatory treatment of black offenders might be due to concern for the welfare of black victims. In other words,

> [Black judges] might see themselves not as representatives of black defendants but as advocates for black victims. This, coupled with the fact that black judges might see themselves as potential victims of black-on-black crime, could help explain the harsher sentences imposed on black offenders by black judges.[118]

Spohn acknowledged that because we do not know with any degree of certainty what goes through a judge's mind during the sentence process, these explanations were highly speculative. As she put it,

> We cannot know precisely how the race of the offender is factored into the sentencing equation. Although the data reveal that both black and white judges sentence black offenders more harshly than white offenders, the data do not tell us *why* this occurs.[119]

All of the studies discussed thus far focus on potential differences in sentencing behavior between black and white judges. One study compares sentences imposed by Anglo and Hispanic judges in El Paso County, Texas.[120] This study found that Hispanic judges imposed similar sentences on Hispanic and Anglo offenders and Anglo judges gave more lenient sentences to Anglo offenders than to Hispanic offenders. Moreover, the sentences given to Hispanic offenders by Anglo and Hispanic judges were similar. As the authors noted, "What is different is that Anglo judges sentence Anglo defendants much less severely, perhaps suggesting that Anglo judges are not so much discriminating against Hispanic defendants as they are favoring members of their ethnic group."[121]

Women on the Bench. As we explained above, those who argue that gender matters in judicial decision making suggest that (a) female judges might be more lenient than male judges (particularly in sentencing nonviolent offenders), (b) female judges might be harsher than male judges (particularly in sentencing offenders convicted of sex offenses and other violent crimes), or (c) female judges might impose more equitable sentences than male

Exhibit 3.4 Adjusted Incarceration Rates: Black and White Offenders Sentenced to Prison by Black and White Judges, Detroit Recorder's Court

	Percentage Sentenced to Prison		
Sentencing Judges	All Judges	Black Judges	White Judges
Race of offender			
Black	73.7	72.9	74.2
White	66.0	65.3	66.5
Race of offender/victim pair			
Black offender/black victim	75.1	75.0	75.2
Black offender/white victim	76.8	75.0	79.2
White offender/black victim	65.8	62.1	67.1
White offender/white victim	68.5	69.3	67.8

SOURCE: From "Sentencing Decisions of Black and White Judges: Expected and Unexpected Similarities" (Table 4), by C. Spohn, 1990.

judges. Others suggest that the differences women bring to the bench will diminish as women are socialized to the judicial role and the expectations of the courtroom workgroup (See Box 3.4 for a discussion of women on the bench in Australia.)

The relatively few studies that address the issue of women on the bench have yielded mixed results. Two early studies, for example, produced evidence in support of the argument that male and female public officials behave differently where issues closely related to sex roles are concerned. Cook[122] found that male and female trial judges "decided" simulated court cases dealing with issues related to women's roles somewhat differently. And Moulds[123] showed that the "gentler" treatment accorded women by the criminal justice system might be due in part to the chivalrous or paternalistic attitudes of men judges toward female defendants.

This was confirmed by two later studies: an analysis of sentencing decisions in "Metro City"[124] and an examination of sentencing patterns in Chicago.[125] Both studies found that female judges were more likely than male judges to sentence offenders to prison but the mean sentences given by female and male judges were nearly identical. Moreover, both studies also found that male judges were reluctant to sentence female offenders to prison but that female judges did not take gender into account in deciding whether to incarcerate or not. In "Metro City," 12 percent of the female offenders sentenced by male judges received prison sentences, compared with 20 percent of those sentenced by female judges. In Chicago, there was a 24-percentage-point difference in the probability of incarceration for male and female offenders sentenced by male judges. These results led the authors of the "Metro City" study to conclude that the presence of women judges has a "twofold impact on women's equality—the obvious one of including women in the politically powerful roles of judges and the less obvious one of reducing the favored treatment which women defendants received in the past."[126]

A more recent and statistically sophisticated study yielded somewhat different results. Steffensmeier and Hebert[127] used data on sentences imposed

---

BOX 3.4

"FEMINIZED JUSTICE" AND
MAGISTRATES' COURTS IN AUSTRALIA

Prior to 1984, there were no female judges on the Magistrates' Courts in Victoria, Australia. A series of controversial decisions in rape cases, however, led to public protests and calls for the appointment of women to the bench. From 1984 to 1992, 30 percent of the new appointees were women. By the mid-1990s, women comprised 15 percent of all judges on the Victoria Magistrates' Court. The Chief Magistrate was also a woman.

A recent study examined the impact of this "sudden and dramatic change" in the gender composition of the Victoria Magistrates' Court, which handles about 90 percent of all criminal cases. Laster and Douglas interviewed 6 female judges and 24 male judges regarding their perceptions of the changes that had taken place on the court.

Laster and Douglas state that the "most striking" finding of their study "is the ready acceptance of women as appropriate appointees to the bench." A number of the male judges reported that "there had been some initial shock when the first women were appointed to the bench." Generally, however, the men believed that the women had made positive contributions to the work environment and had proven themselves to be competent, professional, and hardworking. The male judges, for example, reported that the female judges were "good fun," that they had "livened things up," and that female judges were a "boon" to the working environment. Some of them indicated that the women were more sensitive, more understanding, and more empathic in their decision making.

The male judges also believed that their female colleagues had been accepted and integrated into the organizational culture. According to Laster and Douglas, "Within a relatively short period, the female members of the bench had managed to impress their male colleagues. They seem to have proved to them that if there is any 'difference' between male and female magistrates, the qualities that women bring to the job make them eminently suitable for the career."

The women magistrates maintained that "gender in the courtroom was irrelevant." Although some noted that witnesses seemed uncomfortable when they had to repeat indecent language and that their gender might be commented on by those who were unhappy with the outcome, most of the women magistrates believed that "no one seems to be conscious that you're a man or a woman." Moreover, the attitudes of the men and women toward standards of proof, sentencing standards, and other aspects of the magistrate's job "were marked more by congruence than by divergence." The women magistrates also stated that the overall style of the court reflected feminine values and that both the men and the women on the bench "have female ways of doing things."

Laster and Douglas conclude that the "feminization of the bench" was part of a more general change in perceptions about the administration of justice. "Women did not change practice; rather, politicians allowed women into the all-male preserve because the political imagination suddenly could conceive of them as exercising power under a new ideological regime."

SOURCE: Adapted from "Feminized Justice: The Impact of Women Decision Makers in the Lower Courts in Australia," by K. Laster and R. Douglas, 1995, *Justice Quarterly, 12,* pp. 177-205.

in Pennsylvania from 1991 to 1993. They compared the sentencing decisions of 39 white female judges with those of 231 white male judges. The authors argued that there are "solid reasons for expecting that pre-officeholding attitudinal differences between men and women might carry over and result in some gender-of-judge differences in sentencing practices" and that "fear of crime . . . and sensitivity to risk of recidivism appear to be greater among females than among males." They tested the following hypotheses:[128]

1. Female judges will be more severe in their sentencing decisions than male judges.

2. Prior record, an indicator of dangerousness and recidivism risk, will affect the sentencing decisions of female judges more than it will affect the decisions of male judges.

3. Relative to male judges, female judges will be harsher in their sentencing of defendants who are male, black, and young.

The first hypothesis was confirmed. After controlling for the seriousness of the offense, the offender's prior record, the type of disposition in the case, and other predictors of sentence severity, the authors found that the difference in the probabilities of incarceration between female and male judges was 11 percent. Stated another way, the likelihood of incarceration for offenders sentenced by female judges was 11 percent greater than the likelihood of incarceration for offenders sentenced by male judges. Female judges also gave sentences that averaged 5 months longer than those imposed by males.

The authors' test of the other two hypotheses yielded mixed results. They compared the effects of case and offender characteristics on the sentences imposed by female and male judges on all offenders and found that the offender's prior criminal history score played a very similar role in the sentencing decisions of female and male judges.[129] Each one-unit increase in the criminal history score (which, under the Pennsylvania sentencing guidelines varies from 0 to 6) produced a 12-percentage-point increase in the probability of incarceration for offenders sentenced by female judges and a 10-percentage-point increase for offenders sentenced by male judges. Similarly, both male and female judges added about 7 months to the offender's sentence for each increase in the criminal history score. The authors did find, on the other hand, that *offender characteristics* had a more pronounced effect on the sentencing decisions of female judges. Although both men and women imposed harsher sentences on black offenders than on white offenders, the "race effect" was larger among women. And both men and women sentenced female defendants to prison at a lower rate than male defendants, but the gender effect was larger among women.

Further analysis of the effects of prior record, offender race, offender gender, and offender age revealed a more complex pattern of results. The authors found that the sentences imposed on white female offenders did not vary but that women sentenced black male offenders, black female offenders, and white male offenders more harshly than men did. Women also imposed harsher sentences than men on young adults, but there were no differences in the sentences that men and women imposed on older offenders. Finally, and more important, the authors found that "prior record disproportionately increases the sentence severity of female judges toward both white and black defendants, but the increase is even greater when they sentence black defendants."[130] Stated differently, the authors found that "women judges are particularly harsh toward repeat black offenders."[131]

Although these findings indicate that there are important differences between male and female judges in Pennsylvania, Steffensmeier and

Hebert emphasize that the sentencing patterns of the judges they examined were similar in a number of respects. The incarceration rates and mean sentences of male and female judges were roughly similar, and the factors that influenced their sentencing patterns were, with few exceptions, the same. As they noted, "a coherent picture of 'gendered' reality must recognize both gender differences and gender similarities."[132]

The Interaction of Race and Gender. The findings discussed thus far focus either on differences between black and white judges or differences between female and male judges. Two studies examine the interaction between the race of the judge and the gender of the judge. That is, these studies attempt to determine whether there are significant differences in the sentences imposed by black male judges, black female judges, white male judges, and white female judges. One study examined sentences imposed on offenders convicted of sexual assault in Detroit Recorder's Court.[133] The author of this study found that black judges did not sentence differently than white judges and that there were no differences in the likelihood of incarceration for sexual assault offenders sentenced by female and male judges. Female judges did, on the other hand, impose substantially longer prison sentences than male judges did. Further analysis revealed that this "gender effect" was confined to black judges. Black female judges handed down longer sentences than black male judges, but there were no differences in the sentences imposed by white female and white male judges. According to Spohn, the fact that there were so few differences between female and male judges on an issue, sexual assault, of great concern to women "is indicative of the powerful influence of socialization on the legal profession and the judicial role."[134]

Spears, who examined the sentences imposed on offenders convicted of felonies in Cook County Circuit Court, found a different pattern of results.[135] There were no differences in either the likelihood of incarceration or sentence length for three of the four race-of-judge/gender-of-judge pairs. Comparable offenders sentenced by white female judges, white male judges, and black female judges received similar sentences. There were, on the other hand, significant differences between black male judges and each of the other three categories of judges for both measures of sentence severity. Black male judges were significantly less likely than all other judges to sentence offenders to prison. The differences in the probabilities of incarceration were -12 percent (black males versus white males), -14 percent (black males versus black females), and -18 percent (black males versus white females). Paradoxically, black male judges imposed significantly *lon-*

ger prison sentences than white male judges (+12.96 months), black female judges (+15.53 months), and white female judges (+12.53). As Spears noted, these results suggest that "black male judges are reserving prison sentences for more serious offenders, and, as a result, they hand down longer prison sentences."[136]

Do Members of Racial Minorities or Women Dispense a Different Kind of Justice?

On the basis of the studies that have been conducted to date, what can we conclude about the role played by black and Hispanic judges? By female judges? Most researchers find few overall differences in the sentences imposed by black and white judges. Engle concluded that there were only minor differences in the sentences imposed by black and white judges,[137] Uhlman found that although the sentencing patterns of individual black judges varied considerably, their overall sentencing patterns didn't differ from those of white judges,[138] and Spohn concluded that there were "remarkable similarities" in the sentencing decisions of black and white judges.[139] One study[140] found that black female judges imposed longer sentences on offenders convicted of sexual assault, and another[141] found that black male judges sentenced offenders to prison at a lower rate but imposed longer sentences on those who were incarcerated. Depending on the time period, the jurisdiction, and the types of offenses included in the analysis, black judges sentenced either no differently, more harshly, or more leniently than white judges.

The evidence regarding the degree to which black and Hispanic judges impose more racially equitable sentences is also mixed. Two studies[142] found that black judges imposed similar sentences on black and white offenders, whereas white judges gave more lenient sentences to white offenders than to black offenders. Another[143] found a similar pattern of results for Hispanic judges and Anglo judges. Both studies concluded that white judges discriminate in favor of white offenders. A third study,[144] on the other hand, found no race-of-judge differences in the sentences imposed on black and white offenders convicted of violent felonies.

These inconsistencies suggest that we do not know, on the basis of the limited amount of research that has been conducted to date, whether black judges dispense a different kind of justice than white judges. We do not know the extent to which black judges believe that their role is, to use Judge Crockett's words, "to shake it up."[145]

The degree to which female judges sentence differently than male judges is somewhat more conclusive. There is no evidence that women dispense a "gentler" form of justice; that is, there is no evidence that women, in contrast to men, are "soft on crime." In fact, the differences that do appear suggest just the opposite. Three studies[146] found that offenders sentenced by female judges were significantly more likely to be sent to prison than comparable offenders sentenced by male judges. Female judges in Pennsylvania also imposed longer sentences than their male colleagues,[147] and black female judges in Detroit imposed substantially longer sentences on offenders convicted of sexual assault than black male judges did.[148]

The evidence regarding the treatment of female and male offenders by female and male judges is less consistent. Two studies[149] found that female judges imposed similar sentences on male and female defendants, whereas male judges sentenced female defendants more leniently than male defendants. Although these results suggest that female judges are less likely than male judges to see female defendants through a paternalistic or chivalrous lens, Steffensmeier and Hebert's [150] analysis of sentencing decisions in Pennsylvania found a different pattern of results, which complicates the issue. They found that both women and men sentenced blacks more harshly than whites and sentenced females more leniently than males. Moreover, the race and gender of the offender had a more pronounced effect on the sentencing decisions of females judges, who were particularly harsh toward repeat black offenders.

There is some evidence, then, that female judges speak in a different voice from the bench. Perhaps because of their greater fear of crime, they tend to impose somewhat harsher sentences than their male colleagues. There is also some evidence that female judges, like black and Hispanic judges, are more evenhanded in their sentencing decisions and that the recruitment of increasing numbers of women and members of racial minorities will promote more equitable sentencing decisions.

Overall, however, the differences between male and female judges and between black or Hispanic judges and white judges are not large. All judges, regardless of their race or gender or the race or gender of the person being sentenced, base their sentencing decisions primarily on the seriousness of the crime and the offender's prior criminal record. The similarities in the sentencing practices of judges suggest that "they are governed more by their legal training and legal socialization than by their socially structured personal experiences."[151]

How Do Judges Decide?

The sentencing decision results from a process of gathering and interpreting information about the offense and the offender. Judges use this information to evaluate the harm done by the crime and to paint a portrait of the offender. As John Hogarth wrote, more than 30 years ago, sentencing "is a cognitive process in which information concerning the offender, the offense, and the surrounding circumstances is read, organized in relation to other information and integrated into an overall assessment of the case."[152]

As they attempt to fashion sentences that fit individual offenders and struggle to impose just punishments, judges consider the harm done by the crime, the blameworthiness and culpability of the offender, and the offender's potential for reform and rehabilitation. Their assessment of harm rests squarely on the nature and seriousness of the crime. It rests on both the statutory seriousness of the offense and the gravity and consequences of the crime. Thus, armed robbers will be sentenced more harshly than those who steal cars or write bad checks, and offenders who use deadly weapons or inflict serious injuries on their victims will receive more severe punishment than those who do not. Similarly, offenders who play a primary role in the crime will be punished more harshly than accomplices or those who play secondary roles. The punishment imposed by the judge, in other words, will be proportionate to the harm done by the crime: The punishment will "fit the crime."

Judges also attempt to fashion sentences that "fit the offender." Their evaluation of offenders rests primarily, but not exclusively, on offenders' prior criminal records. In attempting to understand offenders, assess their blameworthiness, and predict their future dangerousness, judges examine the past criminal behavior of offenders, as well as their life histories and current circumstances. They consider the offenders' educational histories, family and work situations, community ties, and conduct since the arrest. Judges also attempt to determine offenders' motivation for crimes, the extent to which they feel remorse for their behavior, and the degree to which they cooperated in the prosecution of their (or another) case. Assessing offenders in this way "allows judges to make substantial and refined distinctions between offenders who might appear quite similar if one looked only at the legal wrong committed and the harm it caused."[153]

To tailor sentences to the facts and circumstances of each case, the judge needs detailed information about the crime and the offender. Although cases tried before a jury may provide the judge with the necessary information, most convictions result from guilty pleas, not trials. Thus, the judge may know little more about the case than the facts necessary to support a guilty plea. A presentence investigation might fill in some of the details about the crime and offender, but the offender might waive the investigation or the probation department might conduct a cursory review. And if the prosecutor and the defense attorney have negotiated a deal that affects the sentence, the judge may believe that gathering additional information about the case would be a waste of the court's resources. Consequently, the judge may have incomplete information about the crime and the offender.

The fact that the information judges have is typically incomplete and the predictions they are required to make are uncertain helps explain why offender characteristics, including the legally irrelevant characteristics of race, gender, and social class, influence sentencing decisions. Because they don't have all the information they need to fashion sentences to fit crimes *and* offenders, judges may resort to stereotypes of dangerousness and threat that are linked to offender characteristics.[154] Thus, men may be perceived as more dangerous than women, younger offenders may be regarded as more crime prone than older offenders, gang members may be viewed as more threatening than non-gang members, the unemployed may be seen as more likely to recidivate than the employed, and those who abuse drugs or alcohol may be viewed as less amenable to rehabilitation than those who abstain from using drugs or alcohol. Similarly, members of racial minorities, particularly those who are also male, young, members of gangs, and unemployed, may be seen as more dangerous and threatening than whites. Judges use these perceptions to simplify and routinize the decision-making process and to reduce the uncertainty inherent in sentencing. As a result, men may be sentenced more harshly than women, blacks and Hispanics may be sentenced more harshly than whites, the unemployed may be sentenced more harshly than the employed, and so on.

The sentences judges impose also may reflect the fact that they are part of a courtroom workgroup[155] or courthouse community[156] with common goals and shared expectations about how cases should be handled and the types of sentences that should be imposed. The members of the courtroom workgroup, for example, may believe that efficiency demands a high rate of guilty pleas; consequently, plea bargaining will be encouraged and defendants who cooperate by pleading guilty will be rewarded. The members of the courthouse community may also believe that there are "normal penalties"[157] or "going rates"[158] for particular types of crimes or particular types of offenders. They may agree on the appropriate penalty for the run-of-the-mill burglary or for the offender who repeatedly appears in court on drug charges. Because judges are concerned about maintaining relationships with other members of the courtroom workgroup and ensuring the smooth flow of cases through the criminal justice system, these expectations will constrain their discretion and affect the sentences they impose.

The ambiguity and uncertainty inherent in the sentencing process —coupled with the fact that judges exercise considerable discretion in deciding what the sentence will be—means that we cannot conclusively determine how a judge arrived at a particular sentence in a particular case. We know that judges' sentencing decisions rest to a considerable degree on their assessments of harm and blameworthiness and their predictions of dangerousness, but we don't know with certainty how these assessments and predictions are made. Moreover, as we explain in the next two chapters, substantial sentencing disparities remain even after the harm caused by the crime and the culpability of the offender are taken into consideration.

Discussion Questions: Chapter 3

1. The federal sentencing guidelines state that the offender's race, gender, age, education, mental and emotional conditions, history of alcohol or drug abuse, employment history, family ties and responsibilities, and community ties are "not ordinarily relevant" in determining the appropriate sentence. Do you agree or disagree with this policy? Why?

2. What are the two "key determinants" of sentences?

3. Explain how victim characteristics affect the sentences that judges impose. Are these legitimate considerations?

4. What is the "trial penalty" or "jury tax"? How do judges justify it? Is their explanation convincing?

5. What explains the fact that defendants who are free pending trial are sentenced more leniently than those who are detained in jail prior to trial?

6. Consider the variables used to explain sentencing decisions in Cook County, Illinois (see Exhibit 3.4). Are there any important variables that are not included in the analysis?

7. Why would we expect women judges and black and Hispanic judges to dispense "a different kind of justice"? Do the results of empirical research confirm or refute these expectations?

Notes

1. Uviller, *Virtual Justice: The Flawed Prosecution of Crime in America*, p. 279.
2. William Spence, Bill Smith, and Ann Harding are pseudonyms; the case is an actual case.
3. See, for example, Cook, Beverly, "Sentencing Behavior of Federal Judges: Draft Cases—1972"; Clancy, Bartolomeo, Richardson, and Wellford, "Sentence Decisionmaking: The Logic of Sentence Decisions and the Extent and Sources of Sentence Disparity"; Ewart and Pennington, "Reasons for Sentence: An Empirical Investigation"; Forst and Wellford, "Punishment and Sentencing: Developing Sentencing Guidelines Empirically from Principles of Punishment"; Kapardis and Farrington, "An Experimental Study of Sentencing by Magistrates"; Spohn and Horney, "'The Law's the Law, But Fair Is Fair': Rape Shield Laws and Officials' Assessment of Sexual History Evidence."
4. Recent examples include Albonetti, "Sentencing Under the Federal Sentencing Guidelines: Effects of Defendant Characteristics, Guilty Pleas, and Departures on Sentence Outcomes for Drug Offenses, 1991-1992"; Britt, "Social Context and Racial Disparities in Punishment Decisions"; Spohn, Gruhl, and Welch, "The Effect of Race on Sentencing: A Re-Examination of an Unsettled Question"; Steffensmeier, Kramer, and Ulmer, "Age Differences in Sentencing"; Steffensmeier, Ulmer, and Kramer, "The Interaction of Race, Gender and Age in Sentencing: The Punishment Cost of Being Young, Black, and Male"; Ulmer, *Social Worlds of Sentencing: Court Communities Under Sentencing Guidelines.*
5. Research has shown, for example, that prior criminal record is a better predictor of the decision to incarcerate or not than of sentence length (Spohn, Gruhl, and, Welch 1981-1982) and that offender characteristics have a stronger effect on the decision to incarcerate than on length of sentence (Chiricos and Crawford 1995; Spohn 2000).
6. For published results of this study, which also included Dade County (Miami), Florida and Jackson County (Kansas City), Missouri, see: Nobiling, Spohn, and DeLone, "A Tale of Two

Counties: Unemployment and Sentencing Severity"; Spohn, "Gender and Sentencing of Drug Offenders: Is Chivalry Dead?" Spohn and Beichner, "Is Preferential Treatment of Female Offenders a Thing of the Past? A Multi-Site Study of Gender, Race, and Imprisonment"; Spohn and DeLone, "When Does Race Matter? An Analysis of the Conditions Under Which Race Affects Sentence Severity"; Spohn, DeLone, and Spears, "Race/Ethnicity, Gender and Sentence Severity in Dade County, Florida: An Examination of the Decision To Withhold Adjudication"; Spohn and Holleran, "The Imprisonment Penalty Paid by Young, Employed Black and Hispanic Male Offenders."

7. Illinois Compiled Statutes Annotated, 730 ILSC 5/5-5-3.1.

8. U. S. Sentencing Commission, *Sentencing Commission Guidelines Manual*, 1997, pt. H, §§5H1.1-5H1.6.

9. Albonetti, "Sentencing Under the Federal Sentencing Guidelines"; Spohn and DeLone, "When Does Race Matter?"; Steffensmeier, Ulmer, and Kramer, "The Interaction of Race, Gender and Age in Criminal Sentencing"; Ulmer, *Social Worlds of Sentencing*.

10. Blumstein, Cohen, Martin and Tonry, *Research on Sentencing: The Search for Reform*, Vol. I, p. 83.

11. For reviews of this research, see Daly and Bordt, "Sex Effects and Sentencing: A Review of the Statistical Literature"; Daly and Tonry, "Gender, Race and Sentencing"; and Steffensmeier, Kramer and Streifel, "Gender and Imprisonment Decisions."

12. Spohn and Holleran, "The Imprisonment Penalty Paid by Young, Unemployed Black and Hispanic Males"; Steffensmeier, Kramer, and Ulmer, "Age Differences in Sentencing"; Steffensmeier, Ulmer and Kramer, "The Interaction of Race, Gender, and Age in Sentencing."

13. For reviews of this research, see Chiricos and Crawford, "Race and Imprisonment: A Contextual Assessment of the Evidence," and Spohn, *Thirty Years of Sentencing Reform: The Quest for a Racially Neutral Sentencing Process*.

14. Spohn and Holleran, "The Imprisonment Penalty Paid by Young, Unemployed, Black and Hispanic Males"; Steffensmeier, Ulmer and Kramer, "The Interaction of Race, Gender, and Age in Sentencing."

15. Smith, *Courts and the Poor*, chap. 2.

16. Albonetti, "Sentencing Under the Federal Sentencing Guidelines."

17. Nobiling, Spohn, and DeLone, "A Tale of Two Counties."

18. Chircos and Bales, "Unemployment and Punishment: An Empirical Assessment." A similar conclusion regarding the effect of unemployment on the likelihood of pretrial detention was reached by Holmes, Hosch, Daudistel, Perez, and Graves (1996).

19. Box, *Recession, Crime and Punishment*; Box and Hale, "Unemployment, Imprisonment, and Prison Overcrowding"; Quinney, *Class, State and Crime*; Spitzer, "Toward a Marxian Theory of Deviance."

20. Box and Hale, "Unemployment, Imprisonment, and Prison Overcrowding," pp. 209-210.

21. Daly, "Neither Conflict nor Labeling nor Paternalism Will Suffice: Intersections of Race, Ethnicity, Gender, and Family in Criminal Court Decisions"; Daly, "Structure and Practice of Familial-Based Justice in a Criminal Court."

22. Daly, "Neither Conflict nor Labeling nor Paternalism Will Suffice," p. 138.

23. From personal interviews with the author during 1995.

24. Ibid.

25. Tonry, *Malign Neglect: Race, Crime, and Punishment in America*, p. 154.

26. Ibid., p. 195.

27. Ibid.

28. Wice, *Judges & Lawyers: The Human Side of Justice*, p. 275.

29. See, for example, Baldus, Woodworth, and Pulaski. *Equal Justice and the Death Penalty: A Legal and Empirical Analysis*; Gross and Mauro, *Death & Discrimination: Racial Disparities in Capital Sentencing*; Paternoster, "Prosecutorial Discretion in Requesting the Death Penalty: A Case of Victim-Based Discrimination."

30. Baldus, Woodworth, and Pulaski, *Equal Justice and the Death Penalty*.

31. LaFree, *Rape and Criminal Justice: The Social Construction of Sexual Assault*; Spohn, "Crime and the Social Control of Blacks"; Walsh, "The Sexual Stratification Hypothesis and Sexual Assault in Light of the Changing Conceptions of Race."

32. Spohn, "Crime and the Social Control of Blacks," p. 260.

33. Quinney, *The Social Reality of Crime.*
34. Hawkins, "Beyond Anomalies: Rethinking the Conflict Perspective on Race and Criminal Punishment," p. 726.
35. LaFree, *Rape and Criminal Justice.*
36. Kingsnorth, MacIntosh, and Wentworth, "Sexual Assault: The Role of Prior Relationship and Victim Characteristics in Case Processing"; McCahill, Meyer and Fischman, *The Aftermath of Rape.*
37. Kingsnorth, MacIntosh, and Wentworth, "Sexual Assault"; Spohn and Spears, "The Effect of Offender and Victim Characteristics on Sexual Assault Case Processing Decisions."
38. McCahill, Meyer, and Fischman, *The Aftermath of Rape.*
39. Kingsnorth, MacIntosh, and Wentworth, "Sexual Assault"; Spohn and Spears, "The Effect of Offender and Victim Characteristics on Sexual Assault Case Processing Decisions."
40. Holmes, Hosch, Daudistel, Perez, and Graves, "Ethnicity, Legal Resources, and Felony Dispositions in Two Southwestern Jurisdictions," p. 12.
41. Alschuler, "The Prosecutor's Role in Plea Bargaining"; Alschuler, "The Defense Attorney's Role in Plea Bargaining"; Alschuler, "The Trial Judge's Role in Plea Bargaining"; Mather, *Plea Bargaining or Trial? The Process of Criminal Case Disposition.*
42. Casper, *American Criminal Justice: The Defendant's Perspective*; Newman, *Conviction: The Determination of Guilt or Innocence Without Trial.*
43. Downie, Justice Denied, p. 24.
44. Albonetti, "Sentencing Under the Federal Sentencing Guidelines"; Kautt and Spohn, "Crack-ing Down on Black Drug Offenders? Testing for Interactions Between Offender Race, Drug Type, and Sentencing Strategy in Federal Drug Sentences."
45. Spohn and DeLone, "When Does Race Matter?"
46. Ibid., Table 2 and Table 4. See also Britt, "Social Context and Racial Disparities in Punishment Decisions"; Holmes, Hosch, Daudistel, Perez, and Graves, "Ethnicity, Legal Resources, and Felony Dispositions in Two Southwestern Jurisdictions"; LaFree, "Adversarial and Nonadversarial Justice: A Comparison of Guilty Pleas and Trials"; and Spohn, "An Analysis of the

'Jury Trial Penalty' and Its Effect on Black and White Offenders."

47. Steffensmeier and Hebert, "Women and Men Policymakers: Does the Judge's Gender Affect the Sentencing of Criminal Defendants?"

48. Personal interview with the author in 1995. I interviewed judges and other criminal justice officials about their sentencing policies and practices for a study of sentencing decisions in Chicago, Miami, and Kansas City.

49. Ibid.

50. U.S. Department of Justice, Bureau of Justice Statistics (BJS), *Felony Defendants in Large Urban Counties, 1996,* Tables 13 and 14.

51. U.S. Department of Justice, BJS, *Federal Pretrial Release and Detention, 1996,* Table 3 and Table A1.

52. The Bail Reform Act of 1984 [18 U.S.C. § 3142] requires the pretrial release of defendants who do not pose a risk of flight or a danger to the community. The defendant can be detained if the court determines (a) that he or she poses a risk of flight or is a danger to the community and (b) that no condition or combination of conditions would reduce this risk. A detention hearing is required. The government must prove by clear and convincing evidence that no condition(s) of release would ensure that the defendant would appear for trial and not pose a risk to anyone in the community.

53. U.S. Department of Justice, BJS, *Pretrial Release of Felony Defendants, 1992,* pp. 13-14.

54. Ibid., pp. 5-6.

55. Chiricos and Bales, "Unemployment and Punishment."

56. Spohn and DeLone, "When Does Race Matter?"

57. Spohn, Gruhl, and Welch, "The Effect of Race on Sentencing."

58. *Powell v. Alabama,* 287 U.S. 45 (1932).

59. *Johnson v. Zerbst,* 304 U.S. 458 (1938).

60. *Gideon v. Wainwright,* 372 U.S. 335 (1963).

61. *Argersinger v. Hamlin,* 407 U.S. 25 (1972).

62. A defendant is entitled to counsel at every stage "where substantial rights of the accused may be affected" that require the "guiding hand of counsel" (*Mempa v. Rhay,* 389 U.S. 128,

[1967]). These critical stages include arraignment, preliminary hearing, entry of a plea, trial, sentencing, and the first appeal.
63. Sterling, "Retained Counsel Versus The Public Defender: The Impact of Type of Counsel on Charge Bargaining," p. 166.
64. Casper, "Did You Have a Lawyer When You Went to Court? No, I Had a Public Defender," p. 4.
65. See, for example, Blumberg, "The Practice of Law as a Confidence Game: Organizational Cooptation of a Profession," and Sudnow, "Normal Crimes: Sociological Features of the Penal Code in the Public Defender's Office."
66. Weitzer, "Racial Discrimination in the Criminal Justice System: Findings and Problems in the Literature," p. 313.
67. Casper, *Criminal Courts*; Levin, *Urban Politics and the Criminal Courts*; McIntyre, *The Public Defender: The Practice of Law in the Shadow of Repute*; Oaks and Lehman, "Lawyers for the Poor"; Silverstein, *Defense of the Poor*; and Wheeler and Wheeler, "Reflections on Legal Representation of the Economically Disadvantaged: Beyond Assembly Line Justice."
68. Skolnick, "Social Control in the Adversary System," p. 67.
69. Wice, *Chaos in the Courthouse: The Inner Workings of the Urban Municipal Courts*, p. 65.
70. U.S. Department of Justice, BJS, *Defense Counsel in Criminal Cases*.
71. Spohn and DeLone, "When Does Race Matter?"
72. Hanson and Ostrom, "Indigent Defenders Get the Job Done and Done Well."
73. Washington, *Black Judges on Justice: Perspectives from the Bench*, p. 248.
74. Carp and Stidham, *Judical Process in America*, p. 261.
75. Ibid.
76. Stumpf, *American Judicial Politics*, p. 184.
77. Carp and Stidham, *Judical Process in America*, p. 210.
78. A similar pattern is found for appointments to the U.S. Court of Appeals. The percentage of appointees who were white males was 60.7 percent (Carter), 92.3 percent (Reagan), 70.3 percent (Bush), and 44.8 percent (Clinton). See Carp and Stidham (1998 Table 8.2).
79. Carp and Stidham, *Judical Process in America*, p. 218.
80. Ibid.

81. Walker and Barrow, "The Diversification of the Federal Bench: Policy and Process Ramifications," p. 615.
82. Frazier and Bock, "Effects of Court Officials on Sentence Severity: Do Judges Make a Difference?"
83. Laster and Douglas, "Feminized Justice: The Impact of Women Decision Makers in the Lower Courts in Australia," p. 182.
84. Wright, "A Black Broods on Black Judges," pp. 22-23.
85. Washington, *Black Judges on Justice*, p. 251.
86. Goldman, "Should There Be Affirmative Action for the Judiciary?" p. 494.
87. Justice Ruth Bader Ginsberg, as cited in Martin, "Women on the Bench: A Different Voice?" p. 126.
88. Gilligan, *In a Different Voice: Psychological Theory and Women's Development*.
89. Berns, *To Speak as a Judge: Difference, Voice, and Power*, p. 197.
90. Fineman, "Feminist Legal Scholarship and Women's Gendered Lives," pp. 239-240.
91. Washington, *Black Judges on Justice*, p. 11.
92. Ibid., pp. 11-12.
93. Crockett, "The Role of the Black Judge," p. 393.
94. Welch, Combs, and Gruhl, "Do Black Judges Make a Difference?" p. 127.
95. Crockett, "The Role of the Black Judge"; and Welch, Combs, and Gruhl, "Do Black Judges Make a Difference?"
96. Spohn, "Decision Making in Sexual Assault Cases: Do Black and Female Judges Make a Difference?"
97. Steffensmeier and Hebert, "Women and Men Policymakers."
98. Gibson, "Race as a Determinant of Criminal Sentences: A Methodological Critique and a Case Study"; Myers, "Social Background and the Sentencing Behavior of Judges"; Steffensmeier and Hebert, "Women and Men Policymakers."
99. Welch, Combs, and Gruhl, "Do Black Judges Make a Difference?"
100. Gibson, "Race as a Determinant of Criminal Sentences"; Welch, Combs, and Gruhl, "Do Black Judges Make a Difference?"
101. Spohn, "Decision Making in Sexual Assault Cases"; Steffensmeier and Hebert, "Women and Men Policymakers."

102. Cook, "Sentencing Behavior of Federal Judges"; Kritzer, "Political Correlates of the Behavior of Federal District Judges: A 'Best Case' Analysis"; Myers, "Social Background and the Sentencing Behavior of Judges"; and Steffensmeier and Hebert, "Women and Men Policymakers."

103. Gibson, "Race as a Determinant of Criminal Sentences"; Myers, "Social Background and the Sentencing Behavior of Judges."

104. Engle, *Criminal Justice in the City: A Study of Sentence Severity and Variation in the Philadelphia Court System.*

105. Ibid., p. 226-227.

106. Uhlman, *Racial Justice: Black Judges and Defendants in an Urban Trial Court.*

107. Ibid., p. 71.

108. Welch, Combs, and Gruhl, "Do Black Judges Make a Difference?"

109. Ibid., p. 134.

110. Ibid.

111. Spears, *Diversity in the Courtroom: A Comparison of the Sentencing Decisions of Black and White Judges and Male and Female Judges in Cook County Circuit Court.*

112. Ibid., p. 135.

113. Spohn, "The Sentencing Decisions of Black and White Judges: Expected and Unexpected Similarities."

114. Ibid., p. 1206.

115. Ibid., p. 1211.

116. Ibid., pp. 1212-1213.

117. Ibid., p. 1213.

118. Ibid., p. 1214.

119. Ibid.

120. Holmes, Hosch, Daudistel, Perez, and Graves, "Judges' Ethnicity and Minority Sentencing: Evidence Concerning Hispanics."

121. Ibid., p. 502

122. Cook, "Judicial Attitudes on Women's Rights: Do Women Judges Make a Difference?"

123. Moulds, "Chivalry and Paternalism: Disparities of Treatment in the Criminal Justice System."

124. Gruhl, Spohn, and Welch, "Women as Policymakers: The Case of Trial Judges."

125. Spears, *Diversity in the Courtroom.*

126. Gruhl, Spohn, and Welch, "Women as Policymakers," p. 320.
127. Steffensmeier and Hebert, "Women and Men Policymakers."
128. Ibid., pp. 1169-1170. The authors tested a number of hypotheses in addition to these; we limit our discussion to the findings concerning these three.
129. Ibid., Table 4.
130. Ibid., p. 1184.
131. Ibid., p. 1186.
132. Ibid., p. 1187.
133. Spohn, "Decision Making in Sexual Assault Cases."
134. Ibid., p. 98.
135. Spears, *Diversity in the Courtroom*.
136. Ibid., p. 135.
137. Engle, *Criminal Justice in the City*.
138. Uhlman, *Racial Justice*.
139. Spohn, "The Sentencing Decisions of Black and White Judges."
140. Spohn, "Decision Making in Sexual Assault Cases."
141. Spears, *Diversity in the Courtroom*.
142. Spears, *Diversity in the Courtroom*; Welch, Combs, and Gruhl,"Do Black Judges Make a Difference?"
143. Holmes et al. ,"Judges' Ethnicity and Minority Sentencing."
144. Spohn, "The Sentencing Decisions of Black and White Judges."
145. Crockett, "The Role of the Black Judge."
146. Gruhl, Spohn, and Welch, "Women as Policymakers: The Case of Trial Judges"; Spears, *Diversity in the Courtroom*; Steffensmier and Hebert, "Women and Men Policymakers."
147. Steffensmier and Hebert, "Women and Men Policymakers."
148. Spohn, "Decision Making in Sexual Assault Cases."
149. Gruhl , Spohn, and Welch, "Women as Policymakers"; Spears, *Diversity in the Courtroom*.
150. Steffensmier and Hebert, "Women and Men Policymakers."
151. Ibid., p. 1187.
152. Hogarth, *Sentencing as a Human Process*, p. 279.
153. Wheeler, Mann, and Sarat, *Sitting in Judgment: The Sentencing of White-Collar Criminals*, p. 120.
154. For a more detailed discussion of this see Hawkins, "Causal Attribution and Punishment for Crime," and Steffensmeier, Ulmer, and Kramer, "The Interaction of Race, Gender, and Age in Sentencing."

155. Eisenstein and Jacob, *Felony Justice: An Organizational Analysis of Communities and Their Courts.*

156. Eisenstein, Flemming, and Nardulli, *The Contours of Justice: Communities and Their Courts.*

157. Sudnow, "Normal Crimes."

158. Eisenstein, Flemming, and Nardulli, *The Contours of Justice*, pp. 30-31.

Chapter Four

Sentencing Disparity and Discrimination

A Focus on Gender

Desperate for money to buy drugs, Jane Simmons, a 22-year-old drug addict with no prior felony convictions, agreed to deliver a package containing 20 grams of cocaine to a waiter at a local restaurant. The waiter turned out to be an undercover police officer, and Jane has been convicted of possession of cocaine with intent to deliver. Under the laws of the state in which she was convicted, Jane could be placed on probation or sentenced to prison for up to 10 years. If she is sentenced by Judge A, a hard-liner who believes that drug use and drug-related crimes are destroying American cities, she will receive the maximum penalty of 10 years in prison. If she is sentenced by Judge B, who believes that imprisonment is not an effective punishment for drug-addicted offenders, she will be placed on probation and will be required to complete a 12-month substance abuse treatment program.

Is this fair? Should the sentence Jane receives depend on the judge who imposes it? Should a sentence depend on a judge's philosophy of punishment or personal beliefs about the dangers of drug abuse? Or should it be

based on an objective evaluation of the seriousness of the crime and the offender's prior criminal record?

Consider another hypothetical situation. Two 19-year-old males have
been convicted of motor vehicle theft. Each of them has one prior conviction for burglary; neither of them has served time in jail or prison. Both appear before the same judge for sentencing. James Jones, who is white and
works part-time at a fast food restaurant, is sentenced to 6 months in jail.
William Barnes, an unemployed African American, receives 2 years in
prison.

Is this fair? Should Barnes receive a longer sentence than Jones because
he is black and unemployed? Should the judge be required to impose the
same sentence on similarly culpable offenders convicted of the same crime?

Critics of the sentencing process contend that the scenarios described
above are real, not hypothetical. They contend that judges who are not
bound by sentencing rules or guidelines and are free to fashion sentences as
they see fit often impose different sentences on similarly situated offenders
or identical sentences on offenders whose crimes and prior criminal histories are different. Echoing Judge Marvin Frankel, these critics suggest that
unstructured discretion leads to "lawlessness" in sentencing.[1]

In this chapter and the next, we examine these allegations. We assess the
degree to which the sentencing process is characterized by disparity and
discrimination. We begin with a discussion of the meaning of these terms.
We then describe the various types of sentencing disparity and discrimination and illustrate that not all sentence disparities are unwarranted. This
chapter goes on to present information about differences in sentences received by men and women, indicating the degree to which such differences
appear to be a result of discrimination. Chapter 5 analyzes disparities in
sentencing based on race and ethnicity and examines the results of research
exploring the interrelationships among race, ethnicity, gender, and sentencing.

Disparity and Discrimination

Allegations of "lawlessness" in sentencing reflect concerns about both
disparity and discrimination. Although these terms are sometimes used
interchangeably, they do not mean the same thing. *Disparity* refers to a
difference in treatment or outcome that does not necessarily result from
intentional bias or prejudice. For example, the fact that very few persons
over the age of 50 enroll at the typical college or university reflects a dis-

parity but not discrimination. There is a difference based on age, but it is not a difference that results from bias or prejudice against older students. No official policies bar older adults from being admitted, and admission decisions are made on the basis of factors other than age. The small number of students over the age of 50, in other words, reflects the fact that most people go to college soon after graduating from high school and applications from persons in the 50-and-over age group are rare.

Discrimination, on the other hand, is differential treatment of individuals based on irrelevant criteria, such as race, gender, or social class. For example, suppose a college or university were to base admission decisions on whether applicants were white or African American, male or female, or rich or poor, rather than on applicants' high school grades or test scores. The fact that most of those admitted were rich, white, and male would be a reflection of discrimination, not simply of disparity. It would reflect intentional bias or prejudice against racial minorities, women, and the poor.

Applied to the sentencing process, disparity exists when similar offenders are sentenced differently or when different offenders receive the same sentence. It exists when (a) judges impose different sentences on two offenders with identical criminal histories who are convicted of the same crime, (b) when judges impose identical sentences on two offenders whose prior records and crimes are very different, or (c) when the sentence depends on the judge who imposes it or the jurisdiction in which it is imposed. In the scenario described at the beginning of this chapter, the fact that Jane Simmons would receive a significantly harsher sentence for possession of cocaine with intent to deliver from Judge A, the hard-liner, than she would from Judge B, the advocate for drug treatment, is an example of sentencing disparity.

In contrast, sentencing discrimination exists when legally irrelevant characteristics of a defendant affect the sentence that is imposed after all legally relevant variables are taken into consideration. It exists when African American and Hispanic offenders are sentenced more harshly than similarly situated white offenders, when male offenders receive more punitive sentences than comparable female offenders, and when poor offenders receive harsher sentences than middle-class or wealthy offenders. In the second scenario presented at the beginning of this chapter, the judge imposed a harsher sentence on William Barnes, an unemployed African American, than he did on James Jones, who is white and employed part-time, despite the fact that the two offenders had identical prior records and were convicted of the same crime. This is an example of sentencing discrimination.

Types of Sentencing Disparity

Defining sentencing disparity as a situation in which similar offenders are treated differently or different offenders are treated the same is overly simplistic. There are actually a number of different types of sentencing disparity (see Exhibit 4.1), and not all sentencing disparities are equally problematic.

Inter-Jurisdictional Disparity

Inter-jurisdictional differences occur when the sentencing patterns of judges in different jurisdictions vary. They come about because certain categories of crimes are viewed as more serious and certain types of offenders are perceived as more dangerous in some jurisdictions than in others. For example, offenders convicted of serious felonies may be sentenced more leniently in large urban court systems, which routinely try such crimes, than in rural areas, where misdemeanors and less serious felonies dominate court dockets. Similarly, offenders convicted of selling drugs may be sentenced more harshly in cities plagued by drug use and drug-related violent crime than in cities in which drug abuse is less

Exhibit 4.1 Types of Sentencing Disparity

Type of Disparity	Definition	Example
Inter-jurisdictional	Judges in different jurisdictions sentence similarly situated offenders differently.	Offenders convicted of possession of crack cocaine are sentenced more harshly by federal court judges than by state court judges.
Intra-jurisdictional	Judges in the same jurisdiction sentence similarly situated offenders differently.	Drug-addicted offenders convicted of burglary in a midwestern county get probation coupled with drug treatment if sentenced by Judge Smith and 3 years in prison if sentenced by Judge Jones.
Intra-judge	An individual judge makes inconsistent sentencing decisions.	Judge Johnson sentences a Hispanic offender convicted of armed robbery to 5 years in prison; she sentences a similarly situated white offender convicted of an identical crime to 2 years in prison.

problematic. These geographic variations in sentence outcomes signal inter-jurisdictional disparity.

Evidence of inter-jurisdictional sentencing disparity is found in studies that compare the sentences imposed by judges serving different communities within a single state. Ulmer, for example, compared the sentencing decisions of judges in three Pennsylvania counties.[2] He found that despite the existence of statewide sentencing guidelines,[3] the sentences imposed by judges in the three counties varied. The sentences handed down by judges in a large urban county were the least severe, those handed down by judges in a medium-sized suburban county were the most severe, and those handed down in a small rural county fell in between. According to Ulmer, "Stiff, retributive sentences were reserved mostly for the serious violent and drug trafficking offenses"[4] in the urban county. In the suburban county, on the other hand, there was "a strong consensus in favor of tougher sentencing standards that reflected an emphasis on deterrence, just deserts, and incapacitation goals."[5]

Evidence of inter-jurisdictional sentencing disparity is also found in studies that examine the sentencing decisions of judges in different states. One study compared the sentencing decisions of judges in nine counties in three different states.[6] When the authors examined the sentences imposed on convicted offenders who were arrested for the same offense, they found significant differences. The incarceration rate for offenders arrested for burglary, for example, ranged from 26 percent in DuPage County, Illinois, to 52 percent in Erie County, Pennsylvania, to 75 percent in Kalamazoo County, Michigan. Judges in Kalamazoo also imposed longer sentences than judges in the other eight counties. The "going rates" in Kalamazoo, in other words, were substantially harsher than those found in the other jurisdictions.

A final type of inter-jurisdictional disparity is disparity in sentences imposed by judges in state and federal courts. The federal sentencing guidelines coupled with mandatory minimum sentences often require harsher sentences than do state criminal codes. This is particularly true for drug offenses, especially those involving crack cocaine. Under the U.S. Sentencing Guidelines, for example, possession of 5 grams of crack cocaine triggers a mandatory minimum prison sentence of 5 years. In contrast, the Illinois Criminal Code, which does not differentiate between crack and powder cocaine, specifies a sentence ranging from 1 to 3 years for possession of up to 15 grams of cocaine, and probation is an option.

As shown in Exhibit 4.2, drug offenders sentenced in U.S. District Courts received substantially harsher sentences than those sentenced in the

75 largest counties in the United States. The federal incarceration rate for drug trafficking was more than double the rate in these counties, and the average sentence handed down by federal court judges was about 2.5 years longer than the mean sentence imposed by state court judges. There were similar disparities in the sentences imposed on offenders convicted of other drug offenses.[7]

Intra-Jurisdictional Disparity

The sentences imposed by judges in the same jurisdiction may also vary. Judges in a particular jurisdiction may have differing perceptions of crime seriousness or may give greater or lesser weight to legally relevant factors, such as the seriousness of the crime and the offender's prior criminal record. As a result, similar offenders sentenced by different judges may receive substantially different sentences. If, for example, some judges routinely sent all burglars with no previous felony convictions to prison, whereas others typically sentenced all such offenders to probation, the result would be intra-jurisdictional sentencing disparity. A similar outcome would result if some judges routinely handed out either substantially harsher or substantially more lenient sentences than their colleagues on the bench. In both cases, the severity of the sentence the offender receives rests in part on the judge who imposes it.

A number of studies document the existence of intra-jurisdictional sentencing disparities.[8] Some of these are simulations in which a group of

Exhibit 4.2 Sentences Imposed on Drug Offenders by Federal and State Court Judges, 1996

	Sentenced to Prison (Percentage)	Mean Prison Sentence (Months)
Sentences imposed in U.S. District Courts[a]		
Drug trafficking	93.2	82.8
Simple possession	47.0	6.0
Sentences imposed in 75 largest U.S. Counties[b]		
Drug trafficking	44.0	54
Other drug offenses	23.0	33

a. Compiled from data presented in the *1996 Sourcebook of Federal Sentencing Statistics* (Table 12 and Table 13), by the U.S. Sentencing Commission, 1997. Washington, DC: Author.
b. Compiled from data presented in the *Sourcebook of Criminal Justice Statistics, 1998* (Table 5.5 and Table 5.6), by the Department of Justice, Bureau of Justice Statistics. Washington, DC: Author.

judges determines sentences in identical hypothetical cases. Two simulation studies of sentencing by federal district court judges,[9] for example, found that some judges were consistently more severe and others consistently more lenient than were their colleagues on the bench. These studies also revealed that judges disagreed about the appropriate sentences for particular types of offenders or particular types of cases. These findings led Clancy and his colleagues to conclude that "Disparity is a widespread phenomenon. . . . Substantial dissensus exists among judges about the sentences that convicted offenders should serve."[10]

Studies of actual sentences imposed by state court judges also reveal intra-jurisdictional disparities. Uhlman's study of sentences imposed by 91 judges in a Pennsylvania county found substantial between-judge variation in mean sentence severity.[11] Uhlman compared the mean sentences imposed by each judge, controlling for the seriousness of the conviction charge. He found that (a) more than half of the judges imposed sentences that were more than 10 percent harsher or more lenient than the overall mean, (b) 16 judges were at least 30 percent harsher than average, and (c) one judge, whom he characterized as a "hanging judge," imposed sentences that were nearly twice as harsh as those imposed by the other 90 judges.[12]

Further evidence of intra-jurisdictional disparity is found in Exhibit 4.3, which displays the sentences imposed on drug offenders by 12 judges in Cook County (Chicago), Illinois. All offenders had at least one prior felony conviction and were convicted in 1993 of either possession of narcotics with intent to deliver or simple possession. Both the incarceration rates and the average sentences vary by judge. Looking first at offenders convicted of possession of narcotics with intent, the incarceration rate varied from 73.2 percent (Judge #12) to 100 percent (Judge #1), and the average sentence varied from 44.3 months (Judge #4) to 55.8 months (Judge #7). The differences for simple possession, which is a less serious offense, were even more pronounced. The incarceration rate for the most severe judge (#6) was 90 percent—more than twice the rate for the least severe judge (#11), who sent only 37.5 percent of the offenders to prison. The average sentences also varied from 14.5 months to 42.0 months. These differences suggest that judges in Cook County based their sentencing decisions on factors other than crime seriousness and prior criminal record.

The reasons that judges in a particular jurisdiction sentence similar offenders differently are complicated. As explained in Chapter 1, judges have different beliefs about the purposes of punishment, and these beliefs may influence the sentences they impose. A judge who is convinced that imprisonment effectively deters offenders from committing future crimes may be

Exhibit 4.3 Sentences Imposed on Drug Offenders by Judges in Cook County (Chicago), Illinois, 1993[a]

	Possess Narcotics With Intent		Simple Possession	
	Sentenced to Prison (Percentage)	Average Prison Sentence (Months)	Sentenced to Prison (Percentage)	Average Prison Sentence (Months)
Judge #1	100.0	45.6	85.0	33.2
Judge #2	95.4	47.6	78.6	17.4
Judge #3	93.8	47.2	70.0	24.0
Judge #4	92.9	44.3	64.3	16.0
Judge #5	92.3	51.0	55.6	19.2
Judge #6	91.7	47.2	90.0	21.8
Judge #7	90.1	55.8	80.0	42.0
Judge #8	88.6	48.6	77.8	16.1
Judge #9	84.2	47.9	84.6	21.5
Judge #10	82.8	45.5	80.0	14.5
Judge #11	78.6	46.9	37.5	24.0
Judge #12	73.2	52.7	79.5	25.5

SOURCE: From *The Effect of Race on Sentencing: Final Report to the National Science Foundation*, by C. Spohn and M. DeLone, 1998. Unpublished data.

a. All offenders had at least one prior felony conviction. All offenders convicted of possession of narcotics with intent were convicted of either Class 1 or Class 2 offenses. All offenders convicted of simple possession were convicted of a Class 4 offense.

more likely to sentence offenders convicted of drug offenses and less serious property crimes to prison than a judge who believes that imprisonment has a criminogenic effect. As one scholar concluded, "Each judge has a point of view, a set of standards and values, a bias, if you will, which will color, influence, and direct the nature of his verdicts independently of the specific condition of the criminal being charged."[13]

It is also possible that judges from different backgrounds sentence differently. A judge who spent many years as a defense attorney may impose more lenient sentences than a judge who came to the bench from the prosecutor's office. A female judge may be more likely than a male judge to view sexual assault, domestic violence, and other crimes that disproportionately victimize women as serious crimes that merit harsh punishment. A Hispanic judge who grew up in a drug-infested inner-city barrio may impose more punitive sentences on drug traffickers than a white judge raised in an upper-middle-class neighborhood in which drug use and drug-related crime were rare. In other words, because the sentencing philosophies and background characteristics of judges in a particular jurisdiction may vary, the sentences they impose may also differ.

Intra-Judge Disparity

A third type of sentence disparity is intra-judge disparity. This type of disparity occurs when an individual judge makes inconsistent sentencing decisions. The judge, in other words, imposes different sentences on equally culpable offenders whose crimes are indistinguishable. Although these sentence variations might be attributable to subtle, and thus not easily observed or measured, differences in crime seriousness and offender blameworthiness, they might also be due to idiosyncratic behavior on the part of the judge. Sentences might vary from case to case depending on the judge's mood; evaluation of the defendant's character, attitude, or demeanor; or feelings about the attorney who is representing the defendant.

Sentencing decisions might also reflect a judge's attitudes toward particular types of offenders or toward offenders who behave in a particular way. As explained in Chapter 3, some judges believe that they are justified in imposing harsher sentences on defendants who refuse to plead guilty. Although most judges claim that they are not penalizing defendants who refuse to plead guilty but rewarding defendants who admit their guilt, skeptics counter that the effect is the same: Those who insist on trials get harsher sentences than those who plead guilty. Judges may also take an offender's truthfulness into account. In one U.S. District Court case, for example, the judge announced at the sentencing hearing that he had decided to impose a harsher sentence than usual because the defendant had lied on the stand. He told the defendant: "It is my view that your defense was a complete fabrication without the slightest merit whatsoever. I feel it is proper for me to consider that fact in the sentencing, and I will do so."[14] When the case was appealed, the U.S. Supreme Court ruled that the judge had not abused his discretion in this case. In fact, the court stated that "the defendant's readiness to lie under oath—especially when, as here, the trial court finds the lie to be flagrant—may be deemed probative of his prospects for rehabilitation."[15]

Intra-judge disparity might also reflect intentional bias or prejudice against certain types of offenders by individual judges. A judge who believes that African American and Hispanic offenders are particularly dangerous and especially likely to recidivate may impose harsher sentences on them than on otherwise identical white offenders. A judge who is concerned about the "social costs" of incarcerating female offenders with young children may refuse to send such offenders to prison but may not hesitate to incarcerate similarly situated male offenders. These types of intra-judge sentencing disparities, then, may signal the presence, not just of disparity, but of *discrimination* based on race, gender, social class, or other legally irrelevant defendant characteristics.

Types of Sentencing Discrimination

Like disparity, discrimination can take a number of forms (see Exhibit 4.4). Walker and his colleagues suggest that discrimination falls along a continuum that ranges from "pure justice," or "no discrimination at any time or place in the criminal justice system," to "systematic discrimination," or "discrimination that occurs at all stages of the criminal justice system, in all places, and at all times."[16] Pure justice, of course, is the ideal, the goal that societies strive to achieve. An example of systematic discrimination would be the treatment of blacks by the criminal justice system during the era of slavery. Another example would be the use of the death penalty for the crime of rape: 405 of the 453 men executed for the crime of rape in the United States from 1930 through 1976 were black.[17]

In the middle of the continuum are institutionalized discrimination, contextual discrimination, and individual acts of discrimination. *Institutionalized discrimination* refers to differences in treatment or outcomes resulting from established policies or procedures that are not themselves based explicitly on race, ethnicity, or gender. The North Carolina sentencing

Exhibit 4.4 Types of Sentencing Discrimination

A. The Discrimination Continuum

Type of Discrimination	Definition	Example
Pure justice	No discrimination at any time or in any place	The ideal toward which societies strive
Institutional discrimination	Discrimination that results from evenhanded application of policies or procedures	Policies that allow judges to consider the offender's employment history or family situation
Contextual discrimination	Discrimination that occurs in some contexts or under some circumstances	Blacks convicted of murdering whites (but not blacks convicted of murdering other blacks) are more likely to be sentenced to death than whites convicted of murder
Individual Acts of Discrimination	Discriminatory decisions made by a few individuals within the system	Judge Miller imposes more lenient sentences on all female offenders; other judges in the jurisdiction do not consider gender in determining the sentence
Systematic Discrimination	Discrimination at all stages, in all places, and during all time periods	Use of the death penalty for rape; 89 percent of those sentenced to death for rape were black

B. Direct Versus Subtle Discrimination

Type of Discrimination	Definition	Example
Direct discrimination (main effect)	Race, ethnicity or gender affects sentence severity when crime seriousness and prior record are held constant	Black and Hispanic offenders face higher odds of incarceration than white offenders who are convicted of identical crimes and have identical prior criminal records
Subtle discrimination (indirect effect)	Race, ethnicity, or gender affects sentence severity through some other factor	Blacks are more likely than whites to be in custody prior to trial; as a result, blacks receive harsher sentences than whites
(Interaction effect)	The effect of race, ethnicity, or gender on sentence severity depends on some other factor; the effect of some other factor depends on race, ethnicity or gender	Blacks receive harsher sentences than whites for drug offenses but not for violent crimes or property offenses; having dependent children reduces the sentence for women but not for men

SOURCE: *The Color of Justice: Race, Ethnicity, and Crime in America*, pp. 16-18, by S. Walker, C. Spohn, and M. DeLone, 2000. Belmont, CA: Wadsworth.

guidelines, for example, allow judges to consider whether the defendant is gainfully employed.[18] The policy, which reflects an assumption that those who are employed have more stakes in conformity and thus will be less likely to commit additional offenses, is intended to be race-neutral. All defendants, regardless of race or ethnicity, get a break at sentencing if they are employed. The effect of the policy, however, may not be race-neutral. Because members of racial minorities are more likely than whites to be unemployed, they may be sentenced more harshly than whites. The evenhanded application of a seemingly race-neutral policy, in other words, might result in institutionalized racial discrimination.

The other two types of discrimination do not result from the evenhanded application of rules or policies, but, rather, from decision makers' biases or prejudice against entire groups of people. *Contextual discrimination* refers to "discrimination in certain situations or contexts."[19] It refers to discrimination that is not systematic but is, instead, confined to certain regions of the country, certain stages of the decision-making process, certain types of crimes, or offenders with particular constellations of characteristics. For example, there is evidence that (a) gender affects the decision to incarcerate or not but does not affect the length of the sentence and (b) the effect of race/ethnicity is confined primarily to less serious crimes. Both of these are examples of contextual discrimination. *Individual discrimination*, which falls closer to the "pure justice" end of the continuum, involves discriminatory acts by particular criminal justice officials. It involves a situation, for example, in which one judge in a particular jurisdiction sentences members of racial minorities more harshly than whites or sentences females more leniently than males, but other judges do not. As Walker and his colleagues note, "These are discriminatory acts, but they do not represent general patterns of how the criminal justice system operates."[20]

Researchers also differentiate between direct and subtle discrimination. *Direct discrimination* refers to a situation in which race, ethnicity, or gender affects sentence severity after all legally relevant case and offender characteristics are taken into consideration. Stated another way, direct discrimination occurs when blacks and Hispanics are sentenced more harshly than whites (or men are sentenced more harshly than women) and these differences cannot be attributed to differences in crime seriousness, prior criminal record, or other legally relevant factors. This type of finding is often referred to as a *main effect*.

Subtle discrimination refers to what researchers characterize as indirect or interaction effects.[21] An *indirect effect* occurs when an independent variable influences a dependent variable through some other factor, rather than directly. Consider a situation in which a researcher discovers that race does not significantly affect the likelihood of incarceration once crime seriousness and prior record are taken into consideration. The researcher also discovers, however, that (a) defendants who are detained in jail prior to trial are substantially more likely to be sentenced to prison than those who are released prior to trial and (b) black defendants are more likely than white defendants to be detained prior to trial. In this case, the researcher could conclude that race indirectly affects sentence severity through its effect on pretrial detention.

An *interaction effect* occurs when either the effects of race or gender vary because of some other factor or when the effects of other variables are conditioned by offender race or gender. If the effect of race is confined to certain types of cases (e.g., to less serious crimes in which judges have greater discretion at sentencing) or to certain types of offenders (e.g., young males), we would conclude that race interacts with crime seriousness or offender age/gender to affect sentence outcomes. We would reach a similar conclusion if we found that, for example, going to trial rather than pleading guilty increased sentence severity for racial minorities but not for whites or that having dependent children reduced sentence severity for females but not for males. As Zatz notes, indirect and interaction effects "reflect more subtle institutionalized biases, but still fall within the purview of discrimination if they systematically favor one group over another."[22]

Warranted Versus Unwarranted Disparity

Not all types of sentencing disparities are necessarily unwarranted. Some of them may be reasonable and justifiable. Although one might question the fairness of a system in which the sentence an offender receives depends on the jurisdiction in which the case is adjudicated, variations in laws and in criminal justice resources might produce inter-jurisdictional sentencing disparity. Within both the federal and state court systems, the judge's discretion at sentencing is constrained by the penalty range, established by the legislature, for crimes of varying seriousness. In one state, the presumptive sentence for burglary might be 5 to 7 years; in another state, the range might be from 7 to 10 years. The fact that an offender convicted of burglary in the first state received 5 years but a seemingly identical offender convicted of burglary in the second state got 7 years is not indicative of unwarranted disparity. In each instance, the judge imposing the sentence determined that the offender deserved the minimum punishment specified for the particular crime.

Jurisdictional and/or regional differences in values and in attitudes toward crime and punishment might also foster sentencing disparity. Public opinion polls reveal that people living in urban areas are substantially more likely than those living in suburban or rural areas to believe that crime is a serious neighborhood problem.[23] These polls also indicate that people residing in the western United States are more likely than those residing in other regions of the country to support the legalization of marijuana.[24] If we assume that the attitudes of judges at least to some extent mirror those of the communities in which they serve, we might expect the sentences imposed by judges in urban areas to differ from those imposed by judges in rural areas. Similarly, we might expect judges in western states to impose more lenient sentences on offenders convicted of possession of marijuana. Principled and thoughtful judges sitting in different jurisdictions, in other words, might come to different conclusions about the appropriate punishment for identical offenders.

The legitimacy of intra-jurisdictional sentencing disparities is more questionable. One might argue that some degree of disparity in the sentences imposed by judges in a particular jurisdiction is to be expected in a system that attempts to individualize punishment and in which there is no universal agreement on the goals of sentences. As long as these differences resulted from the application of legitimate criteria and reflected fundamental differences regarding the purposes of punishment, they might be regarded as warranted.

Alternatively, it could be argued that justice demands that similarly situated offenders convicted of identical crimes in the same jurisdiction receive comparable punishments. In other words, to be fair, a sentencing scheme requires the evenhanded application of objective standards. Thus, the amount of punishment an offender receives should not depend on the values, attitudes, and beliefs of the judge to whom the case is assigned. As Gaylin noted, "These sets of values constitute bias in a non-pejorative sense—but bias nonetheless, and a bias that will influence equality and fairness in exactly the same way as naked bigotry does."[25]

The legitimacy of intra-judge disparity is even more questionable. We expect a particular judge to evaluate cases objectively and to determine sentences based on legally relevant case and offender characteristics. Doing so should result in similar punishments for identical offenders sentenced by that judge. A judge who makes subjective sentencing decisions based on legally irrelevant factors, such as his or her feelings about the attorney handling the case or disapproval of the offender's lifestyle, is not dispensing justice.

The problem is that it is not entirely clear which factors are legally irrelevant and therefore should not be taken into consideration at sentencing. A good example is the offender's employment status. Some might argue that whether an offender is employed or not is irrelevant: It bears no relationship to the offender's blameworthiness and thus has no bearing on the sentence that should be imposed. Those who challenge the use of employment status at sentencing might also point out that unemployment is linked to social class and race/ethnicity: Imposing more severe sentences on those who are unemployed might result in harsher sentences for the poor and for racial minorities. Others might counter that an unemployed offender has fewer financial resources than one who is employed and that because of this, he or she would be more likely to return to a life of crime. The offender's employment status, according to this line of reasoning, is an indicator of his potential for rehabilitation. The use of other offender characteristics might be similarly controversial. As Tonry notes, "Judges . . . make decisions about whole people, and not about generic offenders who have committed offense X and have criminal history Y. Not surprisingly, they often feel moved to take the individual offender's circumstances into account in deciding what to do."[26]

Regardless of how this issue is resolved, it is clear that sentencing disparities that reflect discrimination are unwarranted. This would be true of sentencing disparities between jurisdictions as well as those within jurisdictions. In fact, much of the criticism of sentencing disparity centers on the issue of discrimination based on race, ethnicity, gender, and social class. Allowing judges unrestrained discretion in fashioning sentences, it is argued, opens the door to discrimination, with the result that members of racial minorities are sentenced more harshly than whites, men are sentenced more harshly than women, and the poor are sentenced more harshly than those who are not poor.

In the sections that follow, we examine this issue. We begin with a discussion of gender discrimination in sentencing. In Chapter 5, we discuss the evidence for racial and ethnic discrimination in sentencing.

Gender and Sentencing

In 1997, there were 74,112 females and 1,123,478 males incarcerated in state and federal prisons. Stated another way, there were 15 times as many men as women in our nation's prisons.[27] This clearly is evidence of disparity: There is a striking difference between the number of men and women who are incarcerated. But is it evidence of discrimination? Consider the following statistics. Do they reflect gender disparity, gender discrimination, or both?:

- Of all offenders convicted in U.S. District Courts in 1995, 81.5 percent of the males were sentenced to prison, but only 58.2 percent of the females. The average sentence was 63.3 months for men and 34.0 months for women. Among offenders convicted of violent crimes, 95.0 percent of the males and 81.6 percent of the females were incarcerated. For these offenses, the average sentence was 94.6 months for men and 57.2 months for women.[28]

- Fifty percent of the male offenders sentenced by state court judges in 1994 were sentenced to prison, compared with 33 percent of the female offenders. The average maximum prison sentence was 72 months for males and 54 months for females.[29]

- There were 3,527 prisoners under sentence of death on December 31, 1999; of these, only 49 were women.[30]

- Among offenders convicted of felonies in 1994 in Cook County (Chicago), Illinois, 28.3 percent of the females and 63.9 percent of the males were sentenced to prison. The proportions of offenders who were incarcerated in Jackson County (Kansas City), Missouri, were 16 percent (females) and 45 percent (males). The figures for Dade County (Miami), Florida, were 60.2 percent (females) and 69.2 percent (males).[31]

These data provide compelling evidence of *gender disparity* in sentencing. Women are substantially less likely than men to be sentenced to prison in federal and state courts, the sentences imposed on women are significantly shorter than those imposed on men, and women are much less likely than men to be sentenced to death. But do these data prove that women receive preferential treatment or, alternatively, that judges discriminate against men? Are these gender disparities unwarranted, or are there legitimate explanations for them?

One explanation suggests that women are sentenced more leniently than men because they are convicted of less serious crimes and have less serious prior criminal records than men. In other words, there are substantially more men than women in prison because most offenders arrested for and convicted of the crimes that merit imprisonment (violent crimes and serious property and drug offenses by repeat offenders) are men. According to this explanation, once these legally relevant factors are taken into consideration, the gender differences in sentence severity will disappear: If we compare the sentences imposed on offenders convicted of the same crimes, with identical prior criminal records, we will find that women are sentenced no differently than men. If this is the case, the gender disparities in sentence severity clearly would not be unwarranted. They would be due to legitimate differences in the crimes men and women commit and in the criminal histories that men and women carry with them into court.

It also is possible that women are sentenced less harshly than men because of "gendered presuppositions of crime and justice."[32] One theoretical perspective on judicial decision making contends that judges' sentencing decisions are guided by three focal concerns: their assessment of the blameworthiness or culpability of the offender; their desire to protect the community by incapacitating dangerous offenders or deterring potential offenders; and their concerns about the practical consequences, or social costs, of sentencing decisions.[33] The more lenient sentences imposed on women, then, might reflect the fact that judges believe that women are generally less dangerous, less blameworthy, less likely to recidivate, and more likely to be deterred. They might also reflect judges' beliefs that the social costs of incarcerating women, who are more likely than men to be the sole caretakers of young children, are high. Some might question the legitimacy or fairness of basing sentencing decisions on an offender's child care responsibilities, but sentencing disparities that reflect differences in the way judges evaluate the culpability or dangerousness of male and female offenders are not necessarily unwarranted. These types of disparities reflect differences based on legitimate but gender-linked sentencing goals. (This issue is discussed in more detail in the next section, "Focus on an Issue: Should Men and Women Be Treated the Same?")

It is possible, of course, that gender disparities in sentencing cannot be explained away in this fashion. In fact, some scholars argue that the more lenient treatment of female offenders does reflect discrimination *in favor of women* or, alternatively, discrimination *against* men. According to this view, judges explicitly and inappropriately take gender into account when determining the sentence. Typically, this is attributed either to "chivalry" or "paternalism" on the part of the largely male judiciary. The gentler treatment accorded women, in other words, stems from judges' perceptions of women as childlike and dependent, as well as their desire to protect the "weaker sex" from the harshness of jail or prison. If this is the case, gender differences in sentence severity would remain even after we controlled for crime seriousness, for the offender's prior criminal history, dangerousness, and blameworthiness, and for other legally relevant offender and case characteristics.

We evaluate these competing explanations for gender disparities in sentencing in the section following the "Focus on an Issue." We begin by testing the validity of the assumptions inherent in each explanation. We then discuss the results of empirical research that compares the sentences imposed on men and women, focusing on the results of recent, methodologically sophisticated studies.

Focus on an Issue:
Should Men and Women Be Treated the Same?

Women and the "Imprisonment Binge"

During the past two decades, the number of women incarcerated in state and federal prisons has increased dramatically. 82,716 women were under the jurisdiction of state and federal authorities in mid-1998 compared with only 12,331 in 1980.[34] Much of this growth in women's imprisonment is not attributed to an increase in the seriousness of crimes women commit but to the crime control policies pursued during the past 20 years. Some scholars suggest that these policies, which produced an "unprecedented imprisonment binge,"[35] had a particularly pronounced effect on women. Meda Chesney-Lind, for example, contends that public calls to get tough on crime, "coupled with a legal system that now espouses 'equality' for women with a vengeance when it comes to the punishment of crime, has resulted in a much greater use of imprisonment in response to women's crime."[36]

Several authors suggest that recent increases in the number of women incarcerated in state and federal prisons can be traced directly to the "war on drugs" and the resultant emphasis on increasing the penalties for possession and sale of drugs.[37] Recent data on incarcerated offenders support this assertion. Surveys of state prison inmates, for example, reveal that the number of women incarcerated for drug offenses increased from 2,400 in 1986 to 12,600 in 1991, an increase of 432 percent. Among offenders committed to state prisons in 1996, 39.1 percent of the females were convicted of drug offenses but only 29.3 percent of the males.[38] Among offenders incarcerated in federal prisons in 1997, an astonishing 73.2 percent of the black females and 68.1 percent of the white females were committed for drug offenses.[39] Citing evidence such as this, Chesney-Lind concludes that the "'war on drugs' has translated into a war on women."[40] Other scholars have made analogous arguments. Noting that the increase of women in prison has been fueled by the war on drugs, Durham suggests that "women who had previously been the beneficiary of more lenient sentencing . . . are now being treated like their male counterparts, or even more harshly."[41] Daly and Tonry similarly contend that reformers' attempts to enhance gender equality in sentencing, "coupled with the War on Drugs and the law-and-order campaigns of the 1980s, has yielded dramatically increasing incarceration rates."[42]

These statements imply that chivalrous or paternalistic treatment of female offenders is a thing of the past. More to the point, they imply that equal treatment of male and female offenders, particularly for drug offenses, has resulted in spectacular increases in the female prison population.

The Equal Treatment Controversy

The question of whether female offenders should be treated the same as male offenders has generated considerable controversy. Those on one side of the argument suggest that fairness and justice demand equal treatment.[43] Although they acknowledge that men and women differ in many important respects, the advocates of gender neutrality argue that special treatment of women carries significant risks. With respect to sentencing, they assert that using gender-linked criteria, such as family ties, responsibility for the care of young children, or prior victimization, to determine the appropriate sentence validates traditional sex roles and perpetuates negative stereotypes of female weakness and moral inferiority. They also contend that using these factors to reduce sentence severity may have the unintended consequence of increasing sentences for female offenders without these characteristics. If, in other words, women with family ties or responsibility for raising young children are deemed more reformable, then women without these characteristics may be viewed as less reformable and more in need of harsh punishment.

Those on the other side of the argument suggest that cultural and biological differences between male and female offenders may be relevant and legitimate considerations at sentencing.[44] The fact that women are more likely than men to be the sole caretakers of young children, for example, may be a relevant consideration for judges who believe that it is important to keep families together and to protect the interests of children. As Myrna Raeder argues, "Any cost benefit analysis would seem to dictate that children be considered in the sentencing decision, particularly when societal costs regarding any future criminality of the children are weighed."[45] Other potentially legitimate considerations, according to those in the "special treatment" camp, include pregnancy, prior battering and/or sexual assault victimization, the presence of coercion or abuse by male codefendants, and the offender's subordinate role in the offense. As Kathleen Daly observes, "Allowing for gender-linked criteria is not the same as assuming that men's and women's natures differ. . . . It is to assume that some features of men's and women's lives may differ and ought to be acknowledged in sentencing."[46] If, in other words, the goal of sentencing is justice and not simply equality, then special treatment of women is justified by virtue of their special circumstances.

What do you think? Are the "special circumstances" of female offenders a legitimate consideration at sentencing, or does justice demand equal treatment of similarly culpable male and female offenders who are convicted of the same crime?

Gender and Sentencing: Disparity or Discrimination?

As explained above, there are at least two reasons for concluding that gender disparities in sentencing do not reflect discrimination in favor of women or against men. The first suggests that differences in the sentences imposed on men and women are due to differences in crime seriousness and prior record. According to this line of reasoning, gender differences in sentence severity will disappear once these two legally relevant variables are taken into consideration. The second suggests that male/female sentence differentials are due not only to differences in crime seriousness and prior record but also to differences in judges' perceptions of males' and females' dangerousness, blameworthiness, and child care responsibilities. This explanation, then, assumes that gender differences will disappear once we take these factors into account.

We tested these underlying assumptions using data on offenders convicted of felonies in Cook County (Chicago), Illinois, in 1993. To test the assumption that gender differences will disappear once crime seriousness and prior record are held constant, we compared the sentences imposed on male and female offenders convicted of the same offense (possession of drugs with intent to deliver) with no prior felony convictions. As shown in Part A of Exhibit 4.5, males were still twice as likely as females to be sentenced to prison; 33.6 percent of the males were incarcerated but only 17.4 percent of the females. The mean sentence for men (48.6 months) was also slightly longer than the mean sentence for women (45.0 months).

A more refined test of the validity of the first explanation involves the use of logistic regression, a statistical technique that allows the researcher to

Exhibit 4.5 The Effect of Gender on Sentencing Decisions in Cook County (Chicago), Illinois, 1993

A. Sentences imposed on males and females who were convicted of possession of drugs with intent to deliver and who had no prior felony convictions

	Sentenced to Prison	Sentence Length (Months)
Males	33.6%	48.6
Females	17.4%	45.0

B. Predicted probabilities of incarceration for typical male and female offenders: controlling for crime seriousness and prior criminal record[a]

	Possession of Drugs w/Intent	Simple Possession
Males	61.9%	52.7%
Females	38.1%	29.5%

C. Predicted probabilities of incarceration for typical male and female offenders: controlling for crime seriousness, prior criminal record, use of a weapon, and responsibility for dependent children[b]

	Possession of Drugs w/Intent	Simple Possession
Males	49.4%	37.5%
Females	28.4%	19.9%

SOURCE: The data displayed in this table are unpublished. They were collected by C. Spohn and M. DeLone for their three-city study of sentencing decisions.

a. We used the results of the logistic regression analysis to calculate the predicted probability of incarceration for male and female offenders with the following characteristics: convicted of either possession of drugs with intent or simple possession, convicted of a Class 2 felony, one prior felony conviction, and no prior prison terms of more than 1 year.

b. We used the results of the logistic regression analysis to calculate the predicted probability of incarceration for male and female offenders with the following characteristics: convicted of either possession of drugs with intent or simple possession, convicted of a Class 2 felony, one prior felony conviction, no prior prison terms of more than 1 year, did not use a weapon to commit the crime, and has responsibility for dependent children.

identify the effect of a particular variable (gender) on some outcome (the decision to incarcerate or not) while simultaneously controlling for other variables. We used logistic regression to analyze the likelihood of incarceration, controlling for the offender's gender; the seriousness of the conviction charge (11 different types of offenses); the statutory classification of the conviction charge (Class X, Class 1, Class 2, Class 3, or Class 4 felony); and the offender's prior criminal record (the number of prior felony convictions and the number of prior prison terms of more than 1 year). We found that gender was a statistically significant predictor of the decision to incarcerate or not. In fact, judges were 2.5 times more likely to sentence male offenders to prison than to sentence female offenders to prison, even when we held these legally relevant factors constant.[47]

We used the results of this analysis to calculate the predicted probability of incarceration for "typical" male and female offenders: offenders who had been convicted of Class 2 offenses, had been convicted of either possession of drugs or possession of drugs with intent to deliver, and had one prior felony conviction but had not previously been imprisoned for more than 1 year. As shown in Part B of Exhibit 4.5, there were large differences in the predicted probabilities of incarceration for males and females convicted of these two types of drug offenses. Nearly two thirds (61.9 percent) of the males convicted of possession with intent were sentenced to prison but only 38.1 percent of the females. There were similar differences for simple possession: 52.7 percent of the men and 29.5 percent of the women were incarcerated.

These results raise doubts about the validity of the argument that gender disparities in sentence severity are due primarily to differences in crime seriousness and prior record. The gender differences did not disappear when these legally relevant variables were held constant. The data presented in Part C of Exhibit 4.5 address the validity of the second argument: that gender disparities will disappear once the offender's dangerousness and child care responsibilities are held constant. To test this, we re-ran the analysis, adding a variable measuring the offender's dangerousness (whether the offender used a weapon to commit the crime) and a variable measuring the offender's child care responsibilities (whether the offender had dependent children) to the model. We then calculated predicted probabilities of incarceration for offenders who had been convicted of a Class 2 drug offense, had one prior felony conviction but no prior prison terms of more than 1 year, did not use a weapon during the crime, and did have responsibility for the care of dependent children. As shown in Part C of Exhibit 4.5, although responsibility for dependent children reduced the likelihood of incarceration for both males and females, the gender differences did not disappear. For both offenses, men were substantially more likely than women to be sentenced to prison.

These results suggest that gender disparities in sentence severity cannot be attributed to differences between men and women in crime seriousness, prior criminal record, dangerousness, and child care responsibilities.

Holding these characteristics constant did not cause the sentence differences to disappear. However, we obviously cannot generalize these results, which reflect sentencing decisions made in one jurisdiction during a single year, to other jurisdictions, other time periods, or other types of offenders. We cannot conclude on the basis of these results alone that gender disparities in sentencing are unwarranted.

Gender and Sentencing: The Results of Recent Research

A comprehensive review of research comparing the sentences imposed on male and female offenders is beyond the scope of this book. Instead, we discuss the results of four recent studies: two studies of gender and sentencing for drug offenses and two studies that explore the interrelationships among gender, race/ethnicity, and sentence severity.

Gender and Sentencing for Drug Offenses

As noted in the "Focus on an Issue" presented earlier in this chapter, some commentators attribute the dramatic increases in the female prison population to harsher sentencing of women convicted of drug offenses. Although a number of studies examine the effect of race/ethnicity on sentencing decisions in drug cases,[48] very few studies focus on gender differences in the sentences imposed in these types of cases. One study[49] of the sentences imposed on drug offenders in U.S. District Courts in 1991 to 1992 found that female drug offenders faced lower odds of imprisonment than male drug offenders; they also received substantially shorter sentences than males. Albonetti concluded that the findings of her research "suggest that the federal sentencing guidelines have not eliminated sentence disparity linked to defendant characteristics for defendants convicted of drug offenses in 1991-92."[50]

A study of sentences imposed on offenders convicted of drug offenses in Cook County (Chicago), Illinois, in 1993 also found that female offenders received more lenient sentences than male offenders.[51] Spohn found that women were significantly less likely than men to be detained in jail prior to trial and to be sentenced to prison upon conviction. Noting that pretrial detention was one of the strongest predictors of incarceration, Spohn concluded that these results were indicative of a "pattern of cumulative advantage" for female drug offenders.[52] Female offenders were significantly less likely than male offenders to be in custody at the time of sentence; as a consequence, they were substantially less likely than males to be sentenced to prison. The war on drugs and concern about drug use and drug-related crime notwithstanding, women charged with drug offenses in Chicago faced substantially lower odds of incarceration than their male counterparts.

Spohn also tested for interaction between gender and two variables, responsibility for dependent children and a prior drug conviction, identified by previous research as affecting sentence severity for female offenders. She suggested that female drug offenders with dependent children would *not* benefit from familial paternalism. She reasoned that such women, like women who are convicted of child abuse or prostitution, may be viewed as "bad mothers" whose children would be better off living with relatives or in foster homes. As she noted, "If this is the case, judges may not hesitate to send such women to prison or to impose lengthy terms of incarceration."[53] She similarly suggested that judges would not be reluctant to send female drug offenders to prison if they had a prior conviction for a drug offense.

Consistent with these expectations, Spohn found that preferential treatment of female offenders was confined to cases involving offenders without dependent children and to offenders without prior convictions for drug offenses. Women with children and those who were repeat offenders did not face lower odds of incarceration than their male counterparts. According to Spohn, "This suggests that judges' calculations of the 'social costs of punishment' and assessments of blameworthiness are not invariant but reflect the combined effects of the offender's gender, child care responsibilities, prior criminal record, and type of offense."[54]

Gender, Race/Ethnicity, and Sentencing Decisions

There is evidence that judges' assessments of blameworthiness and dangerousness are affected by the offender's race/ethnicity, as well as the offender's gender. One study, for example, examined the effect of offender characteristics on sentences imposed in Pennsylvania, a state with presumptive sentencing guidelines. Steffensmeier, Kramer, and Streifel[55] used guideline sentencing data to assess the effect of gender on the decision to incarcerate or not and the length of the prison sentence. They also examined departures from the guidelines and judges' reasons for these departures. They found that female offenders faced somewhat lower odds of incarceration than male offenders (a difference of 12 percentage points) but that gender did not affect the length of the prison sentence. When they estimated separate models of sentence length for males and females, however, they found that gender interacted with both race and the type of offense. There were no racial differences in the sentences imposed on males, but black females received sentences that averaged 3 months longer than the sentences imposed on white females. Females received slightly shorter sentences when convicted of serious felonies and slightly longer sentences when convicted of less serious felonies or misdemeanors.

Spohn and Beichner's[56] analysis of the effects of gender and race on sentence outcomes for offenders convicted of felonies in Chicago, Kansas City, and Miami, in 1993, produced different findings regarding the interaction between race and gender. Like Steffensmeier and his colleagues, they found that female offenders faced significantly lower odds of incarceration than male offenders in all three jurisdictions. Further analysis revealed that both black and white females were less likely than their male counterparts to be sentenced to prison in Chicago and Kansas City. In Miami, on the other hand, black females faced lower odds of incarceration than black males, but white females were sentenced to prison at the same rate as white males. As shown in Exhibit 4.6, these gender differences were both statistically significant and nontrivial. In Chicago, for example, the estimated probability of incarceration for a "typical" offender was 48 percent for white men and only 18 percent for white women; it was 55 percent for black men and 32 percent for black women. In Kansas City, the probabilities ranged from 7 percent (white females) to 10 percent (black females) to 20 percent (black males and white males).

The results of these recent studies highlight the importance of testing for intersections among gender, race/ethnicity, and other legal and extralegal variables. It is clear that failure to consider the interaction between gender and race/ethnicity may result in misleading conclusions about the effect of these variables. As these studies reveal, discriminatory treatment of criminal defendants may be restricted primarily to black males, and preferential treatment may be reserved for white females. Alternatively, female offenders, regardless of race/ethnicity, may be treated more leniently than male offenders.

Explanations for More Lenient Treatment of Female Offenders

Researchers have offered a number of explanations for the more lenient treatment of female offenders. Steffensmeier and his colleagues,[57] for example, advanced two complementary explanations for the patterns of findings revealed by their research. They based these explanations on two types of qualitative data: the reasons given by judges for departures from the Pennsylvania Sentencing Guidelines and comments made by judges whom they interviewed. Regarding the more lenient treatment of female offend-

Exhibit 4.6. Predicted Probabilities of Incarceration for Typical Offenders

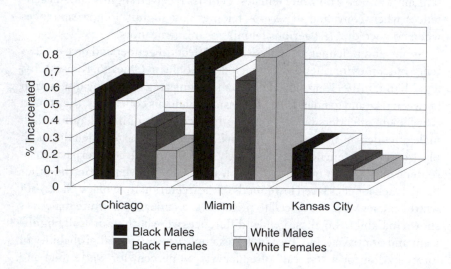

SOURCE: Data are from "Is Preferential Treatment of Female Offenders a Thing of the Past? A Multi-Site Study of Gender, Race, and Imprisonment" (Table 4), by C. Spohn and D. Beichner, *Criminal Justice Policy Review* 11:149-184.

NOTE: A "typical offender" has the following characteristics: age = 29 years; convicted of 1.4 counts of a drug offense; convicted of Class 2 felony (Chicago), third-degree felony (Miami), or Class C felony (Kansas City); one prior prison term of more than a year; not on probation at time of arrest for current crime; represented by a public defender; released prior to trial; and pled guilty. For Miami, the figures represent the predicted probability of being sentenced to jail or prison. For the other two jurisdictions, they represent the predicted probability of being sentenced to prison.

ers, they noted that judges viewed female offenders as less dangerous, less culpable, and more repentant than male offenders. Pennsylvania judges also believed that differential treatment of females was justified and sensible. It was justified because of differences in blameworthiness and sensible because females were more likely than males to have child care responsibilities and mental or health problems that could not be treated in a jail or prison setting.

Similar conclusions are found in Kathleen Daly's influential work.[58] Daly contends that although statistical studies of sentencing "may reveal more lenient outcomes for women, they tell us little about how court officials arrive at these decisions."[59] Her own research suggests that judges' pretrial release and sentencing decisions are affected by defendants' family circumstances. "Familied" defendants (i.e., those who are married and living with a spouse, living with parents or other relatives, or caring for young children) are treated more leniently than "non-familied" defendants. According to Daly, this more lenient treatment of familied defendants reflects judges' beliefs that these offenders have greater informal social control in their lives, as well as judges' concerns about maintaining families and protecting innocent children, which she labels the "social costs of punishment."[60]

Daly's work also reveals that family circumstances have more pronounced mitigating effects on outcomes for female defendants, particularly for black females, than for male defendants. She attributes this to the combined effect of the fact that "court officials see more 'good' mothers than 'good' fathers" and that judges view child care (typically provided by women) as more essential to the maintenance of families than economic support (more often provided by men).[61] She also suggests that judges make "gender-based character judgments."[62] Women are viewed as better candidates for reform than men because of their greater conventionality and less serious prior records. They are perceived as less blameworthy than men because of "blurred boundaries" between their past victimization and their current criminality.[63] Daly concludes that judges' sentencing decisions are not motivated by a desire to protect women but by an intent to protect families, a motivation that she refers to as "familial paternalism."[64]

The explanation offered by Spohn and Beichner[65] also focuses on judges' perceptions and stereotypes of men and women. They suggest that the findings of their study lend credence to assertions that court officials attempt to simplify and routinize the sentencing process by relying on stereotypes that link defendant characteristics such as race/ethnicity and gender to perceptions of blameworthiness, dangerousness, and risk of recidivism. They note that criminal justice officials interviewed for the study admitted that they viewed female offenders, particularly those with dependent children, differently than male offenders. They conclude that judges' assessments of offense seriousness and offender culpability interact with their concerns about protecting society from crime and about the practical effects of incarceration in producing more severe treatment of black and Hispanic male offenders and more lenient treatment of female offenders. As Spohn and Beichner note, "In these three jurisdictions, court officials apparently stereotype black and Hispanic male defendants as particularly blameworthy, violent, and threatening. Conversely, they appear to view all female defendants as less culpable, less likely to recidivate, and more amenable to rehabilitation."[66]

These differences in the way judges view male and female defendants are highlighted by the comments presented in Box 4.1. Judges interviewed for

BOX 4.1

**GENDER AND SENTENCING: PERCEPTIONS OF
CRIMINAL COURT JUDGES IN THREE JURISDICTIONS**

I try not to look at females differently than males. There are very few females in the system and even fewer who have been charged with violent crimes. Sometimes when I have a female offender, I have to stop and ask myself if she's being treated any differently than a male offender. Usually I can honestly say "No." If she's been convicted of possession of a controlled substance and it's her first offense, I'm not going to sentence her to prison; but it's not because she's a female but because she's a first offender.

—Male judge in Cook County (Chicago), Illinois

Of course I look at female offenders differently. They get off easier. I think that the forces that motivate female offenders are different—lack of self esteem as opposed to machismo. In a lot of the cases I see, the woman is more the victim than the offender.

—Male judge in Cook County (Chicago), Illinois

There is a perception that I'm harder on females than on males. I was shocked to learn this because I think I'm very sensitive to women who are trying to raise their kids alone. What I don't like is when they bring their kids to court and try to use them as pawns to get to me. I hate that—using the kids in that way—and I'll tell the woman in no uncertain terms that her children don't belong in court.

—Female judge in Jackson County (Kansas City), Missouri

I'd like to think that being female has no effect on the likelihood of incarceration, but I think that it does. We probably still have that Neanderthal belief that they are the primary caretakers of kids. It may not be irrational to treat women differently—we all know that females are not as likely to commit violent crimes, not as likely to recidivate, and are likely to be the primary caretakers of young children. So, I won't give you the socially desirable answer and tell you that gender is irrelevant in my courtroom.

—Male judge in Jackson County (Kansas City), Missouri

The offender's social and economic circumstances should have no effect on the sentence. However, If the offender is a female with kids at home to take care of, and she's charged with a drug offense, I may be looking for drug treatment rather than jail or prison.

—Male judge in Dade County (Miami), Florida

SOURCE: Personal interviews with the author in 1995.

the three-city study, described above, all indicated that they viewed males and females differently and stated that there were legitimate reasons for sentencing female offenders more leniently than male offenders.[67]

Disparity and Discrimination in Sentencing

Critics of the sentencing process claim that unrestrained judicial discretion leads to disparity and discrimination in sentencing. There are important differences between disparity and discrimination, and both disparity and discrimination can take different forms. Sentencing disparities reflect differences in the sentences imposed on similarly situated offenders by judges in different jurisdictions, by judges in the same jurisdiction, or by individual judges. Sentencing discrimination results from bias or prejudice against racial minorities and the poor or in favor of women. Discrimination in sentencing can be either direct or subtle and can range from systematic to institutional to contextual to individual.

There is compelling evidence of gender disparity in sentencing. Women are substantially less likely than men to be sentenced to prison, women who are incarcerated receive significantly shorter prison terms than men, and women make up less than 2 percent of the death row population. There is also evidence that these differences, which do not disappear when crime seriousness, prior criminal record, and other legally relevant factors are taken into consideration, reflect discrimination in favor of women. The fact that studies of sentencing in federal and state courts found a consistent pattern of preferential treatment of female offenders—coupled with the fact that the gender differences uncovered were large—suggests that contemporary judges evaluate female offenders differently than male offenders. Although some judges and researchers claim there are legitimate reasons for treating women differently than men, these results suggest that gender discrimination in sentencing is not a thing of the past.

Discussion Questions: Chapter 4

1. A researcher collects data on sentences imposed on offenders convicted of felonies in "Midwest City." She discovers that 40 percent of the female offenders and 65 percent of the male offenders were sentenced to prison. What evidence would she need to conclude that this difference was a disparity but did not reflect discrimination? What evidence would suggest that judges were discriminating in favor of women?

2. The researcher conducts further analysis and discovers that women convicted of property crimes are sentenced more leniently than men and women convicted of violent crimes and drug offenses are sentenced no differently than men. Where would this type of discrimination fall on the discrimination continuum?

3. What is the difference between inter-jurisdictional sentencing disparity and intra-jurisdictional sentencing disparity? Why is the latter more problematic than the former?

4. Should judges take the cultural and biological differences between men and women into consideration at sentencing? Why or why not?

5. Daly suggests that "familied" defendants are treated more leniently than "non-familied" defendants. Why? Do Spohn's findings regarding the sentences imposed on female and male drug offenders support this?

6. A reporter for the local newspaper is writing a story on gender differences in sentencing. He asks you to summarize the findings of research on this topic. What will you tell him?

Notes

1. Frankel, *Criminal Sentences: Law Without Order*.
2. Ulmer, *Social Worlds of Sentencing: Court Communities Under Sentencing Guidelines*.
3. The Pennsylvania Sentencing Guidelines are less restrictive than the federal guidelines or than guidelines implemented in states such as Washington and Minnesota. For each combination of crime seriousness and prior criminal record, there is a standard sentence range, an aggravated sentence range, and a mitigated sentence range. Judges are allowed to depart from the guidelines but must provide a written justification for the departure. See Tonry (1996:36-37) and Ulmer (1997:18-19).
4. Ulmer, *Social Worlds of Sentencing*, p. 169.
5. Ibid.
6. Eisenstein, Flemming, and Nardulli, *The Contours of Justice: Communities and Their Courts*.
7. U.S. Department of Justice, Bureau of Justice Statistics (BJS), *Sourcebook of Criminal Justice Statistics, 1998*, Table 5.5 and

Table 5.6; U. S. Sentencing Commission, *1996 Sourcebook of Federal Sentencing Statistics*, Table 12 and Table 13.

8. Forst and Wellford, "Punishment and Sentencing: Developing Sentencing Guidelines Empirically From Principles of Punishment"; Hogarth, *Sentencing as a Human Process*; Uhlman, *Racial Justice: Black Judges and Black Defendants in an Urban Trial Court.*

9. Clancy, Bartolomeo, Richardson and Wellford, "Sentence Decisionmaking: The Logic of Sentence Decisions and the Extent of Sentence Disparity"; Forst and Wellford, "Punishment and Sentencing."

10. Clancy, Bartolomeo, Richardson and Wellford, "Sentence Decisionmaking," p. 553.

11. Uhlman, "Black Elite Decision Making: The Case of Trial Judges."

12. Ibid., p. 890.

13. Gaylin, *Partial Justice: A Study of Bias in Sentencing*, p. 162.

14. *United States v. Grayson*, 438 U.S. 41, 98 S. Ct. 2610 (1978).

15. Ibid.

16. Walker, Spohn, and DeLone, *The Color of Justice: Race, Ethnicity, and Crime in America*, pp. 16-18.

17. Wolfgang and Reidel, "Race, Judicial Discretion and the Death Penalty"; Wolfgang and Reidel, "Rape, Race and the Death Penalty in Georgia."

18. U. S. Department of Justice, Bureau of Justice Assistance, *National Assessment of Structured Sentencing*, p. 80.

19. Walker, Spohn and DeLone, *The Color of Justice*, p. 17.

20. Ibid., p. 18.

21. Zatz, "The Changing Forms of Racial/Ethnic Biases in Sentencing Research," p. 70.

22. Ibid., p. 70.

23. In 1995, 14.5 percent of the urban residents believed that crime was a neighborhood problem, compared with 4.9 percent of suburban residents and 2.2 percent of rural residents. U.S. Department of Justice, BJS, *Sourcebook of Criminal Justice Statistics, 1998*, Table 2.3.

24. In 1998, the proportions who supported the legalization of marijuana were 37 percent (West), 28 percent (Northeast), 27 percent (Midwest), and 22 percent (South). See U.S. Department of Justice, BJS, *Sourcebook of Criminal Justice Statistics, 1998*, Table 2.72.

25. Gaylin, *Partial Justice*, p. 165.
26. Tonry, *Sentencing Matters*, p. 19.
27. U.S. Department of Justice, BJS, *Sourcebook of Criminal Justice Statistics*, 1997, Table 6.35.
28. Ibid., Table 5.19 and Table 5.20.
29. Ibid., Table 5.50 and Table 5.54.
30. U.S. Department of Justice, BJS, *Capital Punishment 1999*, Table 7.
31. Spohn and Beichner, "Is Preferential Treatment of Female Offenders a Thing of the Past? A Multi-Site Study of Gender, Race, and Imprisonment."
32. Daly, *Gender, Crime and Punishment*, p. 197.
33. Steffensmeier, Ulmer, and Kramer, "The Interaction of Race, Gender, and Age in Criminal Sentencing: The Punishment Cost of Being Young, Black, and Male."
34. U.S. Department of Justice, BJS, *Prison and Jail Inmates at Midyear, 1998*.
35. Irwin and Austin, *It's About Time: America's Imprisonment Binge*, p. 1.
36. Chesney-Lind, *The Female Offender: Girls, Women, and Crime*, p. 251.
37. Chesney-Lind, "Rethinking Women's Imprisonment."
38. U.S. Department of Justice, BJS, *New Court Commitments to State Prison*, 1996.
39. U.S. Department of Justice, BJS, *Sourcebook of Criminal Justice Statistics*, 1997, p. 505.
40. Chesney-Lind, "Rethinking Women's Imprisonment," p. 111.
41. Durham, *Crisis and Reform: Current Issues in American Punishment*, p. 111.
42. Daly and Tonry, "Gender, Race and Sentencing," p. 241.
43. Nagel and Johnson, "The Role of Gender in a Structured Sentencing System: Equal Treatment, Policy Choices, and the Sentencing of Female Offenders Under the United States Sentencing Guidelines"; Williams, "Equality's Riddle: Pregnancy and the Equal Treatment/Special Treatment Debate."
44. Wolgast, *Equality and the Rights of Women*.
45. Raeder, "Gender and Sentencing: Single Moms, Battered Women, and Other Sex-Based Anomalies in the Gender-Free World of the Federal Sentencing Guidelines," p. 959.

46. Daly, *Gender, Crime, and Punishment,* p. 270.
47. The coefficients for gender were as follows: $B = .977$; $SE = .184$; *Odds Ratio* = 2.66.
48. Albonetti, "Sentencing Under the Federal Sentencing Guidelines: Effects of Defendant Characteristics, Guilty Pleas, and Departures on Sentence Outcomes for Drug Offenses"; Chiricos and Bales, "Unemployment and Punishment: An Empirical Assessment"; Kramer and Steffensmeier, "Race and Imprisonment Decisions"; Myers, "Symbolic Policy and the Sentencing of Drug Offenders"; Peterson and Hagan, "Changing Conceptions of Race: Toward an Account of Anomalous Findings in Sentencing Research"; Unnever, "Direct and Organizational Discrimination in the Sentencing of Drug Offenders"; Unnever and Hembroff, "The Prediction of Racial/Ethnic Sentencing Disparities: An Expectation States Approach."
49. Albonetti, "Sentencing Under the Federal Sentencing Guidelines."
50. Ibid., p. 818.
51. Spohn, "Gender and Sentencing of Drug Offenders: Is Chivalry Dead?"
52. Ibid., p. 392.
53. Ibid., p. 373.
54. Ibid., p. 392.
55. Steffensmeier, Kramer, and Streifel, "Gender and Imprisonment Decisions."
56. Spohn and Beichner, "Is Preferential Treatment of Female Defendants a Thing of the Past?"
57. Steffensmeier, Kramer, and Streifel, "Gender and Imprisonment Decisions"; Steffensmeier, Ulmer, and Kramer, "The Interaction of Race, Gender, and Age in Criminal Sentencing."
58. Daly, "Gender, Crime and Punishment"; Daly, "Neither Conflict nor Labeling nor Paternalism Will Suffice: Intersections of Race, Ethnicity, Gender, and Family in Criminal Court Decisions"; Daly, "Structure and Practice of Familial-Based Justice in a Criminal Court." See, also, Kruttschnitt, "Social Status and Sentences of Female Offenders."
59. Daly, "Structure and Practice of Familial-Based Justice in a Criminal Court," p. 268.

60. Daly, "Neither Conflict nor Labeling nor Paternalism Will Suffice," p. 138.
61. Daly, "Structure and Practice of Familial-Based Justice in a Criminal Court," p. 279.
62. Daly, *Gender, Crime and Punishment*, p. 227.
63. Ibid., p. 260.
64. Daly, "Structure and Practice of Familial-Based Justice in a Criminal Court"; also see Bickle and Peterson, "The Impact of Gender-Based Family Roles on Criminal Sentencing"; Crew, "Sex Differences in Criminal Sentencing: Chivalry or Patriarchy?"
65. Spohn and Beichner, "Is Preferential Treatment of Female Defendants a Thing of the Past?"
66. Ibid., p. 174-175.
67. These comments were made by judges who were interviewed by Spohn and DeLone for their study of sentencing decisions in three large urban jurisdictions. For a description of that study, see Spohn and DeLone (2000).

Chapter Five

Sentencing Disparity and Discrimination

A Focus on Race/Ethnicity

Racism goes beyond prejudicial discrimination and bigotry.
It arises from outlooks, stereotypes, and fears of which we are vastly
unaware. Our historical experience has made racism an integral
part of our culture even though society has more recently embraced
an ideal that rejects racism as immoral. . . . Most Americans have
grown beyond the evils of overt racial malice, but still have not
completely shed the deeply rooted cultural bias that differentiates
between "them" and "us."

U.S. District Court Judge Clyde S. Cahill[1]

In 1944, Gunnar Myrdal, a Swedish economist who examined race relations in the United States during the late 1930s, concluded in *An American Dilemma* that "the whole judicial system of courts, sentences and prisons in the South is overripe for fundamental reforms."[2] His analysis, which relied primarily on anecdotal accounts of differential treatment of blacks and whites in southern court systems, documented widespread racial discrimination in court processing and sentencing. Myrdal observed that black defendants were handled informally and with a lack of dignity and stated that convictions often were obtained with only "scanty evidence." He noted that grand juries routinely refused to indict whites for crimes against blacks, that those who were indicted were rarely convicted, and that those who were convicted received only the mildest punishment. In contrast, blacks convicted of, or even suspected of, crimes against whites were treated very harshly. Myrdal stated that in cases involving black suspects and white victims, "The court makes no pretense at justice; the Negro must be condemned, and usually condemned to death, before the crowd gets him."[3]

Several highly publicized cases confirm the validity of Myrdal's accusations. Take the case of the "Scottsboro Boys." In March of 1931, nine black teenage boys were accused of raping two white girls on a slow-moving freight train traveling through Alabama. They were arrested and taken to Scottsboro, Alabama, where they were indicted for rape, a capital offense. Within a short time period, all nine were tried and convicted by all-white juries, and eight of the nine were sentenced to death. In 1932, the U.S. Supreme Court overturned their convictions on the grounds that they had been denied the right to counsel at trial.[4] The Scottsboro Boys were quickly retried, reconvicted, and resentenced to death, despite the fact that one of the alleged victims had recanted and questions were raised about the credibility of the other victim's testimony. In 1935, the Supreme Court again reversed their convictions, this time ruling that the exclusion of blacks from jury service deprived black defendants of their right to the equal protection of the laws guaranteed by the Fourteenth Amendment.[5]

Less than 8 months after the Supreme Court's decision, a grand jury composed of 13 whites and 1 black returned new indictments against the nine defendants. The state eventually dropped the charges against four of the nine defendants, and allowed a fifth to plead to a lesser charge, but the other four defendants were convicted of rape a third time. One was sentenced to death, one was sentenced to 99 years in prison, and the remaining two were sentenced to 75 years in prison. Collectively, the nine Scottsboro Boys served 104 years in prison for a crime that many believe was "almost certainly a hoax."[6]

Also consider the case of Ed Johnson, a black man accused of raping a white woman in Chattanooga, Tennessee, in 1906.[7] There was no evidence other than the word of a paid informant to connect Johnson to the crime.

Moreover, more than a dozen witnesses testified that Johnson, who steadfastly maintained his innocence, was working at a local tavern when the crime occurred. The attorneys prosecuting the case described Johnson's alibi witnesses, most of whom were black, as "thugs, thieves and sots—the offscourings of hell" and urged the jurors to "send that black brute to the gallows."[8] Seventeen days after the crime had been committed, the jurors decided to do just that. They convicted Ed Johnson of rape, which, under Tennessee law at that time, resulted in an automatic death sentence. His execution was scheduled for 5 weeks later.

The execution never took place. After the U.S. Supreme Court issued an order staying the execution pending Johnson's appeal to the federal courts, a white lynching mob snatched him from the Hamilton County jail, marched him through town, and hung him from a bridge spanning the Tennessee River. Fifty-three days after he was arrested for rape, Ed Johnson, whose last words were, "God bless you all, I am innocent," was dead.[9] A grand jury was convened to investigate the lynching, but none of the witnesses who were called to testify could identify any of the members of the lynch mob. The grand jury issued no indictments.[10]

Racial Disparity in Sentencing

The two cases described above illustrate overt discrimination directed against black criminal defendants. However, these events took place in the early part of the 20th century, and much has changed since then. The flagrant racism described in *An American Dilemma* and documented in cases such as those involving the Scottsboro Boys and Ed Johnson has been eliminated. Whites who commit crimes against members of racial minorities are not beyond the reach of the criminal justice system, blacks suspected of crimes against whites do not receive "justice" at the hands of white lynching mobs, and racial minorities who victimize other racial minorities are not immune from punishment. As we enter the 21st century, we find little evidence of "widespread systematic racial discrimination in sentencing."[11]

But has equality under the law been achieved? Or is the sentencing process in the United States today characterized by more subtle, but no less real, institutional or contextual discrimination? Consider the following statistics:

- At the end of 1999, there were 3,527 prisoners under sentence of death in the United States. Of these, 1,948 (55.2 percent) were white, 1,514 (43.0 percent) were black, and 65 (1.8 percent) were American Indian, Asian, or other races.[12]

- In 1999, the rate of incarceration (per 100,000 citizens) was 3,408 for black males, 1,335 for Hispanic males, and 417 for white males. For females, the rates ranged from 27 (whites) to 87 (Hispanics) to 212 (blacks). For males aged 25 to 29, the rates were 9,392 for blacks, 3,126 for Hispanics, and 990 for whites. For males in this age group, in other words, the incarceration rate for blacks was nearly 10 times the rate for whites.[13]

- Sixty-five percent of the black offenders convicted of violent crimes in state courts in 1996 were sentenced to prison, but only 51 percent of the white offenders. The figures for offenders convicted of drug offenses were 43 percent (blacks) and 27 percent (whites).[14]

- Black and Hispanic offenders convicted of felonies in Chicago, Miami, and Kansas City faced greater odds of incarceration than whites. In Chicago, 66 percent of the blacks, 59 percent of the Hispanics and 51 percent of the whites were incarcerated. In Miami, 51 percent of the blacks, 40 percent of the Hispanics, and 35 percent of the whites were incarcerated. In Kansas City, the incarceration rates were 46 percent (blacks), 40 percent (Hispanics) and 36 percent (whites).[15]

These statistics, like the statistics documenting preferential treatment of female offenders presented in Chapter 4, provide compelling evidence of *disparity* in sentencing. They indicate that the sentences imposed on black and Hispanic offenders are different—that is, harsher—than the sentences imposed on white offenders. These statistics, however, do not tell us *why* this occurs. They do not tell us whether the racial disparities in sentencing reflect racial discrimination and if so, whether that discrimination is institutional or contextual, direct or subtle.

Explanations for Racial Disparity in Sentencing

We suggest that there are at least four possible explanations for racial disparity in sentencing, only three of which reflect racial discrimination. These explanations are summarized in Box 5.1. First, the differences in sentence severity could be due to the fact that blacks and Hispanics commit more serious crimes and have more serious prior criminal records than whites. As explained in Chapter 3, studies of sentencing decisions have consistently demonstrated the importance of these two legally relevant factors. Offenders who are convicted of more serious offenses, use a weapon to commit the crime, or seriously injure the victim receive harsher sentences, as do offenders who have prior felony convictions. The more severe sentences imposed on black and Hispanic offenders, then, might reflect the influence of these legally prescribed factors rather than the effect of racial prejudice on the part of judges.

The differences could also result from economic discrimination. Poor defendants are not as likely as middle- or upper-class defendants to have private attorneys or to be released prior to trial. They are also more likely to be unemployed. All of these factors may be related to sentence severity. Defendants represented by private attorneys or released prior to trial may receive more lenient sentences than those represented by public defenders or in custody prior to trial. Unemployed defendants may be sentenced more harshly than the employed. Given that black and Hispanic defendants are more likely than white defendants to be poor, economic discrimination amounts to *indirect* racial discrimination.

Third, the differences could be due to *direct* racial discrimination on the part of judges. They could be due to the fact that judges take the race/ethnicity of the offender into account in determining the appropriate sentence. This implies that judges who are confronted with black, Hispanic, and white offenders convicted of similar crimes and with similar prior crim-

---

BOX 5.1

**FOUR EXPLANATIONS FOR
RACIAL DISPARITIES IN SENTENCING**

Blacks and Hispanics are sentenced more harshly than whites. . . .

1. Because they commit more serious crimes and have more serious prior criminal records than whites.

   Conclusion: racial disparity but not racial discrimination.

2. Because they are more likely than whites to be poor. Being poor is associated with a greater likelihood of pretrial detention and unemployment, both of which may lead to harsher sentences.

   Conclusion: indirect (i.e., economic) discrimination.

3. Because of judges' bias or prejudice against racial minorities.

   Conclusion: direct racial discrimination.

4. In some contexts but not in others.

   Conclusion: subtle (i.e., contextual) racial discrimination.

inal records impose harsher sentences on members of racial minorities than on whites. It implies that judges, the majority of whom are white, stereotype black and Hispanic offenders as more violent, more dangerous, and less amenable to rehabilitation than white offenders.[16]

Finally, the sentencing disparities could reflect both equal treatment and discrimination, depending on the nature of the crime, the racial composition of the victim-offender dyad, the type of jurisdiction, the age and gender of the offender, and so on. It is possible, in other words, that racial minorities who commit certain types of crimes (e.g., forgery) are treated no differently than whites who commit these crimes, whereas those who commit other types of crimes (e.g., sexual assault) are sentenced more harshly than their white counterparts. Similarly, it is possible that racial discrimination in the application of the death penalty is confined to the South or to cases involving black offenders and white victims. As we noted earlier, this type of discrimination is what Walker and his colleagues refer to as "contextual discrimination."[17] It is discrimination that is found in particular contexts or under certain circumstances.

As illustrated by the quotes from criminal justice officials in Chicago, Miami, and Kansas City (see Box 5.2), each of these four explanations is plausible. Social scientists have conducted dozens of studies designed to determine which of the explanations is most convincing.[18] These studies generally fall into one of two categories: (a) those that use aggregate data on prison populations and attempt to explain why the incarceration rate for blacks is substantially higher than the rate for whites and (b) those that examine judges' sentencing decisions and attempt to determine if race/ethnicity is a statistically significant predictor of those decisions. Included in the second category are studies that focus explicitly on racial disparities in the use of the death penalty.

In the sections that follow, we discuss the results of empirical research on race/ethnicity and sentencing. We begin by discussing research that focuses on the disproportionate number of racial minorities incarcerated in state and federal prisons. We then present the results of research examining the effect of race on judges' sentencing decisions. We conclude with a discussion of research analyzing racial disparities in the use of the death penalty. Our purpose is not simply to add another voice to the contentious debate over the *existence* of racial discrimination in sentencing. Although we do attempt to determine whether recent research provides convincing evidence of direct racial discrimination, we believe that this is a theoretically unsophisticated and incomplete approach to studying a complex phenomenon. It is overly simplistic to assume that racial minorities will be sentenced

BOX 5.2

DOES RACE/ETHNICITY AFFECT SENTENCE SEVERITY? PERCEPTIONS OF CRIMINAL JUSTICE OFFICIALS IN THREE JURISDICTIONS

Race has absolutely nothing to do with sentence severity. It doesn't come into play in my courtroom at all!

> —Judge in Dade County (Miami), Florida

Race has no effect on my sentencing decisions. The problem is that education and poverty are linked to race, and these things do matter. I resent it when people say we have a racist criminal justice system. The reason more blacks are in prison is because they are more likely to be poor and uneducated and those who are poor and uneducated are more likely to commit crimes.

> —Judge in Cook County (Chicago), Illinois

My judge is out to get everyone, but I swear that she treats whites better than blacks or Hispanics.

> —Prosecutor in Dade County (Miami), Florida

I think that judges do take the race of the offender and the race of the victim into account. For example, about 8 years ago, there was a white guy who was working in a liquor store. A customer—a black guy who was a real jerk—came into the store and started raising hell. The clerk told him to leave, but the guy told him to go to hell. The clerk pumped four slugs into the guy's back as he walked out the door. The defendant originally was charged with first-degree murder, but the prosecutor reduced it to voluntary manslaughter. The judge gave him a 120-day callback sentence and pulled the guy out after he'd spent the 120 days in prison. Now, I can't prove that the judge based his decision on race, but there is absolutely no doubt in my mind that if the defendant had been black he'd still be doing time.

> —Prosecutor in Jackson County (Kansas City), Missouri

A lot of the racism is subtle. You can sit in court and watch the judge's expression and demeanor change when a black or Hispanic defendant who "looks dangerous" comes into court. It's subtle, but it definitely exists.

> —Public Defender in Dade County (Miami), Florida

I believe that race does come into play, particularly if you have a black offender and a white victim. It shouldn't matter, but I know it does.

> —Public Defender in Jackson County (Kansas City), Missouri

SOURCE: Personal interviews with the author in 1995.

more harshly than whites for all types of crimes and under varying sets of circumstances. The more interesting question is this: "When does race matter?" It is this question that we attempt to answer.

Race and Imprisonment: Evidence of Disproportionality

There is irrefutable evidence that blacks comprise a disproportionate share of the U.S. prison population. At the end of 1999, there were 1,222,799 persons incarcerated in state and federal prisons; 46 percent of these inmates were black, 33 percent were white, and 18 percent were Hispanic. Blacks, in other words, comprise only 13 percent of the United States' population but nearly half of the prison population. The disparities are even more dramatic for males, particularly for males in their 20s and 30s. As shown in Exhibit 5.1, the incarceration rates for black males in these age groups are 8 to 9 times higher than the rates for white males and 2.5 to 3 times higher than the rates for Hispanic males. When these data are expressed as percentages, they reveal that 9.4 percent of all black males aged 25 to 29 were in prison, compared with 3.1 percent of Hispanic males and 1.0 percent of white males. Although the absolute numbers are much smaller, the pattern for females is similar. The incarceration rate for black females is significantly greater than the rates for Hispanic or white females.[19]

Other statistics confirm that members of racial minorities face a disproportionately high risk of incarceration. In 1996, for example, more blacks were under some form of correctional supervision (jail, prison, probation, and parole) than were enrolled in college. Among whites, the situation was just the opposite: There were more than 3 times as many whites in college as there were under correctional supervision.[20] There were also substantial racial and ethnic differences in the "lifetime likelihood of imprisonment." A black boy born in 1991 faced a 29-percent chance of being imprisoned at some point in his life, compared with a 16-percent likelihood for a Hispanic boy and a 4-percent likelihood for a white boy.[21]

The crimes for which members of racial minorities and whites are imprisoned also differ. Although the proportions held in state prisons in 1998 for violent offenses were similar, blacks and Hispanics were much more likely than whites to be imprisoned for drug offenses. Twenty-seven percent of the Hispanics and 25.4 percent of the blacks were imprisoned for drug offenses, compared with only 11.5 percent of the whites. Drug of-

Exhibit 5.1 Number of Persons Incarcerated in State and Federal Prison, per 100,000 residents, 1999

	Males			Females		
Age	Black	Hispanic	White	Black	Hispanic	White
20-24	7,326	2,824	832	227	127	44
25-29	9,392	3,126	990	492	215	66
30-34	8,406	2,927	1,106	731	248	96
35-39	7,316	2,315	896	587	214	74

SOURCE: From Prisoners in 1999 (Table 14), by the U.S. Department of Justice, Bureau of Justice Statistics, 2000. Washington, DC: Author.

fenses also constituted a larger share of the growth in state prison inmates for members of racial minorities than for whites. From 1990 to 1998, increases in drug offenders accounted for 25 percent of the total growth among black inmates, 18 percent of the growth among Hispanic inmates, and 12 percent of the growth among white inmates.[22]

As all of these statistics indicate, blacks and Hispanics, particularly black and Hispanic males, are substantially more likely than whites to be locked up in our nation's prisons.

These statistics suggest that state and federal judges sentence a disproportionately high number of racial minorities to prison and/or that racial minorities are sentenced to serve longer terms than whites. The question, of course, is why this occurs.

Race and Imprisonment:
Differential Involvement or Differential Treatment?

In 1918, the Bureau of the Census published a report on the "Negro Population."[23] The authors of the report noted that blacks made up only 11 percent of the population but constituted 22 percent of the inmates of prisons, penitentiaries, jails, reform schools and workhouses. The authors then posed a question that would spark debate and generate controversy throughout the 20th century:

> While these figures . . . will probably be generally accepted as indicating that there is more criminality and lawbreaking among Negroes than among whites and while that conclusion is probably justified by the facts . . . it is a question whether the difference . . . may not be to some extent the result of discrimination in the treatment of white and Negro offenders on the part of the community and the courts.[24]

This question—whether the disproportionate number of racial minorities incarcerated in state and federal prison might be "to some extent the result of discrimination"—is a question that is still being asked today. Those on one side of the debate contend that the war on crime and, particularly, the war on drugs has "caused the ever harsher treatment of blacks by the criminal justice system."[25] They charge that the overrepresentation of blacks in arrest and imprisonment statistics reflects systematic racial discrimination.[26] Those on the other side assert that these results can be attributed primarily to the disproportionate involvement of blacks in serious criminal activity[27] and argue that the idea of systematic discrimination within the criminal justice system is a "myth."[28] Others take a more moderate position, arguing that the disparities result "to some extent" from differential treatment but denying that they reflect systematic discrimination.[29]

Researchers have used a variety of strategies to resolve this issue and to determine whether and to what extent the disparities in imprisonment reflect differential involvement in crime or differential treatment by the criminal justice system. The most frequently cited work compares the racial disparity in arrest rates for serious crimes with the racial disparity in incarceration rates for these crimes. According to Alfred Blumstein, if there is no discrimination following arrest, then "one would expect to find the racial distribution of prisoners who were sentenced for any particular crime type to be the same as the racial distribution of persons arrested for that crime."[30] If, for example, 60 percent of those arrested for robbery were black and 60 percent of those incarcerated for robbery were black, we would conclude (assuming no bias in the decision to arrest or not) that the disproportionate number of blacks imprisoned for robbery reflected differential involvement in robbery by blacks.

To determine the overall portion of the racial disproportionality in prison populations that could be attributed to differential involvement in crime, Blumstein calculated the proportion of the prison population that, based on arrest rates, was expected to be black for 12 separate violent, property, and drug offenses. He then compared these expected rates with the actual rates of incarceration for blacks. Using 1979 data, he found that 80 percent of the racial disproportionality in incarceration rates could be attributed to racial differences in arrest rates.[31] He reached a similar conclusion when he replicated the analysis using 1991 data: 76 percent of the racial disproportionality in incarceration rates was accounted for by racial differences in arrest rates.[32] Blumstein stressed that these results did not mean that racial discrimination did not exist. As he noted, "There are too many anecdotal reports of such discrimination to dismiss that possibility." Rather, his findings implied that "the bulk of the racial disproportionality in prison is attributable to differential involvement in arrest, and probably in crime, in those most serious offenses that tend to lead to imprisonment."[33]

Blumstein's oft-cited conclusion that 80 percent of the racial disproportionality in prison populations can be explained by racial differences in arrest rates has not gone unchallenged.[34] His work has been criticized for assuming that arrests are good measures of criminal involvement and that the number of arrests for serious violent crimes is the primary determinant of the number of persons incarcerated. Tonry, for example, has pointed out that proportions of blacks and whites among those arrested for the offenses most likely to lead to imprisonment did not change appreciably from 1976 to 1992. During this time period, whites accounted for 50 percent to 54 percent of all arrests for violent crimes; blacks accounted for 44 percent to 47 percent.[35] If Blumstein's assumption about the relationship between arrest rates for serious violent crimes and incarceration rates were correct, we would have expected relative stability in the proportions of whites and blacks admitted to prison over this time period. This is not what happened. Instead, the percentage of blacks admitted to state and federal prisons increased from 35 percent in 1976 to 54 percent in 1992.[36] The fact that the percentage of blacks among those arrested for crime was stable while the percentage of blacks among those admitted to prison increased substantially, in other words, raises questions about one of Blumstein's underlying assumptions.

Blumstein has also been criticized for using national-level data, which may mask discrimination in some regions or states.[37] If some states incarcerate more blacks than would be expected (based on arrest) and other states incarcerate fewer blacks than would be expected, the resulting "national average" would hide these between-state differences. In fact, research conducted following the publication of Blumstein's work has revealed considerable interstate variability. Hawkins and Hardy's analysis of state-by-state data found that the percentage of the racial disproportionality in imprisonment that could be explained by arrest ranged from 22 percent in New Mexico to 96 percent in Indiana and Missouri. In nine states, arrest accounted for 40 percent or less of the disproportionality in imprisonment; in six states, arrest accounted for more than 80 percent of the variation.[38] Thus, according to Hawkins and Hardy, "Blumstein's figure of 80 percent would not seem to be a good approximation for all states."[39]

A related criticism of Blumstein's work focuses on his failure to consider the possibility of "off-setting forms of discrimination that are equally objectionable but not observable in the aggregate."[40] If, for example, blacks convicted of murdering whites face a substantially higher likelihood of imprisonment than whites, whereas blacks convicted of murdering other blacks have significantly lower odds of imprisonment than whites, the overall imprisonment rate for blacks might be very similar to the rate for whites. Aggregating the data, as Blumstein did, would mask these differences in the treatment of blacks based on the race of the victim.

Race and Imprisonment: The Impact of the War on Drugs

Blumstein's estimate that 80 percent (76 percent in 1991) of the racial disproportionality in imprisonment could be explained by racial differentials in arrest rates did not apply to each of the crimes he examined. For some crimes, arrest explained more than 80 percent of the disparity, but for others, arrest accounted for substantially less than 80 percent. In both 1979 and 1991, there was a fairly close match between the race distribution in prison and the race distribution at arrest for homicide, robbery, and (to a lesser extent) burglary. For drug offenses, on the other hand, blacks were overrepresented in prison by nearly 50 percent.[41] Racial differences in arrest rates for drug offenses, in other words, could explain only half of the racial disproportionality in imprisonment for drug offenses.

Blumstein himself acknowledged the significance of this finding. He noted that the percentage of drug offenders in the prison population had increased almost fourfold from 1979 to 1991. Drug offenders comprised 5.7 percent of the total prison population in 1979, compared with 21.5 percent in 1991. Blumstein also noted (a) that "arrests for drug offenses are far less likely to be a good proxy for offending patterns than they are for aggravated assault, murder, and robbery" and (b) that the black arrest rate for drug offenses had "grown dramatically in the late 1980s."[42] In other words, the fact that drug offenders comprise an increasing share of the prison population coupled with the fact that blacks are increasingly likely to be arrested for drug offenses means that "a declining proportion of the prison population can be explained by higher rates of crime."[43]

Blumstein concluded that his findings regarding drug offenses "raise serious questions about the degree to which the policy associated with the drug war has significantly exacerbated the racial disproportionality in prison."[44] Other critics contend that the evidence does more than simply "raise questions" about the policies pursued during the war on drugs. Mauer, for example, charges that "Since 1980, no policy has contributed more to the incarceration of African Americans than the 'war on drugs.'"[45]

Lynch and Sabol assert that there has been "an increased targeting of black working-and middle-class areas for discretionary drug enforcement and ultimately increased incarceration for drug offenses."[46] And Miller, who characterizes the war on drugs as a "disaster-in-waiting for African Americans from the day of its conception," contends that "from the first shot fired in the drug war African-Americans were targeted, arrested, and imprisoned in wildly disproportionate numbers."[47]

Tonry's assessment is even more blunt.[48] He charges that officials in the Reagan and Bush administrations knew that the war on drugs would be waged primarily in poor minority communities and that these officials knew, or should have known, that the outcome of the war would be a worsening of racial disparities in imprisonment. He also argues that the architects of the drug war knew, or again, should have known, that (a) imprisonment would not deter drug use or drug-related crime, (b) both drug abuse education and substance abuse treatment were more effective policy choices, and (c) the choice of punishment rather than education or treatment would destroy the lives of countless young blacks. According to Tonry, "The architects of the War on Drugs should be held morally accountable for the havoc they have wrought among disadvantaged members of minority groups."[49]

Randall Kennedy, an African American law professor at Harvard University, disagrees with Tonry's conclusions.[50] Although he acknowledges that the war on drugs "largely explains why, in recent years, the incarceration rate among blacks has exponentially superceded the rate among whites,"[51] Kennedy nonetheless argues that allegations of racial discrimination are "insufficiently substantiated." He asserts that there is little evidence that the policies pursued during the war on drugs resulted from intentional discrimination. He notes, for example, that those who condemn the 100-to-1 punishment disparity for crack and powder cocaine as racist fail to consider the fact that half of the black members of the House of Representatives voted in favor of the disparity and that none of them branded the bill as racist.[52] Kennedy also disagrees with those who assert that punishing crack cocaine more harshly than powder cocaine is racist because it imposes a burden on blacks as a class. As he notes, the enhanced punishment for crack offenses "falls not upon blacks as a class but only upon a distinct subset of the black population—those in violation of the crack law."[53]

Kennedy further suggests that labeling the policies pursued during the war on drugs "racist"—and thus, by implication, those who designed and implemented those policies—is counterproductive. These types of allegations, according to Kennedy, "divert the discussion from the broad ground of whether a given policy is wise to the narrower, more treacherous ground of whether a given policy is racially discriminatory."[54] By calling into question both the judgment and the motives of those who support such policies, assertions of racism also "elevate the stakes and polarize the antagonists."[55] Although he admits that the war on drugs may be mistaken or misguided, Kennedy argues that "being mistaken is different from being racist, and the difference is one that greatly matters."[56]

The Racial Disproportionality in Imprisonment

The research conducted during the past three decades suggests that an answer to the question posed by the Bureau of the Census in 1918 remains elusive. The results of the studies conducted by Blumstein and by those who replicated and refined his approach indicate that some portion of the racial disproportionality in prison populations can be attributed to the fact that blacks are arrested for serious violent crimes at a higher rate than whites. It is true that we do not know whether the percentage that can be explained away in this fashion is 80 percent, 76 percent, or something less. However, even those who criticize Blumstein's approach acknowledge that the higher black arrest rate for violent crimes is the *main reason* that blacks, particularly young black males, are locked up at dramatically higher rates than whites. As Kennedy observes, "That relative to their percentage of the population, blacks commit more street crime than do whites is a fact and not a figment of a Negrophobe's imagination."[57]

It is also true, however, that the black-white disparity in incarceration rates, which has worsened since the Bureau of the Census published its report in 1918, results "to some extent" from racial discrimination. Again, we do not know precisely how much of the disparity can be attributed to discrimination. Blumstein conceded that at least some of the "other 20 percent"—that is, the 20 percent of the racial disproportionality that could not be explained by arrest—might reflect "a residual effect that is explainable only as racial discrimination."[58] The fact that (a) the proportion of blacks arrested for serious violent crime has not increased but the proportion of blacks arrested for drug offenses has skyrocketed and (b) increasingly large proportions of prisoners are incarcerated for drug offenses suggests that the extent to which racial disparity in imprisonment can be accounted for by racial differences in arrests for serious violent crimes may be declining. It also suggests that the source of the discrimination in imprisonment is the war on drugs and the concomitant belief that incarceration is the appropriate penalty for drug offenses.

Considering all the evidence, it seems reasonable to conclude that the racial disproportionality in the prison population results to a large extent from racial disparities in criminal involvement but to some extent from racial discrimination at various stages in the criminal justice process.

Race and Judges' Sentencing Decisions

Prior to the Civil War, state laws provided different levels of punishment for blacks and whites. Slaves, in particular, were subject to harsher punishment. In Virginia, for example, slaves were subject to the death penalty for 73 offenses, whites for 1 offense. Sexual assault statutes also provided different punishments depending on the race of the victim. The Georgia Penal Code of 1816 prescribed the death penalty for the rape of a white woman by a slave or a free person of color. In contrast, the maximum penalty for the rape of a white woman by a white man was 20 years in prison, and a white man convicted of raping a black woman could be fined or imprisoned at the court's discretion.[59] These racially discriminatory punishment differences reflected both a devaluation of black victims and a belief that strong measures were needed to restrain and control blacks, particularly black men, who were regarded as "primitive, wild, inferior beings."[60] As a North Carolina Supreme Court Justice stated in 1830, "The more debased or licentious a class of society is, the more rigorous must be the penal rules of restraint."[61]

Although these types of explicit statutory discrimination have been eliminated, critics of the sentencing process contend that their legacy lives on. Legal scholars and social scientists allege that criminal justice officials continue to regard members of racial minorities, especially young black and Hispanic men, as more dangerous, more threatening, and less reformable than whites. They claim that as a result, judges impose harsher sentences on members of racial minorities, particularly on those who victimize whites. Charges of racial discrimination have been directed at all aspects of the sentencing process, but the harshest criticism is reserved for capital sentencing. Echoing former Supreme Court Justice Harry A. Blackmun, who stated in 1994 that he felt "morally and intellectually obligated simply to concede that the death penalty experiment has failed,"[62] critics charge that "the most profound expression of racial discrimination in sentencing occurs in the use of capital punishment."[63]

In the sections that follow, we address the issue of racial discrimination in sentencing. We focus on the results of research that uses data regarding sentences imposed by judges in a particular jurisdiction to determine whether members of racial minorities are sentenced more harshly than whites. Consistent with the research on gender disparities in sentencing discussed in Chapter 4, these studies attempt to determine whether race/ethnicity is a significant predictor of sentence severity once crime seriousness, prior criminal record, and other legally relevant factors are taken into account. The more sophisticated research also focuses on whether race has indirect effects on sentence outcomes and/or interacts with other predictors of sentencing (see Box 5.1). These more sophisticated studies, in other words, do not focus simply on determining *whether* race makes a difference but on identifying the *contexts in which* race makes a difference.

We begin our discussion of race, ethnicity, and sentencing decisions by summarizing the findings of several reviews of this voluminous body of research. We then present the results of several recent studies, each of which addresses the question "When does race matter?" We conclude the chapter with a discussion of racial discrimination in the use of the death penalty.

Research on Race and Sentencing: A Summary of the Research Findings

Social scientists have conducted dozens of studies designed to untangle the complex relationship between race and sentence severity. In fact, as Zatz notes, this issue "may well have been the major research inquiry for studies of sentencing in the 1970s and early 1980s."[64] The studies that have been conducted vary enormously in theoretical and methodological sophistication. They range from (a) simple bivariate comparisons of incarceration rates for whites and members of racial minorities to (b) methodologically more rigorous multivariate analyses designed to identify direct race effects to (c) more sophisticated designs incorporating tests for indirect race effects and interaction between race and other predictors of sentence severity. The findings generated by these studies and the conclusions drawn by their authors also vary.

Reviews of Recent Research

Studies conducted from the 1930s through the 1960s generally concluded that racial disparities in sentencing reflected overt racial discrimination. For example, the author of one of the earliest sentencing studies, published in 1935, claimed that "equality before the law is a social fiction."[65] Reviews of these early studies,[66] however, found that most of them were methodologically flawed: They typically used simple bivariate statistical techniques, and they failed to control adequately for crime seriousness and prior criminal record.

The conclusions of these early reviews coupled with the findings of its own review of sentencing research[67] led the National Research Council Panel on Sentencing Research to state (in 1983) that the sentencing process was not characterized by "a widespread systematic pattern of discrimination." Rather, "some pockets of discrimination are found for particular judges, particular crime types, and in particular settings."[68] Marjorie Zatz, who reviewed the results of four waves of race and sentencing research conducted from the 1930s through the early 1980s, reached a somewhat different conclusion.[69] Although she acknowledged that "it would be misleading to suggest that race/ethnicity is *the* major determinant of sanctioning," Zatz nonetheless asserted that "race/ethnicity is *a* determinant of sanctioning, and a potent one at that."[70]

The two most recent reviews of research on race and sentencing confirm Zatz's assertion. Chiricos and Crawford reviewed 38 studies published between 1979 and 1991 that included tests for the direct effect of race on sentencing decisions in noncapital cases.[71] Unlike previous reviews, they distinguished results involving the decision to incarcerate or not from those involving the length of sentence decision. Chiricos and Crawford also considered whether the effect of race varied depending on structural or contextual conditions. They asked whether the impact of race would be stronger "in southern jurisdictions, in places where there is a higher percentage of Blacks in the population or a higher concentration of Blacks in urban areas, and in places with a higher rate of unemployment."[72] Noting that two thirds of the studies examined had been published subsequent to Kleck's earlier review, Chiricos and Crawford stated that their assessment "provides a fresh look at an issue that some may have considered all but closed."[73]

The authors' assessment of the findings of these 38 studies revealed "significant evidence of a *direct* impact of race on imprisonment."[74] This effect, which persisted even after the effects of crime seriousness and prior criminal record were controlled, was found only for the decision to incarcerate or not; it was not found for the length of sentence decision. Chiricos and Crawford also identified a number of structural contexts that conditioned the race/imprisonment relationship. Black offenders faced significantly greater odds of incarceration than white offenders in the South, in places where blacks comprised a larger percentage of the population, and in places where the unemployment rate was high.

Spohn's[75] review of noncapital sentencing research that used data from the 1980s and 1990s also highlighted the importance of attempting to identify "the structural and contextual conditions that are most likely to result in racial discrimination."[76] Spohn reviewed 40 studies examining the relationship between race, ethnicity, and sentencing. This included 32 studies of state-level sentencing decisions and 8 studies of sentencing at the federal level. Consistent with the conclusions of Chiricos and Crawford, Spohn reported that many of these studies found a *direct race effect*. At both the state and federal levels, there was evidence that blacks and Hispanics were more likely than whites to be sentenced to prison. At the federal level, there was also evidence that blacks received longer sentences than whites.[77]

Noting that "evidence concerning direct racial effects . . . provides few clues to the circumstances under which race matters,"[78] Spohn also evaluated the 40 studies included in her review for evidence of indirect or contextual discrimination. She did acknowledge that some of the evidence was contradictory: For example, some studies revealed that racial disparities were confined to offenders with less serious prior criminal records, whereas others reported such disparities only among offenders with more serious criminal histories. However, Spohn nonetheless concluded that the studies revealed four "themes" or "patterns" of contextual effects. These themes are summarized in Box 5.3 and discussed in more detail below.

The first theme or pattern revealed by the studies Spohn reviewed was that the combination of race/ethnicity and other legally irrelevant offender characteristics produces greater sentence disparity than race/ethnicity alone. That is, the studies demonstrated that certain minorities—males, the young, the unemployed, the less educated—are singled out for harsher treatment. Some studies found that each of these offender characteristics, including race/ethnicity, had a direct effect on sentence outcomes but the combination of race/ethnicity and one or more of the other characteristics was a more powerful predictor of sentence severity than any characteristic individually. Other studies found that race/ethnicity had an effect only when the offender was male, young, and/or unemployed.[79]

The second pattern of indirect/interaction effects, according to Spohn, was that a number of process-related factors conditioned the effect of race/ethnicity on sentence severity.[80] Some of the studies revealed, for example, that pleading guilty, hiring a private attorney, or providing evidence or testimony in other cases resulted in greater sentence discounts for white offenders than for black or Hispanic offenders. Other studies showed that members of racial minorities paid a higher penalty—received harsher sentences—for being detained prior to trial, having serious prior criminal records, or refusing to plead guilty. As Spohn noted, these results demonstrate that race and ethnicity influence sentence outcomes through their

BOX 5.3

RACE, ETHNICITY, AND SENTENCING DECISIONS: CONTEXTUAL EFFECTS

Spohn's review of recent studies analyzing the effect of race/ethnicity on state and federal sentencing decisions identified four **themes or patterns of contextual effects**. These studies revealed that:

1. Racial minorities are sentenced more harshly than whites if they
   Are young and male
   Are unemployed
   Are male and unemployed
   Are young, male, and unemployed
   Have lower incomes
   Have less education

2. Racial minorities are sentenced more harshly than whites if they
   Are detained in jail prior to trial
   Are represented by a public defender rather than a private
      attorney
   Are convicted at trial rather than by plea
   Have more serious prior criminal records

3. Racial minorities who victimize whites are sentenced more harshly than other race-of- offender/race-of-victim combinations

4. Racial minorities are sentenced more harshly than whites if they are
   Convicted of less serious crimes
   Convicted of drug offenses or more serious drug offenses

SOURCE: "Thirty Years of Sentencing Reform: The Quest for a Racially Neutral Sentencing Process, "by C. Spohn, 2000. In *Criminal Justice 2000: Policies, Process, and Decisions of the Criminal Justice System*. Washington, DC: U.S. Department of Justice.

relationships with earlier decisions and suggest that these process-related determinants of sentence outcomes do not operate in the same way for members of racial minorities and whites.

The third theme or pattern revealed by the studies included in Spohn's review concerned an interaction between the race of the offender and the race of the victim. Consistent with research on the death penalty (which is discussed later in this chapter), two studies found that blacks who sexually assaulted whites were sentenced more harshly than blacks who sexually assaulted other blacks or whites who sexually assaulted whites. Thus, "Punishment is contingent on the race of the victim as well as the race of the offender."[81] The final pattern of indirect/interaction effects, which Spohn admitted was "less obvious" than the other three,[82] was that the effect of race/ethnicity was conditioned by the nature of the crime. Some studies found that racial discrimination was confined to less serious, and thus more discretionary, crimes. Other studies revealed that racial discrimination was most pronounced for drug offenses or, alternatively, that harsher sentencing of racial minorities was found only for the most serious drug offenses.[83]

The fact that a majority of the studies reviewed by Chiricos and Crawford and by Spohn found that blacks and Hispanics were more likely than whites to be sentenced to prison, even after taking crime seriousness and prior criminal record into account, suggests that racial discrimination in sentencing is not a thing of the past. These findings also provide additional evidence that the disproportionate number of racial minorities incarcerated in state and federal prisons reflects "to some extent" racial discrimination within the criminal justice system.

Race and Sentencing Decisions: When Does Race Matter?

Spohn's review of recent research investigating the linkages between race/ethnicity and sentence severity identified the ways in which race/ethnicity interacts with or is conditioned by the following: other legally irrelevant offender characteristics, process-related factors, and the nature and seriousness of the crime. A comprehensive review of these studies is beyond the scope of this book. Instead, we summarize the findings of a few key studies, focusing on (a) the intersections among race, gender, age, employment status, and sentence severity and (b) racial differentials in sentences imposed for drug offenses. Our purpose is to illustrate the subtle and complex ways in which race influences the sentencing process.

Race/Ethnicity, Gender, Age, and Employment: A Volatile Combination?

In a recent article exploring the "convergence of race, ethnicity, gender, and class on court decision making," Zatz urged researchers to consider the ways in which offender (and victim) characteristics jointly affect case outcomes.[84] As she noted, "Race, gender, and class are the central axes undergirding our social structure. They intersect in dynamic, fluid, and multifaceted ways."[85]

The findings of a series of studies conducted by Darrell Steffensmeier and his colleagues at Pennsylvania State University illustrate these "intersections." Research published by this team of researchers during the early 1990s concluded that race,[86] gender,[87] and age[88] each played a role in the sentencing process in Pennsylvania. However, it is interesting to note, especially in light of their later research findings,[89] that the team's initial study of the effect of race on sentencing concluded that race contributed "very little" to our understanding of judges' sentencing decisions.[90] Although the incarceration (jail or prison) rate for blacks was 8 percentage points higher than the rate for whites, there was only a 2-percentage-point difference in the rates at which blacks and whites were sentenced to prison. Race also played "a very small role in decisions about sentence length."[91] The average sentence for black defendants was only 21 days longer than the average sentence for white defendants. These findings led Kramer and Steffensmeier to conclude that "if defendants' race affects judges' decisions in sentencing . . . it does so very weakly or intermittently, if at all."[92]

This conclusion is called into question by Steffensmeier, Ulmer and Kramer's more recent research,[93] which explores the ways in which race, gender, and age interact to influence sentence severity. They found that each of the three legally irrelevant offender characteristics had significant direct effects on both the likelihood of incarceration and the length of the sentence: Blacks were sentenced more harshly than whites, younger offenders were sentenced more harshly than older offenders, and males were sentenced more harshly than females. More important, they found that the three factors interacted to produce substantially harsher sentences for one particular category of offenders—young black males—than for any other age-race-gender combination. According to the authors, their results illustrate the "high cost of being black, young, and male."[94]

Although the research conducted by Steffensmeier and his colleagues provides important insights into the judicial decision-making process, their findings also suggest the possibility that factors other than race, gender, and age may interact to affect sentence severity. The authors suggest that judges impose harsher sentences on offenders perceived to be more deviant, more dangerous, and more likely to recidivate and that these perceptions rest, either explicitly or implicitly, on "stereotypes associated with membership in various social categories."[95] If this is the case, then offenders with constellations of characteristics other than "young, black, and male" may also be singled out for harsher treatment.

The validity of this assertion is confirmed by the results of a recent replication and extension of the Pennsylvania study. Spohn and Holleran examined the sentences imposed on offenders convicted of felonies in Chicago, Miami, and Kansas City.[96] Their study included Hispanics as well as blacks and tested for interactions between race, ethnicity, gender, age and employment status. They found that none of the four offender characteristics had a significant effect on the length of the sentence in any of the three jurisdictions but that each of the characteristics had a significant effect on the decision to incarcerate or not in at least one of the jurisdictions. As shown in Part A of Exhibit 5.2, black offenders in Chicago were 12.1 percent more likely than white offenders to be sentenced to prison. Hispanics were 15.3 percent more likely than whites to be incarcerated. In Miami, the difference in the probabilities of incarceration for Hispanic offenders and white offenders was 10.3 percent. Male offenders were more than 20 percent more likely than female offenders to be sentenced to prison in Chicago and Kansas City, and unemployed offenders faced significantly higher odds of incarceration than employed offenders (+9.3 percent) in Kansas City. In all three jurisdictions, offenders aged 21 to 29 were about 10 percent more likely than offenders aged 17 to 20 to be sentenced to prison.[97] Race, ethnicity, gender, age, and employment status, then, each had a direct effect on the decision to incarcerate or not.

Like Steffensmeier and his colleagues, Spohn and Holleran found that various combinations of race/ethnicity, gender, age, and employment status were better predictors of incarceration than any variable alone. As shown in Part B of Exhibit 5.2, young black and Hispanic males were consistently more likely than middle-aged white males to be sentenced to prison. These offenders, however, were not the only ones singled out for harsher treatment. In Chicago, young black and Hispanic males and middle-aged black males faced higher odds of incarceration than middle-aged white males. In Miami, young black and Hispanic males and older Hispanic males were incarcerated more often than middle-aged white males. And in Kansas City, both young black males and young white males faced higher odds of incarceration than middle-aged whites. These results led Spohn and Holleran to conclude that "in Chicago and Miami the combination of race/ethnicity and age is a more powerful predictor of sentence severity than either variable individually, while in Kansas City age matters more than race."[98]

The findings of the studies conducted by Steffensmeier and his colleagues and by Spohn and Holleran confirm Richard Quinney's assertion, which he made nearly 30 years ago, that "judicial decisions are not made uniformly. Decisions are made according to a host of extra-legal factors, including the age of the offender, his race, and social class."[99] Their findings confirm that dangerous or problematic populations are defined "by a mix of economic *and* racial . . . references."[100] Black and Hispanic offenders who are also male,

Exhibit 5.2 Do Young Unemployed Black and Hispanic Males Pay a Punishment Penalty?

A. *Differences in the Probabilities of Incarceration: The Effect of Race, Ethnicity, Gender, Age, and Employment Status*

Probability Differences	Chicago	Miami	Kansas City
Blacks versus whites	+12.1%	Not significant	Not significant
Hispanics versus whites	+15.3%	+10.3%	Not applicable
Males versus females	+22.8%	Not significant	+21.1%
Unemployed versus employed	Not significant	Not applicable	+9.3%
Aged 21–29 versus aged 17–20	+10.0%	+9.5%	+10.8%

B. *Differences in the Probabilities of Incarceration: Male Offenders Only*

Probability differences between whites aged 30–39 and other groups	Chicago	Miami	Kansas City
Blacks, 17–29	+18.4%	+14.7%	+12.7%
Hispanics, 17–29	+25.1%	+18.2%	Not applicable
Whites, 17–29	Not significant	Not significant	+14.4%
Blacks, 30–39	+23.3%	Not significant	Not significant
Hispanics, 30–39	Not significant	Not significant	Not significant

Probability differences between employed whites and other groups	Chicago	Miami	Kansas City
Unemployed blacks	+16.9%	Not applicable	+13.0%
Unemployed Hispanics	+23.5%		Not applicable
Unemployed whites	Not significant		Not significant
Employed blacks	Not significant		Not significant
Employed Hispanics	Not significant		Not applicable

SOURCE: Data are from "The Imprisonment Penalty Paid by Young, Unemployed Black and Hispanic Male Offenders" (Tables 3, Table 5, and Table 6), by C. Spohn and D. Holleran, 2000, *Criminology* 38:281–306.

young, and unemployed may pay higher punishment penalties than either white offenders or other types of black and Hispanic offenders.

Why Do Young, Unemployed Members of Racial Minorities Pay Punishment Penalties? The question, of course, is *why* young, unemployed members of racial minorities are punished more severely than other types of offenders: why "today's prevailing criminal predator has become a euphemism for young, black males."[101]

A number of scholars suggest that certain categories of offenders are regarded as more dangerous and more problematic than others and thus more in need of formal social control. Spitzer, for example, uses the term "social dynamite"[102] to characterize the segment of the deviant population that is viewed as particularly threatening and dangerous. He asserts that social dynamite "tends to be more youthful, alienated and politically volatile" and contends that those who fall into this category are more likely than other offenders to be formally processed through the criminal justice system.[103] Building on this point, Box and Hale argue that unemployed offenders who are also young, male, and members of racial minorities will be perceived as particularly threatening to the social order and thus will be singled out for harsher treatment.[104] Judges, in other words, regard these types of "threatening" offenders as likely candidates for imprisonment "in the belief that such a response will deter and incapacitate and thus defuse this threat."[105]

Steffensmeier and his colleagues advance a similar explanation for their finding "that young black men (as opposed to black men as a whole) are the defendant subgroup most at risk to receive the harshest penalty."[106] They interpret their results using the "focal concerns" theory of sentencing. According to this perspective, judges' sentencing decisions reflect their assessments of the blameworthiness or culpability of offenders, their desire to protect the community by incapacitating dangerous offenders or deterring potential offenders, and their concerns about the practical consequences, or social costs, of sentencing decisions. Because judges rarely have enough information to accurately determine an offender's culpability or dangerousness, they develop a "perceptual shorthand" based on stereotypes and attributions that are themselves linked to offender characteristics such as race, gender, and age. Thus, according to these researchers,

> Younger offenders and male defendants appear to be seen as more of a threat to the community or not as reformable, and so also are black of-

fenders, particularly those who also are young and male. Likewise, concerns such as 'ability to do time' and the costs of incarceration appear linked to race-, gender-, and age-based perceptions and stereotypes.[107]

The conclusions proffered by Spohn and Holleran, who note that their results are consistent with the focal concerns theory of sentencing, are very similar. They suggest that judges, who generally have both limited time in which to make decisions and incomplete information about offenders, "may resort to stereotypes of deviance and dangerousness that rest on considerations of race, ethnicity, gender, age, and unemployment."[108] Young, unemployed black and Hispanic males, in other words, are viewed as more dangerous, more threatening, and less amenable to rehabilitation; as a result, they are sentenced more harshly.

Race, Ethnicity and Sentences Imposed on Drug Offenders

The task of assessing the effect of race on sentencing is complicated by the war on drugs, which a number of commentators contend has been fought primarily in minority communities (see the "Focus on an Issue"). Tonry, for example, argues that "Urban black Americans have borne the brunt of the War on Drugs."[109] Miller's similarly contends that "the racial discrimination endemic to the drug war wound its way through every stage of the processing—arrest, jailing, conviction, and sentencing."[110] Mauer's criticism is even more pointed; he asserts that "the drug war has exacerbated racial disparities in incarceration while failing to have any sustained impact on the drug problem."[111]

Comments such as these suggest that members of racial minorities will receive more punitive sentences than whites for drug offenses. This expectation is based in part on recent theoretical discussion of the "moral panic" surrounding drug use and the war on drugs.[112] Moral panic theorists argue that society is characterized by a variety of commonsense perceptions about crime and drugs that result in community intolerance for such behaviors and increased pressure for punitive action.[113] Many theorists argue that this moral panic can become ingrained in the judicial ideology of sentencing judges, resulting in more severe sentences for those—that is, blacks and Hispanics—believed to be responsible for drug use, drug distribution, and drug-related crime.[114]

Focus on an Issue

Race and Sentencing for Drug Offenses:
Punishment and Prejudice?

In June of 2000, Human Rights Watch, a New-York-based watchdog organization, issued a report titled "Punishment and Prejudice." The report analyzed nationwide prison admission statistics and presented the results of the first state-by-state analysis of the impact of drug offenses on prison admissions for blacks and whites. The authors of the report alleged that the war on drugs, which is "ostensibly color blind," has been waged "disproportionately against black Americans." As they noted, "The statistics we have compiled present a unique—and devastating—picture of the price black Americans have paid in each state for the national effort to curtail the use and sale of illicit drugs." In support of this conclusion, the report noted the following:

- Blacks constituted 62.6 percent of all drug offenders admitted to state prisons in 1996. In certain states, the disparity was much worse: In Maryland and Illinois, for example, blacks comprised 90 percent of all persons admitted to state prisons for drug offenses.

- Nationwide, the rate of drug admissions to state prison for black men was 13 times greater than the rate for white men. In 10 states, the rates for black men were 26 to 57 times greater than those for white men.

- Drug offenders accounted for 38 percent of all black prison admissions but only 24 percent of all white prison admissions. In New Hampshire, drug offenders accounted for 61 percent of all black prison admissions.

- The disproportionate rates at which blacks were sentenced to prison for drug offenses "originate[d] in racially disproportionate rates of arrest." From 1979 to 1998, the percentage of drug users who were black did not vary appreciably; however, among those arrested for drug offenses, the percentage of blacks rose significantly. In 1979, blacks comprised 10.8 percent of all drug users and 21.8 percent of all drug arrests. In 1998, blacks comprised 16.9 percent of all drug users and 37.3 percent of all drug arrests.

The authors of the report stated that their purpose was "to bring renewed attention to extreme racial disparities in one area of the criminal justice system—the incarceration of drug law offenders." They also asserted that although the high rates of incarceration for all drug offenders are a cause for concern,

> The grossly disparate rates at which blacks and whites are sent to prison for drug offenses raise a clear warning flag concerning the fairness and equity of drug law enforcement across the country, and underscore the need for reforms that would minimize these disparities without sacrificing legitimate drug control objectives.

Critics of the report's conclusions, which they branded "inflammatory," argued that the statistics presented did not constitute evidence of racial discrimination. "There will be inevitably, inherently, disparities of all sorts in the enforcement of any kind of law," said Todd Graziano, a senior fellow in legal studies at the Heritage Foundation. Critics noted that because the illegal drug trade flourishes in inner-city minority neighborhoods, the statistics presented in the report could simply indicate that blacks commit more drug crimes than whites.

What do you think? Do these statistics signal racial discrimination in the criminal justice system? Or do the figures simply indicate that blacks commit more drug crimes—or more serious drug crimes—than whites? What types of reforms might "minimize these disparities"?

SOURCE: "Punishment and Prejudice: Racial Disparities in the War on Drugs," May, 2000, *Human Rights Watch*, 12 (2-G). Available on the World Wide Web at:http://www.hrw.org/reports/2000/usa/

Race/Ethnicity and Sentencing of Drug Offenders in State Courts

Three recent studies focused explicitly on racial disparities in the sentencing of drug offenders.[115] Two of these studies examined sentencing decisions at the state level; the third compared the sentences imposed on members of racial minorities and whites who were convicted of drug offenses in U.S. District Courts. Myers examined the effect of race on sentences imposed on offenders convicted of three types of drug offenses—use, sales/distribution, and trafficking—in Georgia from 1977 to 1985.[116] In 1980, Georgia criminalized drug trafficking and increased the penalties for repeat drug offenders. The new drug-trafficking statutes also restricted judicial discretion, which, according to the author, should have minimized sentencing disparities between blacks and whites. Myers argued that this uniformity in sentencing would be most prevalent during the height of legislative activity (1980-1982) but would decrease thereafter as judges reverted to previous sentencing practices.

Myers's analysis revealed that black offenders were more likely than white offenders to be incarcerated, particularly for the more serious drug offenses. There was a 25-percentage-point difference in the probabilities of incarceration between black and white offenders for drug trafficking, compared with a 19-percentage-point difference for drug distribution and a 12-percentage-point difference for drug use. Contrary to her hypothesis that reducing judicial discretion would produce racially neutral sentence outcomes, Myers found that the racial differential was consistent and significant throughout the time period examined and was actually most pronounced in the midst of the reform effort (1980-1982). As she concluded, "The symbolic crusade against traffickers led to punitiveness that was *selectively* directed toward black traffickers convicted at the height of the crusade."[117]

Spohn and Spears found a different pattern of results in the sentences imposed on drug offenders in Chicago, Kansas City, and Miami during 1993.[118] The authors of this study found that Hispanics—but not blacks—faced greater odds of incarceration than whites in Miami but members of racial minorities and whites were sentenced to prison at about the same rate in Chicago and Kansas City. As illustrated in Exhibit 5.4, they also found that black drug offenders received longer sentences than white drug offenders in Kansas City but the sentences imposed on members of racial minorities and whites were more similar in Chicago and Miami. The mean prison sentence imposed on a "typical" drug offender[119] in Chicago was approximately 39 months for blacks, 41 months for whites, and 47 months for Hispanics. In Miami, the pattern was very similar: The average sentences ranged from 47 months (blacks) to 57 months (whites) to 58 months (Hispanics). In Kansas City, on the other hand, the mean prison sentence for blacks (73 months) was 15 months longer than the sentence for whites.

Further analysis led Spohn and Spears to conclude that race/ethnicity affected sentencing for drug offenses in an unexpected manner. In both Chicago and Miami, the sentences imposed on Hispanic drug offenders were significantly longer than the sentences imposed on black drug offenders. Hispanics received sentences that averaged 15 months longer than those imposed on blacks in Miami; their sentences were 8 months longer than those given to blacks in Chicago. In these two jurisdictions, judges apparently differentiated between blacks and Hispanics, not between blacks and whites. The authors of this study admitted that they were "somewhat puzzled" by these findings.[120] They explained that they expected the moral panic surrounding drug use and drug-related crime to result in harsher sentences for both black and Hispanic offenders, who make up the majority of drug offenders in those jurisdictions. According to Spohn and Spears,

Exhibit 5.3. Adjusted Mean Sentences for Drug Offenders

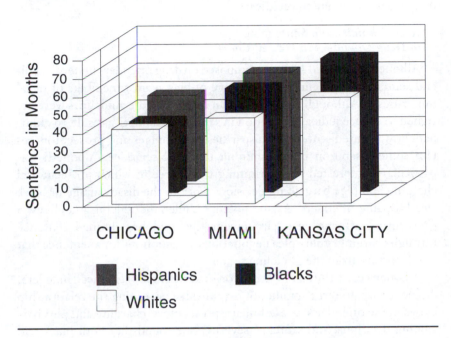

The fact that harsher treatment was reserved for Hispanics in *Miami*, while unexpected, is not particularly surprising; arguably, the most enduring perception about drug importation and distribution in Miami is that these activities are dominated by Hispanics of various nationalities. This explanation, however, is less convincing with regard to our finding that Hispanics received longer sentences than blacks in Chicago.[121]

Further analysis of the sentences imposed in Chicago revealed that only certain types of Hispanic offenders—those convicted of the most serious drug offenses, those with prior felony convictions, and those who were unemployed at the time of arrest—received longer sentences than African American offenders. The authors state that this pattern of results suggests that judges in Chicago "may be imposing more severe sentences on offenders characterized as particularly problematic."[122] It suggests, in other words, that Chicago judges use ethnicity, offense seriousness, prior record, and employment status to define what might be called a "dangerous class"[123] of drug offenders. The Hispanic drug offender who manufactures or sells large quantities of drugs, is a repeat offender, or has no legitimate means of financial support may be perceived as particularly dangerous and likely to recidivate.

Race/Ethnicity and Sentencing of Drug Offenders in Federal Court

Albonetti examined sentences imposed on drug offenders under the federal sentencing guidelines for evidence of bias against members of racial minorities.[124] Although, as we explain in Chapter 6, the guidelines were designed to reduce judicial discretion in sentencing and, as a result, to eliminate unwarranted sentencing disparities, both judges and prosecutors retain some discretion in determining the final sentence. Albonetti was particularly interested in determining the degree to which prosecutorial charging and plea bargaining decisions work to the disadvantage of black and Hispanic offenders. As she noted, "Under the federal guidelines, a prosecuting attorney can circumvent the guideline-defined sentence through charging, guilty plea negotiations, and motions for a sentence that is a departure from the guideline sentence."[125]

Albonetti used 1991 to 1992 data on drug offenders sentenced in federal district courts to test a number of hypotheses concerning the relationship between the offender's race/ethnicity, prosecutors' charging and plea bargaining decisions, and sentence severity. She found that both black and Hispanic drug offenders received more severe sentences than white drug offenders. Albonetti also found that whereas pleading guilty produced similar reductions in sentence severity for all three groups of offenders, whites received significantly greater benefits than either blacks or Hispanics as a result of providing evidence or testimony in other cases. In addition, white offenders received larger sentence reductions than members of racial minorities as a result of being convicted for possession of drugs rather than drug trafficking. Albonetti concluded that the pattern of results found in her study suggests that "the federal sentencing guidelines have not eliminated sentence disparity linked to defendant characteristics for defendants convicted of drug offenses in 1991-1992."[126]

Race and Sentencing: Disparity or Discrimination?

Research conducted during the past several decades has led to conflicting conclusions regarding the effect of race on sentencing. Early reviews of this research concluded that the "race effect" disappeared once crime seriousness and prior criminal record were controlled for adequately. Later reviews challenged the "no-discrimination thesis," arguing that discrimination had not declined or disappeared but had simply become more subtle and difficult to detect. Reviews of the theoretically and methodologically sophisticated research published during the past 20 years reached a similar conclusion, noting that discrimination against members of racial minorities is not universal but is confined to certain types of cases, settings, and defendants. Studies have shown that young, unemployed black and Hispanic men pay a punishment penalty and that black and Hispanic drug offenders are sentenced more harshly than white drug offenders. Although the types of overt discrimination found in the Scottsboro case have been eliminated, racial discrimination in sentencing is not a thing of the past.

Race and the Death Penalty: A Failed Experiment?

In 1987, the U.S. Supreme Court rejected Warren McCleskey's claim that the Georgia capital sentencing process was administered in a racially discriminatory manner.[127] McCleskey, an African American who was convicted of killing a white police officer during the course of an armed robbery, claimed that those who killed whites—particularly blacks who killed whites—were substantially more likely to be sentenced to death than those who killed blacks. In support of his claim, McCleskey offered the results of a study conducted by David Baldus and his colleagues.[128] The "Baldus study," which is widely regarded as the most comprehensive and sophisticated analysis of death penalty decisions to date, concluded that the race of the victim was "a potent influence in the system" and that the state of Georgia was operating a "dual system" for prosecuting homicide cases.[129]

Although the majority accepted the validity of the Baldus study, the Supreme Court nonetheless refused to accept McCleskey's argument that the disparities documented by Baldus signaled the presence of intentional racial discrimination. Writing for the majority, Justice Powell asserted that the disparities were "unexplained" and stated that "at most, the Baldus study indicates a discrepancy that appears to correlate with race."[130] The Court concluded that the Baldus study was "clearly insufficient to support an inference that any of the decisionmakers in McCleskey's case acted with discriminatory purpose."[131]

The four dissenting justices were outraged. Justice Brennan, who was joined in dissent by Justices Blackmun, Marshall, and Stevens, wrote, "The Court today finds that Warren McCleskey's sentence was constitutionally imposed. It finds no fault with a system in which lawyers must tell their clients that race casts a large shadow on the capital sentencing process."[132]

The analysis of legal scholars was similarly harsh. They characterized the decision as a "badge of shame upon America's system of justice"[133] and concluded that "the central message of the McCleskey case is all too plain: de facto racial discrimination in capital sentencing is legal in the United States."[134]

Opponents of the death penalty viewed the issues raised in *McCleskey* as the only remaining challenge to the constitutionality of the death penalty. They predicted that the Court's decision, which effectively closed the door to similar appeals, would speed up the pace of executions and quiet—if not extinguish—the controversy surrounding the death penalty. Although the number of persons executed did increase, from 25 in 1987 to 56 in 1995 to 98 in 1999 and 85 in 2000, the issue of racial discrimination in the capital sentencing process did not die down. In fact, a series of events pushed the issue back on the public agenda:

- In 1990, the U.S. General Accounting Office (GAO) issued a report on the death penalty. The GAO concluded that there was "a pattern of evidence indicating racial disparities in the charging, sentencing, and imposition of the death penalty."[135]

- In January of 2000, George Ryan, the governor of Illinois, issued a moratorium on the use of the death penalty in that state. His decision was motivated by the fact that since the death penalty was reinstated in Illinois, 12 persons were executed but 13 were exonerated. Governor Ryan, who called for a "public dialogue" on "the question of the fairness of the application of the death penalty in Illinois," stated that he favored a moratorium because of his "grave concerns about our state's shameful record of convicting innocent people and putting them on death row."[136]

- In September of 2000, the Department of Justice issued a report on the use of the death penalty for federal offenses from 1988 through 2000. The report noted that the Department of Justice sought the death penalty in 206 cases during this time period. In 155, or 75 percent, of these cases, the defendant was a member of a minority group. In more than half of the cases, the defendant was black.[137] Publication of the report led the American Bar Association to renew its request that President Clinton impose an executive moratorium on the use of the death penalty at the federal level.

- In October of 2000, the Texas Civil Rights Project (TCRP) released a report on the death penalty in Texas. The report identified six critical issues, including the competency of attorneys appointed to represent defendants charged with capital murder, that "decrease due process for low-income death penalty defendants and increase the probability of wrongful convictions."[138] The report called on then-Governor George Bush to institute a moratorium on the death penalty pending the results of two studies, one of which would determine whether race and social class influenced the use of the death penalty in Texas.

As these events demonstrate, controversy continues to swirl around the use of the death penalty in the United States. Although issues other than race and class animate this controversy, these issues clearly are central. The questions asked and the positions taken by those on each side of the controversy mimic to some extent the issues that dominate discussions of the noncapital sentencing process. Supporters of capital punishment contend that the death penalty is administered in an evenhanded manner on those who commit the most heinous murders. They also argue that the restrictions contained in death penalty statutes and the procedural safeguards inherent in the process preclude arbitrary and discriminatory decision making. Opponents contend that the capital sentencing process, which involves a series of highly discretionary charging, convicting, and sentencing decisions, is fraught with race- and class-based discrimination. Moreover, they argue that the appellate process is unlikely to uncover, much less remedy, these abuses.

The controversy surrounding the death penalty differs in one important respect from that surrounding noncapital sentencing. Whereas most researchers and commentators acknowledge that sentencing decisions, including the decision to incarcerate, are not based primarily or even substantially on the race/ethnicity of the offender or victim, many social scientists and legal scholars conclude that the capital sentencing process *is* characterized by systematic racial discrimination.[139] Those who take this position cite historical and contemporary evidence of discrimination based on the race of the offender and the race of the victim. They argue that the data show "a clear pattern unexplainable on grounds other than race."[140]

In this section, we assess the validity of this allegation. We begin with a brief discussion of the constitutionality of the death penalty. We then present the results of research that addresses the issue of racial discrimination in the death penalty. We summarize the results of the early studies and present a more thorough discussion of recent studies, focusing on the findings of the Baldus study.

The Death Penalty: Constitutional Issues

The Eighth Amendment to the U.S. Constitution prohibits "cruel and unusual punishments." In interpreting this amendment, the Supreme Court has ruled that "punishments are cruel when they involve torture or lingering death."[141] The Court has also made it clear, however, that the death penalty itself is not a cruel and unusual punishment. As the Court noted in *Trop v. Dulles*, "Whatever the arguments may be against capital punishment . . . it cannot be said to violate the constitutional concept of cruelty."[142]

The Court's statement that the death penalty per se does not constitute cruel and unusual punishment does not mean that capital punishment has been immune from constitutional challenge. In 1972, the Supreme Court ruled in *Furman v. Georgia*[143] that the death penalty was unconstitutional as it was being administered under the existing statutes. The five-to-four decision, in which nine separate opinions were written, focused on the arbitrary and capricious nature of the procedures by which those arrested for homicide were selected for the death penalty. Justice Douglas, for example, stated that the procedures used in administering the death penalty were "pregnant with discrimination," and Justices Stewart and White focused on the fact that there was little to distinguish those who were sentenced to death from those who were not.[144]

Three of the five justices in the majority also raised the issue of racial discrimination in the administration of the death penalty. Justices Douglas and Marshall cited evidence of discrimination against defendants who were poor, powerless, and black. Marshall, for example, stated that giving juries "untrammeled discretion" to impose a sentence of death was "an open invitation to discrimination."[145] Justice Stewart, who noted that "racial discrimination has not been proved," stated that Douglas and Marshall had "demonstrated that, if any basis can be discerned for the selection of these few to be sentenced to die, it is the constitutionally impermissible basis of race."[146]

The Court's ruling in *Furman* invalidated the death penalty statutes in 39 states. Most of these states responded by enacting new statutes designed to restrict discretion and thus avoid the problems of arbitrariness and discrimination identified by the justices in *Furman*. Some states enacted statutes that required the judge or jury to impose the death penalty on defendants convicted of first-degree murder. Other states enacted *guided-discretion statutes* that allowed the judge or jury to impose the death penalty on offenders convicted of certain crimes, depending on the presence of aggravating and mitigating circumstances. These statutes typically required a bifurcated trial in which the jury first decided guilt or innocence and then decided whether to impose the death penalty or not. They also provided for automatic appellate review of all death sentences.

The Supreme Court ruled on the constitutionality of both types of death penalty statutes in 1976. The mandatory death penalty statutes enacted by Louisiana and North Carolina were ruled unconstitutional,[147] primarily on the grounds that they provided no opportunity for consideration of mitigating circumstances but also because the jury's power to determine whether the defendant would be convicted of first-degree murder (a mandatory death sentence) or of a lesser included offense opened the door to the type of "arbitrary and wanton jury discretion" condemned in *Furman*.[148] The guided-discretion statutes adopted by Georgia, Florida, and Texas, on the other hand, were upheld.[149] In *Gregg v. Georgia*, the Court held that Georgia's statute—which required the jury to weigh 10 specified aggravating circumstances, allowed the jury to consider mitigating circumstances, and provided for automatic appellate review—narrowed the jury's discretion and thereby reduced the likelihood that the jury would impose arbitrary or discriminatory sentences. The majority concluded that these procedural safeguards meant that a jury could no longer "wantonly and freakishly impose the death sentence" and stated that the concerns that motivated their decision in *Furman* were "not present to any significant degree in the Georgia procedure."[150]

Since 1976, the Supreme Court has handed down additional decisions concerning the constitutionality of the death penalty for particular types of crimes or particular types of offenders. The Court has ruled that (a) the death penalty cannot be imposed on a defendant convicted of the crime of rape,[151] (b) the death penalty can be imposed on an offender convicted of felony murder if the offender played a major role in the felony and displayed "reckless indifference to the value of human life,"[152] and (c) that the Eighth Amendment does not prohibit the execution of the mentally retarded[153] or youths who commit crimes at age 16 or older.[154]

As noted at the beginning of this section, in 1987, the Supreme Court directly addressed the issue of racial discrimination in the use of the death penalty. In *McCleskey v. Kemp*,[155] the Court refused to overturn McCleskey's death sentence, ruling five to four that the evidence of victim-based racial disparity documented in the Baldus study (see below) did not signal the presence of intentional, and therefore unconstitutional, racial discrimination. Justice Powell, who wrote the majority opinion, stated that the Court's assumption that the Baldus study was statistically valid did not imply that the study proved "that racial considerations actually enter into any sentencing decisions in Georgia."[156] Noting that "at most," the study indicated "a discrepancy that appears to correlate with race," Powell stated that the Court would not "assume that what is unexplained is invidious."[157] The evidence presented by *McCleskey*, in other words, "did not demonstrate a constitutionally significant risk of racial bias affecting the Georgia capital sentencing process."[158]

The Supreme Court's decisions in *Furman*, *Gregg*, and *McCleskey* have been guided by a number of assumptions about discretion and discrimination in the capital sentencing process. In *Furman*, the Court struck down the death penalty statutes being challenged, on the basis of an assumption that the absence of guidelines and procedural safeguards opened the door to arbitrary, capricious, and discriminatory decisions. In *Gregg*, the Court affirmed the validity of the guided-discretion statutes and assumed that the presence of guidelines and procedural safeguards would eliminate the problems condemned in *Furman*. And in *McCleskey*, the Court assumed that the Baldus study was statistically valid but argued that the evidence of victim-based racial discrimination documented in the study was not sufficient to prove intentional discrimination by criminal justice officials in McCleskey's case.

In the next section, we discuss the results of empirical research investigating the relationship between race and the death penalty. Our purpose is to assess the validity of the assumptions on which *Furman*, *Gregg*, and *McCleskey* rest: that race may have played a role in death penalty decisions prior to *Furman*, that the guided-discretion statutes enacted since 1976 have removed arbitrariness and discrimination from the capital sentencing process, and that the Baldus study merely identified a disparity that seems to correlate with race.

Empirical Research on Race and the Death Penalty

Pre-Furman Studies

Justice Douglas' allegation in *Furman v. Georgia* that the capital sentencing process was "pregnant with discrimination" implied that race was a consideration in death penalty decisions in the pre-*Furman* era. In fact, there is a considerable amount of empirical research documenting that blacks, particularly those who were convicted of murdering or raping whites, were sentenced to death and executed at disproportionately high rates during this time period.[159] The most compelling evidence is found in studies examining the use of the death penalty for the crime of rape. These studies revealed that the death penalty "was largely used for punishing blacks who had raped whites."[160] One study of sentencing decisions for rape in Florida from 1940 to 1964, for example, found that 54 percent of the blacks convicted of raping whites received the death penalty, compared with only 5 percent of the whites convicted of raping whites.[161] Another study of the imposition of the death penalty for rape in 12 southern states from 1945 through 1965 uncovered a similar pattern: Cases in which blacks were convicted of raping whites were 18 times more likely to result in the death penalty than were cases with any other racial combinations.[162] Consistent with these data, 405 of the 455 men executed for the crime of rape from 1930 to 1972 were black.[163]

Evidence of differential treatment is also found in studies of the use of the death penalty for the crime of murder. Most of these studies were conducted in the South. Researchers found, for example, that blacks indicted for murdering whites in North Carolina from 1930 to 1940 faced disproportionately high odds of a death sentence,[164] that whites sentenced to death in nine southern and border states during the 1920s and 1930s were less likely than blacks to be executed,[165] and that blacks sentenced to death in Pennsylvania were less likely than whites to have their sentences commuted to life in prison and more likely than whites to be executed.[166] These early studies also uncovered evidence of victim-based discrimination. Garfinkel's study of the capital sentencing process in North Carolina during the 1930s, for example, revealed that only 5 percent of those who killed blacks were sentenced to death, compared with 24 percent of those who killed whites. Moreover, blacks who killed whites were substantially more likely than any other category of offender/race-of-victim group to be indicted for, charged with, or convicted of first-degree murder (which carried a mandatory death sentence).[167]

Critics have raised questions about the conclusions of these studies, noting that most of them did not control for the defendant's prior criminal history, for the heinous nature of the crime, or for other legally relevant considerations. Gary Kleck, who admitted that controlling for these factors probably would not eliminate "the huge racial differentials in the use of the death penalty for rape," argued that the more modest racial differences found for homicide might disappear if these legally relevant variables were taken into consideration.[168]

Two methodologically sophisticated studies that did take these factors into account found that the racial differences did not disappear. A study of death penalty decisions in the pre-*Furman* era in Georgia found that the death penalty was imposed more often on blacks and on those convicted of murdering whites than on other equally culpable defendants.[169] An examination of the capital sentencing process in pre-*Furman* Texas reached a similar conclusion.[170] In fact, Ralph and her colleagues found that those who killed whites were 25.2 percent more likely to be sentenced to death than those who killed blacks. They concluded that there was a "significant race-linked bias in the death sentencing of non-Anglo-American murderers; the victim's race, along with legal factors taken together, emerged as the pivotal element in sentencing."[171]

Post-Furman Studies

In *Gregg v. Georgia*, the Supreme Court upheld Georgia's guided-discretion statute and stated that the concerns that prompted their decision in *Furman* were not "present to any significant degree" in the Georgia capital sentencing process in the post-*Furman* era.[172] The Court argued that the restrictions on discretion and the procedural safeguards mandated by the new statutes would eliminate arbitrariness and discrimination in death penalty decisions.

Studies conducted in the post-*Furman* era suggest that the Court was overly optimistic. In fact, these studies document substantial discrimination in the application of the death penalty under guided discretion statutes.[173] A report by the GAO,[174] which reviewed 28 post-*Furman* studies, noted that the race of the victim had a significant effect in all but five studies. Those who murdered whites were more likely to be charged with capital murder and to be sentenced to death than those who murdered blacks. Moreover, these differences could not be attributed to differences in the defendant's prior criminal record, the seriousness of the crime, or other legally relevant factors. The GAO noted that although the evidence regarding the race of the defendant was "equivocal," about half of the studies did find that blacks were more likely than whites to be charged with capital crimes and to be sentenced to death.[175] The overall conclusion proffered by the GAO was that there was "a pattern of evidence indicating racial disparities in the charging, sentencing, and imposition of the death penalty after the *Furman* decision."[176] (See the discussion of the Texas death penalty process in Box 5.4.)

The strongest evidence in support of the GAO's conclusion is found in a detailed study of the Georgia capital sentencing process. David Baldus and his colleagues analyzed the effect of race on the outcomes of more than 600 homicide cases in Georgia from 1973 through 1979.[177] As noted earlier, this study is widely regarded as the most comprehensive and methodologically sophisticated study of death penalty decisions to date. The authors controlled for more than 200 variables that might explain racial disparities in the use of the death penalty. They included detailed information on the defendant's background and prior criminal record, information concerning the circumstances and the heinousness of the crime, and measures of the strength of evidence against the defendant. They analyzed both the prosecutor's decision to seek the death penalty and the jury's decision to sentence the offender to death.

Baldus and his colleagues found substantial race-of-victim effects and more modest race-of-defendant effects. As shown in Exhibit 5.4, prosecutors requested the death penalty in 45 percent of the cases involving white victims but in only 15 percent of the cases involving black victims. The jury imposed the death penalty in 57 percent of the cases with white victims and in 42 percent of the cases with black victims. The disparities were even more pronounced for the four defendant/victim racial combinations, particularly for cases involving black defendants and either black or white victims. Prosecutors were almost 4 times more likely to seek the death penalty when the defendant was black and the victim was white (58 percent) than when both the defendant and the victim were black (15 percent). The rate at which juries imposed the death penalty was also higher in black-on-white than in black-on-black cases.[178]

The authors of the Baldus study found that these racial differences in death penalty outcomes did not disappear when they controlled for more

Exhibit 5.4   The Effect of Defendant Race and Victim Race on Death Penalty Decisions in Post-*Furman* Georgia

	Prosecutor's Decision to Seek the Death Penalty (Percentage)	Jury's Decision to Impose the Death Penalty (Percentage)
A. Race of defendant		
Black	30	53
White	37	56
B. Race of victim		
Black	15	42
White	45	57
C. Race of defendant/victim		
Black defendant/white victim	58	58
White defendant/white Victim	38	56
Black defendant/black victim	15	40
White defendant/black victim	21	67

SOURCE: From *Equal Justice and the Death Penalty: A Legal and Empirical Analysis*, by D. Baldus, G. Woodworth, and C. Pulaski Jr, 1990. Boston: Northeastern University Press.

than 200 defendant and case characteristics. Although the race of the offender had only a weak relationship to death penalty decisions once these factors were taken into consideration, the race of the victim continued to exert a strong effect on both the prosecutor's decision to seek the death penalty and the jury's decision to impose a death sentence. Those who killed whites were more than 4 times as likely to be sentenced to death as those who killed blacks. Noting that "the race-of-victim effects are about the same or stronger in the post-*Furman* period," the authors of the study concluded that their findings "are squarely at odds with the Supreme Court's assumption in *Gregg v. Georgia* that the only factors that would influence decisions in post-*Furman* Georgia were the culpability of the offender and the strength of the evidence."[179]

Evidence from other states also contradicts the Court's assumption. Gross and Mauro examined death penalty decisions in eight states: Arkansas, Florida, Georgia, Illinois, Mississippi, North Carolina, Oklahoma, and Virginia.[180] When they analyzed case outcomes in the three states with the largest number of death sentences (Georgia, Florida, and Illinois) they found that the race of the victim had a large and statistically significant effect on the odds of a death sentence in all three states. After controlling for other legally relevant factors, they found that those who killed whites were 4 times more likely than those who killed blacks to be sentenced to death in Illinois; the ratio was 5 to 1 in Florida and 7 to 1 in Georgia.[181] They found a similar pattern in the other five states.[182] These findings led Gross and Mauro to conclude that "the major factual finding of this study is simple: There has been racial discrimination in the imposition of the death penalty under post-*Furman* statutes in the eight states that we examined."[183]

Gross and Mauro suggested that it was unlikely that the racial disparities uncovered by their study resulted entirely from deliberate acts of discrimination by the jurors or criminal justice officials involved in each case. They argued that the disparities were "too great and too widespread" to be blamed on a handful of racial bigots.[184] They suggested that the disparities were more likely due to the fact that the typical juror can more readily empathize with and identify with a white victim than a black victim. As they noted,

> In a society that remains segregated socially if not legally, and in which the great majority of jurors are white . . . jurors are more likely to be horrified by the killing of a white than of a black, and more likely to act against the killer of a white than the killer of a black.[185]

Although they acknowledge that prosecutors and judges might not be as affected by these types of unconscious prejudices, Gross and Mauro suggest that the death penalty decisions of these officials will be influenced by their predictions of the jury's reaction to the case, the defendant, and the victim. According to the authors, "If jurors rely on racial criteria (either consciously or unconsciously), or if prosecutors believe that they do so, the inexorable logic of the adversarial system of adjudicating death sentences" will ensure that the criteria that prosecutors use to decide whether to seek the death penalty will be the same.[186]

BOX 5.4

DEATH AND DISCRIMINATION IN TEXAS

On June 5, 2000, the U.S. Supreme Court set aside Victor Saldano's death sentence after lawyers for the state of Texas admitted that the decision had been based in part on the fact that he is Hispanic. Saldano kidnapped Paul Green at gunpoint from a grocery store parking lot, took him to an isolated area, shot him 5 times, and stole his watch and wallet. At his sentencing hearing, a psychologist testified about Saldano's "future dangerousness." He noted that blacks and Hispanics were overrepresented in prison and stated that the fact that Saldano was Hispanic was an indicator of his future dangerousness. The Texas Court of Criminal Appeals upheld Saldano's death sentence, stating that allowing his ethnicity to be used as an indicator of dangerousness was not a "fundamental error."

In his appeal to the U.S. Supreme Court, Saldano disagreed with that conclusion. He stated that it is "fundamentally unfair for the prosecution to use racial and ethnic stereotypes in order to obtain a death penalty." The Texas Attorney General conceded Saldano's point. He admitted that the state had erred and joined Saldano in asking the Supreme Court to order a new sentencing hearing. After the Court's decision was announced, a spokesperson for the Texas Attorney General's Office stated that an audit had uncovered eight additional cases that might raise similar issues regarding testimony linking race and ethnicity to assessments of future dangerousness.

Questions about the fairness of the Texas death penalty process have been raised in other forums. During the summer of 2000, for example, the *Chicago Tribune* published a two-part series that focused on the 131 executions carried out during the tenure of Texas Governor George W. Bush.[187] (Since 1977, Texas has executed 218 persons, which is more than 3 times the number executed by any other state.[188]) The report noted that in 40 of the 131 cases, the defense attorney either presented no mitigating evidence at all or called only one witness during the sentencing hearing. In 43 of the cases, the defendants were represented by attorneys who had been (or were subsequent to the trial) publicly sanctioned for misconduct by the State Bar of Texas. One attorney, for example, who had been practicing for only 17 months, was appointed in 1985 to represent Davis Losada, who was accused of rape and murder. Losada was found guilty and sentenced to death after the attorney delivered a "disjointed and brief argument" in which he told the jury: "The System. Justice. I don't know. But that's what y'all are going to do."[189] He later admitted that he had had a conflict of interest in the case (he previously had represented the key witness against his client); and in 1994, he was disbarred for stealing money from his clients.

Other problems cited in the *Chicago Tribune* report included the following: use of unreliable evidence, such as testimony by jailhouse informants; the use of questionable testimony from a psychiatrist, nicknamed "Dr. Death," regarding the potential dangerousness of capital offenders; and the refusal of the Texas Court of Criminal Appeals to order new trials or sentencing hearings despite allegations of fundamental violations of defendants' rights. The report noted that since Governor Bush took office in 1995, the Court of Criminal Appeals had affirmed 270 capital convictions, granted new trials eight times, and ordered new sentencing hearings only six times.

In September of 2000, the Texas Civil Rights Project (TCRP) issued a comprehensive report on "The Death Penalty in Texas" that identified many of the same problems.[190] The authors of the report stated that there were "six areas where the probability of error and the probability of wrongful execution grow dramatically":[191] appointment of counsel to represent indigent defendants, the prosecutor's decision to seek the death penalty, the jury selection process, the sentencing process, the appellate process, and the review of cases by the board of pardons and parole. The report emphasized that the issue was not "a possible break at one juncture, but a probable break at two or more critical junctures."[192]

To remedy these deficiencies, the TCRP recommended that Governor Bush call for a moratorium on the death penalty in Texas. They also recommended that Governor Bush appoint a commission to review the convictions of those currently on death row. The commission would be charged with determining whether defendants' rights to due process had been violated and whether race and/or social class affected the death penalty process. According to the report, "If the State of Texas is going to continue to take the lives of people, then it needs to repair the system."[193] The report concluded that "the frightening truth of the matter is that Texas is at greater risk than at any time since it resumed executions in 1982 of killing innocent people."[194]

SOURCE: *Saldano vs. Texas*, 99-8119.

Research on the capital sentencing process confirms that the Supreme Court was correct in assuming that race infected the capital sentencing process in the pre-*Furman* era. There is irrefutable evidence that the death penalty for rape was reserved primarily for black men who raped white women. The evidence regarding homicide, although somewhat less consistent, also suggests that blacks, particularly blacks who murdered whites, were sentenced to death and executed at a disproportionately high rate. It thus appears that "on the issue of racial discrimination, the system pre-*Furman* was as bad as the majority justices in *Furman v. Georgia* feared it to be."[195]

The Court's assumption that the guided-discretion statutes enacted in the wake of the *Furman* decision would eliminate these abuses, on the other hand, appears to be incorrect. Carefully designed and methodologically rigorous research documents the persistence of racial discrimination in the capital sentencing process. Evidence of victim-based discrimination is found in both the prosecutor's decision to seek the death penalty and the jury's decision to impose the death penalty. It is found in nonsouthern as well as southern states. Although evidence concerning discrimination based on the race of the offender is, as the GAO report noted, "equivocal," most studies do reveal that blacks accused of murdering whites are substantially more likely than any other race-of-defendant/race-of-victim category to be charged with a capital crime and sentenced to death.

Most commentators assumed that the Supreme Court's opinion in *McCleskey* delivered a fatal blow to attempts to strike down the death penalty. They based this conclusion on the fact that the Court found the statistical evidence of victim-based discrimination documented in the Baldus study to be unpersuasive. Recent publicity about the race and class inequities inherent in the capital sentencing process—coupled with calls for death penalty moratoriums at both the state and federal level—suggest that the issue has not been laid to rest.

Justice From the Bench?

In 1918, the Bureau of the Census asked whether the disproportionate number of members of racial minorities incarcerated in state and federal prisons might be "to some extent the result of discrimination." This question, which was posed at a time when blacks constituted 11 percent of the population but 22 percent of all prison inmates, is still being asked today. As the proportion of the prison population that is black or Hispanic approaches 50 percent, social scientists and legal scholars continue to ask whether and to what extent racial discrimination infects the sentencing process.

The results of three decades of research suggest that higher arrest rates for serious crimes are the *primary*—but not the *only*—reason that members of racial minorities are locked up at substantially higher rates than whites. Although the flagrant racism of earlier eras has been eliminated, race-linked attributions of dangerousness, threat, and potential for reform continue to influence judges' evaluations of appropriate punishment. As a result, (a) unemployed young black and Hispanic men pay a higher punishment penalty than other offenders, (b) members of racial minorities who engage in drug-distribution or drug-related crime are punished more harshly than whites who commit these crimes, and (c) blacks and Hispanics receive smaller sentence discounts than whites for pleading guilty, cooperating with the prosecution, or securing pretrial release. Blacks and Hispanics who murder whites are also sentenced to death at higher rates than whites or those who murder members of racial minorities. The changes wrought by civil rights legislation and the sentencing reform movement notwithstanding, members of racial minorities who find themselves in the arms of the law continue to suffer discrimination in sentencing.

Discussion Questions: Chapter 5

1. Explain why racial disparities in sentencing do not necessarily reflect racial discrimination.

2. In the United States today, blacks and Hispanics are substantially more likely than whites to be locked up in our nation's prisons. How would Alfred Blumstein explain this? How would critics of Blumstein's work challenge his explanation?

3. Summarize the finding of the "four waves of research" on race and sentencing. What do more recent reviews of this research tell us about the effect of race and sentencing in the 1980s and 1990s?

4. Research conducted in Pennsylvania revealed that young black males were sentenced more harshly than other offenders. Similarly, research conducted in Chicago, Kansas City, and Miami concluded that young, unemployed black and Hispanic males paid an "imprisonment penalty." How would you explain these results?

5. Are black and Hispanic drug offenders sentenced more harshly than white drug offenders in state and federal courts? Do these differences signal racial disparity or racial discrimination?

6. Why have many policymakers concluded that the death penalty is "a failed experiment"?

7. Do the results of empirical studies of death penalty decisions confirm or refute the Supreme Court's assertion in *Gregg v. Georgia* that the guided-discretion statutes enacted in the wake of the *Furman* decision would eliminate arbitrariness and discrimination in the application of the death penalty?

8. Assume that there is racial discrimination in the application of the death penalty. What are the possible solutions to this problem?

Notes

1. *United States v. Clary*, 846 F.Supp. 768 (E.D. Mo).
2. Myrdal, *An American Dilemma: The Negro Problem and Modern Democracy*, p. 555.
3. Ibid., p. 553.
4. *Powell v. Alabama*, 287 U.S. 45 (1932).
5. *Norris v. Alabama*, 294 U.S. 587 (1935).
6. Kennedy, *Race, Crime, and the Law*, p. 104.
7. Curriden and Phillips, *Contempt of Court: The Turn-of-the-Century Lynching That Launched 100 Years of Federalism.*
8. Ibid., pp. 117-118.
9. Ibid., p. 213.
10. Ibid., p. 233. The case, however, did not end there. The U.S. Department of Justice filed contempt of court charges against 26 individuals believed to be responsible for Johnson's lynching. For the first and only time in history, the Justices of the U.S. Supreme Court, who were outraged that Chattanooga officials had defied their court order and had done nothing to stop the lynching, conducted a criminal trial. Six individuals, including the sheriff and one of the jailers, were found guilty of contempt of the Supreme Court. Three of the six were sentenced to serve 90 days in jail; the other three received sentences of 60 days.
11. Blumstein, Cohen, Martin, and Tonry (eds.), *Research on Sentencing: The Search for Reform*, Vol. I, p. 93.
12. U.S. Department of Justice, Bureau of Justice Statistics (BJS), *Capital Punishment 1999*, Table 5.
13. U.S. Department of Justice, (BJS), *Prisoners in 1999.*

14. U.S. Department of Justice, (BJS), *State Court Sentencing of Convicted Felons, 1996.*

15. Spohn and DeLone, "When Does Race Matter? An Analysis of the Conditions Under Which Race Affects Sentence Severity."

16. See Steffensmeier, Ulmer, and Kramer, "The Interaction of Race, Gender, and Age in Criminal Sentencing"; and Spohn and Holleran, "The Imprisonment Penalty Paid by Young, Unemployed Black and Hispanic Male Offenders."

17. Walker, Spohn, and DeLone, *The Color of Justice: Race, Ethnicity, and Crime in America*, p. 18.

18. For comprehensive reviews of this research see Chiricos and Crawford, "Race and Imprisonment: A Contextual Assessment of the Evidence"; Hagan, "Extra-Legal Attributes and Criminal Sentencing: An Assessment of a Sociological Viewpoint"; Hagan and Bumiller, "Making Sense of Sentencing: A Review and Critique of Sentencing Research"; Kleck, "Racial Discrimination in Sentencing: A Critical Evaluation of the Evidence With Additional Evidence on the Death Penalty"; Spohn, *Thirty Years of Sentencing Reform: The Quest for a Racially Neutral Sentencing Process*; and Zatz, "The Changing Forms of Racial/Ethnic Biases in Sentencing."

19. U.S. Department of Justice, BJS, *Prisoners in 1999.*

20. Walker, Spohn, and DeLone, *The Color of Justice*, p. 260.

21. Mauer, *Race To Incarcerate*, p. 125.

22. U.S. Department of Justice, BJS, *Prisoners in 1999.*

23. U.S. Department of Commerce; Bureau of the Census, *Negro Population: 1790-1915.*

24. Ibid., p. 438.

25. Tonry, *Malign Neglect*, p. 52.

26. Mann, *Unequal Justice: A Question of Color.*

27. Blumstein, "On the Racial Disproportionality of United States' Prison Populations"; Blumstein, "Racial Disproportionality of U.S. Prison Populations Revisited."

28. Wilbanks, *The Myth of a Racist Criminal Justice System.*

29. Walker, Spohn, and DeLone, *The Color of Justice.*

30. Blumstein, "On the Racial Disproportionality of Prison Populations," p. 1264.

31. Ibid., p. 1267.

32. Blumstein, "Racial Disproportionality of U.S. Prison Populations Revisited," p. 751.

33. Ibid., p. 750.

34. Crutchfield, Bridges, and Pitchford, "Analytical and Aggregation Biases in Analyses of Imprisonment: Reconciling Discrepancies in Studies of Racial Disparity"; Hawkins and Hardy, "Black-White Imprisonment Rates: A State-by-State Analysis"; Mauer, *Race To Incarcerate*; Sabol, "Racially Disproportionate Prison Populations in the United States: An Overview of Historical Patterns and Review of Contemporary Issues"; Tonry, *Malign Neglect*.

35. Ibid., p. 65.

36. Ibid., p. 59.

37. Crutchfield, Bridges, and Pitchford, "Analytical and Aggregation Biases in Analyses of Imprisonment"; Hawkins and Hardy, "Black-White Imprisonment Rates"; Sabol, "Racially Disproportionate Prison Populations in the United States."

38. Hawkins and Hardy, "Black-White Imprisonment Rates," p. 79.

39. Ibid., p. 79.

40. Tonry, *Malign Neglect*, pp. 67-68.

41. Ibid., p. 751.

42. Ibid., p. 752.

43. Mauer, *Race To Incarcerate*, p. 128.

44. Tonry, *Malign Neglect*, p. 754.

45. Ibid., p. 143.

46. Lynch and Sabol, "The Use of Coercive Social Control and Changes in the Race and Class Composition of U.S. Prison Populations," p. 30.

47. Miller, *Search and Destroy: African-American Males in the Criminal Justice System*, p. 80.

48. Tonry, *Malign Neglect*.

49. Ibid., p. 104.

50. Kennedy, *Race, Crime and the Law*.

51. Ibid., p. 351.

52. Ibid., pp. 370-371.

53. Ibid., p.377.

54. Ibid., p. 352.

55. Ibid., p. 384.

56. Ibid., p. 386.

57. Ibid., p. 22.

58. Blumstein, "On the Racial Disproportionality in U.S. Prison Populations," p. 1230.

59. Wriggens, "Rape, Racism, and the Law."
60. Kennedy, *Race, Crime, and the Law*, p. 77.
61. *State v. Tom*, 13 N.C. 569, 572 (1830).
62. Blackmun expressed this view in an opinion dissenting from the Supreme Court's order denying review in a Texas death penalty case, *Collins v. Collins*, No. 93-7054.
63. Murphy, "Racial Discrimination in the Criminal Justice System," p. 172.
64. Zatz, "The Changing Forms of Racial/Ethnic Biases in Sentencing," p. 69.
65. Sellin, "Race Prejudice in the Administration of Justice," p. 217.
66. Hagan, "Extra-Legal Attributes and Criminal Sentencing"; Kleck, "Racial Discrimination in Sentencing."
67. Hagan and Bumiller, "Making Sense of Sentencing."
68. Blumstein, Cohen, Martin, and Tonry, *Research on Sentencing*, p. 93.
69. Zatz, "The Changing Forms of Racial/Ethnic Biases in Sentencing."
70. Ibid., p. 87.
71. Chiricos and Crawford, "Race and Imprisonment."
72. Ibid., p. 282.
73. Ibid., p. 300.
74. Ibid., p. 300.
75. Spohn, "Thirty Years of Sentencing Reform: A Quest for a Racially Neutral Sentencing Process."
76. Hagan and Bumiller, "Making Sense of Sentencing," p. 21.
77. Spohn, "Thirty Years of Sentencing Reform," pp. 455-456.
78. Ibid., p. 458.
79. Ibid., pp. 460-461.
80. Ibid., pp. 466-467.
81. Ibid., p. 469.
82. Ibid., p. 461.
83. Ibid., pp. 469-473.
84. Zatz, "The Convergence of Race, Ethnicity, Gender, and Class on Court Decisionmaking: Looking Toward the 21st Century."
85. Ibid., p. 540.
86. Kramer and Steffensmeier, "Race and Imprisonment Decisions."
87. Steffensmeier, Kramer, and Streifel, "Gender and Imprisonment Decisions."

88. Steffensmeier, Kramer, and Ulmer, "Age Differences in Criminal Sentencing."

89. Steffensmeier, Ulmer, and Kramer, "The Interaction of Race, Gender, and Age in Criminal Sentencing."

90. Kramer and Steffensmeier, "Race and Imprisonment Decisions," p. 370.

91. Ibid., p. 368.

92. Ibid., p. 373.

93. Steffensmeier, Ulmer, and Kramer, "The Interaction of Race, Gender, and Age in Criminal Sentencing."

94. Ibid., p. 789.

95. Ibid., p. 768.

96. Spohn and Holleran, "The Imprisonment Penalty Paid by Young Unemployed Black and Hispanic Male Offenders."

97. Ibid., pp. 291-293.

98. Ibid., p. 301.

99. Quinney, *The Social Reality of Crime*, p. 142.

100. Melossi, "An Introduction: Fifty Years Later, Punishment and Social Structure in Contemporary Analysis," p. 317.

101. Barak, "Between the Waves: Mass-Mediated Themes of Crime and Justice," p. 137.

102. Spitzer, "Toward a Marxian Theory of Deviance," p. 645.

103. Ibid., p. 646.

104. Box and Hale, "Unemployment, Imprisonment, and Prison Overcrowding."

105. Ibid., p. 217.

106. Steffensmeier, Ulmer, and Kramer, "The Interaction of Race, Gender and Age in Criminal Sentencing," p. 789.

107. Ibid., p. 787.

108. Spohn and Holleran, "The Imprisonment Penalty Paid by Young, Unemployed Black and Hispanic Male Offenders," p. 301.

109. Tonry, *Malign Neglect*, p. 105.

110. Miller, *Search and Destroy*, p. 83.

111. Mauer, *Race To Incarcerate*, p. 143.

112. Chambliss, "Crime Control and Ethnic Minorities: Legitimizing Racial Oppression by Creating Moral Panics"; Tonry, *Malign Neglect*.

113. Jenkins, "'The Ice Age': The Social Construction of a Drug Panic."

114. For a review of this research, see Chiricos and DeLone, "Labor Surplus and Punishment: A Review and Assessment of Theory and Evidence."

115. Two additional studies, which did not focus exclusively on sentencing of drug offenders, did examine the effect of race on sentences imposed for drug offenses as one part of a larger study. Chiricos and Bales (1991) explored the relationship between race, unemployment, and punishment in two Florida counties in 1982. When they estimated separate models for several different types of crimes, they found that race did not directly affect the likelihood of incarceration for drug offenses. Race did, however, interact with the offender's employment status in an unexpected way. *Unemployed* black drug offenders were 3.7 times more likely to be held in jail prior to trial than employed white drug offenders, whereas *employed* black drug offenders were 5.9 times more likely to be incarcerated than employed whites. Crawford, Chiricos, and Kleck (1998), who examined the effect of offender race on the likelihood of being sentenced as a habitual offender, also included a separate analysis of drug offenders. They found that although defendants charged with a drug offense were less likely than defendants charged with other offenses to be habitualized, *blacks* charged with drug offenses were 3.6 times more likely than whites charged with drug offenses to be sentenced as habitual offenders; in fact, 94 percent of the 448 drug offenders habitualized in Florida during 1992 to 1993 were black.

116. Myers, "Symbolic Policy and the Sentencing of Drug Offenders."

117. Ibid., p. 312.

118. Spohn and Spears, "Sentencing of Drug Offenders in Three Cities: Does Race/Ethnicity Make a Difference?"

119. These adjusted sentences control for the seriousness of the crime, the offender's prior criminal record, the offender's age and gender, and for a number of additional variables.

120. Ibid.

121. Spohn and Spears, "Sentencing of Drug Offenders in Three Cities," p. 29.

122. Ibid. pp. 29-30.

123. Adler, "The Dynamite, Wreckage, and Scum in our Cities: The Social Construction of Deviance in Industrial America."

124. Albonetti, "Sentencing Under the Federal Sentencing Guidelines: Effects of Defendant Characteristics, Guilty Pleas, and Departures on Sentence Outcomes for Drug Offenses."

125. Ibid., p. 790.

126. Ibid., p. 496.

127. *McCleskey v. Kemp*, 481 U.S. 279, 107 S.Ct. 1756 (1987).

128. Baldus, Woodworth, and Pulaski, *Equal Justice and the Death Penalty: A Legal and Empirical Analysis.*

129. Ibid., p. 185.

130. *McCleskey v. Kemp*, 107 S. Ct. at 1777.

131. Ibid., at 1769.

132. *McCleskey v. Kemp*, 481 U.S. at 315 (Brennan, J., dissenting).

133. Bright, "Discrimination, Death and Denial: The Tolerance of Racial Discrimination in Infliction of the Death Penalty," p. 947.

134. Gross and Mauro, *Death & Discrimination: Racial Disparities in Capital Sentencing*, p. 212.

135. U.S. General Accounting Office, *Death Penalty Sentencing: Research Indicates Pattern of Racial Disparities*, p. 5.

136. Press Release, January 31, 2000. Available on the World Wide Web at: http://www.state.il.us/gov/press/00/Jan/morat.htm.

137. U.S. Department of Justice, *Survey of the Federal Death Penalty System (1988-2000).*

138. Press Release, Sept. 20, 2000 Available on the World Wide Web at: http://www.state.il.us/gov/press/00/Jan/morat.htm; http://www.igc.org/tcrp/press/HRR/death_penalty.htm.

139. See, for example, Walker, Spohn, and DeLone, *The Color of Justice.*

140. Gross and Mauro, *Death & Discrimination*, p. 110.

141. *In re Kemmler*, 136 U.S. 436, 447 (1890).

142. 356 U.S. 86, 99 (1958).

143. 409 U.S. 238 (1972).

144. Ibid., at 257 (Douglas, J., concurring); at 310 (Stewart, J., concurring); at 313 (White, J., concurring).

145. Ibid., at 257 (Marshall, J., concurring).

146. Ibid., at 310 (Stewart, J., concurring).

147. *Roberts v. Louisiana*, 428 U.S. 325 (1976); *Woodson v. North Carolina*, 428 U.S. 280 (1976).

148. *Woodson v. North Carolina*, 428 U.S. 280 (1976) at 303.

149. *Gregg v. Georgia*, 428 U.S. 153 (1976); *Proffitt v. Florida*, 428 U.S. 242 (1976); *Jurek v. Texas*, 428 U.S. 262 (1976).
150. *Gregg v. Georgia*, 428 U.S. 153 (1976) at 206-207.
151. *Coker v. Georgia*, 433 U.S. 584, 592 (1977).
152. *Tison v. Arizona*, 107 S.Ct. 1676 (1987).
153. *Penry v. Lynaugh*, 109 S.Ct. 2934(1989).
154. *Stanford v. Kentucky*, 109 S.Ct. 1969 (1989).
155. *McCleskey v. Kemp*, 107 S.Ct. 1756 (1987).
156. Ibid., at 1766n.7, 1775.
157. Ibid., at 1775,
158. Ibid., at 1778.
159. See, for example, Garfinkel, "Research Note on Inter- and Intra-Racial Homicides"; Johnson, "The Negro and Crime"; Mangum, *The Legal Status of the Negro*; Ralph, Sorensen, and Marquart, "A Comparison of Death-Sentenced and Incarcerated Murderers in Pre-*Furman* Texas"; Wolfgang, Kelly, and Nolde, "Comparison of the Executed and Commuted Among Admissions to Death Row"; Wolfgang and Reidel, "Race, Judicial Discretion, and the Death Penalty"; Wolfgang and Reidel, "Rape, Race, and the Death Penalty in Georgia."
160. Kleck, "Racial Discrimination in Criminal Sentencing," p. 788.
161. Florida Civil Liberties Union, *Rape: Selective Electrocution Based on Race*.
162. Wolfgang and Reidel, "Race, Judicial Discretion, and the Death Penalty."
163. U.S. Department of Justice, BJS, *Capital Punishment 1991*, p. 8.
164. Johnson, "The Negro and Crime."
165. Mangum, *The Legal Status of the Negro*.
166. Wolfgang, Kelly, and Nolde, "Comparisons Among the Executed and the Commuted."
167. Garfinkel, "Research Note on Inter- and Intra-Racial Homicide."
168. Kleck, "Racial Discrimination in Criminal Sentencing," p. 788.
169. Baldus, Woodworth, and Pulaski, *Equal Justice and the Death Penalty*.
170. Ralph, Sorensen, and Marquart, "A Comparison of Death-Sentenced and Incarcerated Murderers in Pre-*Furman* Texas."
171. Ibid., p. 207.
172. *Gregg v. Georgia*, 428 U.S. 153 (1976) at 206-207.

173. Studies that find either a race-of-victim or race-of-defendant effect include: Arkin, "Discrimination and Arbitrariness in Capital Punishment: An Analysis of Post-*Furman* Murder Cases in Dade County, Florida, 1973-1976"; Baldus, Pulaski, and Woodworth, "Comparative Review of Death Sentences: An Empirical Study of the Georgia Experience"; Baldus, Woodworth and Pulaski, *Equal Justice and the Death Penalty;* Bowers, "The Pervasiveness of Arbitrariness and Discrimination Under Post-*Furman* Capital Statutes"; Bowers and Pierce, "Arbitrariness and Discrimination Under Post-*Furman* Capital Statutes"; Ekland-Olson, "Structured Discretion, Racial Bias, and the Death Penalty: The First Decade After *Furman* in Texas"; Gross and Mauro, *Death & Discrimination;* Keil and Vito, "Race and the Death Penalty in Kentucky Murder Trials: An Analysis of Post-*Gregg* Outcomes"; Paternoster, "Prosecutorial Discretion in Requesting the Death Penalty: A Case of Victim-Based Discrimination"; Radelet, "Racial Characteristics and the Imposition of the Death Penalty"; Radelet and Pierce, "Race and Prosecutorial Discretion in Homicide Cases"; Smith, "Patterns of Discrimination in Assessments of the Death Penalty: The Case of Louisiana."

174. U.S. General Accounting Office, *Death Penalty Sentencing: Research Indicates Pattern of Racial Disparities.*

175. Ibid., p. 6.

176. Ibid., p. 5.

177. Baldus, Woodworth, and Pulaski, *Equal Justice and the Death Penalty.*

178. Ibid., pp. 160-162.

179. Ibid., pp. 185-186.

180. Gross and Mauro, *Death & Discrimination.*

181. Ibid., p. 69.

182. Ibid., p. 91.

183. Ibid., p. 109.

184. Ibid., p. 110.

185. Ibid., p. 113.

186. Ibid., p. 115.

187. Mills, Armstrong, and, Holt, "Flawed Trials Lead to Death Chamber," *Chicago Tribune,* June 11, 2000; Armstrong and Mills, "Gatekeeper Court Keeps Gates Shut," *Chicago Tribune,*

June 12, 2000. Available on the World Wide Web at http://www.chicagotribune.com.

188. U.S. Department of Justice, BJS, *Sourcebook of Criminal Justice Statistics, 1998.*

189. Mills, Armstrong, and Holt, "Flawed Trials Lead to Death Chamber," *Chicago Tribune,* June 11, 2000.

190. Texas Civil Rights Project, *The Death Penalty in Texas: Due Process and Equal Justice . . . or Rush to Execution?*

191. Ibid., p. i.

192. Ibid., p. iii.

193. Ibid., p. iv.

194. Ibid., p. ii.

195. Baldus, Woodworth, and Pulaski, *Equal Justice and the Death Penalty,* p. 185.

Chapter Six

30 Years of Sentencing Reform

What happens to an offender after conviction is the least understood, the most fraught with irrational discrepancies, and the most in need of improvement of any phase in our criminal justice system.

United States v. Waters[1]

Concerns about disparity, discrimination, and unfairness in sentencing led to a "remarkable burst of reform"[2] that began in the mid-1970s and continues today. The initial focus of reform efforts was the indeterminate sentence, in which the judge imposed a minimum and maximum sentence and the parole board determined the date of release. The parole board's determination of when the offender should be released rested on its judgment of whether the offender had been rehabilitated or had served enough time for the particular crime. Under indeterminate sentencing, sentences were tailored to the individual offender, and discretion was distributed not only to the criminal justice officials who determined the sentence but also to corrections officials and the parole board. The result of this process was "a system of sentencing in which there was little understanding or predictability as to who would be imprisoned and for how long."[3]

Both liberal and conservative reformers challenged the principles underlying the indeterminate sentence and called for changes designed to curb discretion, reduce disparity and discrimination, and achieve proportionality and parsimony in sentencing. Liberals and civil rights activists argued that indeterminate sentencing was arbitrary and capricious and therefore violated defendants' rights to equal protection and due process of law.[4] They charged that indeterminate sentences were used to incapacitate those who could not be rehabilitated and that offenders' uncertainty about their dates of release contributed to prison unrest. Liberal critics were also apprehensive about the potential for racial bias under indeterminate sentencing schemes.[5] They asserted that "racial discrimination in the criminal justice system was epidemic, that judges, parole boards, and corrections officials could not be trusted, and that tight controls on officials' discretion offered the only way to limit racial disparities."[6]

Political conservatives, on the other hand, argued that the emphasis on rehabilitation too often resulted in excessively lenient treatment of offenders who had committed serious crimes or had serious criminal histories.[7] They also charged that sentences that were not linked to crime seriousness and offender culpability were unjust.[8] These conservative critics championed sentencing reforms designed to establish and enforce more punitive sentencing standards. Their arguments were bolstered by the findings of research demonstrating that most correctional programs designed to rehabilitate offenders and reduce recidivism were ineffective.[9]

After a few initial "missteps," in which jurisdictions attempted to *eliminate* discretion altogether through flat-time sentencing,[10] states and the federal government adopted structured sentencing proposals designed to *control* the discretion of sentencing judges. A number of states adopted determinate sentencing policies that offered judges a limited number of sentencing options and included enhancements for use of a weapon, presence of a prior criminal record, or infliction of serious injury. Other states and the federal government adopted sentence guidelines that incorporated crime seriousness and prior criminal record into a sentencing "grid" that judges were to use in determining the appropriate sentence. Other reforms enacted at both the federal and state level included mandatory minimum penalties for certain types of offenses (especially drug and weapons offenses), "three-strikes-and-you're out " laws that mandated long prison sentences for repeat offenders, and truth-in-sentencing statutes that required offenders to serve a larger portion of the sentence before being released.

This process of experimentation and reform revolutionized sentencing in the United States. Thirty years ago, every state and the federal government had an indeterminate sentencing system and "the word 'sentencing' generally signified a slightly mysterious process which . . . involved individualized decisions that judges were uniquely qualified to make."[11] The situation today is much more complex. Sentencing policies and practices vary enormously on a number of dimensions, and there is no longer anything that can be described as the American approach.

In this chapter, we discuss the sentencing reform movement. We begin by describing the changes in sentencing policies and practices that have occurred since the mid-1970s. We focus on determinate sentencing and sentencing guidelines, mandatory minimum sentencing statutes, three-strikes-and-you're-out laws, and truth-in-sentencing laws. In Chapter 7, we discuss the impact of these changes. We ask whether the reforms have resulted in more punitive sentences, less crime, or reductions in disparity and discrimination.

The Sentencing Reform Movement

The attack on indeterminate sentencing and the proposals for reform reflected conflicting views of the goals and purposes of punishment, as well as questions regarding the exercise of discretion at sentencing. As discussed in Chapter 1, proponents of retributive or just deserts theories of punishment argue that sentence severity should be closely linked to the seriousness of the crime and the culpability of the offender. Thus, those who commit comparable offenses should receive similar punishments, and those who commit more serious crimes should be punished more harshly than those who commit less serious crimes. Like cases, in other words, should be treated alike. Proponents of utilitarian rationales of punishment, including deterrence, incapacitation, and rehabilitation, on the other hand, argue that the ultimate goal of punishment is to prevent future crime and that the severity of the sanction imposed on an offender should serve this purpose. Thus, the amount of punishment need not be closely proportioned to crime seriousness or offender culpability; it can instead be tailored to reflect individual circumstances related to rehabilitative needs or deterrence and incapacitation considerations.

These conflicting views of the goals of punishment incorporate differing notions of the amount of discretion that judges and juries should be afforded at sentencing. A sentencing scheme based on utilitarian rationales would allow the judge or jury discretion to shape sentences to fit individuals and their crimes. The judge or jury would be free to consider all relevant circumstances, including "the importance of the behavioral norms that were violated, the effects of the crime on the victim, and the amalgam of aggravating and mitigating circumstances that make a defendant more or less culpable and make one sentence more appropriate than another."[12] A retributive or just deserts sentencing scheme, on the other hand, would constrain discretion more severely. The judge or jury would determine the appropriate sentence using only legally relevant considerations (essentially crime seriousness and to a lesser extent, prior criminal record) and would be precluded from considering individual characteristics or circumstances.

The reforms enacted during the sentencing reform movement reflect both retributive and utilitarian principles and are designed to achieve both retributive and utilitarian objectives. Sentencing guidelines, for example, are based explicitly on notions of just desert. Punishments are scaled along a two-dimensional grid measuring the seriousness of the crime and the offender's prior criminal record, and judges are expected to impose the sentence indicated by the intersection of these two factors. By curtailing the judge's discretion, reformers hoped to eliminate disparity and discrimination. By tying sentence severity to crime seriousness and offender culpability, they hoped to achieve proportionality and fairness in sentencing and, at least in the minds of some, to produce more punitive sentences. But most sentencing guidelines also incorporate, implicitly if not explicitly, utilitarian principles and objectives. Most allow the judge to depart from the presumptive sentence if there are good reasons to do so. Although the circumstances under which departures are permitted may be narrowly defined, allowing the judge to depart opens the door to individualization of sentences based on the offender's dangerousness, likelihood of recidivism, or amenability to rehabilitation. The ability to depart, in other words, means that the judge can attempt to achieve utilitarian objectives of incapacitation, deterrence, and rehabilitation.

The other sentencing reforms discussed in this chapter—mandatory minimum sentencing statutes, three-strikes-and-you're-out laws, and truth-in-sentencing laws—are based explicitly on theories of deterrence and incapacitation. These "tough-on-crime" sentencing policies prescribe greater use of imprisonment and longer sentences. Mandatory minimum statutes and three-strikes laws target certain types of offenders: those who use firearms to commit a crime, those who engage in more serious drug offenses, and those who repeat their crimes. Truth-in-sentencing laws, on the other hand, are designed to ensure that all offenders who are imprisoned serve a greater portion of their sentence. Although each of these three reforms reflects a view that justice is served when those who commit very serious crimes receive harsh punishment, their primary purpose is to reduce crime by deterring would-be offenders and/or incapacitating dangerous offenders.

In the sections that follow, we discuss the changes in sentencing policies and practices that have occurred during the past 30 years. We begin with a discussion of three structured sentencing reforms: voluntary or advisory sentencing guidelines, determinate sentencing, and presumptive sentencing guidelines. We then examine mandatory minimum sentencing statutes, three-strikes-and-you're-out laws, and truth-in-sentencing laws.

Structured Sentencing Reforms

In 1972, Marvin Frankel, U. S. District Judge for the Southern District of New York, issued an influential call for reform of the sentencing process.[13] Judge Frankel characterized the indeterminate sentencing system that existed at that time as "a bizarre 'nonsystem' of extravagant powers confided to variable and essentially unregulated judges, keepers, and parole officials."[14] Frankel decried the degree of discretion given to judges, which he maintained led to "lawlessness" in sentencing. As he pointed out,

> The scope of what we call "discretion" permits imprisonment for anything from a day to 1, 5, 10, 20 or more years. All would presumably join in denouncing a statute that said "the judge may impose any sentence he pleases." Given the morality of men, the power to set a man free or confine him for up to 30 years is not sharply distinguishable.[15]

Judge Frankel, who claimed that judges "were not trained at all" for "the solemn work of sentencing,"[16] called for legislative reforms designed to regulate "the unchecked powers of the untutored judge."[17] More to the point, he called for the creation of an administrative agency called a *sentencing commission* that would create rules for sentencing that judges would be required to follow.

Judge Frankel's calls for reform did not go unheeded. Reformers from both sides of the political spectrum joined in the attack on indeterminate sentencing and pushed for reforms designed to curtail judicial discretion and eliminate arbitrariness and disparity in sentencing. In response, state legislatures and the Congress enacted a series of incremental structured sentencing reforms. A number of jurisdictions experimented with voluntary or advisory sentencing guidelines. Other states adopted determinate sentencing policies and abolished release on parole. Still other jurisdictions created sentencing commissions authorized to promulgate presumptive sentencing guidelines. Whereas every jurisdiction had indeterminate sentencing in 1970, by the mid-1990s, 5 states had determinate sentencing, 7 states had voluntary sentencing guidelines, and 11 states had presumptive sentencing guidelines. Indeterminate sentencing survived in 27 states and the District of Columbia.[18]

Voluntary or Advisory Sentencing Guidelines

The first stage in the movement toward structured sentencing was the development of voluntary or advisory sentencing guidelines. These early guidelines typically were *descriptive* rather than *prescriptive*; they were based on the past sentencing practices of judges in the jurisdiction and not on determinations of what the sentence ought to be. The idea, in other words, was to document the sentences that judges in the jurisdiction typically imposed for different types of offenses and different categories of offenders. For example, if the normal penalty for a first-time offender convicted of armed robbery was 5 to 6 years in prison, the guidelines would establish this range as the recommended sentence and judges would be encouraged to sentence within the range. If over time, the sentences imposed by judges in the jurisdiction became more severe or less severe, the guidelines could be revised to reflect these changes.

The primary goal of these voluntary/descriptive guidelines was to reduce intra-jurisdictional disparity in sentencing. Advocates of this reform hoped that identifying the normal penalty or going rate would encourage judges at the two ends of the sentencing continuum to move closer to the middle. The problem, of course, was that the guidelines were, as the name implies, *voluntary*. Judges were not obligated to comply with the guidelines. In fact, the judge could simply ignore them, and the defendant could not appeal a sentence that was harsher than the guidelines prescribed.

The results of early studies of the impact of voluntary guidelines are not surprising. These studies found low rates of compliance and hence, little impact on reducing disparity.[19] Generally, the sentences imposed during the post-reform period were not more consistent than those imposed during the pre-reform period. For example, Rich and his colleagues[20] evaluated the impact of the guidelines in Denver and Philadelphia, two of the first jurisdictions to adopt this particular reform. They found that in each jurisdiction, about 70 percent of the decisions to incarcerate but only about 40 percent of the sentence length decisions were consistent with the guidelines during both time periods. Interviews with judges and lawyers confirmed that few of the judges in either jurisdiction felt obligated to comply with the guidelines.

Although voluntary sentencing guidelines did not produce the instrumental effects that reformers had predicted, they were an important first step in the sentencing reform process. The lessons learned during this early stage in the process helped to guide and structure the efforts of those who subsequently lobbied for determinate sentencing and presumptive sentencing guidelines.

Determinate Sentencing

In the mid- to late 1970s, several states abolished release on parole and replaced the indeterminate sentence with a fixed (i.e., determinate) sentence. Under this system, the state legislature established a presumptive range of confinement for various categories of offenses. The judge imposed a fixed number of years from within this range, and the offender would serve this term minus time off for good behavior. Determinate sentencing was first adopted in California, Illinois, Indiana, and Maine; it was later adopted in Arizona. These five states have retained their determinate sentencing laws, but no other states have enacted them.

Determinate sentencing was seen as a way to restrain judicial discretion and thus to reduce disparity and (at least in the minds of conservative reformers) preclude judges from imposing overly lenient sentences. However, the degree to which the reforms constrain discretion varies. As shown in Exhibit 6.1, which compares the determinate sentencing provisions initially enacted in California and Illinois, the presumptive range of confinement established by the legislature was narrow in California but wide in Illinois. The California Uniform Determinate Sentencing Law, which took effect on July 1, 1977, provides that judges are to choose one of three specified sentences for persons convicted of particular offenses. The judge is to impose the middle term unless there are aggravating or mitigating circumstances that justify imposing the higher or lower term. Thus, the presumptive sentence for robbery is 3 years; if there are aggravating circumstances, the sentence could increase to 4 years, and mitigating circumstances could reduce the sentence to 2 years. The sentence also could be enhanced by 1 year each for prior incarceration, use of a weapon, or infliction of serious injury.

Judges have considerably more discretion under the Illinois Determinate Sentencing Statute. Felonies are divided into six classifications, and the range of penalties is wide, especially for the more serious offenses. Murder and Class X offenses are nonprobationable, but judges can impose prison terms of 20 to 40 years or life for murder and 6 to 30 years for Class X offenses. If there are aggravating circumstances, the sentence range for

Exhibit 6.1 Determinate Sentencing in California and Illinois

Felony Categories and Range of Penalties in California

Presumptive Sentence (Years)	Range in Aggravation	Range in Mitigation	Examples
2	+1 year	-8 months	Burglary, grand theft
3	+1 year	-1 year	Robbery (unarmed), manslaughter
4	+1 year	-1 year	Rape, sale of heroin
6	+1 year	-1 year	Murder (second degree)

Felony Categories and Range of Penalties in Illinois

Felony Category	Regular Term (Years)	Extended Term (Years)	Examples
Murder	Life or 20-40	30-60	Murder
Class X	6-30		Rape, armed robbery, aggravated kidnapping
Class 1	4-15	15-60	Dealing in narcotics
Class 2	3-7	4-15	Burglary, arson, robbery
Class 3	2-5	5-10	Theft (more than $150), aggravated battery
Class 4	1-3	3-6	Possession of marijuana, theft (less than $150)

SOURCE: *National Assessment of Structured Sentencing* (Table 2-1 and Table 2-2), by the U.S. Department of Justice, Bureau of Justice Assistance, 1996. Washington, DC: Author.

Class X felonies increases to 30 to 60 years. As noted above, whereas judges in California were expected to impose a sentence of 3 years for robbery, Illinois judges could impose anywhere from 3 to 7 years. If there were aggravating circumstances, the sentence range for robbery increased to 7 to 14 years in Illinois, compared with 4 years in California.

Although judges in jurisdictions with determinate sentencing retain control over the critical probation or prison decision, their overall discretion is reduced, particularly in states like California. Evaluations of the impact of the California law showed that judges complied with the law and imposed the middle term in a majority of the cases.[21] Despite predictions that discretion would shift to the prosecutor and that plea bargaining would consequently increase, there were no changes in the rate or timing of guilty pleas that could be attributed to the determinate sentencing law. On the other hand, there was some evidence that prosecutors were increasingly likely to use provisions regarding sentence enhancements and probation ineligibility as bargaining chips. One study, for example, found that the sentence enhancement for use of a weapon was dropped in 40 percent of robbery cases and that the enhancement for serious bodily injury was struck in 65 to 70 percent of these cases.[22] As Walker noted, "The net effect of the law seems to have been to narrow and focus the exercise of plea-bargaining discretion. Given the very restricted options on sentence length, the importance of the various enhancements and disqualifiers increased."[23]

Partly as a result of research showing that determinate sentencing laws did not significantly constrain the discretion of judges, the determinate sentencing movement lost steam and eventually sputtered out. No state has adopted determinate sentencing since 1983.

Presumptive Sentencing Guidelines

Since the late 1970s, presumptive sentencing guidelines developed by an independent sentencing commission have been the dominant approach to sentencing reform in the United States. At least 20 states have adopted or are considering sentencing guidelines, and sentencing at the federal level has been structured by guidelines since 1987. In 1994, the American Bar Association (ABA) endorsed sentencing guidelines; it recommended that all jurisdictions create permanent sentencing commissions charged with drafting presumptive sentencing provisions that apply to both prison and nonprison sanctions and are tied to prison capacities.[24]

Although questions have been raised about the effectiveness and fairness of sentencing guidelines, they nonetheless are, as one commentator recently noted, "'alive and well' in the United States."[25]

State Sentencing Guidelines

The guidelines systems adopted by the states have a number of common features. Each of the guideline states established a permanent sentencing commission or committee composed of criminal justice officials and, sometimes, private citizens and legislators. The commission is charged with studying sentencing practices and formulating presumptive sentence recommendations. Some states require legislative approval of the guidelines. In other states, the guidelines either go into effect unless the state legislature rejects them or are issued by administrative order of the state supreme court.[26] The commission is also authorized to monitor the implementation and impact of the guidelines and to recommend amendments.

A second common feature of state guidelines is that the presumptive sentence is based primarily on two factors: the severity of the offense and the seriousness of the offender's prior criminal record. Typically, these two factors are arrayed on a two-dimensional grid; their intersection determines whether the offender should be sentenced to prison and, if so, for how long. The Minnesota Sentencing Guidelines Grid is shown in Exhibit 6.2. The dark line separates offense/criminal history combinations that are probationable (below the line) from those that are not (above the line). The guidelines require prison sentences for all offenders convicted of aggravated robbery. The length of the term depends upon the offender's criminal history. The guideline range is 44 to 52 months if the offender's criminal history score is 0, 54 to 62 months if the criminal history score is 1, and 104 to 112 months if the criminal history score is 6 or more. Offenders convicted of less serious crimes may receive a nonincarceration sentence, again depending upon the criminal history score. Offenders convicted of simple robbery could either be placed on probation or sentenced to prison if their criminal history scores are 2 or less; if their criminal history scores are greater than 2, prison sentences would be required.

States with presumptive sentencing guidelines, as opposed to voluntary or advisory guidelines, require judges to follow them or provide reasons for failing to do so. Judges are allowed to depart from the guidelines and impose harsher or more lenient sentences if there are specified aggravating or mitigating circumstances (see Box 6.1). Some states also list factors that should not be used to increase or decrease the presumptive sentence. For example, the Minnesota guidelines state that the offender's race, gender,

Exhibit 6.2. The Minnesota Sentencing Guidelines Grid

SEVERITY LEVEL OF CONVICTION OFFENSE (Common offenses listed in italics)		CRIMINAL HISTORY SCORE						
		0	1	2	3	4	5	6 or more
Murder, 2nd Degree *(intentional murder, drive-by-shootings)*	X	306 *299-313*	326 *319-333*	346 *339-353*	366 *359-373*	386 *379-393*	406 *399-413*	426 *419-433*
Murder, 3rd Degree Murder., 2nd Degree *(unintentional murder)*	IX	150 *144-156*	165 *159-171*	180 *174-186*	195 *189-201*	210 *204-216*	225 *219-231*	240 *234-246*
Criminal Sexual Conduct, 1st Degree Assault, 1st Degree	VIII	86 *81-91*	98 *93-103*	110 *105-115*	122 *117-127*	134 *129-139*	146 *141-151*	158 *153-163*
Aggravated Robbery 1st Degree	VII	48 *44-52*	58 *54-62*	68 *64-72*	78 *74-82*	88 *84-92*	98 *94-102*	108 *104-112*
Criminal Sexual Conduct, 2nd Degree (a) & (b)	VI	21	26	30	34 *33-35*	44 *42-46*	54 *50-58*	65 *60-70*
Residential Burglary Simple Robbery	V	18	23	27	30 *29-31*	38 *36-40*	46 *43-49*	54 *50-58*
Nonresidential Burglary	IV	12¹	15	18	21	25 *24-26*	32 *30-34*	41 *37-45*
Theft Crimes *(Over $2,500)*	III	12¹	13	15	17	19 *18-20*	22 *21-23*	25 *24-26*
Theft Crimes *($2,500 or less)* Check Forgery *($200-$2,500)*	II	12¹	12¹	13	15	17	19	21 *20-22*
Sale of Simulated Controlled Substance	I	12¹	12¹	12¹	13	15	17	19 *18-20*

 Presumptive commitment to state imprisonment. First Degree Murder is excluded from the guidelines by law and continues to have a mandatory life sentence. See section **II.E. Mandatory Sentences** for policy regarding those sentences controlled by law, including minimum periods of supervision for sex offenders released from prison.

Presumptive stayed sentence; at the discretion of the judge, up to a year in jail and/or other non-jail sanctions can be imposed as conditions of probation. However, certain offenses in this section of the grid always carry a presumptive commitment to a state prison. These offenses include Third Degree Controlled Substance Crimes when the offender has a prior felony drug conviction, Burglary of an Occupied Dwelling when the offender has a prior felony burglary conviction, second and subsequent Criminal Sexual Conduct offenses and offenses carrying a mandatory minimum prison term due to the use of a dangerous weapon (e.g., Second Degree Assault). See section **II.C. Presumptive Sentence** and **II.E. Mandatory Sentences.**

¹ One year and one day   Effective August 1, 1998

and employment status are not legitimate grounds for departure. In North Carolina, on the other hand, judges are allowed to consider the fact that the offender "has a positive employment history or is gainfully employed."[27]

In most states, a departure from the guidelines can be appealed to state appellate courts by either party. If, for example, the judge sentences the defendant to probation when the guidelines call for prison, the prosecuting attorney can appeal. If the judge imposes 60 months when the guidelines call for 36, the defendant can appeal. The standards used by appellate

BOX 6.1

REASONS FOR DEPARTURES IN PENNSYLVANIA

John Kramer and Jeffrey Ulmer examined the official reasons given by judges in Pennsylvania for departing from the guidelines. The most common reasons for downward departures were as follows:

Defendant is remorseful/good candidate for rehabilitation

Guilty plea/plea bargain

Defendant is caring for dependents, court is unwilling to disrupt family ties

Defendant is employed, court is unwilling to disrupt job ties

Offense or prior record is qualitatively less serious than the guideline scores indicate

Kramer and Ulmer also interviewed a number of Pennsylvania judges about the factors that influence decisions to depart from the guidelines. Comments made by these judges included the following:

> In a departure situation, you try and get a sense of whether the person really is likely to return, whether the person really can profit from probation, whether you think they have a sense of remorse. I mean, it's everything that you rely on in your experience and judgment and trying to size a person up.

> You rely on your sense of whether or not, if you give them another chance, are they really not going to commit another crime? You can get a good picture of people in just a few minutes.

> Every case is so different. . . . I always consider the nature of the offense, the defendant's prior record, their character and attitude in general. It is just everything put together.

This study found that the likelihood of a downward departure was affected by the offender's gender and race and by the type of disposition in the case: Judges were more likely to depart if the defendants were women, not members of racial minorities, and pled guilty. The authors contend that both the official reasons given by judges and the comments made during interviews "suggest how race- and gender-linked stereotypes" may affect departure decisions. As they note,

> Although these judges do not explicitly mention factors such as race or gender, it is plausible the process of "sizing up" a defendant's "character and attitude" in terms of whether he or she is a candidate for a departure below guidelines may involve the use of race and gender stereotypes and the behavioral expectations they mobilize.

SOURCE: Adapted from "Sentencing Disparity and Departures From Guidelines," by J. Kramer and J. Ulmer, 1996, *Justice Quarterly* 13: 81-106.

courts to review sentences vary widely. In Minnesota, for example, the appellate court is authorized to determine "whether the sentence is inconsistent with statutory requirements, unreasonable, inappropriate, excessive, unjustifiably disparate, or not warranted by the findings of fact."[28] In contrast, in Oregon, a departure will be upheld as long as it is warranted by "substantial and compelling reasons."[29] If the appellate court rules that the sentence departure is unwarranted, the sentence will be overturned and the offender will be resentenced.

These similarities notwithstanding, state guidelines differ on a number of dimensions. Arguably, the most important difference concerns the purpose or goals of the reform. As the Bureau of Justice Assistance stated,

> States create sentencing commissions for many reasons. . . . The most frequently cited reasons are to increase sentencing fairness, to reduce unwarranted disparity, to establish truth in sentencing, to reduce or control prison crowding, and to establish standards for appellate review of sentences.[30]

Although all state guidelines attempt to make sentencing more uniform and to eliminate unwarranted disparities, the other goals are not universally accepted. Using the guidelines to gain control over rapidly growing prison populations, for example, is a relatively recent development. Minnesota, the first state to incorporate this goal into the guidelines, stated that the prison population should never exceed 95 percent of available capacity. Pennsylvania, on the other hand, initially did not link sentencing decisions to correctional resources; by the time they did, prisons and jails were operating at 150 percent of capacity.[31]

State guidelines systems differ on other dimensions as well. Some guidelines are designed primarily to achieve just deserts, whereas others incorporate utilitarian as well as retributive rationales. Most guidelines cover felony crimes only, but a few, such as those adopted in Pennsylvania, also apply to misdemeanors. Some apply only to the decision to incarcerate or not and the length of incarceration, whereas others also regulate the length and conditions of nonprison sentences. Most guidelines states abolished discretionary release on parole, but a few states have retained it. The procedures for determining offense seriousness and prior record vary widely, as do the presumptive sentences associated with various combinations of offense seriousness and prior record.[32] Even among states with sentencing guidelines, in other words, there is no typical "American approach."

The U.S. Sentencing Guidelines

In 1977, Senator Edward M. Kennedy responded to Judge Marvin Frankel's call for reform of federal sentencing and introduced the Sentencing Guidelines Bill[33]. The purpose of the bill was to establish a U.S. Commission on Sentencing, which would be authorized to develop sentence guidelines for U.S. District Court Judges. Senator Kennedy, who at various times described federal sentencing as "arbitrary," "hopelessly inconsistent," "a national scandal," and "desperately" in need of reform,[34] introduced versions of his sentencing reform bill in the next four Congresses, until it was finally enacted as the Sentencing Reform Act of 1984 (SRA).[35]

The overriding objective of the SRA was to "enhance the ability of the criminal justice system to combat crime through an effective, fair sentencing system."[36] The SRA created the U. S. Sentencing Commission (USSC), which was authorized to develop and implement presumptive sentencing guidelines designed to achieve "honesty," "uniformity," and "proportionality" in sentencing.[37] The SRA also abolished discretionary release on parole, stated that departures from the guidelines would be permitted with written justification, and provided for appellate review of sentences to determine if the guidelines were correctly applied or if a departure was reasonable.

The federal sentencing guidelines promulgated by the USSC went into effect in 1987. In 1989 the U.S. Supreme Court ruled in *Mistretta v. United States*[38] that the SRA, the USSC, and the guidelines were constitutional. The federal guidelines are extremely complex. The first guidelines manual consisted of over 300 pages of directives; the manual is now over 900 pages long and includes nearly 600 amendments enacted since 1987.[39] Like the guidelines adopted by the states, the federal guidelines are based on the seriousness of the offense and the offender's prior criminal record. Unlike the state systems, most of which use 12 or fewer categories of offense seriousness, the federal guidelines use a 43-level sentencing grid (see Exhibit 6.3). They also require the sentencing judge "to follow complex and abstract rules and to make minute arithmetic calculations in order to arrive at a sentence."[40] Judges and other criminal justice officials calculate the sentence using a standardized worksheet that, at least in theory, guides everyone to the same sentence. Critics, however, charge that this process is overly rigid and mechanical. They contend that the "traditional judicial role of deliberation and moral judgment" has been replaced with "complex quantitative calculations that convey the impression of scientific precision and objectivity."[41]

There are other important differences between state and federal guidelines. For example, federal guidelines are based on the defendant's "rele-

Exhibit 6.3. The Federal Sentencing Guidelines Grid

SENTENCING TABLE
(in months of imprisonment)

Offense Level	Criminal History Category (Criminal History Points)					
	I (0 or 1)	II (2 or 3)	III (4, 5, 6)	IV (7, 8, 9)	V (10, 11, 12)	VI (13 or more)
1	0 - 6	0 - 6	0 - 6	0 - 6	0 - 6	0 - 6
2	0 - 6	0 - 6	0 - 6	0 - 6	0 - 6	1 - 7
3	0 - 6	0 - 6	0 - 6	0 - 6	2 - 8	3 - 9
4	0 - 6	0 - 6	0 - 6	2 - 8	4 - 10	6 - 12
5	0 - 6	0 - 6	1 - 7	4 - 10	6 - 12	9 - 15
6	0 - 6	1 - 7	2 - 8	6 - 12	9 - 15	12 - 18
7	0 - 6	2 - 8	4 - 10	8 - 14	12 - 18	15 - 21
8	0 - 6	4 - 10	6 - 12	10 - 16	15 - 21	18 - 24
9	4 - 10	6 - 12	8 - 14	12 - 18	18 - 24	21 - 27
10	6 - 12	8 - 14	10 - 16	15 - 21	21 - 27	24 - 30
11	8 - 14	10 - 16	12 - 18	18 - 24	24 - 30	27 - 33
12	10 - 16	12 - 18	15 - 21	21 - 27	27 - 33	30 - 37
13	12 - 18	15 - 21	18 - 24	24 - 30	30 - 37	33 - 41
14	15 - 21	18 - 24	21 - 27	27 - 33	33 - 41	37 - 46
15	18 - 24	21 - 27	24 - 30	30 - 37	37 - 46	41 - 51
16	21 - 27	24 - 30	27 - 33	33 - 41	41 - 51	46 - 57
17	24 - 30	27 - 33	30 - 37	37 - 46	46 - 57	51 - 63
18	27 - 33	30 - 37	33 - 41	41 - 51	51 - 63	57 - 71
19	30 - 37	33 - 41	37 - 46	46 - 57	57 - 71	63 - 78
20	33 - 41	37 - 46	41 - 51	51 - 63	63 - 78	70 - 87
21	37 - 46	41 - 51	46 - 57	57 - 71	70 - 87	77 - 96
22	41 - 51	46 - 57	51 - 63	63 - 78	77 - 96	84 - 105
23	46 - 57	51 - 63	57 - 71	70 - 87	84 - 105	92 - 115
24	51 - 63	57 - 71	63 - 78	77 - 96	92 - 115	100 - 125
25	57 - 71	63 - 78	70 - 87	84 - 105	100 - 125	110 - 137
26	63 - 78	70 - 87	78 - 97	92 - 115	110 - 137	120 - 150
27	70 - 87	78 - 97	87 - 108	100 - 125	120 - 150	130 - 162
28	78 - 97	87 - 108	97 - 121	110 - 137	130 - 162	140 - 175
29	87 - 108	97 - 121	108 - 135	121 - 151	140 - 175	151 - 188
30	97 - 121	108 - 135	121 - 151	135 - 168	151 - 188	168 - 210
31	108 - 135	121 - 151	135 - 168	151 - 188	168 - 210	188 - 235
32	121 - 151	135 - 168	151 - 188	168 - 210	188 - 235	210 - 262
33	135 - 168	151 - 188	168 - 210	188 - 235	210 - 262	235 - 293
34	151 - 188	168 - 210	188 - 235	210 - 262	235 - 293	262 - 327
35	168 - 210	188 - 235	210 - 262	235 - 293	262 - 327	292 - 365
36	188 - 235	210 - 262	235 - 293	262 - 327	292 - 365	324 - 405
37	210 - 262	235 - 293	262 - 327	292 - 365	324 - 405	360 - life
38	235 - 293	262 - 327	292 - 365	324 - 405	360 - life	360 - life
39	262 - 327	292 - 365	324 - 405	360 - life	360 - life	360 - life
40	292 - 365	324 - 405	360 - life	360 - life	360 - life	360 - life
41	324 - 405	360 - life	360 - life	360 - life	360 - life	360 - life
42	360 - life	360 - life	360 - life	360 - life	360 - life	360 - life
43	life	life	life	life	life	life

Zone labels (left margin): Zone A (Offense Levels 1–8), Zone B (Offense Levels 9–10), Zone C (Offense Levels 11–12), Zone D (Offense Levels 13–43).

vant conduct" at the time of the offense, but state guidelines are not. Federal judges are required to consider not simply the seriousness of the offense for which the defendant has been convicted but also the actual conduct—the relevant conduct—that landed the defendant in court. This can include charges that were never filed, charges that were filed but later dismissed during plea negotiations, and charges that resulted in acquittals.

Consider, for example, the case of an offender who has been convicted of possession of 2 grams of crack cocaine. He was initially charged with possession of 5 grams of crack cocaine and possession of an unregistered firearm, but the U.S. Attorney prosecuting the case agreed to reduce the amount of cocaine he would be held accountable for and drop the firearms charge in exchange for a guilty plea. If at the sentencing hearing, the prosecutor can prove—simply by a preponderance of the evidence, as opposed to beyond a reasonable doubt—that the offender did in fact possess an unregistered firearm and 5 rather than 2 grams of cocaine, the judge is required to take this into consideration in determining the offense severity score.

The relevant conduct principle—which Judge William Wilkins, the first Chairman of the USSC, characterized as the "cornerstone"[42] of the federal sentencing guidelines—is designed to prevent circumvention of the guidelines through charging and plea-bargaining decisions by the prosecutor. According to Judge Wilkins, this feature of the guidelines "significantly reduces the impact of prosecutorial charge selection and plea bargaining by ensuring that the court will be able to consider the defendant's real-offense behavior in imposing a guideline sentence."[43] Critics of real-offense sentencing charge that the concept of relevant conduct, which is an "invention of the United States Sentencing Commission" that is unknown outside the federal sentencing guidelines, is "remarkably abstract and difficult to apply."[44] They also contend that manipulation of the guidelines by prosecutorial charging and plea bargaining decisions "is less undesirable than a sentencing policy that trivializes the significance of convictions based on proof beyond a reasonable doubt or a voluntary, informed confession."[45]

Although the federal sentencing guidelines are fairly rigid, they are not inflexible. The guidelines provide for a spread of about 25 percent between the minimum and the maximum sentence for each combination of offense seriousness and prior record; judges therefore have discretion to impose sentences within that range. In addition, defendants who plead guilty may qualify for a two- or three-level reduction in the guideline range for "acceptance of responsibility." This results in a sentence reduction of approximately 25 percent. Defendants who provide "substantial assistance"—that is, information that leads to the prosecution and conviction of another offender—can also be sentenced outside the applicable guideline range. This type of departure is especially common in cases involving drug offenses, many of which carry mandatory minimum sentences. A substantial assistance motion made by the prosecutor and granted by the court removes the mandatory minimum sentence that otherwise would be binding at sentencing. If the case involves unusual circumstances, the judge can depart from the sentence range indicated by the guidelines, either upward or downward.

There are, however, very limited grounds for these upward or downward departures. The statute states that judges may depart from the guidelines only on a finding that "there exists an aggravating or mitigating circumstance of a kind, or to a degree, not adequately taken into consideration by the Sentencing Commission in formulating the guidelines."[46] Moreover, the guidelines expressly state that certain factors "are not ordinarily relevant in determining whether a sentence should be outside the applicable guideline range."[47] Included among the "specific offender characteristics" that are "not ordinarily relevant" are the defendant's age, education and vocational skills, mental and emotional conditions, physical conditions (including drug or alcohol dependence or abuse), employment record, family ties and responsibilities, and community ties. These provisions, then, effectively preclude judges from considering what many regard as the "commonsense bases for distinguishing among offenders."[48]

Another important—and highly criticized—feature of the federal guidelines is their severity. In developing the guidelines, the USSC apparently interpreted the SRA, which stated that "the guidelines were to correct the fact that current federal sentences often did not accurately reflect the seriousness of the offense,"[49] to mean that sentences generally should be more severe than they had been in the past. Accordingly, under the guidelines, sentences for probation were greatly reduced, sentences for career offenders and for those convicted of violent crimes, drug crimes, and white-collar crimes were significantly increased, and sentences for crimes involving mandatory minimum sentences were set substantially above statutory minimums. Although the commissioners asserted that they developed the guidelines "by taking an empirical approach that used as a starting point data estimating pre-guidelines sentencing practice,"[50] Stith and Cabranes contend that they did no such thing. They state that the categories of offenses "for which the Commission conceded it purposely deviated from past practice—drug cases, fraud and other white collar cases, and cases involving threatened or actual violence—actually far outnumber the remaining categories of cases."[51]

These essential differences between state and federal guidelines help explain why the guidelines enacted by the states are generally supported by both citizens and criminal justice practitioners, whereas the federal guidelines are, in the words of one of their staunchest critics, "the most controversial and disliked sentencing reform initiative in U.S. history."[52] They are deeply unpopular with the judges and lawyers who are required to apply them, and they have been condemned by legal scholars, social scientists, and civil rights activists. According to Stith and Cabranes, "The greatest challenge facing policymakers today is the restoration of the legitimacy of sentencing in the eyes of victims, litigants, the bar, the bench, and the general public."[53]

Sentencing Guidelines: Compliance or Circumvention?

Sentencing guidelines are intended to change sentencing practices. Their intent is to alter the procedures used by the judge to determine the appropriate sentence and, at least in some cases, enhance the severity of the sentence imposed by the judge. In the preguidelines era, the trial judge had the ultimate discretion to fashion the sentence. He or she could determine which factors were relevant or irrelevant to criminal punishment, weigh all of the relevant circumstances in the case, and tailor a sentence designed to meet one or more of the four general purposes of punishment. The sentencing process in the postguidelines era is much less discretionary and, some would say, substantially more mechanical. Unless there are aggravating or mitigating circumstances that justify a departure, the judge is directed to impose the sentence indicated by the intersection of offense seriousness and prior criminal record.

Because the movement from indeterminate sentencing to sentencing guidelines represented a major change in sentencing policies and practices, some observers predicted that members of the courtroom workgroup would find ways to circumvent or sabotage the guidelines. Skeptics, for example, predicted that discretion simply would shift from the judge to the prosecutor, who would manipulate the charges so that the defendant's sentence would approximate the going rate for the offense in the preguidelines era.[54] If, in other words, the going rate for a first offender convicted of armed robbery in the preguideline period was 7 years but the guidelines called for 10 years, the prosecutor could reduce the defendant's sentence liability by downgrading the charge to unarmed robbery. Because the prosecutor's discretion is essentially unregulated, the courtroom workgroup could effectively undermine the guidelines in this way.

Evidence regarding the "hydraulic displacement of discretion"[55] from the judge at sentencing to the prosecutor at charging can be found in studies of offenders sentenced before and after the guidelines were implemented in Minnesota and Washington State. The studies conducted in Minnesota reached contradictory conclusions. One study found that prosecutors manipulated charges for property offenders, who faced a lower likelihood of imprisonment under the guidelines than in the preguideline era, and for sex offenders, who faced substantially more serious penalties under the guidelines.[56] Prosecutors required property offenders to plead guilty to multiple counts, which enhanced the odds of imprisonment. Conversely, prosecutors would agree to a downward departure from the guidelines for offenders convicted of sex offenses. Miethe and Moore,[57] who examined charging and plea-bargaining practices before and after the Minnesota guidelines were implemented, reached a different conclusion. They found that charging and plea-bargaining practices did not change dramatically and that the changes that did occur were related to changes in case attributes. Miethe concluded there was little evidence that members of the workgroup were using charging and plea bargaining to undermine the guidelines.[58]

Engen and Steen's[59] analysis of sentencing in Washington State led them to the opposite conclusion. They examined charging and sentencing decisions in cases involving drug offenders before and after three amendments to the Washington Sentencing Guidelines. The first change, which went into effect in 1988, eliminated the First-Time Offender Waiver (FTOW) for offenders convicted of delivery of heroin or cocaine. Enactment of this amendment meant that these offenders would no longer be eligible for a reduced sentence of up to 90 days confinement. The second change, effective in 1990, significantly increased the presumptive sentence for offenders convicted of delivery of heroin or cocaine. The third change resulted from a 1992 Washington Court of Appeals decision, *State v. Mendoza*.[60] The court ruled that conspiracy to deliver was an unranked offense that carried with it a presumptive sentencing range of 0 to 12 months. As Engen and Steen note, this decision meant that "an offender—even a repeat offender—convicted of one or more counts of conspiracy to deliver heroin or cocaine could receive a shorter sentence than a first-time offender convicted of a single count of simple possession."[61]

Consistent with the hydraulic displacement argument, Engen and Steen found changes in charging practices that corresponded to these changes in the sentencing guidelines. From 1986 to 1990, the proportion of drug offenders convicted of simple possession increased, whereas the proportion convicted of delivery decreased. Moreover, the proportion of convictions for conspiracy, which did not change much from 1986 to 1992, increased fivefold from 1993 to 1995. Further analysis revealed that "the *changes over time* in the severity of charges are *entirely contingent upon the mode of conviction*."[62] Prosecutors in Washington, in other words, were using their charging and plea bargaining discretion to minimize the effect of the sentencing guideline amendments. As Engen and Steen conclude, "The severity of charges at conviction changed significantly following each change in the law, which suggests the manipulation of charges (and subsequent sentences) rather than a strict application of charges to the crimes committed."[63]

There also is evidence of guideline manipulation at the federal level. As explained above, the USSC attempted to short-circuit circumvention of the guidelines through charging and plea-bargaining decisions by requiring federal judges to base the sentence on defendants' relevant conduct. In addition, the *Prosecutor's Handbook on Sentencing Guidelines* states that "readily provable" charges should not be bargained away and that a guilty plea should not be used as a basis for recommending a sentence that departs from the guidelines.[64] These rules and policies clearly were designed to prevent circumvention of the guidelines through charging and plea bargaining.

Nagel and Schulhofer's analysis of charging and bargaining practices in three federal districts revealed that the rules and practices implemented to preclude manipulation of the guidelines were "more impressive on paper than in practice."[65] According to the authors, the procedures designed to regulate charging and bargaining practices were not rigorously enforced and "fact bargaining, charge bargaining, and guideline-factor bargaining continue unabated."[66] Nagel and Schulhofer found that prosecutors sometimes dropped charges, including use of a weapon, which were "readily provable." They also used the substantial assistance motion to avoid severe sentences for sympathetic defendants who provided no genuine substantial assistance. Although the authors were careful to point out that guideline compliance, not guideline circumvention, was the norm, they nonetheless concluded that "unwarranted manipulation and evasion do occur in a substantial minority of guilty-plea cases."[67]

The changes in charging and plea-bargaining practices documented by these studies obviously make it difficult to determine the extent of compliance with the guidelines. If compliance is defined simply as the percentage of sentences that conform to the guidelines, with no consideration of the degree to which the charges at conviction mirror the seriousness of the offender's behavior, then a high rate of formal compliance may mask substantial informal or organizational noncompliance. As Tonry points out, "If judges are willing to give plea bargaining free rein, compliance may be more apparent than real."[68]

With these important caveats in mind, the research conducted to date does reveal substantial formal compliance with sentencing guidelines. Consider, for example, the following findings:

In Minnesota, compliance with the guidelines was very high during the first year of the postguideline period. Judges departed only 6.2 percent of the time on the disposition (prison versus probation) and only 8.5 percent of the time on the duration of the prison sentence. By 1996, the departure rate had more than doubled, but compliance remained the norm.[69]

During the first 5 years following adoption of sentencing guidelines in Oregon, judges followed the guidelines and imposed the presumptive sentence in 87.5 percent of the cases.[70]

Judges in Washington State complied with a series of sentencing guideline amendments. When the FTOW was eliminated for defendants convicted of delivery of heroin or cocaine, judges responded by sentencing 94 percent of these offenders to prison in accordance with the increased presumptive ranges.[71]

Judges in Pennsylvania from 1985 to1987 and 1989 to1991 imposed the disposition called for by the guidelines in 86 percent of the cases. Dispositional departures ranged from a low of 4 percent for rape and involuntary deviate sexual intercourse to a high of 33 percent for weapons offenses.[72] From 1984 to 1997, overall conformity to the guidelines ranged between 83 and 89 percent.[73]

The proportions of offenders sentenced in U.S. District Courts who received a sentence within the guideline range were as follows: 71.1 percent (1995), 69.6 percent (1996), 67.9 percent (1997), 66.3 percent (1998), and 64.9 percent (1999). Most offenders whose sentences fell outside the guideline range received downward departures. Fewer than 1 percent of the offenders in any year received upward departures.[74]

As these data indicate, "Judges much more often than not impose sentences that comply with applicable guidelines."[75] Although we do not know how often charging and plea-bargaining decisions distort the process and produce misleading estimates of the overall compliance rate, it appears that judges do fashion sentences that conform to the guidelines in a majority of the cases.

Mandatory Minimum Sentencing Statutes

In 1985, Donald Clark, a Myakka City, Florida, farmer, was arrested by local police for growing marijuana on his farm. He was sentenced to probation and 2 years house arrest. In 1990, federal agents descended on Myakka City, where many of the local residents grew marijuana, and arrested 28 people, including Donald Clark, for conspiracy to grow more than a million marijuana plants; the crime carried a mandatory life sentence. All of the others arrested in the conspiracy case entered into plea bargains for sentences of less than 12 years. Donald, who contended that he had not grown marijuana since his arrest in 1985, took his case to trial. He was convicted and sentenced to life in prison. He later appealed his sentence, which was reduced to 27 years. On January 20, 2001, outgoing President Bill Clinton commuted his sentence and Donald Clark was freed. He had spent 9 years in prison for a nonviolent drug offense.[76]

Donald Clark's story is not atypical. Each year, thousands of state and federal offenders are sentenced under mandatory minimum statutes that require the judge to impose specified sentences on offenders convicted of certain types of crimes, such as violent offenses, firearms offenses, drug offenses, or drunk driving, and on habitual or repeat offenders.[77] These "tough-on-crime" statutes are designed to prevent future crime by deterring potential offenders and incapacitating those who are not deterred. The implicit assumption is that *everyone* convicted of a targeted offense is dangerous and likely to recidivate. In imposing the sentence, therefore, the judge is supposed to consider *only* the fact that the defendant has been convicted of an offense carrying a mandatory sentence. He or she is not permitted to consider the defendant's role in the offense, the defendant's family situation or background characteristics, or other mitigating factors.

Mandatory penalty statutes proliferated during the "war on crime" and "war on drugs" that were waged during the 1970s, 1980s, and early 1990s. Candidates from both political parties campaigned on "tough-on-crime" platforms and decried "lenient sentences" imposed by "soft" judges; they championed "reforms" designed to ensure that offenders "who do the crime will do the time." State and federal legislators responded enthusiastically. Consider these examples:[78]

- In 1973, New York enacted the Rockefeller Drug Laws, which required long prison terms for a variety of drug offenses. For example, the law provided a mandatory penalty of 15 years to life for anyone convicted of selling 2 ounces or possessing 4 ounces of a narcotics substance.

- In 1975, the Massachusetts Bartley-Fox Amendment was enacted. This law required a 1-year prison term for unlawfully carrying (but not necessarily using) an unlicensed firearm.

- In 1977, Michigan's Felony Firearm Statute went into effect. Publicized with the catchy slogan "one with gun gets you two," the Michigan law required a 2-year sentence enhancement for use of a firearm in the course of committing a felony.

- In 1978, Michigan passed the "650 Lifer Law," which requires a life sentence for offenders convicted of delivering or attempting to deliver 650 grams (about 1.4 pounds) of cocaine or heroin. In 1998, the law, which originally required a life sentence with no possibility of parole, was revised to make prisoners eligible for parole after 20 years.

- In 1984, Congress enacted the Comprehensive Crime Control Act of 1984, which required a 5-year sentence enhancement for using or carrying a gun during a crime of violence or a drug crime. The law also mandated a 15-year sentence for possession of a firearm by a person with three state or federal convictions for burglary or robbery.

- In 1986, Congress enacted the Anti-Drug Abuse Act, which established 5- and 10-year mandatory sentences for a variety of drug offenses. Passage of this law was spurred by the death of Len Bias, a University of Maryland basketball star who had just been signed by the Boston Celtics. Bias died of heart failure, apparently as a result of an accidental cocaine overdose.

Despite the fact that evaluations of these early statutes revealed that they had not achieved their objectives (see Chapter 7), the mandatory penalty movement continued unabated. By the mid-1990s, mandatory penalties had been enacted in every state, and Congress had passed over 60 mandatory sentencing laws covering more than 100 federal offenses.[79]

Criticisms of Mandatory Minimums

Although the primary objection to mandatory penalties, particularly those for drug offenses, is their excessive severity, opponents also criticize their inflexibility. They charge that mandatory statutes turn judges into sentencing machines: The type of drug plus the amount of drugs equals the sentence.[80] As noted above, in sentencing a defendant convicted of an offense carrying a mandatory minimum sentence, the judge is not supposed to consider anything other than the type and amount of drugs involved. Thus, "It matters not at all whether the offender is a 17-year-old transporting drugs from one location to another (a 'mule'), the battered girlfriend of a small-time distributor, or a genuine 'drug kingpin.'"[81] State and federal judges echo these criticisms (see Box 6.2). Large majorities disapprove of mandatory minimums,[82] want mandatory penalties for drug offenses eliminated,[83] and support changes designed to increase the discretion of the judge.[84]

Critics also charge that mandatory minimum sentencing statutes, like presumptive sentencing guidelines, shift discretion from the sentencing judge to the prosecutor. Because sentencing for offenses carrying mandatory penalties is, by definition, nondiscretionary and because the applica-

---

BOX 6.2 _____

**MANDATORY MINIMUM SENTENCES:
JUDICIAL EXASPERATION AND DESPAIR**

In 1993, Bill Langston, who was on probation for driving while intoxicated, and a friend were stopped by the police as they were transporting chemicals used to manufacture PCP. He was convicted of conspiracy to manufacture 70 kilograms of PCP after a DEA agent testified that Billy had admitted he was going to use the chemicals to make PCP.

Billy Langston's codefendant, who provided information to the government to help convict the man who was to receive the chemicals, received a 60-month sentence. The alleged recipient received probation. Billy Langston, who contended that he had played only a minimal role in the crime and maintained that his codefendant bought the chemicals, was sentenced to 30 years in prison.

At the sentencing hearing, U.S. District Court Judge David V. Kenyon stated that "there is no question that this is an unjust, unfair sentence"; he lamented the fact that his hands were tied by the mandatory minimum sentencing statute. As he stated from the bench, "it is clear that what's going on here is a far greater sentence than what this man deserves. But there's nothing I can do about it, at least that I can figure out."

Judge Kenyon's comments were echoed by the prosecuting attorney, who stated that "the 30-year sentence in this case, which is mandated, is extraordinarily heavy. I don't think that it's anything that anyone feels good about. I certainly don't."

_____

SOURCE: "Victims of MMS," *Families Against Mandatory Minimums* , available on the World Wide Web at http://www.famm.org

---

tion of a mandatory minimum sentence depends on conviction for a charge carrying a mandatory penalty, prosecutors, not judges, determine what the ultimate sentence will be. If, in other words, a defendant is convicted of a drug offense carrying a mandatory minimum sentence of 5 years in prison, the judge's hands are tied: He or she must impose the mandatory 5-year term. The prosecutor, on the other hand, is not required to charge the defendant with the drug offense carrying the mandatory term. If the prosecutor does file the charge, he or she can reduce it to an offense without a mandatory penalty if the defendant agrees to plead guilty. By manipulating the charges that defendants face, prosecutors can circumvent the mandatory penalty statutes.

A study conducted by the USSC[85] confirmed that prosecutors often did not file charges carrying mandatory minimum penalties when the evidence indicated that such charges were warranted. In fact, prosecutors did not file the expected charges in about a fourth of the cases. To avoid the mandatory minimum penalty, prosecutors filed drug charges that did not specify the amount of drugs or that specified a lower amount than appeared supportable, failed to file charges for mandatory weapons enhancements, and did not request increased minimums in cases involving offenders with prior convictions. Plea-bargaining decisions also had an impact. A substantial proportion of the defendants who were charged with mandatory minimum offenses pled guilty to offenses that carried lower mandatory minimum sentences or no mandatory minimums at all.[86] The USSC study also found that 40 percent of the defendants received shorter sentences than would have been warranted under the applicable mandatory minimum statute.

The commission acknowledged that prosecutors might have legitimate reasons for not filing charges that carried mandatory penalties or for allowing defendants to plead guilty to lesser offenses. Nonetheless, they concluded that the results of their study indicated that mandatory minimums were not working. As they noted, "Since the charging and plea negotiation processes are neither open to public review nor generally reviewable by the courts, the honesty and truth in sentencing intended by the guidelines system is compromised."[87] According to the USSC, "There are a number of ways in which Congress effectively can shape sentencing policy without resorting to mandatory minimum provisions."[88] (See Box 6.3 for a discussion of the "safety valve" provision.)

Evaluations of mandatory minimum sentences in New York, Massachusetts, and Michigan also revealed high levels of noncompliance and circumvention. An examination of the impact of New York's Rockefeller Drug Laws,[89] touted as the "nation's toughest drug laws," found that the proportion of felony arrests that resulted in indictment declined, as did the percentage of indictments that led to conviction. Although the likelihood of incarceration and the average sentence imposed on offenders convicted of drug felonies did increase, the lower rates of indictment and conviction meant that the overall likelihood that someone arrested for a drug felony would be sentenced to prison remained about the same. A similar pattern was observed in Massachusetts[90] and Michigan,[91] which adopted mandatory sentencing provisions for carrying or using a firearm. For offenses targeted by these gun laws, the rate at which charges were dismissed increased and the conviction rate decreased. In all three states, as in the federal system, prosecutors and judges devised ways to avoid application of mandatory penalties.

BOX 6.3
_____

MANDATORY MINIMUMS AND THE "SAFETY VALVE"

In 1994, the Department of Justice issued a report that revealed that 1 in 5 federal prisoners were low-level drug offenders with no records of violence, no involvement in sophisticated criminal enterprises, and no prior sentences to prison. Among federal prisoners locked up for drug offenses, over a third were low-level offenders.[a]

Publication of these findings led Congress to search for ways to revise, but not repeal, mandatory minimum penalties for drug offenses. Senator Strom Thurmond (R-SC) and Senator Alan Simpson (R-WY) cosponsored legislation establishing a "safety valve" for nonviolent drug offenders. Under this provision, first-time, nonviolent offenders would be exempt from mandatory penalties if they met specified criteria.

Although the safety-valve provision was attacked by conservative legislators, the National Rifle Association (which claimed, incorrectly, that the provision would eliminate mandatory minimums for gun crimes), and the National Association of U.S. Attorneys, it was included in the final version of the Omnibus Crime Control Act of 1994.

_____

a. Mauer (1999). *Race to Incarcerate.* New York: The New Press.

21st-Century Backlash?

In 1996, Michael Tonry, a staunch critic of mandatory penalties, predicted that "sooner or later, the combination of chronic prison overcrowding, budgetary crises, and a changed professional climate will make more public officials willing to pay attention to what we have long known about mandatory penalties."[92]

By the late 1990s, it appeared that Tonry might be correct. Prison populations continued to grow even as the crime rate declined, and mandatory minimum sentencing statutes came under increasing criticism. In July of 1998, Michigan Governor John Engler signed a law reforming Michigan's "650 Lifer Law."[93] Under the old law, anyone convicted of possessing, delivering, or intending to deliver more than 650 grams of cocaine or heroin received a mandatory life sentence without the possibility of parole. The new law requires a sentence of "life or any term of years, not less than 20"[94] for future offenders. A companion bill made the change applicable to offenders sentenced under the old law. In February of 1999, DeJonna Young became the first person released from prison as a result of the legal changes. She had been sentenced to life in prison without parole in 1979 after she and her boyfriend were stopped by the police, who found 3 pounds of heroin in her car. Young, who was 24 years old at the time of her arrest, maintained that she didn't know the drugs were in her car.

New York's draconian Rockefeller Drug Laws also came under attack.[95] In early 2001, New York Governor George Pataki proposed changing the laws. He recommended shorter mandatory terms, treatment instead of incarceration in some cases, and enhanced sentencing discretion for judges. Although state legislators were generally supportive of the governor's recommendations, the New York State District Attorneys Association came out against the changes. The president of the association stated, "We can't live with a system that takes out of prosecutors' hands the right to send predatory drug dealers to prison."[96]

Federal officials also are questioning the wisdom of mandatory minimums, particularly for drug offenders. In the spring of 2000, for example, the House Subcommittee on Criminal Justice, Drug Policy, and Human Resources held hearings on mandatory minimum drug sentences.[97] After hearing testimony regarding the quadrupling of the federal prison population since 1980, Representative Elijah Cummings (D-MD) stated, "It appears the only thing that mandatory minimums have accomplished is growth in the federal prison system."[98] Both former Attorney General Janet Reno and Supreme Court Chief Justice William Rehnquist also called for reexamining mandatory minimums. Rehnquist, who characterized mandatory penalties as "the law of unintended consequences," said that "these mandatory minimums impose unduly harsh punishment for first-time offenders and have led to an inordinate increase in the prison population."[99]

These direct attacks on mandatory minimums, coupled with the drug court movement and the increasing emphasis on drug treatment rather than incarceration (see the next section, "Focus on an Issue: Sentencing Drug Offenders"), suggest that state and federal officials are willing to rethink mandatory minimum sentencing statutes, particularly for nonviolent, low-level drug offenders. Although it is unlikely that mandatory penalties will be repealed, there appears to be growing consensus that reform is needed.

Focus on an Issue

Sentencing Drug Offenders:
Incarceration or Treatment—What Works?

The past two decades have witnessed dramatic growth in the United States prison population. There were nearly 1.3 million persons incarcerated in state and federal prisons as of midyear 1999, compared with less than a quarter of a million in 1975.[100] Most commentators attribute this fivefold increase to increasingly severe sentencing practices for drug offenses.[101] Statistics concerning the offenses for which state and federal prisoners are incarcerated support this conclusion. The percentage of state prisoners incarcerated for a drug offense nearly quadrupled from 1980 (6%) to 1996 (23%). Similarly, the percentage of federal prisoners serving time for drug offenses increased from 25 percent in 1980 to 60 percent in 1996. In fact, the increase in drug offenders accounted for nearly three quarters of the total increase in federal inmates and one third of the total increase in state inmates during this 16-year period.[102]

These statistics reflect a crime control policy premised on a theory of deterrence that Skolnick characterizes as "superficially persuasive."[103] The assumption is that sentencing drug offenders to prison for long periods of time will deter current and prospective offenders, leading eventually to a reduction in drug abuse and drug-related crime. As numerous commentators have observed, however, this assumption rests on the false premise that altering criminal penalties will alter behavior.[104] In fact, scholarly research generally concludes that increasing the severity of penalties will have little, if any, effect on crime.[105] As Cohen and her colleagues recently noted,

> Observers of the criminal justice system who in general agree on little else have joined in arguing that increased penalties for drug use and distribution at best have had a modest impact on the operation of illicit drug markets, on the price and availability of illicit drugs, and on consumption of illicit drugs.[106]

Critics of the crime control approach, who maintain that the war on drugs has failed and that "public safety has not improved as a result of the imprisonment binge,"[107] have called for a new approach that balances public safety and public health interests. While acknowledging that imprisonment may be an appropriate penalty for some offenders, those who advocate a public health approach argue for expansion in the use of a variety of alternatives to incarceration. Skolnick, for example, suggests that two thirds of the $13 billion the United States spends annually to wage the war on drugs be allocated to treatment and prevention.[108]

These calls for expansion of drug treatment programs are premised on the notion that in contrast to incarceration, treatment "works."[109] In fact, there is substantial evidence in support of the efficacy of treatment. There is now a sizeable literature that documents the ability of drug abuse treatment programs to reduce drug use and drug-related crime.[110] Positive results have been noted for both community-based treatment[111] and for treatment within a correctional institution.[112]

Demands for expanding drug treatment programs also are fueled by research documenting a strong relationship between drug use and crime. Evidence of this comes from the National Institute of Justice's Arrestee Drug Abuse Monitoring (ADAM) program, which has been testing arrestees for a variety of drugs since 1987. Results from the program indicate that the percentage of arrestees testing positive for any drug has rarely fallen below 50 percent in any of the 23 sites and has been as high as 85 percent in some.[113] In 1996, for example, more than 60 percent of adult males and at least 50 percent of adult females tested positive for any drug in all but three sites; the median rate for all sites was 68 percent.

These figures are consistent with the results of self-report studies of substance-abusing offenders. State prison inmates surveyed in 1991, for example, reported high rates of drug use: 80 percent reported that they had used illegal drugs at least once, about half stated that they had been using drugs in the month before the offense for which they were incarcerated, and 31 percent indicated that they were under the influence of drugs at the time of the crime.[114] Self-report studies also indicate that substance-abusing offenders are responsible for a disproportionate amount of crime. One study found that violent offenders who used heroin committed 15 times more robberies, 20 times more burglaries, and 10 times more thefts than offenders who did not use drugs.[115]

The Drug Court Movement

Increases in the number of drug offenders appearing in state and federal courts—coupled with mounting evidence of both the linkages between drug use and crime and the efficacy of drug treatment programs—led a number of jurisdictions "to rethink their approach to handling defendants charged with drug and drug-related offenses."[116] Some jurisdictions, such as Cook County (Chicago), Illinois, established specialized dockets designed to manage the drug caseload more efficiently and to alleviate stress on the felony court system.[117] Other jurisdictions, such as Dade County (Miami), Florida, created "drug treatment courts," which incorporated intensive judicial supervision of drug offenders, mandatory drug treatment, and rehabilitation programs providing vocational, education, family, and medical services.

The drug treatment court concept spread rapidly during the 1990s. As of June of 1999, 377 drug courts were operating, and an additional 217 drug courts were in the planning stages in 49 of the 50 states, the District of Columbia, Puerto Rico, Guam, several Native American tribal courts, and two federal district courts.[118] Many jurisdictions were also planning, or had implemented, drug courts for juveniles.

Although the nature and characteristics of drug courts throughout the United States vary widely, they share several "key elements:"[119]

- Integration of substance abuse treatment with justice system case processing

- Use of a nonadversarial approach

- Early identification and prompt placement of eligible participants

- Access to a continuum of treatment, rehabilitation and related services

- Frequent testing for alcohol and illicit drugs

- A coordinated strategy among judge, prosecutor, defense, and treatment providers to govern offender compliance

- Ongoing, judicial interaction with each participant

In the typical preadjudication drug court,[120] drug offenders who meet the eligibility criteria for the program are given a choice between participation in the drug court and traditional adjudication. Although the eligibility criteria vary, most programs exclude offenders who have prior convictions for violent offenses or whose current offense involved violence or use of a weapon. They target offenders whose involvement with the criminal justice system is due primarily to their substance abuse. The program may last 12 months, 18 months, or longer. Offenders who are accepted and agree to abide by the requirements of the program are immediately referred to a substance abuse treatment program for counseling, therapy, and education. They also are subject to random urinalysis and are required to appear frequently before the drug court judge. Offenders who do not show up for treatment sessions or drug court or who fail drug tests are subject to sanctions. Repeated violations may result in termination from the program and in adjudication and sentencing on the original charges. The charges against the offender are dismissed upon completion of the program.

The Effectiveness of Drug Court. There is mounting evidence that drug courts reduce offender recidivism and prevent drug relapse. A report by the U.S. General Accounting Office (GAO) summarized the results of 20 evaluations of 16 drug courts that had been completed by early 1997.[121] The

GAO report indicated that these early evaluations generally concluded that drug courts were effective in reducing drug use and criminal behavior. A later review by Belenko[122] summarized the results of 30 evaluations of 24 drug courts that had been completed by May of 1998. Belenko observed that most of these evaluations concluded "that criminal behavior was substantially reduced during participation in the program."[123] For example, an evaluation of a Ventura County, California, drug court, which tracked recidivism over an 8-month period, found that only 12 percent of the drug court participants were rearrested, compared with 32 percent of those in a comparison group. A Jackson County, Missouri, evaluation similarly revealed 6-month rearrest rates of 4 percent for program participants and 13 percent for nonparticipants. Belenko's review also included studies that assessed the impact of drug court participation on postprogram recidivism. Eight of the nine evaluations reported lower recidivism rates for the drug court group, compared with a group of similarly situated offenders who did not participate in the drug court program.[124] An evaluation of the Multnomah County, Oregon, drug court, for example, found statistically significant differences between drug court participants (0.59 new arrests) and drug-court-eligible nonparticipants (1.53 new arrests) over a 24-month tracking period. Belenko concluded,

> Although the evaluations vary considerably in scope, methodology and quality, the results are consistent in finding that . . . drug courts provide more comprehensive and closer supervision of the drug-using offender than other forms of community supervision, drug use and criminal behavior are substantially reduced while clients are participating in drug court, [and] criminal behavior is lower after program participation.[125]

New Approaches: More Effective Solutions?

Recent developments in New York and California suggest that criminal justice officials and the general public are becoming increasingly concerned about the costs of incarcerating nonviolent drug offenders and increasingly skeptical about the benefits of doing so. In June of 2000, the Chief Judge of New York, who has wide latitude to restructure state courts, issued an order requiring that nearly all nonviolent, drug-addicted offenders be offered treatment instead of jail time.[126] To be eligible for the program, offenders must test positive for drugs, agree to plead guilty, and be willing to enter a rigorous substance abuse treatment program. Chief Judge Judith Kaye said that about 10,000 offenders per year would be diverted from jail or prison to treatment. Court officials predicted that the program would lead to a 10-percent reduction in the state prison population and would save $500 million a year in prison, foster care, and mental health costs.

In November of 2000, California voters voted overwhelmingly to approve Proposition 36, to provide drug treatment instead of prison for first- and second-time drug offenders who are not charged with other crimes.[127] The law, which was described as "the most sweeping change" in the California criminal justice system in decades, was expected to divert 36,000 offenders each year from prison and into treatment programs.[128] Although the law was widely praised, there were concerns that it was not adequately funded, that there were not enough treatment slots available, and that the law would dissuade drug offenders from pleading guilty.

In February of 2001, Senator Orrin Hatch (R–UT) introduced the Drug Abuse Education, Prevention, and Treatment Act.[129] This legislation, which was backed by a bipartisan group of U.S. senators, called for $2.7 billion in spending over 3 years to increase the scope of drug treatment programs in prisons and jails and to expand drug testing throughout the criminal justice system. The bill also proposed stricter sentencing guidelines for those who commit drug offenses in the presence of minors or use children in drug trafficking. According to Senator Hatch, chairman of the Senate Judiciary Committee, "Our law enforcement efforts to reduce the supply of illegal drugs must be complemented by a substantial commitment to reduce our demand for these substances."[130]

It is too early to tell whether these calls for expanded drug treatment signal a major change in the philosophy of punishment for drug offenders. It does appear, however, that both voters and lawmakers are disillusioned with current crime control efforts, which have resulted in the imprisonment of increasingly large numbers of drug offenders but have not produced the expected reduction in crime.

Three-Strikes-and-You're-Out Laws

Laws bearing the catchy "three-strikes-and-you're-out" slogan were enacted in the early 1990s in Washington State and California. These laws, which impose extremely long prison terms on repeat offenders—sometimes, life without parole—proved immensely popular. As one commentator noted, "The laws appeal to a certain intuitive notion of justice."[131] Like the baseball player in the batter's box, an offender is allowed to strike out once, even twice, but the three-time loser is "out" of the game, at least temporarily and sometimes, for good. By 1997, about half of the states and the federal government had adopted some variation of three-strikes-and-you're out laws.

Although touted as a major innovation, in reality, three-strikes laws are simply more punitive versions of habitual offender statutes that date back to the late 18th century. Like their predecessors, three-strikes laws target repeat offenders. They are designed to prevent future crime by locking up offenders who repeatedly commit serious crimes for long periods of time, in many cases for life. They are designed, in other words, to incapacitate dangerous career criminals. The main difference between the three-strikes laws and the earlier habitual criminal statutes is the size of the sentence enhancement. Whereas the typical habitual criminal statute might have added 5 or 10 years to the sentence, three-strikes laws provide for sentence enhancements of 25 years, 40 years, or longer; some laws mandate life in prison with no possibility of parole. The three-strikes laws also are less flexible and apply to a longer list of felonies than the habitual offender statutes.[132]

Not all laws that carry the "three-strikes-and-you're-out" moniker are alike. They differ in three important ways: how the "strike zone" is defined, how many strikes are required to be "out," and what it means to be "out."[133] The "strike zone" refers to the offenses that constitute a strike. All states include violent felonies, but some state laws also include drug offenses and property crimes. In Maryland and Tennessee, only prior offenses that resulted in incarceration qualify as strikes. And in California, the first two strikes must be from the list of "strikeable" felonies, but the third strike can be *any* felony offense, no matter how minor. Under California's law, individuals were sentenced to 25 years to life for stealing a slice of pizza, stealing cookies from a restaurant, and stealing meat from a grocery store.[134]

In most states, offenders are not "out" until they have three strikes, but many of these states also have enhanced sentences for a second strike. In Montana and South Carolina, a person convicted a second time for a serious violent crime is sentenced to life in prison without parole. In California, a conviction for any felony doubles the sentence that otherwise would be imposed if the offender has one prior conviction for a strikeable offense. Typically, a three-time loser receives a mandatory sentence of life without parole. In a few states, offenders who strike out can be released but only after serving 25, 30, or 40 years in prison.

Critics of three-strikes laws predicted that they would have a substantial impact on local courts and jails. They predicted that offenders facing mandatory life sentences would demand jury trials and that the additional time needed to process cases through trial—coupled with local officials' reluctance to release three-strikes defendants prior to trial—would cause jail populations to explode. An early report on the projected impact of the law in Santa Clara County, California, for example, stated that "the 'three-strikes, you're out' law is expected to create a crisis in the administration of justice in Santa Clara County and elsewhere in the State."[135] Although early evaluations of the implementation of three-strikes in California did reveal substantial increases in trials and jail populations, more recent data showed that these trends were beginning to moderate.[136] One study noted that although trials in six California counties had increased in third-strike cases, the trial rate in nonstrike cases had decreased dramatically.[137] This study also found that criminal justice officials had devised a number of ways to circumvent the law. Judges have attempted to encourage guilty pleas by offering two-strike defendants the lowest possible sentences, and the prosecuting attorney in one county announced that third-strike cases would be filed only when the current offense was serious or violent.[138]

The results of these studies suggest that the dire predictions of clogged courts and skyrocketing jail populations as a result of three-strikes laws were overly pessimistic (see Chapter 7 for discussion of the impact of the laws on sentence severity and prison populations). Although the laws may have produced an "initial period of hyper-concern and confusion," over time, the members of the courtroom workgroup used "a host of discretionary devices to adapt to the laws in ways that reinstitute long-standing operating procedures."[139] Over time, in other words, the criminal justice system may adapt to and, eventually, nullify the law.

Truth-in-Sentencing Laws

In July of 2000, *The Birmingham News*, in Alabama, ran a story headlined "Lies in Sentencing."[140] The article cited two recent cases in which offenders served only a portion of their sentences. The first involved two brothers who were sentenced to prison for 40 years for kidnapping and rape. They were released on parole after serving less than half of their sentences. The second involved a woman who was sentenced to 25 years in prison for murdering another woman but was up for parole after spending only 8 years behind bars. Noting that most offenders in Alabama served only one third of their prison sentences, the author of the article asked, "So where is 'truth in sentencing,' where 40 years means 40 years and 25 years means 25 years?"[141]

Widespread concerns about "lies in sentencing" led to a number of interrelated reforms. About half of the states abolished early release from prison at the discretion of the parole board, either for all offenders or for certain categories of offenders. Many states also tightened policies regarding good-time reductions for satisfactory behavior in prison and earned-time reductions for participation in prison-based educational and vocational programs. At the same time, most states enacted truth-in-sentencing laws that require offenders to serve a substantial portion of the prison sentence imposed before being eligible for release. These laws were enacted in the wake of the passage of the 1994 Crime Act, which authorized grants to states to build or expand correctional facilities. To qualify for the federal money, states must require persons convicted of violent crimes to serve at least 85 percent of the prison sentence imposed by the judge.

By 1999, 27 states and the District of Columbia had adopted truth-in-sentencing laws that met the 85-percent federal standard.[142] The laws enacted by 13 other states require offenders to serve from 50 percent to 75 percent of the sentence. Maryland and Texas have a 50-percent requirement for violent offenders, Nebraska and Indiana require all offenders to serve 50 percent, and Arkansas requires certain offenders to serve 70 percent. In Colorado, violent offenders with two previous violent felony convictions serve 75 percent of the sentence, and those with one prior violent conviction serve 56 percent. Several states with indeterminate sentencing require offenders to serve 100 percent of the minimum sentence imposed by the judge. Federal offenders serve a uniform 85 percent of the sentence.

Truth-in-sentencing laws are designed to ensure that offenders, particularly violent offenders, serve a substantial portion of their sentences. Assuming that the judge does not discount the sentence he or she imposes, anticipating that the offender will serve a larger percentage of the sentence, these laws should result in longer prison terms. Early data from states that qualified for federal funding by enacting an 85-percent requirement showed that the average time served by violent offenders did, in fact, increase between 1993 and 1997. For the United States as a whole, the mean time served by offenders who were released from prison increased by only 6 months, from 43 months in 1993 to 49 months in 1997. Among states with the 85-percent rule, the increase was much more dramatic. Vermont reported the largest increase (32 months to 82 months), followed by Florida (28 months to 50 months), and North Dakota (31 months to 47 months). The percent of time served by offenders who were released in 1997 varied widely among the states; it ranged from 25 percent in Arkansas to 87 percent in Vermont.[143]

Like three-strikes laws and mandatory minimum sentencing statutes, truth-in-sentencing laws are premised on assertions that offenders who commit violent crimes or repeat their crimes are responsible for a disproportionate amount of crime and that locking them up for long periods of time will reduce the crime rate. As Princeton University Professor John DiLulio wrote in 1995, "Letting violent and repeat criminals out of prison or jail and putting them on probation, parole, or pretrial release results in countless murders, rapes, assaults, weapons offenses, robberies, and burglaries each year."[144] Although it may be too early to tell whether truth-in-sentencing laws will prevent "countless" crimes by violent and repeat offenders, one study concluded that the laws did not have a significant effect on crime rates.[145]

Three Decades of Reform

Three decades of experimentation and reform have transformed sentencing policies and practices in the United States. Thirty years ago, indeterminate sentencing based on the philosophy of rehabilitation was the norm. Judges had substantial though not unlimited discretion to determine the sentence range, and parole boards decided how long offenders would actually serve. Judges considered the facts and circumstances of the case and the characteristics of the offender and attempted to tailor sentences that fit individuals and their crimes. With few exceptions, judges were not required to impose specific sentences on particular types of offenders.

Concerns about disparity and discrimination in sentencing—coupled with widespread disillusionment with rehabilitation and a belief that more punitive sentences were both necessary and just—led to a series of incremental sentencing reforms that revolutionized the sentencing process. Sentencing policies and practices today are much more complex and substantially more fragmented than they were in the past. Some jurisdictions retained indeterminate sentencing; others replaced it with more tightly structured determinate sentencing or sentencing guidelines. Mandatory minimum sentencing statutes that eliminated judicial discretion and targeted violent offenders, drug offenders, and career criminals proliferated at both the state and federal levels. Other tough-on-crime reforms also proved popular. More than half of the states adopted "three-strikes-and-you're-out" laws, and most jurisdictions enacted truth-in-sentencing laws designed to ensure that offenders served a larger portion of the sentence imposed by the judge.

Although there is evidence that the members of the courtroom workgroup have been able to circumvent some of the requirements of these laws and that state and federal lawmakers are beginning to have doubts about the wisdom of imprisoning drug-addicted offenders, the reforms adopted during the past 30 years have significantly altered the sentencing process in the United States. As a result of these changes, sentencing today is less discretionary, less individualized, and more mechanical.

Discussion Questions: Chapter 6

1. Calls for sentencing reform came from both ends of the political spectrum. How did the arguments put forth by liberal reformers differ from those put forth by conservative reformers?

2. Assume that your state legislature is considering sentencing guidelines. You have been asked to testify before the committee on the judiciary. Would you recommend voluntary/advisory guidelines or presumptive guidelines? Why?

3. What are the common features of state sentencing guidelines? How do the guidelines adopted by the states differ?

4. Explain how the defendant's "relevant conduct" affects sentencing under the federal sentencing guidelines.

5. Why are the federal sentencing guidelines "the most controversial and disliked sentencing reform initiative in U.S. history"?

6. Critics charge that sentencing guidelines and mandatory minimum sentencing statutes result in "hydraulic displacement of discretion." Explain what this means.

7. How do the sentences imposed by drug courts differ from those imposed in traditional courts?

8. Your state is considering enacting a "three-strikes-and-you're out" law. You send an e-mail to your state senator explaining why you are opposed to this. What will you say?

9. How has the sentencing process been changed as a result of the reforms enacted during the past 30 years?

Notes

1. 457 F. 2d 722 (D.C. Cir. 1970).
2. Walker, *Taming the System: The Control of Discretion in Criminal Justice, 1950-1990*, p. 112.
3. U.S. Department of Justice, Bureau of Justice Assistance, *National Assessment of Structured Sentencing*, p. 6.
4. American Friends Service Committee, *Struggle for Justice: A Report on Crime and Punishment in America*; Davis, *Discretionary Justice: A Preliminary Inquiry*; Frankel, *Criminal Sentences: Law Without Order*.
5. See, for example, van den Haag, *Punishing Criminals: Confronting a Very Old and Painful Question*; Wilson, *Thinking About Crime*.
6. Tonry, *Malign Neglect*, p. 164.
7. See, for example, van den Haag, *Punishing Criminals*; Wilson, *Thinking About Crime*.
8. von Hirsch, *Doing Justice: The Choice of Punishments*.
9. Martinson, "What Works? Questions and Answers about Prison Reform."
10. Walker, *Taming the System*, p. 123.
11. Tonry, *Sentencing Matters*, p. 3.
12. Ibid.
13. Frankel, *Criminal Sentence*; Frankel, "Lawlessness in Sentencing."
14. Frankel, "Lawlessness in Sentencing," p. 1.
15. Ibid., p. 4.
16. Ibid., p. 6.
17. Ibid., p. 41.
18. U.S. Department of Justice, Bureau of Justice Assistance, *National Assessment of Structured Sentencing*, p. 19; Frase, "Sentencing Guidelines Are 'Alive and Well' in the United States," p. 12.
19. Ibid.
20. Rich, Sutton, Clear, and Saks, *Sentencing Guidelines: Their Operation and Impact on the Courts*.
21. Cohen and Tonry, "Sentencing Reforms and Their Impacts," p. 363.
22. Casper, Brereton, and Neal, *The Implementation of the California Determinate Sentencing Law: Executive Summary*.
23. Walker, *Taming the System*, p. 129.

24. American Bar Association, *Standards for Criminal Justice—Sentencing Alternatives and Procedures*.

25. Frase, "Sentencing Guidelines Are 'Alive and Well' in the United States," p. 12. However, the Florida legislature abolished the guidelines for that state effective October 1, 1998. (See Hogenmuller, "Structured Sentencing in Florida: Is the Experiment Over?")

26. U.S. Department of Justice, Bureau of Justice Assistance, *National Assessment of Structured Sentencing*, pp. 45-46.

27. Ibid., pp. 79-80.

28. Laws of Minnesota 1978 CA. 723 § 244.11.

29. Oregon Criminal Justice Council, *1989 Oregon Sentencing Guidelines Manual*.

30. U.S. Department of Justice, Bureau of Justice Assistance, *National Assessment of Structured Sentencing*, p. 31.

31. Frase, "Sentencing Guidelines Are 'Alive and Well' in the United States," pp. 15-16.

32. For a comparison of sentencing policies and outcomes in Minnesota, Pennsylvania, and Washington, see Kramer, Lubitz, and Kempinen, "Sentencing Guidelines: A Quantitative Comparison of Sentencing Policies in Minnesota, Pennsylvania, and Washington."

33. S. 1437, 95th Cong. (1977).

34. As quoted in Stith and Cabranes, *Fear of Judging: Sentencing Guidelines in the Federal Courts*, p. 38.

35. 18 U.S.C. §§ 3551-3626 and 28 U.S.C. §§ 991-998. For a detailed discussion of the history of the federal sentencing guidelines, also see Stith and Cabranes, *Fear of Judging: Sentencing Guidelines in the Federal Courts*.

36. U.S. Sentencing Commission, *Federal Sentencing Guidelines Manual*, chap. 1, pt. A-3.

37. U.S. Sentencing Commission, *Federal Sentencing Guidelines Manual*, chap. 1, pt. A, p. 2.

38. 488 U.S. 361 (1989).

39. Stith and Cabranes, p. 58, *Fear of Judging*.

40. Ibid., p. 83.

41. Ibid., p. 82.

42. Wilkins and Steer, "Relevant Conduct: The Cornerstone of the Federal Sentencing Guidelines."

43. Ibid., p. 504.

44. Stith and Cabranes, *Fear of Judging*, p. 70.
45. Tonry, *Sentencing Matters*, p. 78.
46. 18 U.S.C. §3553 (b).
47. U.S. Sentencing Commission, *Federal Sentencing Guidelines Manual*, chap. 5, pt. H, §5H.1-13.
48. Tonry, *Sentencing Matters*, p. 77.
49. 28 U.S.C.§994 (m).
50. U.S. Sentencing Commission, *Federal Sentencing Guidelines Manual*, chap. 1, pt. A, p. 4.
51. Stith and Cabranes, *Fear of Judging*, pp. 60-61.
52. Tonry, *Sentencing Matters*, p. 72.
53. Stith and Cabranes, *Fear of Judging*, p. 143.
54. Miethe, "Charging and Plea Bargaining under Determinate Sentencing: An Investigation of the Hydraulic Displacement of Discretion."
55. Ibid., p. 156.
56. Knapp, "Implementation of the Minnesota Guidelines: Can the Innovative Spirit Be Preserved?"
57. Miethe and Moore, "Socioeconomic Disparities Under Determinate Sentencing Systems: A Comparison of Pre-Guideline and Post-Guideline Practices in Minnesota."
58. Miethe, "Charging and Plea Bargaining Under Determinate Sentencing."
59. Engen and Steen, "The Power to Punish: Discretion and Sentencing Reform in the War on Drugs."
60. Engen and Steen, "The Power to Punish," p. 1365.
61. Ibid., p. 1365.
62. Ibid., p. 1382.
63. Ibid., p. 1384.
64. U.S. Department of Justice, *Prosecutor's Handbook on Sentencing Guidelines* 50.
65. Nagel and Schulhofer, "A Tale of Three Cities: An Empirical Study of Charging and Bargaining Practices Under the Federal Sentencing Guidelines," p. 544.
66. Ibid., p. 547.
67. Ibid., p. 552.
68. Tonry, *Sentencing Matters*, p. 33.
69. Dailey, "Minnesota Sentencing Guidelines: A Structure for Change," p. 315.
70. Bogan and Factor, "Oregon Guidelines, 1989-1994," p. 53.

71. Engen and Steen, "The Power to Punish," p. 1384.
72. Kramer and Ulmer, "Sentencing Disparity and Departures From Guidelines," Table 1 and Table 2.
73. Pennsylvania Commission on Sentencing, *1997 Annual Report*, Figure M.
74. U.S. Sentencing Commission. *1999 Sourcebook of Federal Sentencing Statistics*, Figure G.
75. Tonry, *Sentencing Matters*, p. 39.
76. Available on the World Wide Web at://www.famm.org.
77. In 1999, 7,089 offenders were convicted of marijuana offenses in U.S. District Courts; of these, 1,836 received 5-year mandatory minimum sentences and 477 received 10-year sentences. Considering all federal offenders convicted of drug offenses in 1999, 6,365 received mandatory minimum sentences of 5years, 6,903 received 10 years, and 459 received more than 10 years (see U.S. Sentencing Commission, *1999 Sourcebook of Federal Sentencing Statistics*, Table 43).
78. For a description of these reforms, see Beckett and Sasson, The Politics of Injustice; Mauer, *Race to Incarcerate*; and Tonry, Sentencing Matters.
79. Tonry, *Sentencing Matters*, chap. 5.
80. Beckett and Sasson, *The Politics of Injustice*, p. 177-178.
81. Ibid., pp. 176-177.
82. ABA Journal, "The Verdict Is In: Throw Out Mandatory Sentences: Introduction."
83. U.S. Sentencing Commission, *Special Report to the Congress: Mandatory Minimum Penalties in the Federal Criminal Justice System*.
84. Federal Judicial Center, *Planning for the Future: Results of a Federal Judicial Center Survey of United States Judges*.
85. U.S. Sentencing Commission, *Special Report to the Congress*, p. 57.
86. Ibid., p. 58.
87. Ibid., p. ii.
88. Ibid., p. 124.
89. Joint Committee on New York Drug Law Evaluation, *The Nation's Toughest Drug Law: Evaluating the New York Experience*.
90. Beha, "'And Nobody Can Get You Out': The Impact of a Mandatory Prison Sentence for the Illegal Carrying of a Firearm on the Use of Firearms and on the Administration of

Criminal Justice in Boston"; Rossman, Floyd, Pierce, McDevitt, and Bowers, "Massachusetts' Mandatory Minimum Sentence Gun Law: Enforcement, Prosecution, and Defense Impact."

91. Loftin, Heumann, and McDowall, "Mandatory Sentencing and Firearms Violence: Evaluating an Alternative to Gun Control."

92. Tonry, *Sentencing Matters*, p. 135.

93. Michigan Compiled Laws, chap. 333§7401(2).

94. Public Act 314 of 1998.

95. "Who's Defending Rockefeller Drug Laws? The Prosecutors," the *New York Times*, February 6, 2001. Available on the World Wide Web at http://www.nytimes.com

96. Ibid.

97. "Lawmakers Hear Arguments On Mandatory Minimum Drug Sentences," May 11, 2000. Available on the World Wide Web at http://www.cnn.com/2000/LAW/05/11/bc.drugsentences.ap/

98. Posted on the World Wide Web at http://www.famm.org

99. "Judges Decry Mandatory Minimum Sentences," *Pittsburgh Post-Gazette*, June 6, 1999, p. A-18.

100. U.S. Department of Justice, Bureau of Justice Statistics (BJS), *Sourcebook of Criminal Justice Statistics*, 1998.

101. Mauer, *Race To Incarcerate*; Skolnick, "Rethinking the Drug Problem"; Tonry, *Malign Neglect: Race, Crime, and Punishment in America*.

102. U.S. Department of Justice, BJS, *Prisoners in 1997*.

103. Skolnick, "Rethinking the Drug Problem," p. 411.

104. Austin and Irwin, *It's About Time: America's Imprisonment Binge*; Paternoster, "The Deterrent Effect of the Perceived Certainty and Severity of Punishment: A Review of the Evidence and Issues"; Tonry, *Sentencing Matters*.

105. For research that assesses the deterrent effects of punishment for drug offenders, see Caulkins, Rydell, Schwabe, and Chiesa, *Mandatory Minimum Sentences: Throwing Away the Key or the Taxpayers' Money?* and Speckart, Anglin, and Deschenes, "Modeling the Longitudinal Impact of Legal Sanctions on Narcotics Use and Property Crime."

106. Cohen, Nagin, Wallstrom, and Wasserman, "A Hierarchical Bayesian Analysis of Arrest Rates," p. 1260.

107. Irwin and Austin, *It's About Time*, p. 140.

108. Skolnick, "Rethinking the Drug Problem."

109. An alternative view, Martinson (1974), concluded that "rehabilitative efforts that have been reported so far have no appreciable effect on recidivism."

110. See Anglin and Hser, "Treatment of Drug Abuse," for a summary of this research.

111. Benedict, Huff-Corzine, and Corzine, "'Clean Up and Go Straight:' Effects of Drug Treatment on Recidivism Among Felony Probationers"; McCorkel, Harrison, and Inciardi, "How Treatment Is Constructed Among Graduates and Dropouts in a Prison Therapeutic Community"; Smith and Akers, "A Comparison of Recidivism of Florida's Community Control and Prison: A Five-Year Survival Analysis."

112. Field, "The Cornerstone Program: A Client Outcome Study"; Inciardi, Lockwood, and Hooper, "Delaware Treatment Program Presents Promising Results"; Mullen, "Therapeutic Communities in Prisons: Dealing with Toxic Waste"; Tunis, Austin, Morris, Hardyman, and Bolyard, *Evaluation of Drug Treatment in Local Corrections*; Wexler, Falkin, and Lipton, "Outcome Evaluation of a Prison Therapeutic Community for Substance Abuse Treatment."

113. National Institute of Justice, *Drug Use Forecasting 1996: Annual Report on Adult and Juvenile Arrestees.*

114. U.S. Department of Justice, BJS, *Survey of State Prison Inmates*, 1991.

115. Chaiken, "Crime Rates and Substance Abuse Among Types of Offenders."

116. Drug Court Clearinghouse and Technical Assistance Project, *Looking at a Decade of Drug Courts*, p. 3.

117. Inciardi, McBride, and Rivers, *Drug Control and the Courts.*

118. Drug Court Clearinghouse and Technical Assistance Project, *Looking at a Decade of Drug Courts*, p. 1.

119. National Association of Drug Court Professionals, *Defining Drug Courts*: The Key Components.

120. Drug Court Clearinghouse and Technical Assistance Project, *Looking at a Decade of Drug Courts*, p. 3.

121. U.S. General Accounting Office, *Drug Courts: Overview of Growth, Characteristics, and Results.*

122. Belenko, "Research on Drug Courts: A Critical Review."

123. Ibid., p. 29.

124. Ibid., pp. 29-30.

125. Ibid., pp. 17-18.
126. "New York to Send Criminal Addicts to Treatment Instead of Jail," *Omaha World Herald*, June 26, 2000, p. 8.
127. "Drug Policy Challenges California," Omaha World Herald, November 13, 2000, p. 3.
128. "California Lacks Resources for Law on Drug Offenders, Officials Say," the *New York Times*, February 12, 2001. Available on the World Wide Web at: http://www.nytimes.com
129. "Bill Calls for Big Bucks for Addiction Treatment," the *New York Times*, February 13, 2001. Available on the World Wide Web at: http://www.nytimes.com
130. Ibid.
131. Caulkins, "How Large Should the Strike Zone Be in 'Three Strikes and You're Out' Sentencing Laws?" p. 1. Available on the World Wide Web at http://www.heinz.cmu.edu/cgi
132. Wright, "Three Strikes Legislation and Sentencing Commission Objectives," p. 442.
133. Clark, Austin, and Henry, *"Three Strikes and You're Out:" A Review of State Legislation*, p. 7.
134. Beckett and Sasson, *The Politics of Injustice*, p. 180.
135. Cushman, "Effects on a Local Criminal Justice System," p. 93.
136. Clark, Austin, and Henry, *"Three Strikes and You're Out,"* p. 3.
137. Harris and Jesilow, "It's Not the Old Ball Game: Three Strikes and the Courtroom Workgroup."
138. Ibid.
139. Feeley and Kamin, "The Effect of 'Three Strikes and You're Out' on the Courts: Looking Back to See the Future," p. 136.
140. Birmingham News, "Lies in Sentencing," July 28, 2000. Available on the World Wide Web at http://www.bhmnews.com
141. Ibid.
142. U.S. Department of Justice, BJS, *Truth in Sentencing in State Prisons*, Table 1.
143. Ibid., Table 8.
144. DiLulio, "Criminals and Gutting Truth-in-Sentencing Laws," p. 2.
145. Turner, Greenwood, Chen, and Fain, "The Impact of Truth-in-Sentencing and Three Strikes Legislation: Prison Populations, State Budgets, and Crime Rates."

Chapter Seven

The Impact of the Sentencing Reform Movement

The sentencing reforms enacted during the past 30 years reflect diverse views of the purposes of punishment, the degree of discretion that should be accorded to judges and other criminal justice officials, and the extent to which crime and criminals can be controlled by sentencing policies. Those who proposed the reforms and lobbied for their enactment believed that they would result in more punitive, more effective, and fairer sentence outcomes. But have the changes in sentencing policy produced these results? Are sentences today more punitive than they were in the past? Are offenders being sent to prison at higher rates and for longer periods of time? If so, has this punitiveness translated into reductions in crime? Are sentences today fairer or more equitable than they were in the past? Is there less disparity and gender or racial bias today than there was 30 years ago?

We address these questions in the sections that follow. We begin by examining changes in sentence severity. We first examine trends in the severity of sentences imposed in jurisdictions that adopted sentencing guidelines, mandatory minimum sentences, and three-strikes-and-you're-out laws. We then examine the late-20th-century phenomenon of "mass imprisonment"[1] and summarize recent research designed to determine whether increases in imprisonment have led to reductions in crime. We conclude with a discussion of the extent to which the reforms have reduced disparity and discrimination in sentencing.

Have Sentencing Reforms Led to More Punitive Sentences?

There are at least two ways to answer the question "Are sentences today more severe than they were in the past?" One way is to compare the sentences imposed before and after the adoption of sentencing reforms. Thus, one would ask whether sentences are more severe in jurisdictions that adopted sentencing guidelines, mandatory minimum penalties, or three-strikes statutes. The second way to answer the question is to compare the number and rate of persons incarcerated in state and federal prisons today with imprisonment statistics from earlier years. In taking this approach, one would ask whether an increasingly large proportion of the population is being locked up in our nation's prisons. As we will see, the two approaches rely on different data but lead to relatively similar conclusions.

Sentencing Reforms and Sentence Severity

In the next three sections, we examine the results of research evaluating the impact of three reforms: sentencing guidelines, mandatory minimum sentences, and three-strikes-and-you're-out laws. Our goal is to determine whether these "tough-on-crime" sentencing reforms produced the predicted increase in sentence severity.

Sentencing Guidelines

Sentencing guidelines have the potential to increase sentence severity; they link sentence severity explicitly to the seriousness of the offense and the offender's criminal history and generally prohibit judges from reducing sentences based on the offender's personal circumstances. Moreover, as explained in Chapter 6, most commissions adopted prescriptive guidelines that were intended to change sentence patterns by reducing use of probation, increasing use of prison, and lengthening sentences, particularly for violent offenses.

One way to assess the impact of guidelines on sentence severity is to examine overall sentencing trends in jurisdictions with guidelines. Exhibit 7.1

displays the percentages of offenders incarcerated from 1984 to 1999 in Minnesota, Washington, and Pennsylvania, as well as the percentage of federal offenders incarcerated during this time period.[2] These data reveal that the overall likelihood of incarceration increased over time in Minnesota, Washington, and for federal offenders but decreased over time in Pennsylvania.[3] In Minnesota, the total incarceration rate grew from 73 percent in 1984 to 88 percent in 1999. This was primarily due to increases in the percentage of offenders sentenced to local jails. The jail rate increased from 53 percent to 66 percent, whereas the imprisonment rate increased by only 2 percentage points (from 20 percent to 22 percent).[4] In Washington, the odds of imprisonment for nonviolent offenses increased from 18.6 percent in 1990 to 25.7 percent in 1999. The likelihood of incarceration for offenders convicted in U.S. District Courts also increased substantially, from 49 percent in 1984 to 77 percent in 1999. In contrast, the odds of incarceration in Pennsylvania declined from 58 percent to 46 percent.

Exhibit 7.1. Percent Incarcerated in Jurisdictions with Sentencing Guidelines, 1984–1999

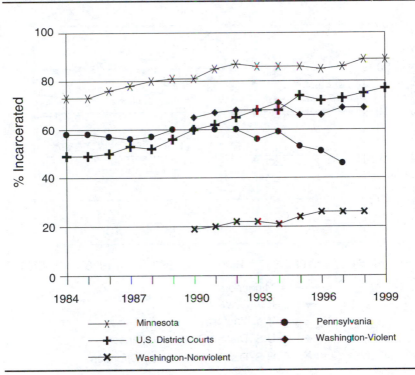

Further evidence of the impact of sentencing guidelines is presented in Exhibit 7.2, which displays the average prison sentences in the four jurisdictions over time. The trends in Washington and Minnesota are very similar; in these two jurisdictions, the average prison sentence increased from 1989 to 1994 and then decreased slightly from 1994 to 1999. In Pennsylvania and at the federal level, on the other hand, sentences have fluctuated over time; the average sentence for all offenses generally increased from 1984 to 1988, declined in 1989 and 1990, and increased in 1991. The average sentence imposed on offenders in U.S. District Courts declined somewhat from 1991 to 1999, and sentences in Pennsylvania increased from 1993 to 1995 but declined in 1996 and 1997.

Exhibit 7.2 also displays the prison sentences imposed on federal drug offenders. The mean sentence for these offenders increased from a low of 64.8 months in 1984 to a high of 95.7 months in 1991. Since 1991, judges have imposed somewhat shorter sentences on federal drug offenders. It is

Exhibit 7.2. Average Prison Sentence in Jurisdictions with Sentencing Guidelines, 1984-1999

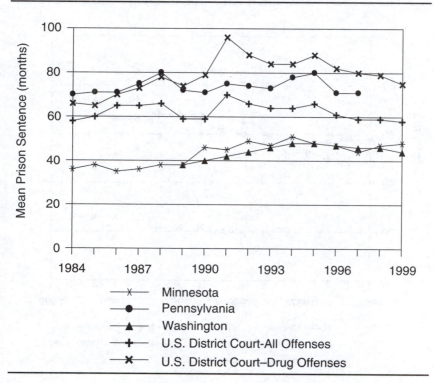

important to note, however, that since 1990, the sentences given to offenders convicted of drug offenses in U.S. District Courts have been longer than the sentences imposed on all of the felony offenders in Minnesota, Pennsylvania, and Washington. Federal drug offenders, in fact, received sentences that were twice as long as those imposed on offenders convicted of felonies in Minnesota and Washington.

Research on Sentence Outcomes in State Courts. The data presented in Exhibits 7.1 and 7.2 (which may mask trends for individual offenses) suggest that sentences overall are somewhat more severe in Minnesota, Washington, and at the federal level than they were in the past but are somewhat less severe in Pennsylvania. The conclusion that sentences are more severe in the postguideline era in Minnesota and Washington is confirmed by the results of empirical research evaluating the impact of the guidelines in those states. Research in Minnesota, for example, revealed that the postguideline imprisonment rate was generally similar to the preguideline rate[5] but the jail incarceration rate increased substantially in the post-reform period.[6] In fact, D'Alessio and Stolzenberg reported that "the onset of the guidelines increased jail incarceration by 26%."[7] The authors of this study also found that when the prison population was high, judges departed from the guidelines and sentenced offenders to jail rather than prison. Because the Minnesota guidelines placed limits on the growth of the prison population, in other words, judges attempted "to circumvent the guidelines by shifting the burden of incarcerating offenders from the state to the local level."[8] Consistent with this, Marvel and Moody, who used time-series analysis to investigate the effect of the guidelines on court commitments to prison and on prison populations, found that the guidelines did not affect court commitments but did have a negative effect on the prison population in Minnesota.[9]

A more recent evaluation found that the Minnesota prison population began to increase in the late 1980s.[10] The number of offenders imprisoned in Minnesota grew by 29 percent from 1984 to 1988 and by another 37 percent from 1988 to 1992. Frase attributed this growth in the prison population to three factors: a significant increase in the number of felony convictions, increases in the number of probation and parole revocations, and substantially more severe penalties for violent crimes that were adopted by the Minnesota legislature in 1989. The 1989 Omnibus Crime Bill also amended the sentencing guidelines enabling legislation "by specifying that the sentencing commission's 'primary' goal in writing guidelines should be *public safety*" and that prison capacity should no longer be a "substantial" consideration.[11] Recent data provided by the Minnesota Sentencing Guidelines Commission suggest that the prison population has continued to increase.[12] The number of offenders sentenced to prison increased from 1,925 in 1992 to 2,451 in 1999.[13]

Two studies evaluating the impact of sentencing guidelines in the state of Washington reported that sentence severity increased in the post-reform period.[14] Boerner compared the sentences imposed for a variety of offenses in the preguideline and postguideline periods. He found that changes in the severity of sentences prescribed by the guidelines were followed by increases in the severity of sentences imposed by judges for the targeted offenses. For example, he compared the sentences imposed before and after the enactment of guideline amendments that divided second-degree burglary into residential and nonresidential burglary and increased the penalties for both. In 1991, the year after these changes went into effect, the mean sentence for residential burglary (20.8 months) was more than twice the average sentence for second-degree burglary in 1990 (10.2 months). Boerner found a similar pattern for first-degree statutory rape and first-degree rape of a child. In 1988, some types of statutory rape were redefined as rape of a child; the penalties prescribed for the latter were also more severe than those for the former. The mean sentence for first-degree statutory rape was 32.5 months in 1988. In contrast, the average sentence for first-degree rape of a child was 58.6 months in 1989 and 75.7 months in 1992. In this jurisdiction, then, changes in sentencing policy did lead to more punitive sentences.

A recent study of sentences imposed on drug offenders in Washington provides even more dramatic evidence of the impact of sentencing guidelines on sentence outcomes in that state.[15] Engen and Steen examined the effect of two amendments to Washington's Sentencing Reform Act. The first, which went into effect in 1988, eliminated the First-Time Offender Waiver (FTOW) for offenders convicted of delivery of cocaine or heroin. Under the FTOW, first-time offenders were eligible for a sentence of only 90 days confinement. As Engen and Steen explain, the principal effect of this change was that "every convicted dealer would receive a prison sentence within the standard range (12-14 months for a first offender)."[16] The second amendment, which went into effect in 1990, substantially increased the presumptive sentence for offenders convicted of delivering cocaine or heroin.

To determine whether these changes affected sentence severity, Engen and Steen examined sentencing data for first-time offenders convicted of drug offenses from 1985 to 1995. As shown Exhibit 7.3, the sentences for offenders convicted of delivering drugs increased dramatically. The FTOW was ordered in 64.5 percent of the cases in 1986 but in only 5.9 percent of the cases in 1989, the year after the FTOW reform went into effect. Consistent with this, the percentage of offenders sentenced to prison increased substantially, from 23.6 percent in 1986 to 87.5 percent in 1989. The average sentence also increased; it more than doubled from 1986 to 1989 and doubled again from 1989 to 1991.

Evidence on the impact of the guidelines in Pennsylvania also suggests that sentences are more punitive in the post-reform era. One early study, for example, compared sentences imposed in 1980 (preguideline) with those imposed in 1983 (postguideline).[17] Kramer and Lubitz found that both the rate of incarceration and the average sentence length increased in the postguideline era. The likelihood of incarceration increased from 44 percent to 64 percent for aggravated assault, from 47 percent to 69 percent for burglary, from 74 percent to 86 percent for rape, and from 67 percent to 74 percent for robbery. The average minimum sentence increased from 8.5 months to 13.6 months for aggravated assault, from 10.3 months to 15.1 months for burglary, and from 41.5 months to 51.9 months for rape.[18] A later study by the Pennsylvania Commission on Sentencing reached a similar conclusion.[19]

Data released by the Pennsylvania Commission reveal that this upward trend has continued.[20] The incarceration rate for aggravated assault, which

Exhibit 7.3 Sentences Imposed on First-Time Offenders Convicted of Delivery of Cocaine or Heroin in Washington State, 1986-1995

	FTOW Sentences (Percentage of All Sentences)	Percentage Sentenced to Prison	Average Sentence (Months)
1986	64.5	23.6	6.3
1987	51.3	42.9	8.3
1988	42.5	49.2	8.9
1989	5.9	87.5	13.3
1990	0.9	90.9	22.6
1991	0.5	92.1	25.9
1992	0.4	94.5	28.7
1993	0.5	92.8	25.6
1994	0.0	94.6	26.9
1995	0.4	93.5	27.9

SOURCE: Adapted from "The Power to Punish: Discretion and Sentencing Reform in the War on Drugs" (Table 2), by R. Engen and S. Steen, *American Journal of Psychology* 105:1357-1395.

was 64 percent in 1983, was 83 percent in 1997. The rates for the other three offenses were also higher in 1997 than in 1983: 78 percent versus 69 percent for burglary, 96 percent versus 86 percent for rape, and 90 percent versus 74 percent for robbery. The average lengths of incarceration sentences also continued to increase: from 13.6 months to 26 months for aggravated assault and from 51.9 months to 67.9 months for rape. Contrary to the patterns revealed by Exhibits 7.1 and 7.2, which showed that sentences imposed in Pennsylvania from 1984 to 1997 had become less severe, these data reveal that sentences *for these four offenses* were substantially harsher in 1997 than in either 1983 or 1980. This suggests that the overall downward trend in sentence severity in Pennsylvania is due at least in part to changes in the composition of the offender pool. It suggests that a larger proportion of the offenders sentenced in Pennsylvania courts have been convicted of less serious crimes or have less serious prior criminal records.

Research on Sentence Outcomes in Federal Courts. There is relatively little research on the impact of the federal sentencing guidelines on sentence outcomes. The most oft-cited study is an analysis conducted by the U.S. Sentencing Commission (USSC).[21] The USSC used a sophisticated time-series design to compare the sentences imposed on offenders overall and on three categories of offenders (those convicted of robbery, heroin or cocaine trafficking, and embezzlement) from July of 1984 to June of 1990. As shown in Exhibit 7.4, the proportion of offenders sentenced to prison increased over the 5-year time period for all offenders and for each category of offenders. Mean sentence lengths also increased substantially for robbery and drug offenses. In fact, the mean prison term for drug offenders was 27 months in 1984 and 67 months in 1990, an increase of 248 percent. (The USSC noted that changes in the severity of sentences imposed on drug offenders were probably due to the harsher penalties prescribed by the guidelines and the mandatory minimum sentences contained in the Anti-Drug Abuse Act of 1986.)[22]

Although the sentencing commission concluded that these increases in sentence severity signaled "major system changes," they did not conclude that the sentencing reforms caused these changes. They pointed out that the new laws might have resulted in the conviction of more higher-level offenders or individuals involved in more serious offenses. If this were the case, the more severe sentences would simply reflect changes in the nature of the offenders processed. As the commission report notes, "Due to considerable changes that occurred not only in legislation and sentencing policy but also in the volume, seriousness, and composition of the criminal be-

Exhibit 7.4 Sentences Imposed on Offenders Sentenced in U.S. District Courts, 1984 to 1990

	Percentage Incarcerated		Mean Prison Sentence (Months)	
	July 1984	June 1990	July 1984	June 1990
All Offenders	52	65	24	46
Robbery	84	99	60	78
Cocaine/heroin Trafficking	72	87	27	67
Embezzlement	39	51	12	10

SOURCE: *The Federal Sentencing Guidelines: A Report on the Operation of the Guidelines System and Short-Term Impacts on Disparity in Sentencing, Use of Incarceration, and Prosecutorial Discretion and Plea Bargaining* (pp. 56-63), by the U.S. Sentencing Commission, 1991. Washington, DC: Author.

havior they seek to regulate, any causal influences are too confounded and close in proximity to be separately assessed and evaluated."[23]

A study of sentence outcomes in two federal district courts also found that sentences were more severe in the postguideline period.[24] Lacasse and Payne compared the average sentences imposed on offenders convicted of nine types of offenses in the Southern District of New York and the Eastern District of New York from 1981 to 1987 (pre-reform) and from 1988 to 1995 (post-reform). Like the USSC, they found that sentences for most offenses increased substantially in both jurisdictions. In the Southern District of New York, for example, sentences increased from 8.2 months to 23.7 months for forgery, from 8.9 months to 14.8 months for fraud, from 30.9 months to 60.2 months for drug offenses, and from 20.9 months to 48.8 months for weapons offenses.

Considered together, the results of these evaluations of the effect of state and federal sentencing guidelines suggest that sentences are more severe in the postguideline era. They suggest that offenders are more likely to be sentenced to prison and that those who are imprisoned serve longer terms in the post-reform era. Although it would be inappropriate to conclude that there is a *causal relationship* between the adoption of sentencing guidelines and more punitive sentences, the fact that these evaluations consistently revealed that sentences became more severe suggests that the guidelines did have an effect. As Tonry concludes, "The record, though not uncomplicated, shows that commissions through their policy choices can alter sentencing patterns substantially."[25]

The Impact of Mandatory Minimum Sentencing Statutes

Mandatory minimum sentencing statutes tie judges' hands by requiring them to impose minimum sentences on offenders convicted of targeted crimes: murder, drug offenses, driving while intoxicated, and use of a firearm during the commission of a felony. Supporters of these laws, which were designed to imprison some offenders who might otherwise not get prison sentences and to lengthen prison terms for others, expected that they would lead to increases in overall sentence severity at both the state and federal level. But have they?

One problem with mandatory penalties is noncompliance. Researchers have consistently demonstrated that mandatory penalties do not work as predicted. They shift discretion from judges to prosecutors and result in widespread circumvention by judges who regard the penalties as too severe. This obviously reduces their potential impact on sentence severity. Although offenders convicted of the targeted offenses, or at least some portion of them, might well receive harsher sentences, if fewer offenders are prosecuted or convicted for these offenses, the effect on overall sentence severity might be negligible (or even nonexistent).

As shown in Box 7.1, which summarizes cases posted on the "Families Against Mandatory Minimums" Web site, there is anecdotal evidence that mandatory minimum penalty laws do result in severe sentences. But are sentences generally more severe than they would have been in the absence of the mandatory minimum statutes?

A number of studies have addressed this question. One of the earliest was an evaluation of New York's Rockefeller Drug Laws, [26] which took effect in 1973 and required long prison terms for offenders convicted of narcotics offenses.[27] This study found that arrests, indictments, and convictions for felony drug offenses declined after the law took effect. The percentage of felony drug arrests resulting in indictment for felony drug offenses declined from 39.1 percent in 1972 to 25.4 percent in 1976, and the percentage of indictments that resulted in convictions declined from 87.3 percent to 79.3 percent. As predicted, sentences imposed on offenders who were not diverted out of the mandatory minimum pipeline did increase. The likelihood that an offender convicted of a drug felony would be incarcerated increased from 33.8 percent to 54.8 percent, and substantially more offenders received sentences of 3 years or longer.[28] However, the fact that a smaller proportion of the defendants arrested for drug offenses were convicted of drug offenses meant that the likelihood that a person arrested for a drug felony would go to prison remained about the same.

BOX 7.1

SENTENCES IMPOSED ON DRUG OFFENDERS IN THE 1990s

Gloria Van Winkle

Gloria Van Winkle, a 33-year-old mother of two young children, was sentenced to life in prison for possession of $40 worth of cocaine in Kansas in 1992. Van Winkle had two prior convictions for cocaine possession and had been addicted to cocaine for a number of years. She was befriended by a convicted thief working as a paid government informant. The informant sold her a small amount of cocaine for $40. Because this was her "third strike," she received a mandatory life sentence. She currently is incarcerated in a maximum security prison and will not be eligible for parole until she has served 15 years of her sentence.

Nancy Simmons

In the early 1990s, a group of Colombians offered Nancy Simmons and three of her friends an all-expense-paid trip to Colombia and $1,500 to smuggle gold into the United States from Colombia. Nancy and her friends spent 3 days in a house in Colombia where the Colombians showed them the gold pebbles and how they were packaged. Each woman received a package and was instructed to strap it to her body. When they landed in Miami, customs officers stopped them, searched them, and arrested them. The government offered the women sentences of less than 1 year if they would plead guilty to knowingly importing cocaine. Because the women had believed that they were smuggling gold, they refused the offer and went to trial. All of them were convicted and sentenced to 10 years in prison. Nancy Simmons, who was 35 years old at the time of her sentencing, had four children ranging in age from 4 to 20. She had no prior convictions.

John Patillo

John Patillo, who was facing serious financial problems, agreed to deliver a package to a Federal Express office in Los Angeles for $500. The package contained 681 grams of crack cocaine. John admitted that he knew the package contained illegal drugs but denied knowing what type of drug or what quantity was involved. At the time of his arrest, he was working for a cable television company and was a student at San Diego State University.

The U.S. District Court Judge who imposed the mandatory 10-year sentence commented on the unfairness of John's sentence. As he noted, "Statutory mandatory minimum sentences create injustice because the sentence is determined without looking at the particular defendant. . . .

Under this sledgehammer approach, it can make no difference whether the defendant actually owned the drugs with which he was caught or whether, at a time when he had an immediate need for cash, he was suckered into taking the risk of being caught with someone else's drugs. . . . One of the basic precepts of criminal justice has been that the punishment fit the crime. This is the principle which, as a matter of law, I must violate in this case."

SOURCE: "Families Against Mandatory Minimums, Victims of MMS," available on the World Wide Web.

A second evaluation of mandatory minimum sentences focused on Michigan's Felony Firearm Statute,[29] which went into effect in 1977.[30] As explained in Chapter 6, the "Gun Law" mandated a 2-year sentence enhancement for offenders who possessed firearms while committing felonies[31] The major objectives of the Gun Law were to increase the likelihood that offenders convicted of violent crimes with a gun would serve some time in prison and to lengthen the sentence of those who were incarcerated. To determine whether the law met its objectives, Loftin, Heumann, and McDowall compared sentences imposed by judges in Detroit Recorder's Court for violent felonies committed with and without guns before and after the implementation of the law.

Loftin and his colleagues found that the law had little impact on sentence severity for five of the six violent offenses examined. For these five offenses—murder, criminal sexual conduct, armed robbery, assault with intent to commit murder, and assault with intent to do great bodily harm—the Gun Law did not increase the likelihood of imprisonment or the length of the prison sentence. For felonious assault, the law reduced the likelihood of conviction but increased the likelihood of incarceration and the length of sentence for those who were convicted. According to the authors, these findings suggest that "the situation stayed pretty much the same after the introduction of the mandatory 2-year sentence."[32]

To explain these results, the authors point to the "centrality of the notion of a 'going rate' to court participants."[33] Members of the courtroom workgroup, in other words, generally agreed that certain types of cases "were 'worth' a certain price."[34] As a result, they adjusted the sentence for the primary felony downward so that the total sentence would not exceed the going rate. For example, if the going rate for armed robbery were 10 years, the sentence for the robbery would be scaled back to 8 years and the 2-year enhancement for use of a firearm would bring the sentence back up to 10 years. For felonious assault cases in which the norm was "no time in prison," the workgroup preserved the going rate by dismissing the case, acquitting the defendant, or finding the defendant guilty of a misdemeanor (in which case the felony firearm charge automatically disappeared). As the authors note, the changes in conviction and sentencing in the post-reform period "were not systematic, were not across-the-board, and were not, therefore, congruent with one of the goals of the Gun Law—namely, equal punishment across sets of similarly situated gun offenders."[35]

The highly controversial federal mandatory minimum sentencing statutes have also been the subject of a number of evaluations.[36] The U.S. Sentencing Commission, for example, compared sentences over time for drug offenders whose offense behavior was sufficient to invoke mandatory minimum sentences. They found that from 1985 to 1990, the median sentence length increased from 36 to 66 months for drug offenders who did not possess or use a firearm; for drug offenders who did possess or use a firearm, the median sentence more than doubled, from 84 to 180 months.[37] Moreover, the USSC report noted that these figures actually understated the increase in sentence severity. Because the Sentencing Reform Act of 1984 [38]eliminated parole and curtailed the amount of good-time credit that offenders could receive, the actual time that offenders would serve in prison increased. A defendant who received the median 36 months in 1984 would serve only 12 months, but a defendant who received the median 66 months in 1990 would serve 85 percent of the sentence, or 56 months. The time that a typical drug offender would serve, then, increased more than fourfold, from 12 months to 56 months.[39] Although the USSC was careful to point out that these changes in sentence severity could not be attributed *solely* to the mandatory minimum sentencing statutes, they did conclude that the mandatory minimums, along with other factors, resulted in increasing sentence length.

Subsequent research by the Federal Judicial Center revealed that many of the drug offenders sentenced under the mandatory minimum statutes were low-level offenders "who present no threat to society and who could be adequately punished with shorter sentences."[40] Of the 16,834 offenders convicted of drug offenses in 1992, about half received 0 or 1 criminal history point and did not use a dangerous weapon or play a major role in the offense. Research conducted by the Department of Justice reached a similar conclusion.[41] They found that half of the 90,000 offenders in the custody of the Bureau of Prisons in June of 1993 were drug offenders and over one third of them had no record of violence, no evidence of sophisticated criminal activity, and no prior prison confinement. Moreover, the majority of these low-level drug offenders had never been arrested before their present offenses but were serving an average of 81.5 months in federal prison. As Vincent and Hofer concluded,

> There is substantial evidence that the mandatory minimums result every year in the lengthy incarceration of thousands of low-level offenders who could be effectively sentenced to shorter periods of time at an annual savings of several hundred million dollars, and that the mandatory minimums do not narrowly target violent criminals or major drug traffickers.[42]

It thus appears that the enactment of mandatory minimum sentencing statutes, like the adoption of sentencing guidelines, did lead to more punitive sentences, particularly for low-level drug offenders. As one vocal critic of these laws stated, "They do little that is good and much that is bad, both to the integrity of the legal system and to offenders who are often punished more severely than anyone directly involved believes is appropriate."[43]

The Impact of Three-Strikes-and-You're Out Laws

Like mandatory minimum sentencing statutes, three-strikes-and-you're-out laws reduce judicial discretion in sentencing. These laws, which typically require judges to enhance sentences for second felonies and to sentence "three-time losers" to life in prison, were designed to increase the use of imprisonment and to extend the sentences of those who were incarcerated.

Evaluating the impact of three-strikes laws on sentence severity is difficult. The reason for this is that each state that enacted a three-strikes law already had provisions in place to increase penalties for repeat or habitual offenders.[44] Although the mandatory penalties for those found to be repeat offenders were increased substantially in some states and the definition of a repeat offender was expanded in others, the statutes that existed prior to the enactment of the three-strikes laws provided harsh sentences for repeat offenders. The North Carolina Habitual Criminal Statute, for example, required the judge to impose an additional consecutive term of 25 years for a third conviction for any felony. The preexisting California statute provided for a mandatory term of life for a third violent felony conviction and specified that the offender would not be eligible for parole before 20 years.[45] As a result, a substantial majority of the offender population targeted by three-strikes laws were already serving long prison terms.

Critics contend that the three-strikes-and-you're-out movement was "largely symbolic."[46] In states other than California, the laws were carefully worded to ensure that only the most serious offenders, who comprise a very small portion of the total offender population, would be affected by the law. And even in California, the law's impact was less than initially predicted. Prior to the law's passage, the California Department of Corrections (CDC) predicted that the prison population would more than double between January of 1994 and December of 1999. Each year since then, the CDC has lowered its estimation of the impact of the strike law. By 1998, the projected 1999 prison population was 170,000, about 75,000 less than what was predicted in 1994.[47]

Most analysts attribute this to the fact that there were not as many offenders sentenced under California's two-strikes provision as originally predicted. Exhibit 7.5 presents the number of two- and three-strikes cases admitted to California prisons from April of 1994 through December of 1998. The number of two-strikes cases increased dramatically in the first 12 months but then leveled off after that, and the number of three-strikes cases stayed well below 200 during the entire time period. A second explanation focuses on changes in judge's sentencing patterns in two-strike cases. The CDC initially estimated that about 40 percent of second-strikers would be sentenced at the low end of the determinate sentencing range for each offense, but found that 60 percent were being sentenced in this range.[48] Thus, the second-strike provision was being used less often than predicted, and sentences imposed on those who were sentenced under the provision were shorter than expected.

The three-strikes laws, like the mandatory minimum sentencing statutes, were designed to incapacitate violent, dangerous, repeat offenders. In states with "narrow strike zones," which require the second or third strike to be a violent crime, most of those sentenced under the laws' provisions have in fact been convicted of violent crimes. In Washington, 108 of the 115 third-strikers were convicted of crimes against persons. Similarly, in Georgia, all 88 two-strikers and 3,046 one-strikers were convicted of crimes against persons.[49] In contrast, in California, 31.5 percent of the offenders sentenced for a second strike and 19.3 percent of those sentenced for a third strike were convicted of drug offenses: Most of them were convicted of drug possession rather than drug distribution. Another third of the two- and three-strikers were convicted of property offenses, particularly burglary.[50] According to Austin and Irwin, by 1998, over 600 offenders convicted of drug possession and more than 1,500 convicted of property crimes had been sentenced to 25 years to life for a third strike.[51]

Exhibit 7.5. Number of 2- and 3-Strike Cases Admitted to the California Department of Corrections, by Month

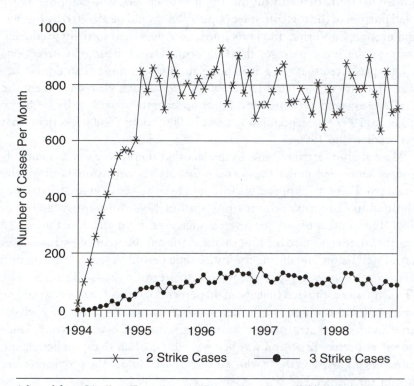

Adapted from *It's About Time: America's Imprisonment Binge* (Table 9-6), by J. Austin and J. Irwin, 2001. Belmont, CA: Wadsworth.

The lack of a comprehensive evaluation of the nationwide impact of three-strikes laws coupled with widespread variation in the nature of the statutes enacted make it difficult to generalize about the laws' effect on sentence severity. It appears that the laws have had minimal impact in states with laws that apply only to the most violent repeat offenders. The impact of the law enacted in California, although less than initially predicted, has been more significant. Over 40,000 felony offenders, many of whom were convicted of minor drug offenses and property crimes, are now serving long prison sentences as second- and third-strikers in California.

The results of evaluations of the sentencing reforms adopted during the past 30 years indicate that sentences are more punitive in the post-reform era. In the next section, we examine the effect of the reforms on state and federal prison populations.

The "Imprisonment Binge"

In 1971, David Rothman, one of the foremost authorities on the history and development of the prison system, wrote, "We have been gradually emerging from institutional responses, and one can foresee the period when incarceration will be used still more rarely than it is today."[52] Two years later, the National Advisory Commission on Criminal Justice Standards and Goals, which concluded that "the prison, the reformatory and the jail have achieved only a shocking record of failure,"[53] recommended that "no new institutions for adults should be built and existing institutions for juveniles should be closed."[54]

By the year 2000, it was clear that Rothman's prediction would not come true and that the commission's recommendations would not be followed. Their calls for reductions in the use of incarceration, which were voiced at a time when the inmate population was just over 300,000, fell on deaf ears. Rather than declining, America's imprisonment rate, which had fluctuated around a relatively steady mean of 110 individuals per 100,000 for most of the 20th century, increased every year from 1975 to 2000. In fact, the prison population quadrupled from 1972 to 2000: It increased from 300,000 to just under 2 million in less than 30 years. Stated another way, the incarceration rate increased from 110 persons incarcerated for every 100,000 persons in the population to about 450 per 100,000. If inmates in local jails are included, the rate is even higher: 680 per 100,000.[55]

As these figures demonstrate, for the past 30 years, the United States "has been engaged in an unprecedented imprisonment binge."[56] The question, of course, is whether these dramatic increases in the prison population are due to changes in crime rates or changes in sentencing policies and practices. If there are more crimes—or more serious violent crimes—today than there were three decades ago, we would expect the prison population to increase, irrespective of whether new sentencing policies had been enacted. If, on the other hand, the crime rate has remained relatively stable as the incarceration rate has skyrocketed, we could conclude that at least some of the increase in the prison population is due to the crackdown on crime and criminals.

Most criminologists believe that the escalating prison population cannot be attributed to increases in crime. Zimring[57] suggests that the overall upward trend actually reflects three different patterns at three different time periods. He contends that from 1973 to the mid-1980s, the imprisonment binge was fueled by "general increases in the commitment of marginal felons to prison."[58] During this time period, in other words, judges were generally sending more borderline offenders convicted of felonies to prison rather than giving them probation. The yearly increases from 1985 to 1992, on the other hand, reflected a greater likelihood of incarceration and longer sentences in one category: drug offenders.[59] Zimring argues that during the most recent time period, which he characterizes as "the period of time when imprisonment rates defy gravity and continue to grow even as crime rates are dropping," the emphasis shifted from "'lock em up' to 'throw away the key.'" As he notes, during this time period, "The lengthening of sentences has begun . . . to play a much larger role in sustaining the growth of [the] prison population."[60]

Other scholars similarly contend that changes in sentencing policy—and not changes in crime—fueled the growing use of imprisonment in the United States. Garland, for example, maintains that "America did not collectively decide to get into the business of mass imprisonment."[61] Instead, mass imprisonment emerged as the overdetermined outcome of a converging series of policies and decisions. Determinate sentencing structures, the war against drugs, mandatory sentencing, truth in sentencing, the emergence of private corrections, the political events and calculations that made everyone tough on crime—these developments built on one another and produced the flow of prisoners into custody.[62]

Mauer makes an analogous argument, asserting that "the impact of these sentencing changes on prison populations has been dramatic, and far outweighs any change in crime rates as a contributing factor."[63]

This was confirmed by a careful and methodologically rigorous analysis of growth in the prison population from 1980 to 1996. Blumstein and Beck[64] concluded that 88 percent of the tripling of the prison population from 1980 to 1996 could be explained by changes in the imposition of punishment: 51 percent of the increase was due to a greater likelihood of incarceration following conviction and 37 percent could be attributed to longer prison sentences. In contrast, changes in the crime rate explained only 12 percent of the growth in the prison population during this time period.

It thus appears that the answer to the question posed earlier—are sentences more punitive today than they were in the past?—is "yes." In the post-reform period, offenders convicted of felonies in state and federal courts face a greater likelihood of incarceration and longer prison sentences than they did in the pre-reform era. These changes, in turn, have led to dramatic increases in the nation's prison population.

Have the Sentencing Reforms Led to a Reduction in Crime?

The sentencing reforms enacted during the past 30 years were premised on a belief that harsher sentences would reduce crime. They were based on the argument that more punitive penalties would deter and incapacitate would-be offenders and that crime rates would therefore fall. We have seen that the reforms did in fact lead to more punitive sentences and to dramatic increases in the prison population. But did these changes in sentence severity produce the predicted reduction in crime?

A comprehensive discussion of this issue, which has generated dozens of research reports (many of which reach conflicting conclusions) is beyond the scope of this book. Instead, we briefly summarize the results of research on the deterrent effect of punishment. We then evaluate the validity of the arguments made by those on each side of the "incarceration reduces crime" debate.

The Deterrent Effect of Punishment: Rhetoric Versus Reality

Skyrocketing increases in the state and federal prison populations reflect a crime control policy premised on a somewhat unpersuasive theory of deterrence. The assumption is that sentencing offenders to prison for long periods of time will deter current and prospective offenders, leading eventually to a reduction in crime. As numerous commentators have observed, however, this assumption rests on the false premise that altering criminal penalties will alter behavior.[65] Tonry and others question the validity of this assumption, noting that scholarly research generally concludes that increasing the severity of penalties will have little, if any, effect on crime. The voluminous body of research on the deterrent effect of the death penalty,[66] for example, reveals that "capital punishment is no better at deterring would-be murderers than a prolonged period of incarceration."[67]

Research examining the effect of increased use of imprisonment similarly fails to support the deterrence argument.[68] In 1978, for instance, the National Academy of Sciences Panel on Deterrent and Incapacitative Effects concluded that the evidence did not support the deterrence hypothesis.[69] The National Academy of Sciences Panel on the Understanding and Control of Violent Behavior similarly concluded in 1993 that greatly increased use of imprisonment had not led to significant reductions in violent crime rates.[70] An even more damning assessment was provided by McGuire and Priestly, who reviewed recent evaluations of the deterrent effects of incarceration and alternatives to incarceration. They concluded that this body of research revealed that punitive measures "have a net destructive effect, in that they serve primarily to worsen rates of recidivism."[71]

A recent study of sentencing options and outcomes reached a similarly negative conclusion about the deterrent effect of imprisonment.[72] Gottfredson examined the crime control effects of sentences imposed on offenders convicted of felonies in Essex County, New Jersey, in 1976 and 1977. Using a 20-year follow-up period, he compared recidivism rates of offenders who were incarcerated (in a youth facility, jail, or prison) with those for offenders who received suspended sentences and were placed on probation. He controlled for the factors associated with judges' sentencing decisions and for the judge's assessment of the likelihood that the offender would commit new crimes. As shown in Exhibit 7.6, Gottfredson found that neither the type of sentence (confined versus not confined) nor the length of confinement affected the likelihood of recidivism. In fact, the percentages of offenders with new arrests during the initial 5-year follow-up period were nearly identical: 55.1 percent for offenders who were incarcerated and 55.0 percent for offenders placed on probation. These results led Gottfredson to conclude that although incarceration "may have served as a warning to others or as deserved punishment,"[73] it was not a more effective deterrent than noncustodial sentences. As he observed, "These results offer little support for the policy trends, prominent since this project began, that have supported increased use of confinement as a sentencing choice, emphasized longer terms, or accepted specific deterrence to reduce offenders' recidvisim."[74]

The results of studies evaluating laws requiring mandatory minimum sentences for crimes committed with firearms, although somewhat inconsistent, also fail to provide strong support for the deterrence thesis. Those who lobbied for mandatory minimum sentences assumed that the laws would deter gun use and reduce crime; they assumed that would-be offenders would be deterred by the fear of imprisonment and the threat of long prison sentences. As a number of commentators have pointed out, however, even if the gun laws deterred offenders from committing crimes with guns, they would not necessarily reduce crime rates.[75] Although armed robbers who were deterred by the law's harsher penalties might commit fewer crimes, they might also substitute less lucrative crimes without guns, such as burglary or larceny, for more lucrative robberies with guns or switch to gun crimes with less risk of apprehension. If they did switch from robbery to burglary or larceny, they might actually commit more crimes to maintain the income that gun robberies provided.

Exhibit 7.6 Percentage of Offenders With Any New Arrest: Essex County, New Jersey

	Percentage With New Arrests
Type of sentence	
Confined	55.1
Not confined	55.0
Length of sentence	
Up to 12 months	87.8
12-18 months	87.0
19-36 months	93.5
37-84 months	81.4
More than 84 months	75.2

SOURCE: Adapted from "Effects of Judges' Sentencing Decisions on Criminal Careers" (Exhibit 11 and Exhibit 14), by D. Gottfredson, 1999, in *National Institute of Justice: Research in Brief*. Washington, DC: U.S. Department of Justice.

Evaluations of the deterrent effect of the felony firearm statutes have yielded inconsistent results. Some studies found that the laws produced significant reductions in armed robbery and assault with a gun. but not in homicide,[76] whereas others found that homicide, but not robbery or assault, declined in the wake of the law's passage.[77] Some found that all three types of crimes were reduced,[78] whereas others found that the law's passage had no effect on crime rates at all.[79] A recent and methodologically sophisticated study of gun laws nationwide attempted to sort out these conflicting conclusions.[80] Marvel and Moody analyzed the impact of mandatory penalties for use of a firearm in all 50 states and conducted a widespread search for conditions under which the laws might work. They found little evidence that the laws reduced crime rates or gun use.[81] In fact, reductions in crime were found in only three states and for only some crimes. These findings led Marvel and Moody to conclude that the felony firearms enhancement laws "do little nationwide to reduce crime or gun use."[82]

It thus seems clear that evidence for the deterrent effect of punishment is weak or nonexistent. Critics of the crime control policies pursued during the past two decades have used these results to support their contention that the war on crime has been a failure. For example, Early concludes that the crime control strategies "have been relatively impotent" and that "at best, they have been successful in temporarily removing these malefactors from society."[83] Tonry is even more critical, charging that "there are no sound, knowledge-based justifications for current crime control policies."[84] Even James Q. Wilson, a leading conservative scholar on crime and punishment, acknowledged in 1994 that "many (probably most) criminologists think we use prison too much and at too great cost and that this excessive use has had little beneficial effect on the crime rate."[85]

The "Incarceration Reduces Crime" Debate

Despite the negative findings and pessimistic conclusions about the deterrent effect of punishment, some researchers and a substantial number of politicians have embraced the "incarceration reduces crime" argument. They argue that the policy of locking up and thereby incapacitating increasingly large numbers of felony offenders has led to substantial reductions in crime, including violent crime. As Steven Dillingham, the former director of the Bureau of Justice Statistics, stated in 1991, "Statisticians and criminal justice researchers have consistently found that falling crime rates are associated with rising imprisonment rates, and rising crime rates are associated with falling imprisonment rates."[86]

Conclusions such as these are based primarily on studies by the Department of Justice comparing national violent crime rates with imprisonment rates between 1960 and 1990. One study, for example, revealed that during the 1960s, the imprisonment rate declined by 17 percent, and reported violent crimes increased by 104 percent. During the 1970s, the imprisonment rate increased by 39 percent, and the violent crime rate continued to increase, but only by 47 percent. And in the 1980s, imprisonment rates increased by 99 percent, and violent crime rates increased by only 11 percent.[87] These results led one Department of Justice spokesperson to predict further reductions in the violent crime rate during the 1990s:

> No one knows for sure what the 1990s will bring. But my guess, based on the lessons learned over the past three decades, is this: If imprisonment rates continue to rise, violent crime rates will not increase and eventually could fall in the 1990s. A big "if," of course, is whether imprisonment rates will continue their steady upward climb.[88]

The fact that this is exactly what happened—imprisonment rates continued to escalate, and overall crime rates and violent crime rates steadily declined throughout the 1990s—led many commentators to conclude that imprisonment "works." It led them to conclude that incarceration does in fact reduce crime.

Those on the other side of the debate maintain that there are a number of conceptual and methodological flaws in the "incarceration reduces crime" argument. A major problem, according to Austin and Irwin,[89] is its overly simplistic view of the factors affecting the crime rate. As they point out, the crime rate is not simply a product of the number of people incarcerated but also of "a very complex set of individual, social, economic, political, and even random circumstances."[90] Studies, for example, have consistently shown that changes in the demographic characteristics of the population are associated with crime: As the number of males aged 15 to 24 increases or decreases, the crime rate also increases or decreases. Similarly, crime rates respond to changes in the unemployment rate, to changes in other indicators of social well-being, and to changes in patterns of drug distribution and drug use. As Austin and Irwin correctly note, "In order for the 'incarceration reduces crime' thesis to be valid, it must be shown that these other crime-related factors remained constant or were controlled in the analysis."[91]

A second problem with the "prison 'works'" conclusion is that the 10-year trends in crime and imprisonment rates that are used to support the conclusion mask significant inconsistencies within each decade. Although it is true that the incarceration rate has increased every year since the early 1970s, the crime rate has fallen during some time periods and increased during others. For example, the crime rate increased during the 1970s, fell from 1980 to 1984, increased from 1985 to 1991, and declined from 1992 to 2000. In fact, from 1984 to 1991, the number of prison inmates grew by 79 percent; meanwhile, the overall crime rate increased by 17 percent, and the violent crime rate increased by 41 percent.[92] As a result of these fluctuations, by the late 1990s, violent crime rates were about the same as they had been in 1973, when there were only 300,000 people in prison.

A related problem is that the incarceration/crime rate trends for the nation as a whole are not found in all 50 states or in all cities throughout the United States. Not only do states with the highest incarceration rates tend to have the highest crime rates but the relationship between changes in incarceration and crime rates varies among the states.[93] From 1990 to 1998, California increased its prison population by 53 percent, and its crime rate fell by 34 percent. Texas, which increased its prison population by *141 percent*, saw crime drop by an almost identical 35 percent. And in New York, there was a relatively modest increase in the prison population (+26 percent), but a more substantial decline in the crime rate (-44 percent) than in either California or Texas.[94] Similar inconsistencies are found for two counties in California. In Los Angeles, the number of persons incarcerated increased by 27 percent from 1990 to 1998, and the crime rate declined by 49 percent. In San Francisco, the crime rate went down by 38 percent, even though the number of persons sentenced to prison declined by 61 percent.[95] Changes in incarceration rates, in other words, are not associated with the same changes in crime rates in all jurisdictions throughout the United States.

In summary, although the sentencing reforms enacted since 1970 *have* led to more punitive sentences, they *have not* produced the predicted reduction in crime. There is little evidence that making criminal penalties more severe deters would-be offenders or that incarcerating increasingly large numbers of citizens is an effective crime control policy.

Have Sentencing Reforms Reduced Disparity and Discrimination?

The goals of those who championed sentencing reform varied. Liberals argued that structured sentencing practices would enhance fairness and hold judges accountable for their decisions, and conservatives asserted that the reforms would lead to harsher penalties that eventually would deter criminal behavior. Reformers on both sides of the political spectrum, however, agreed that the changes were designed to curb discretion and reduce unwarranted disparity. Both conservatives and liberals urged sentencing reform as a means of reducing "lawlessness"[96] in sentencing.

In the sections that follow, we attempt to determine whether the sentencing reforms have achieved this goal. We begin by asking whether sentences in the post-reform period are "fairer" and more uniform. That is, are sentences today more closely tied to offense seriousness and prior criminal record and more consistent from one judge to the next? We then shift our focus to an even more important issue: the degree to which the reforms have reduced or eliminated *discrimination* in sentencing. We ask whether there is evidence that race, gender, or social class influence sentencing decisions in the post-reform era.

Our assessment focuses on the effect of sentencing guidelines. There are two reasons for this. First, one of the explicit goals of sentencing guidelines was to reduce disparity and discrimination in sentencing. The enabling legislation in Louisiana, for example, states that one purpose of the guidelines is "to provide rational and consistent criteria for imposing criminal sanctions in a uniform and proportionate manner," whereas the legislation in Minnesota specifies that "sentencing should be neutral with respect to the race, gender, and social or economic status of convicted felons."[97] Similarly, the *Federal Sentencing Guidelines Manual* states that one of the "three objectives Congress sought to achieve in enacting the Sentencing Reform Act of 1984" was "reasonable uniformity in sentencing by narrowing the wide disparity in sentences imposed for similar criminal offenses committed by similar offenders."[98] The second reason for concentrating on sentencing guidelines is that there is relatively little research on the effect of the other reforms on disparity and discrimination. A handful of studies examine the degree to which mandatory penalties and three-strikes provisions are applied in a racially neutral manner, but the dearth of research makes it difficult to draw conclusions about the impact of these reforms.

Have the Sentencing Guidelines Reduced Disparity?

Determining whether sentencing guidelines have reduced disparity is complicated. The researcher must decide how to define and measure disparity, ensure that the cases being compared in the pre- and post-reform periods are similar, and devise some way of separating out the effect of the guidelines from the effects of other changes that occurred during the time period from which the cases are drawn.[99]

Devising valid and reliable measures of disparity and disparity reduction is obviously critical. Most researchers compare sentence outcomes in the preguideline and postguideline eras. They attempt to determine whether sentences are more consistent, or more predictable, in the post-reform period. Although some researchers use sophisticated statistical techniques to model sentencing in the two time periods, others simply compare the degree to which sentences in the pre- and post-reform eras reflect the relationship between crime seriousness and prior record expressed in the guidelines. Use of this latter approach fails to consider factors, such as age or employment history, which may have been legitimate determinants of sentencing in the pre-reform era but are deemed irrelevant in the post-reform era; this approach almost guarantees that guideline sentences will appear more uniform than preguideline sentences.

Ensuring that comparable cases are being compared in the two time periods is also important. As discussed in Chapter 6, critics charge that sentencing guidelines have shifted discretion from the judge at sentencing to the prosecutor at charging. They maintain that prosecutors use charging and plea bargaining to circumvent the guidelines and to achieve "more appropriate" outcomes in cases in which the sentence prescribed by the guidelines appears too harsh. If this represents a change from charging and bargaining practices in the preguidelines era, the cases falling into the various crime seriousness/prior record categories in the two time periods may be very different. Assume, for example, that in the preguideline period, sentence agreements were the norm. A defendant charged with a less serious first-degree burglary would plead guilty as charged, with an agreement for a reduced sentence. In order to achieve the same result under the sentencing guidelines, the prosecutor may have to reduce the charge to second-degree burglary. As Tonry points out, removing the less serious burglaries from the first-degree burglary pool will result in a more homogeneous pool of first-degree burglary cases, and "apparently reduced disparity may be a product of that greater homogeneity."[100]

The final methodological challenge is separating the effect of the guidelines from the effects of other changes. If mandatory minimums went into effect at about the same time as the guidelines, how do we know which reform produced the observed reduction in disparity?[101] How do we separate the reform's impact from such factors as changes in judges' attitudes toward crime and punishment, the occurrence of a high-profile crime, or fallout from a controversial sentencing decision? How do amendments to the guidelines affect our assessment of the long-term impact of the guidelines on disparity reduction? Although these obviously are important issues, most researchers do not confront them directly.

With these caveats in mind, we turn to an examination of the research on disparity reduction under state and federal sentencing guidelines.

Disparity and State Sentencing Guidelines

There is convincing evidence that the guidelines adopted by the Minnesota Sentencing Guidelines Commission (MSGC) reduced disparity in sentencing, at least in the early years. Research conducted by the MSGC, for example, concluded that during the first 3 years, there was more "uniformity and proportionality" in sentencing under the guidelines.[102] This reflected the fact that there were very few departures from the prescribed guidelines during these early years. Two independent evaluations confirmed this finding. Miethe and Moore compared sentence outcomes in 1978 (preguideline) and 1981, 1982, and 1984. They found that "uniformity, neutrality, and proportionality improved as a result of the guidelines."[103] Like the MSGC study, they found that rates of departure from the guidelines during these early years were relatively low.

The conclusions of a third, more methodologically sophisticated study are similar. Stolzenberg and D'Alessio used time-series analysis to examine the long-term effect of the guidelines on disparity reduction.[104] Unlike previous studies, which defined sentencing disparity in terms of the effect of legally irrelevant variables on sentence outcomes, this study defined unwarranted disparity as "sentencing variation not attributable to legally mandated sentencing factors."[105] Implementation of the guidelines had a dramatic effect on unwarranted disparity both in the decision to incarcerate or not and the length of the prison sentence. Further analysis revealed that the substantial reductions in disparity were maintained over time for sentence length but that disparity in the decision to incarcerate or not began to revert to preguideline levels during the later years of the time period. Over the entire time period, there was an 18 percent reduction in disparity for the decision to incarcerate or not but a 60 percent reduction in disparity for the length of sentence decision.[106]

Studies conducted in Pennsylvania also found that sentencing disparities had been reduced by the guidelines. An early evaluation by the Pennsylvania Commission on Sentencing concluded that sentences were more uniform throughout the state,[107] and a comparison of pre- and postguideline sentencing patterns found that sentences had become substantially more consistent with the guidelines.[108] Kramer and Lubitz found, for example, that only 25 percent of the sentences for aggravated assault in the preguideline period were consistent with the guidelines; in the postguideline period, the overall compliance rate for aggravated assault was 67 percent.[109] They also found that sentences were based more squarely on crime seriousness and prior criminal record in the postguideline period. The variation in sentence length that could be attributed to these two factors more than doubled, from 24.1 percent to 49.3 percent. According to the authors, these results signal greater "sentencing uniformity" and "a corresponding reduction in sentencing variability."[110]

Evidence regarding the effect of the guidelines on disparity reduction in other states also comes primarily from research conducted by those states' sentencing commissions. The Washington State Sentencing Guidelines Commission reviewed that state's first 10 years of experience with guidelines, concluding that "the high degree of compliance with sentencing guidelines has reduced variability in sentencing among counties and among judges."[111] The Oregon Criminal Justice Council, which compared case outcomes during the first year under the guidelines to those in previous years, found that sentencing under the guidelines was substantially more uniform. As they noted, "Dispositional variability for offenders with identical crime seriousness and criminal history scores has been reduced by 45 percent over the variability under the preguidelines system."[112] A follow-up report indicated that disparity was "most pronounced in areas where judges retain most discretion, such as in decisions about departures and use of sentencing options."[113] Likewise, a preliminary evaluation of results in North Carolina reported that sentencing had become more predictable.[114]

In summary, there is substantial evidence that the presumptive sentencing guidelines adopted in Minnesota, Pennsylvania, Washington, and Oregon have made sentencing more consistent and more uniform. In all four states, sentencing disparity has declined in the post-reform period. Although these findings no doubt strike a positive chord with those who lobbied for structured sentencing reform, they are not particularly surprising. As Tonry has pointed out, "Because guidelines set standards for sentences where none existed, it would be astonishing if they had no effect on sentencing decisions."[115]

Disparity and the Federal Sentencing Guidelines

Evidence regarding the reduction of unwarranted disparity under the federal sentencing guidelines is, to put the most positive spin on it, "mixed." In fact, "Opinions vary from those who believe disparity has been reduced, to those who cannot tell whether there has been significant change, to those who think disparity has actually gotten worse under the guidelines."[116] Although divergent points of view on an issue as controversial as the federal sentencing guidelines are to be expected, "Such a range of opinion about an important *empirical* matter indicates a failure of research to provide objective, quantified answers to these essentially factual questions."[117]

Evaluating the impact of the U.S. Sentencing Guidelines is complicated by the complexity of the guidelines[118] and more important, by the fact that federal sentencing is based on relevant conduct. As explained in Chapter 6, the judge's determination of the offense seriousness score is based on the offender's "actual offense behavior," which may or may not be identical to the offense for which he has been convicted. Information concerning drug quantity, presence or use of a weapon, the offender's role in the offense, and the existence of uncharged criminal conduct—all of which may be highly relevant to sentencing under the guidelines—was not consistently recorded in the preguideline era; thus, it is difficult, if not impossible, to precisely "match" offenders in the two time periods. This, in turn, makes it difficult to determine whether sentencing practices and outcomes have been altered in the post-reform period.

The USSC issued a detailed report on the short-term effects of the federal sentencing guidelines in 1991.[119] The Commission acknowledged that "the preguideline and guideline periods present quite different contexts for studying disparity in sentencing" and cautioned that their results "should be interpreted keeping these contextual differences in mind."[120] Using data on offenders convicted of four categories of bank robbery, cocaine distribution, heroin distribution, and two categories of bank embezzlement, the USSC attempted to determine whether "the range of sentences for defendants with similar criminal records convicted of similar criminal conduct has narrowed as a result of guideline implementation."[121] They found that both the range of sentences imposed and time to be served narrowed considerably for all eight types of offenses following guideline implementation but only three of the differences were statistically significant.

A second major study of the federal sentencing guidelines was conducted by the U.S. General Accounting Office (GAO). The GAO reanalyzed the USSC data using different statistical techniques. Critics of the USSC study identified a number of methodological problems: (a) small sample sizes for some of the offenses, (b) the fact that the eight offenses were not representative of all federal offenses, (c) the elimination of cases in which the judge departed from the guidelines because the offender provided substantial assistance to the government (which meant that the judge did not have to sentence within the guidelines), and (d) the fact that drug offenses became subject to mandatory minimum sentences during the time period examined.[122] The GAO, which titled its report, *Sentencing Guidelines: Central Questions Remain Unanswered*, concluded that these methodological problems "made it impossible to determine how effective the sentencing guidelines have been in reducing overall sentencing disparity."[123]

The inconsistent results of these two major studies of the federal sentencing guidelines led Tonry to suggest that "the best conclusion at present is that we do not know whether disparities have increased or decreased."[124] The results also led researchers to search for more effective ways of measuring disparity and calculating disparity reduction. Hofer and his colleagues, for example, employed several techniques designed to determine whether inter-judge disparity had declined in the postguideline period. These researchers argued that "the most important source of unwarranted disparity in the preguideline era" was "philosophical differences among judges."[125] They attempted to determine (a) whether the sentences imposed by the same judges before and after the guidelines went into effect were more consistent in the post-reform period and (b) whether sentences imposed by the judges in a particular district in the preguideline period were more disparate than those imposed by judges in that district under the guidelines. The findings of their study are summarized below:

- The comparison of sentences imposed by the same judges in the two time periods revealed that the guidelines reduced—but did not eliminate—inter-judge disparity. The sentences imposed on defendants in the preguideline period were 7.87 months longer or shorter depending on the judge. In the guideline period, the difference attributable to the judge was 7.61 months.[126]

- The comparison of sentences imposed by all judges in 44 different districts revealed a similar pattern of results: The guidelines had "modest success at reducing inter-judge disparity."[127]

- The effect of the guidelines on reducing inter-judge disparity was not uniform across all offense types. Although there was less inter-judge disparity for most offenses in the guideline era than the preguideline period, there was *greater* inter-judge disparity for robbery and immigration offenses in the guideline era.[128]

- The effect of the guidelines on reducing inter-judge disparity varied among the districts examined. In some jurisdictions the "judge effect" decreased, but in others, it increased.[129]

Although the authors of this study acknowledged that the inconsistent results of their analysis "might cause some to question whether the guidelines have been worth the trouble," they nonetheless concluded that "there are reasons to judge the sentencing guidelines as a qualified success and reason to hope that additional improvements would reduce disparity further."[130]

A second study of inter-judge disparity reached a very similar conclusion.[131] Using a somewhat different definition of inter-judge disparity, the authors of this study found that sentencing disparity attributable to the judge declined substantially from 1986 to 1987 and from 1988 to 1989 and that it remained relatively stable from 1990 to 1993. As they noted, "The Guidelines have reduced the net variation in sentence attributable to the happenstance of the identity of the sentencing judge."[132]

It thus appears that the sentencing patterns of federal judges *have* become less variable. Although questions have been raised about the methods used to define and analyze disparity, the weight of the evidence suggests that federal sentences are more uniform in the guideline period than in the preguideline era. As a number of critics have noted, however, this objective may have been purchased "at the price of undue severity in sentences, undue uniformity of those sentenced, and unwarranted complexity."[133] Moreover, as we discuss below, there is evidence that the guidelines have *not* eliminated discrimination in sentencing.

Sentencing Reform and Sentencing Discrimination

Those who lobbied for sentencing reform, particularly those who championed sentencing guidelines, argued that unchecked judicial discretion opened the door to discrimination in sentencing. Citing the results of research conducted in the pre-reform era, they asserted that members of racial minorities were sentenced more harshly than similarly situated whites (see Chapter 5) and that women received more severe sentences than comparable men (see Chapter 4). They called for reforms designed to structure the sentencing process, constrain judicial discretion, and thereby eliminate disparity and discrimination.

The reforms enacted during the past 30 years clearly were *designed* to ameliorate discrimination in sentencing. Sentencing guidelines explicitly prohibit consideration of the offender's race, gender, or social class. They shift the focus of sentencing away from the personal characteristics of the offender to the nature and seriousness of the offense and the culpability of the offender. Mandatory minimum sentence statutes and three-strikes laws are applicable to *all* offenders, regardless of race, gender, or social class, whose offense conduct and prior record qualify them for these sentence enhancements. If these laws are applied as intended, legally irrelevant offender characteristics should not affect sentencing decisions in jurisdictions with sentencing guidelines. Likewise, offender characteristics should not affect the application of mandatory minimum penalties or three-strikes-and-you're out provisions.

Offender Characteristics and the Federal Sentencing Guidelines

The findings of a comprehensive review of recent federal and state sentencing research suggest that the sentencing reforms have not achieved their goal of eliminating unwarranted racial disparity.[134] Spohn reviewed eight methodologically sophisticated studies of sentences imposed under the federal sentencing guidelines.[135] She found that each of these studies revealed that members of racial minorities were sentenced more harshly than whites, either for all offenses or for some types of offenses. Moreover, racial disparities were not confined to the decision to incarcerate or not and to the length of the prison sentence. Compared to whites, blacks and Hispanics were less likely to be offered sentence reductions for acceptance of responsibility[136] or for providing substantial assistance in the prosecution of other offenders.[137] Among those who did receive departures for substantial assistance, the sentence discounts that blacks and Hispanics received were less than the discounts that whites received.[138] And blacks and Hispanics were more likely than whites to be sentenced at or above the minimum sentence indicated by applicable mandatory minimum sentencing provisions.[139]

The fact that significant racial differences were found for each of the various alternative measures of sentence severity is interesting. The federal sentencing guidelines severely constrain judges' discretion in deciding between prison and probation and in determining the length of the sentence, but they place only minimal restrictions on the ability of judges (and prosecutors) to reduce sentences for substantial assistance or acceptance of responsibility. Mandatory minimum sentences can also be avoided through charge manipulation. As Albonetti notes, "These process-related decisions offer potential avenues through which prosecutors [and judges] can circumvent guideline-defined sentence outcomes."[140] The validity of this assertion is confirmed by the fact that each of the six federal-level studies that examined an alternative measure of sentence severity found evidence of direct discrimination against both black and Hispanic offenders.

These findings are confirmed by a recent study of federal sentencing decisions.[141] Using data on male offenders convicted of drug and non-drug offenses from 1993 to 1996, Steffensmeier and Demuth compared sentence outcomes for four groups of offenders: whites, blacks, white Hispanics, and black Hispanics. As shown in Part A of Exhibit 7.7, which presents descriptive data on sentence outcomes, the likelihood of incarceration was substantially less and the mean prison sentence significantly shorter for white offenders than for members of racial minorities. Whites were also more likely than minority individuals to receive downward departures and departures for providing substantial assistance.

These differences did not disappear when the authors controlled for offense seriousness, prior criminal record, and other relevant predictors of sentence severity. As shown in Part B of Exhibit 7.7, which presents the differences in the likelihood of incarceration and the mean prison sentence for members of minorities compared with whites, minority individuals were sentenced more harshly than whites. The differences were particularly pronounced for drug offenses. Black Hispanics were 20 percent more likely than whites to be sentenced to prison, and their sentences averaged 23 months longer than those imposed on whites. Similarly, white Hispanics faced a 16-percent-greater likelihood of incarceration and 19 months longer in prison than whites. Blacks were 11 percent more likely than whites to be sentenced to prison; blacks who were incarcerated received sentences that averaged 16 months longer than those imposed on whites.[142] Further analysis revealed that a considerable amount of the differential treatment of Hispanics was due to the fact that they were less likely than whites to receive either downward departures or substantial assistance departures. These findings led Steffensmeier and Demuth to conclude that "the ethnic disparities found in our analysis are real and meaningful—they support our theoretical hypotheses and they also raise some concerns about the equal appli-

Exhibit 7.7 Race/Ethnicity and Sentence Outcomes: Male Offenders in U.S. District Courts, 1993 to 1996

A. Descriptive Data

	Non-Drug Offenses				Drug Offenses			
			Hispanic				Hispanic	
	White	Black	White	Black	White	Black	White	Black
Percentage imprisoned	67.1	78.1	73.2	75.2	88.1	96.7	95.7	97.2
Mean sentence (months)	44.0	70.6	53.4	77.2	70.5	122.6	78.2	95.3
Downward departure (percentage)	9.0	5.4	7.7	4.0	5.4	4.8	6.8	6.0
Substantial assistance departure (percentage)	14.1	10.4	12.8	6.7	38.0	31.2	28.0	26.1

B. Differences in the Probability of Incarceration and Mean Prison Sentence

	Non-Drug Offenses				Drug Offenses			
			Hispanic				Hispanic	
	White	Black	White	Black	White	Black	White	Black
Probability of incarceration (percentage)		+5	+7	+6		+11	+16	+20
Mean prison sentence (difference in months)		+1	+4	+16		+16	+19	+23

SOURCE: Adapted from "Ethnicity and Sentencing Outcomes in U.S. Federal Courts: Who Is Punished More Harshly? Table 2 and Table 3, by Steffensmeier and Demuth, 2000, *American Sociological Review* 65:705–729.

cation of the law and the wherewithal of the sentencing guidelines in reducing sentencing disparities of any kind."[143]

There is less evidence regarding the effect of offender characteristics other than race/ethnicity on federal guidelines sentence outcomes. The GAO evaluation[144] concluded that females received more lenient sentences than males, but an analysis of mandatory minimum penalties found that gender did not affect sentence severity once offense seriousness and prior criminal record were taken into consideration.[145] Studies of sentences imposed on federal drug offenders, on the other hand, revealed that females were sentenced more leniently than males,[146] that defendants with fewer years of education received harsher sentences than those with more education,[147] and that more education produced greater sentence discounts for white offenders than for black or Hispanic offenders.[148]

Offender Characteristics and State Sentencing Guidelines

There is also evidence that race and ethnicity affect state sentencing decisions in the post-reform era.[149] Studies of sentences imposed on felony offenders[150] and drug offenders[151] in Miami found that Hispanics (but not blacks) were significantly more likely than whites to be sentenced to prison; one study also found that Hispanic drug offenders were sentenced more harshly than black drug offenders.[152] A third study[153] of sentence outcomes in Miami found that *young black and Hispanic males* faced significantly higher odds of imprisonment than middle-aged white males. Researchers also found that blacks were substantially more likely than whites to be sentenced as habitual offenders in Florida.[154]

A series of studies of sentence outcomes in Pennsylvania[155] also revealed that blacks were sentenced more harshly than whites: They were more likely than whites to be incarcerated, and they received longer sentences than whites. Moreover, in Pennsylvania, both blacks and Hispanics were less likely than whites to receive either dispositional or durational departures. Consistent with the results in Miami, one study found that young black males were singled out for the harshest treatment under the Pennsylvania Sentencing Guidelines. An early evaluation of guidelines sentencing in Washington found that blacks were less likely than whites to benefit from departures.[156] A later study of sentence outcomes for drug offenders found that Hispanics were more likely than whites to be incarcerated; Hispanic drug offenders also received longer sentences than white drug offenders.[157]

These studies, then, revealed that black and/or Hispanic offenders received more punitive sentences in Florida, Pennsylvania, and Washington.

In contrast, research conducted in Minnesota generally found that race did not affect sentence severity. In fact, Miethe and Moore[158] found that blacks were more likely than whites to be sentenced to prison in the preguideline period but that race did not affect sentence outcomes under the guidelines. Three other studies of sentencing decisions in Minnesota also found no racial differences in the likelihood of incarceration or the length of sentence.[159] In fact, the only statistically significant racial difference revealed by this research was that blacks were less likely than whites to receive downward departures.[160]

There is also evidence that offender characteristics other than race/ethnicity affect state sentencing outcomes. The most consistent finding is that females are sentenced more leniently than males. In Miami, female offenders were less likely than male offenders to be sentenced to prison.[161] In Pennsylvania, females faced lower odds of incarceration and shorter sentences than their male counterparts;[162] females were also more likely than males to get sentence discounts for downward departures from the guidelines.[163] In Minnesota, females benefited more than males from departures from the guidelines,[164] and in Washington, female drug offenders faced a lower likelihood of incarceration and longer sentences than male drug offenders.[165] There is also some evidence that age and employment status affect sentencing decisions in the postguideline era. These studies reveal that older teenagers and young adults receive harsher sentences than other offenders and that unemployed offenders are sentenced more harshly than those who are employed.[166]

It thus appears that federal and state sentencing guidelines have not eliminated disparities based on race, gender, and other legally irrelevant offender characteristics. The guidelines notwithstanding, racial minorities receive harsher sentences than whites, males are sentenced more severely than females, and the unemployed receive more punitive punishment than the employed.

Assessing the Impact of the Sentencing Reform Movement

The advocates of sentencing reform believed that the enactment of sentencing guidelines, mandatory minimum sentencing statutes, three-strikes laws, and truth-in-sentencing laws would result in more punitive, more effective, and fairer sentence outcomes. But have they?

Although the evidence is somewhat mixed, it does appear that sentences are more punitive today than they were in the past. The movement away from indeterminate sentencing and the rehabilitative ideal to determinate sentencing and an emphasis on just deserts—coupled with laws mandating long prison terms—have resulted in harsher sentences. As a result of these changes in sentencing policy, offenders convicted of felonies in state and federal courts face a greater likelihood of incarceration and longer prison sentences than they did in the pre-reform era. These changes, in turn, have led to dramatic increases in the nation's prison population.

This punitiveness, however, has not produced the predicted reduction in crime. Conservative advocates of harsh crime control policies claim that locking up increasingly large numbers of felony offenders for increasingly long periods of time has caused the crime rate to fall; however, conceptual and methodological flaws in the "prison 'works'" argument call this conclusion into question. Critics suggest that a more careful examination of the evidence "demonstrates major inconsistencies in their argument and lends greater support to the conclusion that more imprisonment has little to do with crime rates."[167] If crime rates decline by a similar amount regardless of whether or how much incarceration rates change, it seems illogical to argue that there is a strong relationship between incarceration and crime. And if violent crime rates today are about the same as they were when one sixth as many persons were locked up in our nation's prisons, it seems unreasonable to contend that imprisonment prevents crime. Furthermore, as Mauer notes, focusing on trends during the 1990s, as advocates of the incarceration reduces crime position tend to do, is "rather myopic, given the scale of the race to incarcerate over a quarter century."[168]

The evidence regarding the third question posed in this chapter is mixed: Are sentencees today fairer or more equitable than they were in the past? Critics of sentencing reform contend that members of the courtroom workgroup have been able to circumvent—or even sabotage—the reforms enacted during the past 30 years; they argue that this makes it difficult to assess the impact of the reforms. Nonetheless, most studies of sentences imposed under federal and state guidelines conclude that guideline sentences are more uniform and less disparate. There is less inter-judge disparity in jurisdictions with sentencing guidelines, and sentences are more tightly linked to the seriousness of the offense and the offender's prior criminal record. These findings are not surprising; presumptive sentencing guidelines are based explicitly on the seriousness of the crime and the offender's prior record, and judges are *required* to take these two factors into account in determining the appropriate sentence. As Tonry has noted, it would be "astonishing" if guidelines had not reduced disparity in sentencing.[169]

The evidence regarding the effect of legally irrelevant offender characteristics—race, gender, age, education, and employment status—is less inconsistent and, unfortunately, more negative. There is a lack of longitudinal research comparing the effect of offender characteristics on sentence outcomes before and after the implementation of guidelines; this makes it difficult to assess the degree to which the guidelines have *reduced* unwarranted disparities in sentencing. Nonetheless, the studies of sentences imposed in federal and state jurisdictions operating under sentencing guidelines showed that racial minorities and women were sentenced differently than whites and men. This suggests that attempts to constrain judicial discretion have not *eliminated* unwarranted disparities in sentencing. The guidelines notwithstanding, judges mete out harsher sentences to black and Hispanic offenders than to similarly situated white offenders. They impose more lenient sentences on females than on males, and the unemployed and less educated receive harsher sentences than their counterparts.

These conclusions apply to sentences imposed under the more restrictive federal sentencing guidelines as well as the looser guidelines at the state level. They imply that judges and prosecutors are reluctant to place offenders into cells of sentencing grids defined only by crime seriousness and prior criminal record and thus, that statutorily irrelevant factors such as race, gender, age, employment status, and social class may be factually relevant to criminal justice officials' assessments of dangerousness, threat, and culpability. In sum, these conclusions attest to the validity of Tonry's assertion that "There is, unfortunately, no way around the dilemma that sentencing is inherently discretionary and that discretion leads to disparities."[170]

Discussion Questions: Chapter 7

1. There is convincing evidence that state and federal guidelines resulted in more punitive sentences. Why did the guidelines produce this effect?

2. Explain why the enactment of mandatory minimum sentences might not produce the expected increase in sentence severity.

3. Why do critics contend that the three-strikes-and-you're-out movement was "largely symbolic"?

4. Why do most scholars conclude that the "imprisonment binge" of the past 30 years is due to changes in sentencing policies and practices rather than changes in crime rates?

5. Most studies conclude that increasing the severity of punishment does not have a deterrent effect. Why not?

6. Steven Dillingham, former director of the Bureau of Justice Statistics, stated in 1991 that "statisticians and criminal justice researchers have consistently found that falling crime rates are associated with rising imprisonment rates, and rising crime rates are associated with falling imprisonment rates."[171] What are the major conceptual and methodological flaws in this argument?

7. You have been awarded a research grant to determine whether sentences imposed under the federal sentencing guidelines are more uniform—more consistent—than those imposed in the preguideline era. What methodological problems will you encounter? How will you address these problems?

8. How would you answer the question, "Are sentences today fairer and more equitable than they were in the past?"

Notes

1. See, for example, *Punishment & Society* 3 (January, 2001), a special issue on mass imprisonment in the USA.
2. Data for Pennsylvania were not available for 1998 and 1999; data for Washington were not available for 1984 to 1988. Source of data: Minnesota Sentencing Guidelines Commission, *Sentencing Practices: Annual Summary Statistics for Felony Offenders Sentenced in 1999*, p. 12; Pennsylvania Commission of Sentencing, *Annual Report for 1997*, Figure N and Figure P; U.S. Department of Justice, Bureau of Justice Statistics (BJS), *Sourcebook of Criminal Justice Statistics, 1998*, Table 5.31 and Table 5.37; Washington Sentencing Guidelines Commission, *The Sentencing Reform Act at Century's End*, Appendix B.
3. It is important to note that the data for Minnesota include only offenders convicted of felonies, whereas the data for Pennsylvania include offenders convicted of misdemeanors and felonies.
4. Minnesota Sentencing Guidelines Commission, *Sentencing Practices*, p. 12.

5. Miethe and Moore, *Sentencing Guidelines: Their Effect in Minnesota.*
6. D'Alessio and Stolzenberg, "The Impact of Sentencing Guidelines on Jail Incarceration in Minnesota."
7. Ibid., p. 294.
8. Ibid., p. 296.
9. Marvel and Moody, "Determinate Sentencing and Abolishing Parole: The Long-Term Impacts on Prisons and Crime."
10. Frase, "Prison Population Growing Under Minnesota Guidelines."
11. Ibid., p. 42.
12. Minnesota Sentencing Guidelines Commission, *Sentencing Practices.*
13. Ibid., p. 13.
14. Boerner, "The Legislature's Role in Guidelines Sentencing in 'The Other Washington'"; Engen and Steen, "The Power to Punish: Discretion and Sentencing Reform in the War on Drugs."
15. Engen and Steen, "The Power to Punish."
16. Ibid., p. 1364.
17. Kramer and Lubitz, "Pennsylvania's Sentencing Reform: The Impact of Commission-Established Guidelines."
18. Ibid., Table 6.
19. Pennsylvania Commission on Sentencing, *1986-1987 Report: Sentencing in Pennsylvania.*
20. Pennsylvania Commission on Sentencing. *Annual Report: 1997,* Table 14.
21. U.S. Sentencing Commission, *The Federal Sentencing Guidelines: A Report on the Operation of the Guidelines System and Short-Term Impacts on Disparity in Sentencing, Use of Incarceration, and Prosecutorial Discretion and Plea Bargaining.*
22. Pub. Law 99-570 (H.R. 5484 1986).
23. U.S. Sentencing Commission, *The Federal Sentencing Guidelines,* p. 63.
24. Lacasse and Payne, "Federal Sentencing Guidelines and Mandatory Minimum Sentences: Do Defendants Bargain in the Shadow of the Judge?"
25. Tonry, *Sentencing Matters,* p. 54.
26. New York State Penal Law, Article 220.

27. Joint Committee on New York Drug Law Evaluation, *The Nation's Toughest Drug Law: Evaluating the New York Experience.*
28. Ibid., pp. 99-103.
29. Michigan Compiled Laws Ann. § 750.227
30. Loftin, Heumann, and McDowall, "Mandatory Sentencing and Firearms Violence: Evaluating an Alternative to Gun Control."
31. Mich. Comp. Laws Ann. § 750.227(b)
32. Ibid., p. 298.
33. Ibid.
34. Ibid.
35. Ibid., p. 302.
36. Caulkins, Rydell, Schwabe, and Chiesa, *Mandatory Minimum Drug Sentences: Throwing Away the Key or the Taxpayers' Money?*; Meierhoefer, *The General Effect of Mandatory Minimum Prison Terms*; U.S. Department of Justice, BJS, *An Analysis of Non-Violent Drug Offenders with Minimal Criminal Histories*; U.S. General Accounting Office, *Mandatory Minimum Sentences: Are They Being Imposed and Who Is Receiving Them?*; U.S. Sentencing Commission, *Special Report to Congress: Mandatory Minimum Penalties in the Federal Criminal Justice System*; Vincent and Hofer, *The Consequences of Mandatory Minimum Prison Terms: A Summary of Recent Findings.*
37. U.S. Sentencing Commission, *Special Report to Congress*, p. 44.
38. 18 U.S.C. §§ 3551-3626 and 28 U.S.C. §§ 991-998.
39. Ibid.
40. Vincent and Hofer, *The Consequences of Mandatory Minimum Prison Terms*, chap. II, p. 4.
41. U.S. Department of Justice, BJS, *An Analysis of Non- Violent Drug Offenders with Minimal Criminal Histories*
42. Vincent and Hofer, *The Consequences of Mandatory Minimum Prison Terms*, p. 1.
43. Tonry, *Sentencing Matters*, p. 191.
44. Austin and Irwin, *It's About Time: America's Imprisonment Binge*, p. 191.
45. Ibid., Table 9-2.
46. Ibid., p. 195.
47. Ibid., p. 202 and Table 9.5.
48. Clark, Austin, and Henry, *"Three Strikes and You're Out": A Review of State Legislation.*
49. Austin and Irwin, *It's About Time*, Table 9-7.

50. Ibid., Table 9-8.
51. Ibid., pp. 205-207.
52. Rothman, *The Discovery of the Asylum: Social Order and Disorder in the New Republic*, p. 295.
53. National Advisory Commission on Criminal Justice Standards and Goals, *Task Force Report on Corrections*, p. 597.
54. Ibid., p. 358.
55. Garland, "Introduction: The Meaning of Mass Imprisonment," p. 5.
56. Austin and Irwin, *It's About Time*, p. 1.
57. Zimring, "Imprisonment Rates and the New Politics of Criminal Punishment."
58. Ibid., p. 162.
59. This is confirmed by the results of a study showing that 70 percent of the federal prison growth from 1985 to 1992 could be attributed to increases in drug sentence length (Simon 1993).
60. Zimring, "Imprisonment Rates and the New Politics of Criminal Punishment," p. 162.
61. Garland, "Introduction," p. 6.
62. Ibid.
63. Mauer, "The Causes and Consequences of Prison Growth in the U.S.A.," p. 11.
64. Blumstein and Beck, "Population Growth in U.S. Prisons, 1980-1996."
65. Austin and Irwin, *It's About Time*; Paternoster, "The Deterrent Effect of the Perceived Certainty and Severity of Punishment: A Review of the Evidence and Issues"; and Tonry, *Sentencing Matters*.
66. For summaries of this research, see Cochran, Chamblin, and Seth, "Deterrence or Brutalization? An Impact Assessment of Oklahoma's Return to Capital Punishment," and Paternoster, *Capital Punishment in America*.
67. Paternoster, *Capital Punishment in America*, p. 241.
68. Blumstein, Cohen, and Nagin, *Deterrence and Incapacitation*; Gibbs, *Crime, Punishment and Deterrence*; Reiss and Roth, *Understanding and Preventing Violence*.
69. Blumstein, Cohen, and Nagin, *Deterrence and Incapacitation*.
70. Reiss and Roth, *Understanding and Preventing Violence*.
71. McGuire and Priestly, "Reviewing 'What Works': Past, Present and Future."

72. Gottfredson, "Effects of Judges' Sentencing Decisions on Criminal Careers." See also, Spohn and Holleran, "The Effect of Imprisonment on Recidivism Rates: A Focus on Drug Offenders."

73. Ibid., p. 8.

74. Ibid., p. 9.

75. Cook, "The Effect of Gun Availability on Violent Crime Patterns"; Marvel and Moody, "The Impact of Enhanced Prison Terms for Felonies Committed With Guns."

76. Berk, Hoffman, Maki, Rauma, and Wong, "Estimation Procedures for Pooled Cross-Sectional and Time-Series Data"; Deutsch and Alt, "The Effect of Massachusetts' Gun Control Law on Gun-Related Crimes in the City of Boston."

77. Loftin and McDowall, "One With a Gun Gets You Two: Mandatory Sentencing and Firearms Violence in Detroit"; Loftin and McDowall, "The Deterrent Effects of the Florida Firearm Law"; Loftin, Heumann and McDowall, "Mandatory Sentencing and Firearms Violence: Evaluating an Alternative to Gun Control"; McDowall, Loftin, and Wiersema, "A Comparative Study of the Preventive Effects of Mandatory Sentencing Laws for Handgun Crimes"; Roth, *Firearms and Violence.*

78. Deutsch, "Intervention Modeling: Analysis of Changes in Crime Rates"; Pierce and Bowers, "The Bartley-Fox Gun Law"; Rossman, Floyd, Pierce, McDevitt, and Bowers, "Massachusetts' Mandatory Minimum Sentence Gun Law: Enforcement, Prosecution, and Defense Impact."

79. Beha, "'And Nobody Can Get You Out:' The Impact of a Mandatory Prison Sentence for the Illegal Carrying of a Firearm on the Use of Firearms and on the Administration of Criminal Justice in Boston"; Carlson, *Mandatory Sentencing: The Experience of Two States;* Kleck, *Point Blank: Guns and Violence in America.*

80. Marvel and Moody, "The Impact of Enhanced Prison Terms for Felonies Committed With Guns."

81. Marvel and Moody, "The Impact of Enhanced Prison Terms for Felonies Committed With Guns.

82. Ibid., p. 280.

83. Early, *Drug Treatment Behind Bars: Prison-Based Strategies for Change,* p. 3.

84. Tonry, *Malign Neglect: Race, Crime, and Punishment in America*, p. 47.
85. Wilson, "Crime and Public Policy," p. 499.
86. Dillingham, *Remarks*, p. 10.
87. Barr, *Combating Violent Crime: 24 Recommendations to Strengthen Criminal Justice*, p. 5.
88. Dillingham, *Remarks*, p. 10.
89. Austin and Irwin, *It's About Time*, p. 227.
90. Ibid.
91. Ibid., p. 234. In fact, they show that changes in the crime rate are associated with changes in the number of males aged 15 to 24 and suggest that improvements in the economy and in other social indicators correspond to reductions in crime.
92. Mauer, "The Causes and Consequences of Prison Growth in the U.S.A.," p. 12.
93. Austin and Irwin, *It's About Time*, p. 228.
94. Ibid., p. 229.
95. Ibid., Table 10-4.
96. Frankel, *Criminal Sentences: Law Without Order*.
97. U.S. Department of Justice, BJS, *National Assessment of Structured Sentencing*, Table 4-2.
98. U.S. Sentencing Commission, *Federal Sentencing Guidelines Manual*, chap. 1, pt. A-3.
99. For a discussion of these methodological issues, see U.S. Department of Justice, BJS, *National Assessment of Structured Sentencing*, pp. 81-84, and Tonry, *Sentencing Matters*, pp. 40-41.
100. Tonry, *Sentencing Matters*, p. 40.
101. A study that attempts to separate the effects of these two sentencing strategies is described in Kautt and Spohn, "*Crack*-ing Down on Black Drug Offenders? Testing for Interactions Between Offender Race, Drug Type, and Sentencing Strategy in Federal Drug Sentences."
102. Knapp, *The Impact of the Minnesota Sentencing Guidelines: Three-Year Evaluation*, p. vi.
103. Miethe and Moore, "Sentencing Guidelines," p. 4.
104. Stolzenberg and D'Alessio, "Sentencing and Unwarranted Disparity: An Empirical Assessment of the Long-Term Impact of Sentencing Guidelines in Minnesota."
105. Ibid., p. 303.
106. Ibid., p. 306.

107. Pennsylvania Commission on Sentencing, *1984 Report: Sentencing in Pennsylvania.*

108. Kramer and Lubitz, " Pennsylvania's Sentencing Reform."

109. Ibid., Table 3.

110. Ibid., p. 497.

111. Washington State Sentencing Guidelines Commission, *A Decade of Sentencing Reform: Washington and Its Guidelines*, p. 12.

112. Ashford and Mosbaek, *First Year Report on Implementation of Sentencing Guidelines, November 1989 to January 1991*, p. viii.

113. Bogan and Factor, "Oregon Guidelines, 1989-1994," p. 54.

114. Wright, "Managing Prison Growth in North Carolina Through Structured Sentencing."

115. Tonry, *Sentencing Matters*, p. 42.

116. Hofer, Blackwell, and Ruback, "The Effect of the Federal Sentencing Guidelines on Inter-Judge Sentencing Disparity," p. 263.

117. Ibid.

118. For a detailed discussion of the guideline's complexity, see Ruback, "Warranted and Unwarranted Complexity in the U.S. Sentencing Guidelines."

119. U.S. Sentencing Commission, *The Federal Sentencing Guidelines.*

120. Ibid., p. 31.

121. Ibid.

122. Hofer, Blackwell, and Ruback, "The Effect of the Federal Sentencing Guidelines on Inter-Judge Sentencing Disparity."

123. U.S. General Accounting Office, *Sentencing Guidelines: Central Questions Remain Unanswered*, p. 10.

124. Tonry, *Sentencing Matters*, p. 42.

125. Hofer, Blackwell, and Ruback, "The Effect of the Federal Sentencing Guidelines on Inter-Judge Sentencing Disparity," p. 246.

126. Ibid., pp. 287-288.

127. Ibid., pp. 290-291.

128. Ibid., p. 294.

129. Ibid., p. 295.

130. Ibid., p. 297.

131. Anderson, Kling, and Stith, "Measuring Interjudge Sentencing Disparity: Before and After the Federal Sentencing Guidelines."

132. Ibid., p. 303.

133. Ibid., p. 303.

134. Spohn, "Thirty Years of Sentencing Reform: The Quest for a Racially Neutral Sentencing Process."

135. The eight studies of federal sentencing decisions included in the review were: Albonetti, "Sentencing Under the Federal Sentencing Guidelines: Effects of Defendant Characteristics, Guilty Pleas, and Departures on Sentence Outcomes for Drug Offenses, 1991-1992"; Everett and Nienstedt, "Race, Remorse, and Sentence Reduction: Is Saying You're Sorry Enough?" Langan, "Sentence Reductions for Drug Traffickers for Assisting Federal Prosecutors"; Maxfield and Kramer, *Substantial Assistance: An Empirical Yardstick Gauging Equity in Current Federal Policy and Practice;* McDonald and Carlson, *Sentencing in Federal Courts: When Does Race Matter?* Smith and Damphouse, "Punishing Political Offenders: The Effect of Political Motive on Federal Sentencing Decisions"; U.S. Sentencing Commission, *Special Report to the Congress;* U.S. Sentencing Commission, *Substantial Assistance Departures in the United States Courts.*

136. Everett and Nienstedt, "Race, Remorse, and Sentence Reduction."

137. Langan, "Sentence Reductions for Drug Traffickers for Assisting Federal Prosecutors"; Maxfield and Kramer, *Substantial Assistance;* U.S. Sentencing Commission, *Substantial Assistance Departures in the United States Courts.*

138. Maxfield and Kramer, *Substantial Assistance.*

139. U.S. Sentencing Commission, *Special Report to the Congress.*

140. Albonetti, "Sentencing Under the Federal Sentencing Guidelines," p. 790.

141. Steffensmeier and Demuth, "Ethnicity and Sentencing Outcomes in U.S. Federal Courts: Who Is Punished More Harshly?"

142. Ibid., p. 718.

143. Ibid., p. 725.

144. U.S. General Accounting Office, *Sentencing Guidelines: Central Questions Remain Unanswered.*

145. United States Sentencing Commission, *Special Report to Congress.*

146. Albonetti, "Sentencing Under the Federal Sentencing Guidelines"; Kautt and Spohn, "*Crack*-ing Down on Black Drug Offenders."

147. Albonetti, "Sentencing Under the Federal Sentencing Guidelines"; Steffensmeier and Demuth, "Ethnicity and Sentencing Outcomes in U.S. Federal Courts."
148. Albonetti, "Sentencing Under the Federal Sentencing Guidelines."
149. Spohn, "Thirty Years of Sentencing Reform."
150. Spohn and DeLone, "When Does Race Matter? An Analysis of the Conditions Under Which Race Affects Sentence Severity."
151. Spohn and Spears, "Sentencing of Drug Offenders in Three Cities: Does Race/Ethnicity Make a Difference?"
152. Ibid.
153. Spohn and Holleran, "The Imprisonment Penalty Paid by Young, Unemployed Black and Hispanic Male Offenders."
154. Crawford, Chiricos, and Kleck, "Race, Racial Threat, and Sentencing of Habitual Offenders."
155. Kramer and Steffensmeier, "Race and Imprisonment Decisions"; Kramer and Ulmer, "Sentencing Disparity and Departures from Guidelines"; Steffensmeier, Ulmer, and Kramer, "The Interaction of Race, Gender, and Age in Criminal Sentencing: The Punishment Cost of Being Young, Black, and Male"; Ulmer, *Social Worlds of Sentencing*; Ulmer and Kramer, "Court Communities Under Sentencing Guidelines: The Dilemmas of Formal Rationality and Sentencing Disparity."
156. Washington State Sentencing Guidelines Commission, *Preliminary Statistical Summary of 1986 Sentencing Data*.
157. Engen and Steen, "The Power to Punish."
158. Miethe and Moore, "Racial Differences in Criminal Processing: The Consequences of Model Selection on Conclusions About Differential Treatment."
159. Dixon, "The Organizational Context of Criminal Sentencing"; Frase, "Implementing Commission-Based Sentencing Guidelines: The Lessons of the First Ten Years in Minnesota"; Miethe and Moore, "Socioeconomic Disparities Under Determinate Sentencing Systems: A Comparison of Preguideline and Postguideline Practices in Minnesota."
160. Frase, "Implementing Commission-Based Sentencing Guidelines"; Miethe and Moore, "Racial Differences in Criminal Processing."

161. Spohn and Beichner, "Is Preferential Treatment of Female Offenders a Thing of the Past? A Multisite Study of Gender, Race, and Imprisonment."

162. Ulmer and Kramer, "Court Communities Under Sentencing Guidelines."

163. Kramer and Ulmer, "Sentencing Disparity and Departures from Guidelines."

164. Frase, "Implementing Commission-Based Sentencing Guidelines"; Moore and Miethe, "Regulated and Unregulated Sentencing Decisions: An Analysis of First-Year Practices Under Minnesota's Felony Sentencing Guidelines."

165. Engen and Steen, "The Power to Punish."

166. Spohn and Holleran, "The Imprisonment Penalty Paid by Young, Unemployed Black and Hispanic Male Offenders"; Steffensmeier, Ulmer, and Kramer, "The Interaction of Race, Gender, and Age in Criminal Sentencing."

167. Austin and Irwin, *It's About Time*, p. 227.

168. Mauer, *Race to Incarcerate*, p. 190.

169. Tonry, *Sentencing Matters*, p. 42.

170. Ibid., p. 180.

171. Dillingham, *Remarks*, p. 10.

References

ABA *Journal*. 1994. "The Verdict Is In: Throw Out Mandatory Sentences: Introduction." *ABA Journal* 79:78.

Abel, Charles F. and Frank H. Marsh. 1984. *Punishment and Restitution*. Westport, CT: Greenwood.

Adler, Jeffrey S. 1994. "The Dynamite, Wreckage, and Scum in Our Cities: The Social Construction of Deviance in Industrial America." *Justice Quarterly* 11:33-49.

Albonetti, Celesta A. 1985. "Sentencing: The Effects of Uncertainty." Paper presented at the Law & Society Association Annual Meeting, San Diego, CA.

———. 1997. "Sentencing Under the Federal Sentencing Guidelines: Effects of Defendant Characteristics, Guilty Pleas, and Departures on Sentence Outcomes for Drug Offenses, 1991-1992." *Law & Society Review* 31:789-822.

Alschuler, Albert W. 1968. "The Prosecutor's Role in Plea Bargaining." *University of Chicago Law Review* 36:50-112.

———. 1975. "The Defense Attorney's Role in Plea Bargaining." *Yale Law Journal* 84:1179-1313.

———. 1976. "The Trial Judge's Role in Plea Bargaining." *Columbia Law Review* 76:1059-1154.

American Bar Association. 1994. *Standards for Criminal Justice: Sentencing Alternatives and Procedures*. 3rd ed. Boston, MA: Little, Brown.

American Friends Service Committee. 1971. *Struggle for Justice: A Report on Crime and Punishment in America*. Boston. MA: Little, Brown.

Anderson, James M., Jeffrey R. Kling, and Kate Stith. 1999. "Measuring Interjudge Sentencing Disparity: Before and After the Federal Sentencing Guidelines." *Journal of Law and Economics* XLII:271-307.

Anglin, Douglas M. and Yih-lng Hser. 1990. "Treatment of Drug Abuse." In *Prisons, Crime and Justice: A Review of Research*, Vol. 13, edited by M. Tonry and J. Q. Wilson. Chicago, IL: University of Chicago Press.

Arkin, Stephen. 1980. "Discrimination and Arbitrariness in Capital Punishment: An Analysis of Post-Furman Murder Cases in Dade County, Florida, 1973-1976." *Stanford Law Review* 33:75-101.

Ashford, Kathryn and Craig Mosbaek. 1991. *First Year Report on Implementation of Sentencing Guidelines, November 1989 to January 1991*. Portland, OR: Oregon Criminal Justice Council.

Austin, James and John Irwin. 2001. *It's About Time: America's Imprisonment Binge*. 3rd ed. Belmont, CA: Wadsworth.

Baldus, David C., Charles A. Pulaski, and George G. Woodworth. 1983. "Comparative Review of Death Sentences: An Empirical Study of the Georgia Experience." *The Journal of Criminal Law and Criminology* 74:661-673.

Baldus, David C., George G. Woodworth, and Charles A. Pulaski, Jr. 1990. *Equal Justice and the Death Penalty: A Legal and Empirical Analysis*. Boston, MA: Northeastern University Press.

Barak, Gregg. 1994. "Between the Waves: Mass-Mediated Themes of Crime and Justice." *Social Justice* 21:133-147.

Barr, William. 1992. *Combating Violent Crime: 24 Recommendations to Strengthen Criminal Justice*. Washington, DC: U.S. Department of Justice, Office of the Attorney General.

Baumer, Terry L. and Robert I. Mendelsohn. 1992. "Electronically Monitored Home Confinement: Does It Work?" In *Smart Sentencing: The Emergence of Intermediate Sanctions*, edited by J. M. Byrne, A. J. Lurigio, and J. Petersilia. Newbury Park, CA: Sage.

Bazemore, Gordon. 1998. "Restorative Justice and Earned Redemption: Communities, Victims, and Offender Reintegration." *American Behavioral Scientist* 41:768-813.

Beccaria, Cesare. 1964. *On Crimes and Punishments*, trans. by J. Grigson. In *The Column of Infamy*, edited by A. Manzoni. Oxford, England: Oxford University Press.

Beckett, Katherine and Theodore Sasson. 2000. *The Politics of Injustice*. Thousand Oaks, CA: Pine Forge.

Beha, James A. II. 1977. "'And Nobody Can Get You Out:' The Impact of a Mandatory Prison Sentence for the Illegal Carrying of a Firearm on the Use of Firearms and on the Administration of Criminal Justice in Boston." *Boston University Law Review* 57:97-146 (pt. 1), 289-333 (pt. 2).

Belenko, Steven. 1998. "Research on Drug Courts: A Critical Review." *National Drug Court Institute Review*, 1:3-43.

Benedict, William. R., Lin Huff-Corzine, and Jay Corzine. 1998. "'Clean Up and Go Straight:' Effects of Drug Treatment on Recidivism Among Felony Probationers." *American Journal of Criminal Justice* 22:169-187.

Bentham, Jeremy. 1970. *Introduction to the Principles of Morals and Legislation*, edited by J. Burns and H. L. A. Hart. London, England: Athlone Press, University of London.

———. 1995. "Punishment and Deterrence." In *Principled Sentencing*, edited by A. von Hirsch and A. Ashworth. Boston, MA: Northeastern University Press.

Berk, Richard A., Donnie M. Hoffman, Judith E, Maki, David Rauma, and Herbert Wong. 1979. "Estimation Procedures for Pooled Cross-Sectional and Time-Series Data." *Evaluation Quarterly* 3:385-411.

Berns, Sandra. 1999. *To Speak as a Judge: Difference, Voice, and Power*. Aldershot, England: Ashgate.

Bickle, Gayle. S. and Ruth D. Peterson. 1991. "The Impact of Gender-Based Family Roles on Criminal Sentencing." *Social Problems* 38:373-394.

Blomberg, Thomas and Karol Lucken. 1993. "Intermediate Punishment and the Piling Up of Sanctions." *Howard Journal of Criminal Justice* 33:62-80.

Blumberg, Abraham S. 1967. "The Practice of Law as a Confidence Game: Organizational Cooptation of a Profession." *Law & Society Review* 1:15-39.

Blumstein, Alfred. 1982. "On the Racial Disproportionality of United States' Prison Populations." *Journal of Criminal Law and Criminology* 73:1259-1281.

———. 1993. "Racial Disproportionality of U.S. Prison Populations Revisited." *University of Colorado Law Review* 64:743-760.

Blumstein, Alfred and Allen J. Beck. 1999. "Population Growth in U.S. Prisons, 1980-1996." In *Prisons, Crime and Justice: A Review of Research*, Vol. 26, edited by M. Tonry and J. Petersilia. Chicago, IL: University of Chicago Press.

Blumstein, Alfred, Jacqueline Cohen, Susan E. Martin, and Michael H. Tonry (Eds.). 1983. *Research on Sentencing: The Search for Reform*, Vol. I. Washington, DC: National Academy Press.

Blumstein, Alfred, Jacqueline Cohen, and Daniel Nagin. 1978. *Deterrence and Incapacitation*. Report of the National Academy of Sciences Panel on Research on Deterrent and Incapacitative Effects. Washington, DC: National Academy Press.

Boerner, David. 1993. "The Legislature's Role in Guidelines Sentencing in 'The Other Washington,'" *Wake Forest Law Review* 28:381-420.

Bogan, Kathleen and David Factor. 1997. "Oregon Guidelines, 1989-1994." In *Sentencing Reform in Overcrowded Times*, edited by M. Tonry and K. Hatlestad. New York: Oxford University Press.

Bottomley, A. Keith. 1990. "Parole in Transition: A Comparative Study of Origins, Developments, and Prospects for the 1990s." In *Crime and Justice: A Review of Research*, Vol. 12, edited by M. Tonry and N. Morris. Chicago, IL: University of Chicago Press.

Bowers, William. 1983. "The Pervasiveness of Arbitrariness and Discrimination Under Post-*Furman* Capital Statutes." *Journal of Criminal Law and Criminology* 74:1067-1100.

Bowers, William and Glenn L. Pierce. 1980. "Arbitrariness and Discrimination Under Post-*Furman* Capital Statutes." *Crime and Delinquency* 26:563-575.

Box, Steven. 1987. *Recession, Crime and Punishment*. Totowa, NJ: Barnes and Noble.

Box, Steven and Chris Hale. 1985. "Unemployment, Imprisonment, and Prison Overcrowding." *Contemporary Crises* 9:209-238.

Braithwaite, John. 1998. "Restorative Justice: Assessing Optimistic and Pessimistic Accounts." In *The Handbook of Crime and Punishment*, edited by M. Tonry. New York and Oxford, England: Oxford University Press.

Braithwaite, John and Philip Pettit. 1990. *Not Just Deserts: A Republican Theory of Criminal Justice*. New York and Oxford, England: Oxford University Press.

Bright, Stephen B. 1995. "Discrimination, Death and Denial: The Tolerance of Racial Discrimination in Infliction of the Death Penalty." *Santa Clara Law Review* 35:901-950.

Britt, Chester L. 2000. "Social Context and Racial Disparities in Punishment Decisions." *Justice Quarterly* 17:707-732.

Butler, Paul. 1995. "Racially Based Jury Nullification: Black Power in the Criminal Justice System." *Yale Law Journal* 105:677-725.

Caputo, Gail A. 1998. *Community Service for Repeat Misdemeanor Offenders in New York City*. New York: Vera Institute of Justice.

Carey, Mark. 1996. "Restorative Justice in Community Corrections." *Corrections Today* 58:152-155.

Carlson, Kenneth. 1982. *Mandatory Sentencing: The Experience of Two States*. Washington, DC: U.S. Department of Justice.

Carp, Robert A. and Ronald Stidham. 1998. *Judicial Process in America*. 4th ed. Washington, DC: Congressional Quarterly.

Carter, Robert M. and Leslie T. Wilkins. 1967. "Some Factors in Sentencing Policy." *Journal of Criminal Law, Criminology, and Police Science* 58:503-514.

Casper, Jonathan D. 1971. "Did You Have a Lawyer When You Went to Court? No, I Had a Public Defender." *Yale Review of Law & Social Action* 1:4-9.

———. 1972. *American Criminal Justice: The Defendant's Perspective*. Englewood Cliffs, NJ: Prentice-Hall.

———. 1978. *Criminal Courts: The Defendant's Perspective*. Englewood Cliffs, NJ: Prentice-Hall.

Casper, Jonathan D., David Brereton, and David Neal. 1982. *The Implementation of the California Determinate Sentencing Law: Executive Summary*. Washington, DC: Government Printing Office.

Caulkins, Jonathan P. 1999. "How Large Should the Strike Zone Be in 'Three Strikes and You're Out' Sentencing Laws?" Available on the World Wide Web at http://www.heinz.cmu.edu/cgi

Caulkins, Jonathan P., Peter Rydell, William L. Schwabe, and James Chiesa. 1997. *Mandatory Minimum Drug Sentences: Throwing Away the Key or the Taxpayers' Money?* Santa Monica, CA: RAND.

Chaiken, M. R. 1986. "Crime Rates and Substance Abuse Among Types of Offenders." In *Crime Rates Among Drug-Abusing Offenders: Final Report to the National Institute of Justice*, edited by B. D. Johnson and E. D. Wish. New York: Narcotic and Drug Research.

Chambliss, William J. 1995. "Crime Control and Ethnic Minorities: Legitimizing Racial Oppression by Creating Moral Panics." In *Ethnicity, Race, and Crime*, edited by D. Hawkins. Albany, NY: State University of New York Press.

Chesney-Lind, Meda. 1995. 2nd ed. "Rethinking Women's Imprisonment." In *The Criminal Justice System and Women: Offenders, Victims, and Workers*, edited by B. R Price and N. J. Sokoloff. New York: McGraw-Hill.

———. 1997. *The Female Offender: Girls, Women, and Crime.* Thousand Oaks, CA: Sage.

Chiricos, Theodore G. and William D. Bales. 1991. "Unemployment and Punishment: An Empirical Assessment." *Criminology* 29:701-724.

Chiricos, Theodore G. and Charles Crawford. 1995. "Race and Imprisonment: A Contextual Assessment of the Evidence." In *Ethnicity, Race, and Crime*, edited by D. Hawkins. Albany, NY: State University of New York Press.

Chiricos, Theodore G. and Miriam DeLone. 1992. "Labor Surplus and Punishment: A Review and Assessment of Theory and Evidence." *Social Problems* 39:421-446.

Clancy, Kevin, John Bartolomeo, David Richardson, and Charles Wellford. 1981. "Sentence Decisionmaking: The Logic of Sentence Decisions and the Extent and Sources of Sentence Disparity." *The Journal of Criminal Law & Criminology* 72:524-554.

Clark, John, James Austin, and D. Alan Henry. 1997. *"Three Strikes and You're Out": A Review of State Legislation.* Washington, DC: U.S. Department of Justice, National Institute of Justice.

Clear, Todd R. 1994. *Harm in American Penology: Offenders, Victims, and Their Communities.* Albany, NY: State University of New York Press.

Clear, Todd R., Val B. Clear, and William D. Burrell. 1989. *Offender Assessment and Evaluation.* Cincinnati, OH: Anderson.

Clear, Todd. R. and Patricia L. Hardyman. 1990. "The New Intensive Supervision Movement." *Crime & Delinquency* 36:42-60.

Cochran, John K., Mitchell B. Chamblin and Mark Seth. 1994. "Deterrence or Brutalization? An Impact Assessment of Oklahoma's Return to Capital Punishment." *Criminology* 32:107-134.

Cohen, Jacqueline, Daniel Nagin, Garrick Wallstrom, and Larry Wasserman. 1998. "A Hierarchical Bayesian Analysis of Arrest Rates." *Journal of the American Statistical Association* 93:1260-1270.

Cohen, Jacqueline and Michael H. Tonry. 1983. "Sentencing Reforms and Their Impacts." In *Research on Sentencing: The Search for Reform*, Vol. I, edited by A. Blumstein, J. Cohen, S. E. Martin, and M. H. Tonry. Washington, DC: National Academy Press.

Cole, George F., Barry Mahoney, Marlene Thornton, and Roger A. Hanson. 1987. *The Practices and Attitudes of Trial Court Judges Regarding Fines as a Criminal Sanction.* Washington, DC: U.S. Department of Justice, National Institute of Justice.

Cook, Beverly B. 1973. "Sentencing Behavior of Federal Judges: Draft Cases, 1972." *University of Cincinnati Law Review* 42:597.

———. 1979. "Judicial Attitudes on Women's Rights: Do Women Judges Make a Difference?" Paper presented at the International Political Science Round Table, University of Essex, England.

Cook, Philip J. 1981. "The Effect of Gun Availability on Violent Crime Patterns." *The Annals of the Academy of Political and Social Science* 455:63-79.

Council of Judges, National Council on Crime and Delinquency. 1972. "Model Sentencing Act, 2nd Edition." *Crime and Delinquency* 18:335.

Crawford, Charles, Ted Chiricos, and Gary Kleck. 1998. "Race, Racial Threat, and Sentencing of Habitual Offenders." *Criminology* 36:481-511.

Crew, Keith B. 1991. "Sex Differences in Criminal Sentencing: Chivalry or Patriarchy?" *Justice Quarterly* 8:59-84.

Crockett, George. 1984. "The Role of the Black Judge." In *The Criminal Justice System and Blacks*, edited by D. Georges-Abeyie. New York: Clark Boardman.

Crutchfield, Robert D., George S. Bridges, and Susan R. Pitchford. 1994. "Analytical and Aggregation Biases in Analyses of Imprisonment: Reconciling Discrepancies in Studies of Racial Disparity." *Journal of Research in Crime and Delinquency* 31:166-182.

Cullen, Francis T. and Karen E. Gilbert. 1982. *Reaffirming Rehabilitation*. Cincinnati, OH: Anderson.

———. 1992. "Reaffirming Rehabilitation." In *Principled Sentencing*, edited by A. von Hirsch and A. Ashworth. Boston, MA: Northeastern University Press.

Curriden, Mark and Leroy Phillips, Jr. 1999. *Contempt of Court: The Turn-of-the-Century Lynching That Launched 100 Years of Federalism*. New York: Faber and Faber.

Cushman, Robert C. 1996. "Effects on a Local Criminal Justice System." In *Three Strikes and You're Out: Vengeance as Public Policy*, edited by D. Shichor and D. K. Sechrest. Thousand Oaks, CA: Sage.

Dailey, Debra A. 1998. "Minnesota Sentencing Guidelines: A Structure for Change." *Law & Policy* 20:311-332.

D'Alessio, Stewart J. and Lisa Stolzenberg. 1995. "The Impact of Sentencing Guidelines on Jail Incarceration in Minnesota." *Criminology* 33:83-302.

Daly, Kathleen. 1987. "Structure and Practice of Familial-Based Justice in a Criminal Court." *Law & Society Review* 21:267-290.

———. 1989. "Neither Conflict nor Labeling nor Paternalism Will Suffice: Intersections of Race, Ethnicity, Gender, and Family in Criminal Court Decisions." *Crime & Delinquency* 35:136-168.

———. 1994. *Gender, Crime, and Punishment*. New Haven, CT: Yale University Press.

Daly, Kathleen and Rebecca Bordt. 1995. "Sex Effects and Sentencing: A Review of the Statistical Literature." *Justice Quarterly* 12:143-177.

Daly, Kathleen and Michael Tonry. 1997. "Gender, Race and Sentencing." In *Crime and Justice: A Review of Research*, Vol. 22, edited by M. Tonry. Chicago, IL: University of Chicago Press.

Davis, Kenneth C. 1969. *Discretionary Justice: A Preliminary Inquiry*. Baton Rouge, LA: Louisiana State University Press.

Deutsch, Stuart J. 1981. "Intervention Modeling: Analysis of Changes in Crime Rates." In *Methods in Quantitative Criminology*, edited by J. A. Fox. New York: Academic Press.

Deutsch, Stuart J. and Francis B. Alt. 1977. "The Effect of Massachusetts' Gun Control Law on Gun-Related Crimes in the City of Boston." *Evaluation Quarterly* 1:543-568.

Dillingham, Steven D. (1991, March 4-5). *Remarks*. Presented at the Attorney General's Summit on Law Enforcement Responses to Violent Crime: Public Safety in the Nineties, Washington, DC.

DiLulio, John J. (1995, February 25). "Criminals and Gutting Truth-in-Sentencing Laws." *The Heritage Foundation Backgrounder*, No. 1020. Available on the World Wide Web at: www.heritage.org/library/categories/crimelaw/bg1020.html

Dixon, Jo. 1995. "The Organizational Context of Criminal Sentencing." *American Journal of Sociology* 100:1157-1198.

Dodge, Mary and John C. Harris. 2000. "Calling a Strike a Ball: Jury Nullification and 'Three Strikes' Cases." In *Courts & Justice: A Reader*, 2nd ed., edited by G. L. Mays and P. R. Gregware. Prospect Heights, IL: Waveland.

Downie, Leonard, Jr. 1971. *Justice Denied*. Baltimore, MD: Penguin Books.

Drug Court Clearinghouse and Technical Assistance Project. 1999. *Looking at a Decade of Drug Courts*. Washington, DC: U.S. Department of Justice.

Durham, Alexis M., III. 1994. *Crisis and Reform: Current Issues in American Punishment*. Boston, MA: Little, Brown.

Early, Kevin E. (Ed.). 1996. *Drug Treatment Behind Bars: Prison-Based Strategies for Change*. Westport, CT: Praeger.

East, E. R. 1947. "Is Reformation Possible in Prison Today?" *Journal of Criminal Law and Criminology* 38.

Eisenstein, James, Roy B. Flemming and Peter F. Nardulli. 1988. *The Contours of Justice: Communities and Their Courts*. Boston, MA: Little, Brown.

Eisenstein, James and Herbert Jacob. 1977. *Felony Justice: An Organizational Analysis of Communities and Their Courts*. Boston, MA: Little, Brown.

Ekland-Olson, Sheldon. 1988. "Structured Discretion, Racial Bias, and the Death Penalty: The First Decade After *Furman* in Texas." *Social Science Quarterly* 69:853-873.

Engen, Rodney L. and Sara Steen. 2000. "The Power to Punish: Discretion and Sentencing Reform in the War on Drugs." *American Journal of Sociology* 105:1357-1395.

Engle, Charles Donald. 1971. *Criminal Justice in the City: A Study of Sentence Severity and Variation in the Philadelphia Court System*. Doctoral dissertation, Temple University, Philadelphia, PA.

Everett, Ronald S. and Barbara C. Nienstedt. 1999. "Race, Remorse, and Sentence Reduction: Is Saying You're Sorry Enough?" *Justice Quarterly* 16:99-122.

Ewart, Brian W. and Donald C. Pennington. 1997. "Reasons for Sentences: An Empirical Investigation." In *The Sentencing Process*, edited by M. Wasik. Aldershot, England: Dartmouth Publishing.

Federal Bureau of Investigation. 2000. *Uniform Crime Reports, Crime in the United States–1999*. Washington, DC: Author.

Federal Judicial Center. 1994. *Planning for the Future: Results of a Federal Judicial Center Survey of United States Judges*. Washington, DC: Author.

Feeley, Malcolm M. and Sam Kamin. 1996. "The Effect of 'Three Strikes and You're Out' on the Courts: Looking Back to See the Future." In *Three Strikes and You're Out: Vengeance as Public Policy*, edited by D. Shichor and D. K. Sechrest. Thousand Oaks, CA: Sage.

Field, Gary. 1984. "The Cornerstone Program: A Client Outcome Study." *Federal Probation* 48:50-55.

Fineman, Martha. 1994. "Feminist Legal Scholarship and Women's Gendered Lives." In *Lawyers in a Postmodern World: Translation and Transgression*, edited by C. M. Harrington and C. B. Harrington. New York: New York University Press.

Finnis, John. 1980. *Natural Law and Natural Rights*. Oxford, England: Clarendon.

Florida Civil Liberties Union. 1964. *Rape: Selective Electrocution Based on Race*. Miami, FL: Author.

Floud, Jean and Warren Young. 1981. *Dangerousness and Criminal Justice*. London, England: Heinemann.

Forst, Brian and Charles Wellford. 1981. "Punishment and Sentencing: Developing Sentencing Guidelines Empirically from Principles of Punishment." *Rutgers Law Review* 33:799-837.

Frankel, Marvin. 1972a. *Criminal Sentences: Law Without Order.* New York: Hill and Wang.

———. 1972b. "Lawlessness in Sentencing." *University of Cincinnati Law Review* 41:1-54.

Frase, Richard. 1993. "Implementing Commission-Based Sentencing Guidelines: The Lessons of the First Ten Years in Minnesota." *Cornell Journal of Law and Public Policy* 2:279-337.

———. 1997a. "Prison Population Growing Under Minnesota Guidelines." In *Sentencing Reform in Overcrowded Times,* edited by M. Tonry and K. Hatlestad. New York: Oxford University Press.

———. 1997b. "Sentencing Guidelines Are 'Alive and Well' in the United States." In *Sentencing Reform in Overcrowded Times,* edited by M. Tonry and K. Hatlestad. New York: Oxford University Press.

Frazier, Charles E. and E. Wilbur Bock. 1982. "Effects of Court Officials on Sentence Severity: Do Judges Make a Difference?" *Criminology* 20:257-272.

Frazier, Charles E., Wilbur E. Bock, and John C. Henretta. 1980. "Pretrial Release And Bail Decisions: The Effects of Legal, Community, and Personal Variables." *Criminology* 18:162-181.

Garfinkel, Harold. 1949. "Research Note on Inter- and Intra-Racial Homicides." *Social Forces* 27:369-381.

Garland, David. 1999. "Punishment and Society Today." *Punishment & Society* 1:5-10.

———. 2001. "Introduction: The Meaning of Mass Imprisonment." *Punishment & Society* 3:5-7.

Gaylin, Willard. 1974. *Partial Justice: A Study of Bias in Sentencing.* New York: Knopf.

Gibbs, Jack P. 1975. *Crime, Punishment, and Deterrence.* New York: Elsevier.

———. 1995. "Deterrence Theory and Research." In *Law & Society: Readings on the Social Study of Law,* edited by S. Macaulay, L. M. Friedman, and J. Stookey. New York: Norton.

Gibson, James L. 1978. "Race as a Determinant of Criminal Sentences: A Methodological Critique and a Case Study." *Law & Society Review* 12:455-478.

Gilligan, Carol. 1982. *In a Different Voice: Psychological Theory and Women's Development.* Cambridge, MA: Harvard University Press.

Goldman, Sheldon. 1979. "Should There Be Affirmative Action for the Judiciary?" *Judicature* 62:488-495.

Gottfredson, Don M. 1999. "Effects of Judges' Sentencing Decisions on Criminal Careers." *National Institute of Justice: Research in Brief.* Washington, DC: U.S. Department of Justice.

Gottfredson, Michael R. and Don M. Gottfredson. 1988. *Decision Making in Criminal Justice: Toward the Rational Exercise of Discretion,* 2nd ed. New York: Plenum.

Gottfredson, Don M., Leslie T. Wilkins, and Peter B. Hoffman. 1978. *Guidelines for Parole and Sentencing.* Lexington, MA: Lexington Books.

Gross, Samuel R. and Robert Mauro. 1989. *Death & Discrimination: Racial Disparities in Capital Sentencing.* Boston, MA: Northeastern University Press.

Gruhl, John, Cassia Spohn, and Susan Welch. 1981. "Women as Policymakers: The Case of Trial Judges." *American Journal of Political Science* 25:308-322.

Hagan, John. 1974. "Extra-Legal Attributes and Criminal Sentencing: As Assessment of a Sociological Viewpoint." *Law & Society Review* 8:357-383.

———. 1975. "The Social and Legal Construction of Criminal Justice: A Study of the Presentence Process." *Social Problems* 22:620-637.

Hagan, John and Kristin Bumiller. 1983. "Making Sense of Sentencing: A Review and Critique of Sentencing Research." In *Research on Sentencing: The Search for Reform*, Vol. I, edited by A. Blumstein, J. Cohen, S. E. Martin, and M. H. Tonry. Washington, DC: National Academy Press.

Hagan, John, John Hewitt, and Duane Alwin. 1979. "Ceremonial Justice: Crime and Punishment in a Loosely Coupled System." *Social Forces* 58:506-525.

Hahn, Paul H. 1998. *Emerging Criminal Justice: Three Pillars for a Proactive Justice System.* Thousand Oaks, CA: Sage.

Hanson, Roger A. and Brian J. Ostrom. 1993. "Indigent Defenders Get the Job Done and Done Well." In *Criminal Justice: Law and Politics*, 6th ed., edited by G. W. Cole. Belmont, CA: Wadsworth.

Harris, John C. and Paul Jesilow. 2000. "It's Not the Old Ball Game: Three Strikes and the Courtroom Workgroup." *Justice Quarterly* 17:185-203.

Hart, Herbert L. A. 1968. "Prolegomenon to the Principles of Punishment." In *Punishment and Responsibility*, edited by H. L. A. Hart, New York: Oxford University Press.

Hawkins, Darnell. 1981. "Causal Attribution and Punishment for Crime." *Deviant Behavior* 1:191-215.

———. 1987. "Beyond Anomalies: Rethinking the Conflict Perspective on Race and Criminal Punishment." *Social Forces:* 65:719-745.

Hawkins, Darnell and Kenneth A. Hardy. 1987. "Black-White Imprisonment Rates: A State-by- State Analysis." *Social Justice* 16:75-94.

Heumann, Milton and Colin Loftin. 1979. "Mandatory Sentencing and the Abolition of Plea Bargaining: The Michigan Felony Firearms Statute." *Law & Society Review* 13:393-430.

Hobbes, Thomas. 1651. *Leviathan*. New York: Dutton.

Hofer, Paul J., Keven R. Blackwell, and R. Barry Ruback. 1999. "The Effect of the Federal Sentencing Guidelines on Inter-Judge Sentencing Disparity." *The Journal of Criminal Law & Criminology* 90:239-321.

Hogarth, John. 1971. *Sentencing as a Human Process*. Toronto, Canada: University of Toronto Press.

Hogenmuller, John. 1998. "Structured Sentencing in Florida: Is the Experiment Over?" *Law & Policy* 20:281-309.

Holmes, Malcolm D., Harmon M. Hosch, Howard C. Daudistel, Dolores A. Perez, and Joseph B. Graves. 1993. "Judges' Ethnicity and Minority Sentencing: Evidence Concerning Hispanics." *Social Science Quarterly* 74:496-506.

———. 1996. "Ethnicity, Legal Resources, and Felony Dispositions in Two Southwestern Jurisdictions." *Justice Quarterly* 13:11-30.

Hood, Roger. 1972. *Sentencing the Motoring Offender.* London, England: Heinemann.

Hospers, John. 1977. "Punishment, Protection, and Rehabilitation." In *Justice and Punishment*, edited by J. Cederblom and W. L. Blizek, Cambridge, MA: Ballinger.

Inciardi, James A., Dorothy Lockwood, and Robert M. Hooper. (1994, February). "Delaware Treatment Program Presents Promising Results." *Corrections Today*, pp. 34-42.

Inciardi, James A., Duane C. McBride, and James E. Rivers. 1996. *Drug Control and the Courts.* Thousand Oaks, CA: Sage.

Irwin, John and James Austin. 1997. *It's About Time: America's Imprisonment Binge*. Belmont, CA: Wadsworth.

Jacobs, Bruce. 1996. "Crack Dealers and Restrictive Deterrence: Identifying Narcs." *Criminology* 34:409-431.

Jenkins, Phillip. 1994. "'The Ice Age': The Social Construction of a Drug Panic." *Justice Quarterly* 11:7-31.

Johnson, Guy. 1941. "The Negro and Crime." *Annals of the American Academy* 217:93-104.

Joint Committee on New York Drug Law Evaluation. 1978. *The Nation's Toughest Drug Law: Evaluating the New York Experience.* Washington, DC: U.S. Government Printing Office.

Kant, Immanuel. 1887. *The Philosophy of Law,* trans. by W. Hastie. Edinburgh, Scotland: T. T. Clark.

Kapardis A. and David P. Farrington. 1982. "An Experimental Study of Sentencing by Magistrates." *Law and Human Behavior* 5:107-121.

Kaufman, Irving R. (1960, January). "Sentencing: The Judge's Problem." *Atlantic Monthly.* Available on the World Wide Web at: http://www.theatlanticmonthly/unbound/flashbks/death/kaufman.htm

Kautt, Paula and Cassia Spohn. (in press) "*Crack*-ing Down on Black Drug Offenders? Testing for Interactions Between Offender Race, Drug Type, and Sentencing Strategy in Federal Drug Sentences." *Justice Quarterly.*

Keil, Thomas and Gennaro Vito. 1990. "Race and the Death Penalty in Kentucky Murder Trials: An Analysis of Post-*Gregg* Outcomes." *Justice Quarterly* 7:189-207.

Kennedy, Randall. 1997. *Race, Crime, and the Law.* New York: Vintage.

Kerstetter, Wayne. 1990. "Gateway to Justice: Police and Prosecutorial Response to Sexual Assaults Against Women." *Criminology* 81:267-313.

Kingsnorth, Rodney F., Randall C. MacIntosh, and Jennifer Wentworth. 1999. "Sexual Assault: The Role of Prior Relationship and Victim Characteristics in Case Processing." *Justice Quarterly* 16:275-302.

Kingsnorth, Rodney and Louis Rizzo. 1979. "Decision-Making in the Criminal Courts: Continuities and Discontinuities." *Criminology* 17:3-14.

Kleck, Gary. 1981. "Racial Discrimination in Sentencing: A Critical Evaluation of the Evidence With Additional Evidence on the Death Penalty." *American Sociological Review* 43:783-805.

———. 1991. *Point Blank: Guns and Violence in America.* New York: Aldine de Gruyter.

Knapp, Kay A. 1984. *The Impact of the Minnesota Sentencing Guidelines: Three-Year Evaluation.* St. Paul, MN: Minnesota Sentencing Guidelines Commission.

———. 1987. "Implementation of the Minnesota Guidelines: Can the Innovative Spirit Be Preserved?" In *The Sentencing Commission and Its Guidelines,* edited by A. von Hirsch, K. A. Knapp, and M. Tonry. Boston, MA: Northeastern University Press.

Kramer, John H. and Robin L. Lubitz. 1985. "Pennsylvania's Sentencing Reform: The Impact of Commission-Established Guidelines." *Crime & Delinquency* 31:481-500.

Kramer, John H., Robin L. Lubitz, and Cynthia A. Kempinen, "Sentencing Guidelines: A Quantitative Comparison of Sentencing Policies in Minnesota, Pennsylvania, and Washington." *Justice Quarterly* 6:565-587.

Kramer, John H. and Darrell Steffensmeier. 1993. "Race and Imprisonment Decisions." *The Sociological Quarterly* 34:357-376.

Kramer, John H. and Jeffery T. Ulmer. 1996. "Sentencing Disparity and Departures From Guidelines." *Justice Quarterly* 13:81-106.

Kritzer, Herbert M. 1978. "Political Correlates of the Behavior of Federal District Judges: A 'Best Case' Analysis." *Journal of Politics* 40:25-58.

Kruttschnitt, Candace. 1980-1981. "Social Status and Sentences of Female Offenders." *Law & Society Review* 15:247-265.

Kurki, Leena. 2000. "Restorative and Community Justice." In *Crime and Justice: A Review of Research,* Vol. 27, edited by M. Tonry. Chicago, IL: University of Chicago Press.

Lacasse, Chantale and Abigail Payne. 1999. "Federal Sentencing Guidelines and Mandatory Minimum Sentences: Do Defendants Bargain in the Shadow of the Judge?" *Journal of Law and Economics* XLII:245-269.

LaFree, Gary D. 1985. "Adversarial and Nonadversarial Justice: A Comparison of Guilty Pleas and Trials." *Criminology* 23:289-312.

———. 1989. *Rape and Criminal Justice: The Social Construction of Sexual Assault.* Belmont, CA: Wadsworth.

Langan, Patrick. 1996. "Sentence Reductions for Drug Traffickers for Assisting Federal Prosecutors." Unpublished manuscript.

Laster, Kathy and Roger Douglas. 1995. "Feminized Justice: The Impact of Women Decision Makers in the Lower Courts of Australia." *Justice Quarterly* 12:177-205.

Levin, Martin A. 1977. *Urban Politics and the Criminal Courts.* Chicago, IL: University of Chicago Press.

Lilly, J. Robert, Richard A. Ball, G. David Curry, and John McMullen. 1993. "Electronic Monitoring of the Drunk Driver: A Seven-Year Study of the Home Confinement Alternative." *Crime and Delinquency* 39:462-484.

Lipsey, Mark W. 1992. "The Effect of Treatment on Juvenile Delinquents: Results From Meta-Analysis." In *Psychology and Law: International Perspectives*, edited by F. Losel, T. Bliesener and D. Bender. Berlin, Germany: W. de Gruyter.

Lipton, Douglas S. 1995. *The Effectiveness of Treatment for Drug Abusers Under Criminal Justice Supervision.* Washington, DC: U.S. Department of Justice, National Institute of Justice.

Loftin, Colin, Milton Heumann, and David McDowall. 1983. "Mandatory Sentencing and Firearms Violence: Evaluating an Alternative to Gun Control." *Law & Society Review* 17:287-318.

Loftin, Colin and David McDowall. 1981. "One With a Gun Gets You Two: Mandatory Sentencing and Firearms Violence in Detroit." *The Annals of the Academy of Political and Social Science* 455:150-181.

———. 1984. "The Deterrent Effects of the Florida Firearm Law." *Journal of Criminal Law and Criminology* 75:50-259.

Longfellow, Henry Wadsworth. 1875. *The Masque of Pandora.* Boston, MA: James R. Osgood.

Lynch, James P. and William J. Sabol. (1994, November). "The Use of Coercive Social Control and Changes in the Race and Class Composition of U.S. Prison Populations." Paper presented at the annual meeting of the American Society of Criminology, Chicago, IL.

MacKenzie, Doris L. and Robert Brame. 1995. "Shock Incarceration and Positive Adjustment During Community Supervision." *Journal of Quantitative Criminology* 11:111-142.

MacKenzie, Doris L., Robert Brame, David McDowall, and Claire Souryal. 1995. "Boot Camp Prisons and Recidivism in Eight States." *Criminology* 33:401-430.

MacKenzie, Doris L. and Eugene E. Herbert (Eds.). 1996. *Correctional Boot Camps: A Tough Intermediate Sanction.* Washington, DC: U.S. Department of Justice.

MacKenzie, Doris L. and Dale G. Parent. 1991. "Shock Incarceration and Prison Crowding in Louisiana." *Journal of Criminal Justice* 19:225-237.

Mangum, Charles S., Jr. 1940. *The Legal Status of the Negro.* Chapel Hill, NC: North Carolina Press.

Mann, Coramae R. 1993. *Unequal Justice: A Question of Color.* Bloomington, IN: Indiana University Press.

Martin, Elaine. 1993. "Women on the Bench: A Different Voice?" *Judicature* 77:126.

Martinson, Robert. 1974. "What Works? Questions and Answers about Prison Reform." *Public Interest* 24:22-54.

Marvel, Thomas B. and Carlisle E. Moody. 1995. "The Impact of Enhanced Prison Terms for Felonies Committed With Guns." *Criminology* 33:247-281.

———. 1996. "Determinate Sentencing and Abolishing Parole: The Long-Term Impacts on Prisons and Crime." *Criminology* 34:107-128.

Mather, Lynn M. 1979. *Plea Bargaining or Trial? The Process of Criminal Case Disposition.* Lexington, MA: Lexington Books.

Mauer, Marc. 1999. *Race to Incarcerate.* New York: The New Press.

———. 2001. "The Causes and Consequences of Prison Growth in the U.S.A." *Punishment & Society* 3:9-20.

Maxfield, Linda D. and John H. Kramer. 1998. *Substantial Assistance: An Empirical Yardstick Gauging Equity in Current Federal Policy and Practice.* Washington, DC: U.S. Sentencing Commission.

McCahill, Thomas W., Linda C. Meyer, and Arthur M. Fischman, *The Aftermath of Rape.* Lexington, MA: Lexington Books.

McCorkel, Jill, Lana D. Harrison, and James A. Inciardi. 1998. How treatment is constructed among graduates and dropouts in a prison therapeutic community. *Journal of Offender Rehabilitation* 27:37-59.

McDonald, Douglas. 1986. *Punishment Without Walls: Community Service Sentences in New York City.* New Brunswick, NJ: Rutgers University Press.

McDonald, Douglas C. and Kenneth E. Carlson. 1993. *Sentencing in the Federal Courts: Does Race Matter?* Washington, DC: U.S. Department of Justice.

McDonald, Douglas C., Judith Greene, and Charles Worzella. 1992. *Day Fines in American Courts: The Staten Island and Milwaukee Experiments.* Washington, DC: U.S. Department of Justice.

McDowall, David, Colin Loftin, and Brian Wiersema. 1992. "A Comparative Study of the Preventive Effects of Mandatory Sentencing Laws for Handgun Crimes." *Journal of Criminal Law and Criminology* 83:378-394.

McGuire, James and P. Priestly. 1995. "Reviewing 'What Works': Past, Present and Future." In *What Works? Reducing Offending*, edited by J. McGuire. West Sussex, England: Wiley.

McIntyre, Lisa. 1987. *The Public Defender: The Practice of Law in the Shadows of Repute.* Chicago, IL: University of Chicago Press.

Meierhoefer, Barbara S. 1992. *The General Effect of Mandatory Minimum Prison Terms.* Washington, DC: Federal Judicial Center.

Melossi, Dario. 1989. "An Introduction: Fifty Years Later, Punishment and Social Structure in Contemporary Analysis." *Contemporary Crises* 13:311-326.

Miethe, Terence D. 1987. "Charging and Plea Bargaining under Determinate Sentencing: An Investigation of the Hydraulic Displacement of Discretion." *Journal of Criminal Law and Criminology* 78:155-176.

Miethe, Terence D. and Charles A. Moore. 1985. "Socioeconomic Disparities Under Determinate Sentencing Systems: A Comparison of Pre-Guideline and Post-Guideline Practices in Minnesota." *Criminology* 23:337-363.

———. 1986. "Racial Differences in Criminal Processing: The Consequences of Model Selection on Conclusions About Differential Treatment." *The Sociological Quarterly* 27:217-237.

———. 1989. "Sentencing Guidelines: Their Effect in Minnesota." *National Institute of Justice Research in Brief.* Washington, DC: U.S. Department of Justice.

Miller, Frank, Robert O. Dawson, George E. Dix, and Raymond I. Parnas. 1991. *Prosecution and Adjudication.* Westbury, NY: Foundation Press.

Miller, Jerome G. 1996. *Search and Destroy: African-American Males in the Criminal Justice System*. New York: Cambridge University Press.

Minnesota Sentencing Guidelines Commission. 2001. *Sentencing Practices: Annual Summary Statistics for Felony Offenders Sentenced in 1999*. St. Paul, MN: Author.

Moore, Charles A. and Terence D. Miethe. 1986. "Regulated and Unregulated Sentencing Decisions: An Analysis of First-Year Practices Under Minnesota's Felony Sentencing Guidelines." *Law & Society Review* 20:253-277.

Moore, Herbert. 1968. "Persons and Punishment." *The Monist* 52:476-479.

Moore, Michael S. 1992. "The Moral Worth of Retribution." In *Principled Sentencing*, edited by A. von Hirsch and A. Ashworth. Boston, MA: Northeastern University Press.

Morris, Norval. 1992. *The Brothel Boy and Other Parables of the Law*. New York: Oxford University Press.

Morris, Norval and Michael Tonry. 1990. *Between Prison and Probation: Intermediate Punishments in a Rational Sentencing System*. New York: Oxford University Press.

Moulds, Elizabeth. 1980. "Chivalry and Paternalism: Disparities of Treatment in the Criminal Justice System." In *Women, Crime, and Justice*, edited by S. K. Datesman and F. R. Scarpitti. New York: Oxford University Press.

Mullen, R. 1996. "Therapeutic Communities in Prisons: Dealing with Toxic Waste." In *Drug Treatment Behind Bars: Prison-Based Strategies for Change* , edited by K. Early. Westport: CN: Praeger.

Murphy, Clyde E. 1988. "Racial Discrimination in the Criminal Justice System." *North Carolina Central Law Journal* 17:171-190.

Murphy, Jeffrie G. 1979. *Retribution, Justice and Therapy*. Boston, MA: Reidel.

Myers, Martha A. 1988. "Social Background and the Sentencing Behavior of Judges." *Criminology* 26:649-675.

———. 1989. "Symbolic Policy and the Sentencing of Drug Offenders." *Law & Society Review* 23:295-315.

Myrdal, Gunnar. 1944. *An American Dilemma: The Negro Problem and Modern Democracy*. New York: Harper and Brothers. Chicago, IL: University of Chicago Press.

Nagel, Ilene H. and Barry L. Johnson. 1994. "The Role of Gender in a Structured Sentencing System: Equal Treatment, Policy Choices, and the Sentencing of Female Offenders Under the United States Sentencing Guidelines." *Journal of Criminal Law and Criminology* 85:181-221.

Nagel, Ilene H. and Stephen J. Schulhofer. 1992. "A Tale of Three Cities: An Empirical Study of Charging and Bargaining Practices Under the Federal Sentencing Guidelines." *Southern California Law Review* 66:501-566.

Nardulli, Peter F., James Eisenstein, and Roy B. Flemming. 1988. *The Tenor of Justice: Criminal Courts and the Guilty Plea Process*. Urbana and Chicago, IL: University of Illinois Press.

National Advisory Commission on Criminal Justice Standards and Goals. 1973. *Task Force Report on Corrections*. Washington, DC: Government Printing Office.

National Association of Drug Court Professionals. 1997. *Defining Drug Courts: The Key Components*. Washington, DC: U.S. Department of Justice, Drug Courts Program Office.

National Institute of Justice. 1997. *Drug Use Forecasting 1996: Annual Report on Adult and Juvenile Arrestees*. Washington, DC: U.S. Department of Justice, Office of Justice Programs.

National Law Enforcement and Corrections Technology Center. 1999. *Keeping Track of Electronic Monitoring*. Washington, DC: U.S. Department of Justice.

Newman, Donald J. 1966. *Conviction: The Determination of Guilt or Innocence Without Trial.* Boston, MA: Little, Brown.

Nobiling, Tracy, Cassia Spohn, and Miriam DeLone. 1998. "A Tale of Two Counties: Unemployment and Sentence Severity." *Justice Quarterly* 15:401-427.

Oaks, Dallin H. and Warren Lehman. 1970. "Lawyers for the Poor." In *The Scales of Justice,* edited by A. S. Blumberg. Hawthorne, NY: Aldine.

Oregon Criminal Justice Council, *1989 Oregon Sentencing Guidelines Manual.* Portland, OR: Oregon Criminal Justice Council.

Packer, Herbert L. 1968. *The Limits of the Criminal Sanction.* Stanford, CA: Stanford University Press.

Palmer, Ted. 1991. "The Effectiveness of Intervention: Recent Trends and Current Issues." *Crime and Delinquency* 37:330-342.

Paternoster, Raymond. 1984. "Prosecutorial Discretion in Requesting the Death Penalty: A Case of Victim-Based Discrimination." *Law & Society Review* 18:437-478.

———. 1987. "The Deterrent Effect of the Perceived Certainty and Severity of Punishment: A Review of the Evidence and Issues." *Justice Quarterly* 4:173-217.

———. 1991. *Capital Punishment in America.* New York: Lexington Books.

Pennsylvania Commission on Sentencing. 1985. *1984 Report: Sentencing in Pennsylvania.* State College, PA: Author.

———. 1987. *1986-1987 Report: Sentencing in Pennsylvania.* State College, PA: Author.

———. 1998. *1997 Annual Report.* State College, PA: Author.

Petersilia, Joan. 1987. *Expanding Options for Criminal Sentencing.* Santa Monica, CA: RAND.

Petersilia, Joan and Susan Turner. 1993. "Intensive Probation and Parole." In *Crime and Justice: A Review of Research,* Vol. 17, edited by M. Tonry. Chicago, IL: University of Chicago Press.

Petersilia, Joan, Susan Turner, James Kahan, and Joyce Peterson. 1985. *Granting Felons Probation: Public Risks and Alternatives.* Santa Monica, CA: RAND.

Peterson, Ruth and John Hagan. 1984. "Changing Conceptions of Race: Toward an Account of Anomalous Findings in Sentencing Research." *American Sociological Review* 49:56-70.

Pierce, Glenn L. and William J. Bowers. 1981. "The Bartley-Fox Gun Law." *The Annals of the Academy of Political and Social Science* 455:120-137.

Quinney, Ricard. 1970. *The Social Reality of Crime.* Boston, MA: Little, Brown.

———. 1977. *Class, State and Crime.* New York: David McKay.

Radelet, Michael L. 1981. "Racial Characteristics and the Imposition of the Death Penalty." *American Sociological Review* 46:918-927.

Radelet, Michael L. and Glenn L. Pierce. 1985. "Race and Prosecutorial Discretion in Homicide Cases." *Law & Society Review* 19:587-621.

Raeder, Myrna. 1993. "Gender and Sentencing: Single Moms, Battered Women, and Other Sex-Based Anomalies in the Gender-Free World of the Federal Sentencing Guidelines." *Pepperdine Law Review* 20:905.

Ralph, Paige H., Jonathan R. Sorensen, and James W. Marquart. 1992. "A Comparison of Death-Sentenced and Incarcerated Murderers in Pre-*Furman* Texas." *Justice Quarterly* 9:185-209.

Reiss, Albert J., Jr. and Jeffrey A. Roth. 1993. *Understanding and Preventing Violence.* Report of the National Academy of Sciences Panel on the Understanding and Control of Violence. Washington, DC: National Academy Press.

Renzema, Marc. 1992. "Home Confinement Programs: Development, Implementation, and Impact." In *Smart Sentencing: The Emergence of Intermediate Sanctions*, edited by J. M. Byrne, A. J. Lurigio, and J. Petersilia. Newbury Park, CA: Sage.

Rich, William D., L. Paul Sutton, Todd D. Clear, and Michael J. Saks. 1981. *Sentencing Guidelines: Their Operation and Impact on the Courts*. Williamsburg, VA: National Center for State Courts.

Rosecrance, John. 1993. "Maintaining the Myth of Individualized Justice: Probation Presentence Reports," 6th ed. In *Criminal Justice: Law & Politics*, edited by G. F. Cole. Belmont, CA: Wadsworth.

Rossman, David, Paul Floyd, Glenn L. Pierce, John McDevitt and William J. Bowers. 1979. "Massachusetts' Mandatory Minimum Sentence Gun Law: Enforcement, Prosecution, and Defense Impact." *Criminal Law Bulletin* 16:150-163.

Roth, Jeffrey A. 1994. *Firearms and Violence*. Washington, DC: National Institute of Justice.

Rothman, David J. 1971. *The Discovery of the Asylum: Social Order and Disorder in the New Republic*. Boston, MA: Little, Brown.

Ruback, R. Barry. 1998. "Warranted and Unwarranted Complexity in the U.S. Sentencing Guidelines." *Law & Policy* 20:357-382.

Sabol, William J. 1989. "Racially Disproportionate Prison Populations in the United States: An Overview of Historical Patterns and Review of Contemporary Issues." *Contemporary Crises* 13:405-432.

Sadurski, Wojciech. 1985. *Giving Desert Its Due*. Dordrecht, Netherlands: Reidel.

Scheflin, Alan W. and Jon M. Van Dyke. 2000. "Merciful Juries: The Resilience of Jury Nullification," 2nd ed. In *Courts & Justice: A Reader*, edited by G. L. Mays and P. R. Gregware. Prospect Heights, IL: Waveland.

Sellin, Thorsten. 1935. "Race Prejudice in the Administration of Justice." *American Journal of Sociology* 41:212-217.

Shichor, David and Dale K. Sechrest. 1996. *Three Strikes and You're Out: Vengeance as Public Policy*. Thousand Oaks, CA: Sage.

Silverstein, Lee. 1965. *Defense of the Poor*. Chicago, IL: American Bar Foundation.

Simon, Eric. 1993. "The Impact of Drug-Law Sentencing on the Federal Prison Population." *Federal Sentencing Reporter* 6:29.

Skolnick, Jerome. 1967. "Social Control in the Adversary System." *Journal of Conflict Resolution* 11:67.

———. 1997. "Rethinking the Drug Problem." In *Drugs, Crime, and Justice*, edited by L. K. Gaines and P. B. Kraska. Prospect Heights, IL: Waveland.

Smith, Brent L. and Kelly R. Damphouse. 1996. "Punishing Political Offenders: The Effect of Political Motive on Federal Sentencing Decisions." *Criminology* 34:289-321.

Smith, Christopher E. 1991. *Courts and the Poor*. Chicago, IL: Nelson-Hall.

Smith, Dwayne M. 1987. "Patterns of Discrimination in Assessments of the Death Penalty: The Case of Louisiana." *Journal of Criminal Justice* 15:279-286.

Smith, Linda G. and Ron L. Akers. 1993. "A Comparison of Recidivism of Florida's Community Control and Prison: A Five-Year Survival Analysis." *Journal of Research in Crime and Delinquency* 30:267-292.

Spears, Jeffrey W. 1999. *Diversity in the Courtroom: A Comparison of the Sentencing Decisions of Black and White Judges and Male and Female Judges in Cook County Circuit Court*. Doctoral dissertation, University of Nebraska at Omaha.

Speckart, George, Douglas M. Anglin, and Elizabeth P. Deschenes. 1989. "Modeling the Longitudinal Impact of Legal Sanctions on Narcotics Use and Property Crime." *Journal of Quantitative Criminology* 5:33-56.

Spitzer, Steven. 1975. "Toward a Marxian Theory of Deviance." *Social Problems* 22:638-651.

Spohn, Cassia. 1990a. "Decision Making in Sexual Assault Cases: Do Black and Female Judges Make a Difference?" *Women & Criminal Justice* 2:83-105.

———. 1990b. "The Sentencing Decisions of Black and White Judges: Expected and Unexpected Similarities." *Law & Society Review* 24:1197-1216.

———. 1992. "An Analysis of the 'Jury Trial Penalty' and Its Effect on Black and White Offenders." *The Justice Professional* 7:93-112.

———. 1994. "Crime and the Social Control of Blacks." *Inequality, Crime, and Social Control*, edited by G. S. Bridges and M. A. Myers. Boulder, CO: Westview.

———. 1998. "Gender and Sentencing of Drug Offenders: Is Chivalry Dead?" *Criminal Justice Policy Review* 9:365-399.

———. 2000. *Thirty Years of Sentencing Reform: The Quest For a Racially Neutral Sentencing Process*. Washington, DC: U.S. Department of Justice.

Spohn, Cassia and Dawn Beichner. 2000. "Is Preferential Treatment of Female Offenders a Thing of the Past? A Multi-Site Study of Gender, Race, and Imprisonment." *Criminal Justice Policy Review* 11:149-184.

Spohn, Cassia and Miriam DeLone. 2000. "When Does Race Matter? An Analysis of the Conditions Under Which Race Affects Sentence Severity." *Sociology of Crime, Law, and Deviance* 2:3-37.

Spohn, Cassia, Miriam DeLone, and Jeffrey Spears. 1998. "Race/Ethnicity, Gender and Sentence Severity in Dade County, Florida: An Examination of the Decision To Withhold Adjudication." *Journal of Crime & Justice* XXI:111-138.

Spohn, Cassia, John Gruhl, and Susan Welch. 1981-1982. "The Effect of Race on Sentencing: A Re-Examination of an Unsettled Question." *Law & Society Review* 16:71-88.

Spohn, Cassia and David Holleran. (2000, November). "The Effect of Imprisonment on Recidivism Rates: A Focus on Drug Offenders." Paper presented at the annual meeting of the American Society of Criminology, San Francisco, CA.

Spohn, Cassia and David Holleran. 2000. "The Imprisonment Penalty Paid by Young, Unemployed Black and Hispanic Offenders." *Criminology* 38:281-306.

Spohn, Cassia and Julie Horney. 1991. "'The Law's the Law But Fair Is Fair:' Rape Shield Laws and Officials' Assessment of Sexual History Evidence." *Criminology* 29:137-160.

Spohn, Cassia and Jeffrey Spears. 1996. "The Effect of Offender and Victim Characteristics on Sexual Assault Case Processing Decsions." *Justice Quarterly* 13:649-679.

———. 2001. "Sentencing of Drug Offenders in Three Cities: Does Race/Ethnicity Make a Difference?" In *Crime Control and Social Justice: A Delicate Balance*, edited by D. F. Hawkins, S. L. Myers, Jr., and R. N. Stone. Westport, CT: Greenwood.

Steffensmeier, Darrell and Stephen Demuth. 2000. "Ethnicity and Sentencing Outcomes in U.S. Federal Courts: Who Is Punished More Harshly?" *American Sociological Review* 65:705- 729.

Steffensmeier, Darrell and Chris Hebert. 1999. "Women and Men Policymakers: Does the Judge's Gender Affect the Sentencing of Criminal Defendants?" *Social Forces* 77:1163-1196.

Steffensmeier, Darrell, John Kramer, and Cathy Streifel. 1993. "Gender and Imprisonment Decisions." *Criminology* 31:411-446.

Steffensmeier, Darrell, Jeffery Ulmer, and John Kramer. 1995. "Age Differences in Sentencing." *Justice Quarterly* 12:701-719.

———. 1998. "The Interaction of Race, Gender, and Age in Criminal Sentencing: The Punishment Cost of Being Young, Black, and Male." *Criminology* 36:763-797.

Sterling, Joyce S. 1983. "Retained Counsel Versus The Public Defender: The Impact of Type of Counsel on Charge Bargaining." In *The Defense Counsel*, edited by W. F. McDonald. Beverly Hills, CA: Sage.

Stith, Kate and Jose A. Cabranes. 1998. *Fear of Judging: Sentencing Guidelines in the Federal Courts*. Chicago, IL: University of Chicago Press.

Stolzenberg, Lisa and Steward J. D'Alessio. 1994. "Sentencing and Unwarranted Disparity: An Empirical Assessment of the Long-Term Impact of Sentencing Guidelines in Minnesota." *Criminology* 32:301-310.

Stumpf, Harry P. 1988. *American Judicial Politics*. San Diego. CA: Harcourt Brace Jovanovich.

Sudnow, David. 1965. "Normal Crimes: Sociological Features of the Penal Code in the Public Defender's Office." *Social Problems* 12:255-277.

Texas Civil Rights Project. 2000. *The Death Penalty in Texas: Due Process and Equal Justice . . . or Rush to Execution?* Austin, TX: Texas Civil Rights Project.

Thornburgh, Richard. (1989, May). *Opening Remarks*. Presented at the National Drug Conference, Washington, DC.

Tonry, Michael. 1992. "Selective Incapacitation: The Debate Over Its Ethics." In *Principled Sentencing*, edited by A. von Hirsch and A. Ashworth. Boston, MA: Northeastern University Press.

———. 1995. *Malign Neglect: Race, Crime, and Punishment in America*. New York: Oxford University Press.

———. 1996. *Sentencing Matters*. New York: Oxford University Press.

Tunis, Sandra, James Austin, Mark Morris, Patricia Hardyman, and Melissa Bolyard. 1996. *Evaluation of Drug Treatment in Local Corrections*. Washington, DC: U.S. Department of Justice, National Institute of Justice.

Turner, Susan, Peter W. Greenwood, Elsa Chen, and Terry Fain. 1999. "The Impact of Truth-in-Sentencing and Three Strikes Legislation: Prison Populations, State Budgets, and Crime Rates." *Stanford Law and Policy Review* 11:75-92.

Uhlman, Thomas M. 1978. "Black Elite Decision Making: The Case of Trial Judges." *American Journal of Political Science* 22:884-895.

———. 1979. *Racial Justice: Black Judges and Black Defendants in an Urban Trial Court*. Lexington, MA: Lexington Books.

Ulmer, Jeffrey T. 1997. *Social Worlds of Sentencing: Court Communities Under Sentencing Guidelines*. Albany, NY: State University of New York Press.

Ulmer, Jeffery T. and John H. Kramer. 1996. "Court Communities Under Sentencing Guidelines: Dilemmas of Formal Rationality and Sentencing Disparity." *Criminology* 34:383-408.

Unnever, James D. 1982. "Direct and Organizational Discrimination in the Sentencing of Drug Offenders." *Social Problems* 30:212-225.

Unnever, James D. and Larry A. Hembroff. 1987. "The Prediction of Racial/Ethnic Sentencing Disparities: An Expectation States Approach." *Journal of Research in Crime and Delinquency* 25:53-82.

U.S. Department of Commerce. Bureau of the Census. 1918. *Negro Population: 1790-1915*. Washington, DC: Government Printing Office.

U.S. Department of Justice. 1987. *Prosecutors Handbook on Sentencing Guidelines 50*. Washington, DC: Author.

U.S. Department of Justice. Bureau of Justice Assistance. 2000. *Survey of the Federal Death Penalty System (1988-2000)*. Washington, DC: Author.

———. 1996. *National Assessment of Structured Sentencing*. Washington, DC: Author.

U.S. Department of Justice. Bureau of Justice Statistics. 1992. *Capital Punishment 1991*. Washington, DC: Author.

———. 1993a. *An Analysis of Non-Violent Drug Offenders with Minimal Criminal Histories*. Washington, DC: Author.

————. 1993b. *Pretrial Release of Felony Defendants, 1992.* Washington, DC: Author.

————. 1993c. *Survey of State Prison Inmates, 1991.* Washington, DC: Author.

————. 1996. *Indigent Defense.* Washington, DC: Author.

————. 1997a. *Characteristics of Adults on Probation, 1995.* Washington, DC: Author.

————. 1997b. *Lifetime Likelihood of Going to State or Federal Prison.* Washington, DC: Author.

————. 1997c. *New Court Commitments to State Prison, 1996.* Washington, DC: U.S. Department of Justice, National Corrections Reporting Program.

————. 1998. *Sourcebook of Criminal Justice Statistics, 1997.* Washington, DC: Author.

————. 1999a. *Federal Criminal Case Processing, 1998.* Washington, DC: Author.

————. 1999b. *Federal Pretrial Release and Detention, 1996.* Washington, DC: Author.

————. 1999c. *Felony Defendants in Large Urban Counties, 1996.* Washington, DC: Author.

————. 1999d. *Felony Sentences in the United States, 1996.* Washington, DC: Author.

————. 1999e. *Prison and Jail Inmates at Midyear 1998.* Washington, DC: Author.

————. 1999f. *Sourcebook of Criminal Justice Statistics, 1998.* Washington, DC: Author.

————. 1999g. *Truth in Sentencing in State Prisons.* Washington, DC: Author.

————. 2000a. *Capital Punishment, 1999.* Washington, DC: Author.

————. 2000b. *Compendium of Federal Justice Statistics, 1998.* Washington, DC: Author.

————. 2000c. *Correctional Populations in the United States, 1997.* Washington, DC: Author.

————. 2000d. *Defense Counsel in Criminal Cases.* Washington, DC: Author.

————. 2000e. *Prisoners in 1999.* Washington, DC: U.S. Department of Justice.

————. 2000f. *Probation and Parole in the United States, 1998.* Washington, DC: Author.

————. 2000g. *State Court Sentencing of Convicted Felons, 1996.* Washington, DC: Author.

U.S. General Accounting Office. 1990a. *Death Penalty Sentencing: Research Indicates Pattern of Racial Disparities.* Washington, DC: Author.

————. 1990b. *Intermediate Sanctions: Their Impacts on Prison Crowding, Costs, and Recidivism Are Still Unclear.* Washington, DC: Author.

————. 1992. *Sentencing Guidelines: Central Questions Remain Unanswered.* Washington, DC: Author.

————. 1993. *Mandatory Minimum Sentences: Are They Being Imposed and Who Is Receiving Them?* Washington, DC: Author.

————. 1997. *Drug Courts: Overview of Growth, Characteristics, and Results.* Washington, DC: Author.

U.S. Sentencing Commission. 1991a. *The Federal Sentencing Guidelines: A Report on the Operation of the Guidelines System and Short-Term Impacts on Disparity in Sentencing, Use of Incarceration, and Prosecutorial Discretion and Plea Bargaining.* Washington, DC: Author.

————. 1991b. *Special Report to Congress: Mandatory Minimum Penalties in the Federal Criminal Justice System.* Washington, DC: Author.

————. 1993. *Federal Sentencing Guidelines Manual,* 1994 Edition. St Paul, MN: West.

————. 1995. *Substantial Assistance Departures in the United States Courts.* (Draft final report). Washington, DC: Author.

————. 1997. *1996 Sourcebook of Federal Sentencing Statistics.* Washington, DC: Author.

————. 2000. *1999 Sourcebook of Federal Sentencing Statistics.* Washington, DC: Author.

Uviller, H. Richard. 1996. *Virtual Justice: The Flawed Prosecution of Crime in America.* New Haven, CT: Yale University Press.

van den Haag, Ernest. 1975. *Punishing Criminals: Confronting a Very Old and Painful Question.* New York: Basic Books.

Vincent, Barbara S. and Paul J. Hofer. 1994. *The Consequences of Mandatory Minimum Prison Terms: A Summary of Recent Findings.* Washington, DC: Federal Judicial Center.

von Hirsch, Andrew. 1976. *Doing Justice: The Choice of Punishments.* New York: Hill and Wang.

———. 1992. "Prediction and False Positives." In *Principled Sentencing,* edited by A. von Hirsch and A. Ashworth. Boston, MA: Northeastern University Press.

von Hirsch, Andrew and Andrew Ashworth. 1992. *Principled Sentencing.* Boston, MA: Northeastern University Press.

von Hirsch, Andrew and Lisa Maher. 1992. "Should Penal Rehabilitationism Be Revived?" In *Principled Sentencing,* edited by A. von Hirsch and A. Ashworth. Boston, MA: Northeastern University Press.

Walker, Nigel. 1985. *Sentencing: Theory, Law, and Practice.* London, England: Butterworths.

———. 1991. *Why Punish?* Oxford, England and New York: Oxford University Press.

Walker, Samuel. 1993. *Taming the System: The Control of Discretion in Criminal Justice, 1950-1990.* New York: Oxford University Press.

Walker, Samuel, Cassia Spohn, and Miriam DeLone. 2000. *The Color of Justice: Race, Ethnicity, and Crime in America.* Belmont, CA: Wadsworth.

Walker, Thomas G. and Deborah J. Barrow. 1985. "The Diversification of the Federal Bench: Policy and Process Ramifications." *Journal of Politics* 47:596-617.

Walsh, Anthony. 1985. "The Role of the Probation Officer in the Sentencing Process." *Criminal Justice and Behavior* 12:289-303.

———. 1987. "The Sexual Stratification Hypothesis and Sexual Assault in Light of the Changing Conceptions of Race." *Criminology* 25:153-173.

Washington, Linn. 1994. *Black Judges on Justice: Perspectives from the Bench.* New York: The New Press.

Washington State Sentencing Guidelines Commission. 1987. *Preliminary Statistical Summary of 1986 Sentencing Data.* Olympia, WA: Author.

———. 1992. *A Decade of Sentencing Reform: Washington and Its Guidelines, 1981-1991.* Olympia, WA: Author.

———. 2000. *The Sentencing Reform Act at Century's End: An Assessment of Adult Felony Sentencing Practices in the State of Washington.* Olympia, WA: Author.

Weitzer, Ronald. 1966. "Racial Discrimination in the Criminal Justice System: Findings and Problems in the Literature." *Journal of Criminal Justice* 24:309-322.

Welch, Susan, Michael Combs, and John Gruhl. 1988. "Do Black Judges Make a Difference?" *American Journal of Political Science* 32:126-136.

Wexler, Harry K., Gregory P. Falkin, and Douglas S. Lipton. 1990. "Outcome Evaluation of a Prison Therapeutic Community for Substance Abuse Treatment." *Criminal Justice and Behavior* 17:71-92.

Wheeler, Gerald R. and Carol L. Wheeler. 1980. "Reflections on Legal Representation of the Economically Disadvantaged: Beyond Assembly Line Justice." *Crime and Delinquency* 26:319-332.

Wheeler, Stanton, Kenneth Mann, and Austin Sarat. 1988. *Sitting in Judgment: The Sentencing of White-Collar Criminals.* New Haven, CT: Yale University Press.

Wice, Paul. 1985. *Chaos in the Courthouse: The Inner Workings of the Urban Municipal Courts.* New York: Praeger.

———. 1991. *Judges & Lawyers: The Human Side of Justice.* New York: HarperCollins.

Wilbanks, William. 1985. *The Myth of a Racist Criminal Justice System.* Monterey, CA: Brooks/Cole.

Wilkins, William W. Jr. and John R. Steer. 1990. "Relevant Conduct: The Cornerstone of the Federal Sentencing Guidelines." *South Carolina Law Review* 41:495-531.

Williams, Wendy W. 1984-1985. "Equality's Riddle: Pregnancy and the Equal Treatment/Special Treatment Debate." *New York University Review of Law and Social Change* 13:325-363.

Wilson, James Q. 1975. *Thinking About Crime*. New York: Basic Books.

———. 1992. "Selective Incapacitation." In *Principled Sentencing*, edited by A. von Hirsch and A. Ashworth. Boston, MA: Northeastern University Press.

———. 1994. "Crime and Public Policy." In *Crime*, edited by J. Q. Wilson and J. Petersilia. San Francisco, CA: Institute for Contemporary Studies.

Wolfgang, Marvin E., Arlene Kelly, and Hans C. Nolde, "Comparison of the Executed and Commuted Among Admissions to Death Row." *Journal of Criminal Law, Criminology, and Police Science* 53:301.

Wolfgang, Marvin E. and Marc Reidel. 1973. "Race, Judicial Discretion and the Death Penalty." *Annals of the American Academy of Political and Social Science* 407:119-133.

———. 1975. "Rape, Race, and the Death Penalty in Georgia." *American Journal of Orthopsychiatry* 45:658-668.

Wolgast, Elizabeth H. 1980. *Equality and Rights of Women*. Ithaca, NY: Cornell University Press.

Wriggens, Jennifer. 1983. "Rape, Racism, and the Law." *Harvard Women's Law Journal* 6:104-141.

Wright, Bruce M. 1973. "A Black Broods on Black Judges." *Judicature* 57:22.

Wright, Ronald F. 1998a. "Managing Prison Growth in North Carolina Through Structured Sentencing." *National Institute of Justice Program Focus*. Washington, DC: U.S. Department of Justice, National Institute of Justice.

Wright, Ronald F. 1998b. "Three Strikes Legislation and Sentencing Commission Objectives." *Law & Policy* 20:429-463.

Zatz, Marjorie. 1987. "The Changing Forms of Racial/Ethnic Biases in Sentencing." *Journal of Research in Crime and Delinquency* 25:69-92.

———. 2000. "The Convergence of Race, Ethnicity, Gender, and Class on Court Decisionmaking: Looking Toward the 21st Century." Pp. 503-552 in *Policies, Processes, and Decisions of the Criminal Justice System*, Vol. 3, *Criminal Justice 2000*. Washington, DC: U.S. Department of Justice.

Zimring, Franklin E. 2001. "Imprisonment Rates and the New Politics of Criminal Punishment." *Punishment and Society* 3:161-166.

Index

About the Author

Cassia Spohn is Professor of Criminal Justice at the University of Nebraska at Omaha, where she holds a Kayser Professorship. She is the coauthor of two books: *The Color of Justice: Race, Ethnicity, and Crime in America* (with Sam Walker and Miriam DeLone) and *Rape Law Reform: A Grassroots Movement and Its Impact* (with Julie Horney). She has published a number of articles examining prosecutors' charging decisions in sexual assault cases and exploring the effect of race/ethnicity on charging and sentencing decisions. Her current research interests include the effect of race and gender on court processing decisions, victim characteristics and case outcomes in sexual assault cases, judicial decision making, sentencing of drug offenders, and the deterrent effect of imprisonment. In 1999, she was awarded the University of Nebraska Outstanding Research and Creative Activity Award.